D1557481

A History of the Iraq Crisis

A History of the Iraq Crisis

France, the United States, and Iraq, 1991–2003

Frédéric Bozo

Translated by Susan Emanuel

Woodrow Wilson Center Press
Washington, D.C.

Columbia University Press
New York

Woodrow Wilson Center Press
Washington, D.C.
www.wilsoncenter.org

Columbia University Press
Publishers Since 1893
New York Chichester, West Sussex
cup.columbia.edu

Library of Congress Cataloging-in-Publication Data

Names: Bozo, Frédéric, author. | Emanuel, Susan, translator.
Title: A history of the Iraq crisis : France, the United States, and Iraq, 1991–2003 / Frédéric Bozo ;
    translated by Susan Emanuel.
Other titles: Histoire secrète de la crise irakienne. English
Description: Washington, D.C. : Woodrow Wilson Center Press ; New York : Columbia University
    Press, [2016] | Includes bibliographical references and index.
Identifiers: LCCN 2016013007 (print) | LCCN 2016015085 (ebook) | ISBN 9780231704441
    (cloth : alk. paper) | ISBN 9780231801393 (ebook)
Subjects: LCSH: Persian Gulf War, 1991—Diplomatic history. | Iraq War, 2003–2011—Diplomatic
    history. | France—Relations—United States. | United States—Relations—France. | France—
    Military relations—United States. | United States—Military relations—France.
Classification: LCC DS79.75 .B6913 2016 (print) | LCC DS79.75 (ebook) | DDC 956.7044/32—dc23
LC record available at http://lccn.loc.gov/2016013007

Woodrow Wilson Center Press and Columbia University Press books are printed on permanent and
durable acid-free paper.
Printed in the United States of America

c 10 9 8 7 6 5 4 3 2 1

Cover photo: US president George W. Bush meeting with French president Jacques Chirac
in New York, ahead of the 61st United Nations General Assembly, September 19, 2006. AFP
Photo/Jim Watson
Design and layout: Station 10 Creative

To Stanley Hoffmann (1928–2015)

Contents

Contents

Acknowledgments

My first encounter with Stanley Hoffmann more than three decades ago influenced my intellectual journey more than any other. When this book was first published in France in 2013, it seemed to me obvious to dedicate to him a study of historic events that I knew had profoundly affected him. We (or rather he, as my role was that of a modest interviewer) had discussed these events in a book that had appeared shortly after the fact in France, and later in the United States. In rereading our 2003 conversation, I am amazed by Stanley's extraordinary perceptiveness, his clairvoyance, and his moral integrity. I hoped that he would see the present book as a testimonial of my gratitude and affection, and I was pleased that he was able to read it when it appeared in France. Stanley has since passed away, creating an immense loss—in particular for his former students and colleagues, many of whom, like me, had become his friends. He was a formidable intellectual and an exceptional individual.

This book owes a great deal to the many institutions and individuals who made it possible. As the happy few know, the Nobel Institute in Oslo, Norway, offers an incomparable working environment for historians and international relations specialists. By inviting me there for two months in the spring of 2007 for the second time, the institute's director, Geir Lundestad, and its academic director, Olav Njølstad, allowed me to begin to reflect on this book under the best possible conditions, for which I am very thankful.

By granting me a semester's sabbatical leave for research in 2009–10, my home university enabled me to devote the time necessary for the launch of my research in the archives and a first series of interviews. I am grateful to the scientific council of the university for having thus given me the possibility to advance this project more quickly.

Access to archives was a precondition, and many people under various guises helped to make this possible, among whom I want to thank Gérard Araud, Anne de la Blache, Jérôme Bonnafont, Monique Constant, Jay Dharmadhikari, Philippe Errera, Franck Gellet, Pascal Geneste, Emmanuelle Flament-Guelfucci, Manuel Lafont-Rapnouil, Bertrand Landrieu, Alexis Morel, and Hughes Moret.

It would not have been possible for me to bring my research to fruition without the year's stay I was able to enjoy in 2010–11 as a public policy scholar at the Woodrow Wilson International Center for Scholars in Washington, D.C., another key place for the study of international relations. I want to thank in particular Christian Ostermann, Samuel Wells, Michael Van Dusen, and Robert S. Litwak for having invited and hosted me and for thus allowing me to benefit from an exceptionally conducive research environment. Daily conversations with my colleagues at the Wilson Center who shared with me the same focus on the Iraq issue, foremost among whom were Melvyn P. Leffler and Joseph Sassoon, were essential. My research assistants, Yannek Smith, Whitney Wallace, and Aniseh Bassiri, greatly contributed to the effectiveness of my work. Great thanks for their help are also due to those in charge at the library: Janet Spikes, Dagne Gizaw, and Michelle Kamalich.

My stay in Washington would not have offered such fine conditions without the help of two other institutions to which I would also like to express my gratitude. France's Centre national de la recherche scientifique (CNRS) granted me a one-year secondment to its Washington bureau. I am thankful to Alain Laquièze, Claudio Galderisi, Diane Brami, Jean Favero, and Bernard Bobe, who helped me in various ways. Last but not least, the Franco-American Commission for Educational Exchange granted me a Fulbright scholarship for the duration of my American stay. I thank Arnaud Roujou de Boubée and Séverine Peyrichou for their support.

In the United States, in France, and elsewhere, many people helped me with their advice or shared their contacts, notably Michael Brenner, Charles Cogan, Stephen Flanagan, Jolyon Howorth, David Malone, Eric Méchoulan, Leo Michel, Vincent Nouzille, John Prados, Marie-Pierre Rey, Kori Schake, and Justin Vaïsse. I am grateful to them all.

Many other people listed at the end of this volume agreed to give me their testimony in the form of interviews conducted in Paris, Washington, or elsewhere. I thank them all.

At the French publishing house Éditions Perrin, where the book first appeared three years ago, I owe thanks to the late Anthony Rowley and then to Benoît Yvert for having believed in this project and having trusted me to achieve it, and for demonstrating their patience as I was struggling to keep deadlines. I also want to thank Séverine Courtaud for her efficient and wise assistance. Christophe Carle, François Godement, Jane Muret, Pauline Schnapper, and Jean-Frédéric Schaub read the manuscript in part or in whole and suggested useful improvements. As usual, Christophe Carle gave me precious suggestions.

For a book to be translated and published in another language means acquiring a second life. The present outcome is the result of the efforts and tenacity of several individuals whom I want to thank especially here, including Rebecca Byers at Perrin and, not least, Joe Brinley at the Wilson Center, who essentially made this happen. Susan Emanuel once again took on the demanding task of transposing my prose into English with her usual patience and commitment, and Shannon Granville did a marvelous job editing the manuscript with a view to making it fluid for English-speaking readers. Financial support for the translation came in part from France's Agence nationale de la recherche.

Finally, my family bore with stoicism my investment in a project that would prove time-consuming beyond all reason. For this, I ask the pardon of Jane, Pauline, André, and Clémence.

Abbreviations

BND	Bundesnachrichtendienst; Federal Intelligence Service (Germany)
CAP	Common Agricultural Policy (EU)
CEA	Commissariat à l'Énergie Atomique; Atomic Energy Commission (France)
CENTCOM	United States Central Command
CFSP	Common Foreign and Security Policy (EU)
CIA	Central Intelligence Agency (US)
DGSE	Direction Générale de la Sécurité Extérieure; General Directorate for External Security (France)
DPC	Defense Planning Committee (NATO)
DRM	Direction du Renseignement Militaire; Directorate of Military Intelligence (France)
DST	Direction de la Surveillance du Territoire; Directorate of Territorial Surveillance (France)
EU	European Union
IAEA	International Atomic Energy Agency

INC	Iraqi National Congress
ISAF	International Security Assistance Force
ISG	Iraq Survey Group
NAC	North Atlantic Council (NATO)
NATO	North Atlantic Treaty Organization
NIE	*National Intelligence Estimate*
NSC	National Security Council (US)
OMV	ongoing monitoring and verification
P3	Western permanent members of the United Nations Security Council (France, the United Kingdom, and the United States)
P5	permanent members of the United Nations Security Council (China, France, the Soviet Union/Russia, the United Kingdom, and the United States)
PNAC	Project for the New American Century
RPR	Rassemblement pour la République; Rally for the Republic (France)
SGDN	Secrétariat Général de la Défense Nationale; Secretariat-General for National Defense (France)
SISMI	Servizio per le Informazioni e la Sicurezza Militare; Military Intelligence Service (Italy)
UN	United Nations
UNMOVIC	United Nations Monitoring, Verification, and Inspection Commission
UNSCOM	United Nations Special Commission
US	United States
VFW	Veterans of Foreign Wars (US)
WMD	weapons of mass destruction

A History of the Iraq Crisis

Introduction

More than a dozen years later, the scene remains in everybody's memory: In the center of Baghdad on April 9, 2003, Iraqi citizens, with the help of American soldiers, overturned a statue of Saddam Hussein, putting a symbolic end to his regime and marking the outcome of a war launched three weeks earlier by the United States and Great Britain. Twelve years after the Gulf War—conducted in January and February 1991 by the Americans and their allies, including the French, to liberate Kuwait from an Iraqi invasion launched by the same Saddam Hussein in August 1990—the Americans "finished the job" that former US president George H. W. Bush had left incomplete. After an early success against al-Qaeda and the Taliban in Afghanistan in November 2001, two months after the September 11 attacks, America euphorically celebrated a second victory less than eighteen months later. On May 1, 2003, President George W. Bush landed on the aircraft carrier *Abraham Lincoln* to declare that major combat operations in Iraq were over. Although Bush did not say the exact words in his speech, a banner displayed on the carrier deck read "Mission Accomplished."

The launch of Operation Iraqi Freedom in March 2003, against the backdrop of global opposition to the war, had marked the apogee of the greatest international crisis since the Cold War. For weeks, millions of antiwar demonstrators had paraded in the streets of the world's great capitals, while France, Germany, and Russia stood in the front rank of opponents that had rejected American policy. The "peace camp" expressed not only its disagreement with the United States on the nature of the Iraq problem and the way of solving it, but also its opposition to the logic of preventive war that Washington had

1

made into a doctrine in the wake of 9/11, as well as its refusal of the US uni-lateralism that had culminated in the war against Iraq. In his speech to the United Nations (UN) Security Council on February 14, 2003, French foreign minister Dominique de Villepin famously spoke against the coming war in the name of "an old country, France" and "an old continent, Europe." Villepin's statement provoked applause from the audience—an unusual response in that normally quiet body—and has since remained emblematic of the worldwide confrontation played out at the UN.

The Iraq crisis in the first months of 2003 triggered a tension between Europe and the United States of an intensity unequaled since the 1956 Suez Crisis. On one side stood the United States and those of its allies for whom American leadership ought to remain at any cost the alpha and omega of the transatlantic relationship. On the other side stood those European countries that wanted to work for more balanced relations between the United States and a Europe that now was capable of asserting itself on the international scene, even at the price of its detachment from America. The Atlantic alliance and the European Union (EU) were shaken by the Iraq earthquake along preexisting fault lines, between a Franco-German–led "old Europe" hoping for more autonomy from the United States and an Atlanticist "new Europe" of soon-to-be EU members who had belonged to the former communist bloc and now assumed a "let's-follow-Washington's-lead" attitude under the aegis of Great Britain.

But the most spectacular aspect of the international crisis over Iraq was the confrontation that took place between France and America—the most serious one since the 1960s, when President Charles de Gaulle (1958–69) had challenged the United States' hegemony and its waging of the war in Vietnam. This new confrontation culminated in the spring of 2003, leading the Bush administration to proclaim its desire to "punish" France for its opposition and to allow, if not encourage, a wave of virulent Francophobia in the United States. The most derisory expression of this antagonism was the replacement of the term "French fries" by "freedom fries" on the menu of the US House of Representatives' cafeterias. For many months, Franco-American relations experienced a new chilling period; only when Bush's second term began in 2005 did they enjoy a rapprochement, which eventually led to reconciliation with the election of Nicolas Sarkozy as French president in 2007.

Meanwhile, the war in Iraq had turned into a fiasco. Already in the summer of 2003, it had become clear that the United States' proclaimed motive—eliminating the weapons of mass destruction (WMD) allegedly held by the

Saddam Hussein regime—was specious. Far from the anticipated transition to democracy, a long occupation had begun, even after the formal return of Iraq's sovereignty a year later. The country sank into chaos and violence, justifying critics like French president Jacques Chirac (1995–2007), who had constantly warned the United States against the danger of a military adventure in Iraq. Ultimately, this adventure would last more than eight years, until President Barack Obama ordered the complete withdrawal of American forces in December 2011: eight years of war for which Americans would pay dearly (more than 4,000 killed and 30,000 wounded; a financial and economic cost calculated in trillions of dollars) and which had fatal consequences for America's formerly uncontested status as a "hyperpower." As for the Iraqis, although the war put an end to thirty years of a brutal, bloody dictatorship, they paid an even higher price and suffered a new destructive conflict, followed by a civil war that to date has resulted in more than a hundred thousand victims. This new conflict came on top of a long and devastating war with Iran (1980–88), the 1991 Gulf War, and more than a dozen years of UN sanctions (1990–2003).

* * *

Over the past twelve years, the events surrounding the Iraq crisis have aroused an interest commensurate with their historical stakes and sheer magnitude. Innumerable books, most of them written from an American point of view, have been devoted to the Iraq crisis, starting of course with the journalistic accounts published in its immediate aftermath.[1] Numerous documentaries and other televised reports about it have also been created. And although US government archives remain for the most part inaccessible, a considerable amount of first-hand sources—beginning with the testimony of individuals who participated directly in these events, whether the heads of states or governments (notably George W. Bush, Jacques Chirac, Tony Blair, and Gerhard Schröder) and their immediate entourages (Condoleezza Rice, Dick Cheney, Donald Rumsfeld, and George Tenet) or actors of lower rank whose testimony is nevertheless important—are available.[2] In addition, a series of public inquiries, parliamentary or otherwise, especially American or British, have focused on particular aspects of the crisis. Some have focused on intelligence, the most controversial issue, while others have reviewed the whole decision-making process.[3] This wealth of evidence makes for an unparalleled corpus; as a result, the Iraq crisis is now the best-documented international episode since the end of the Cold War.[4]

This does not mean that it is the subject of consensus; nor is it exempt from shadowy areas. Questions and controversies remain substantial more than a decade later. This is true for the US decision-making process, about which the polemics, unsurprisingly, remain the most virulent. Schematically, there are two opposing narratives. The first comes from those who were in charge at the time—beginning with Bush himself—and are concerned with defending the core of their decisions. According to them, taking on Iraq after 9/11 was necessary in light of the danger of seeing a hostile regime one day allow terrorist networks to lay hands on WMD and commit even more murderous attacks. In this context, they aver, the American president made decisive choices and exercised leadership commensurate with the magnitude of the challenge, not only to prevent an inevitable new attack but also to profoundly transform the Middle East and even the world. As for the mistakes that were made, starting with the WMD issue, they allegedly were attributable not to the administration itself but to intelligence failures.[5] Detractors of this narrative have replied with their own opposing narrative: that the so-called Iraqi threat, if not a wholesale fabrication, was at least deliberately exaggerated by a manipulative administration and became the pretext for an intervention whose real motives were of a different nature—such as Bush's supposed desire to "finish the job" left incomplete by his father in 1991, or to take revenge on his father's behalf for an attempted assassination plot that Baghdad allegedly had hatched against him in 1993, or even Washington's purported desire to secure American domination over the region and its oil. This counternarrative suggests that US decision-making was marked by unprecedented institutional dysfunctions (illustrated, for example, by the exorbitant role of Vice President Dick Cheney) and by the warping of the American democratic system by the means of a politics of fear and the manipulation of public opinion.[6]

Questions and controversies, although lesser in scope, also exist about French policy during the Iraq crisis. Admittedly, former French leaders have an easier time addressing these concerns, as events largely have validated their choices. Their own narrative has tended to highlight their clairvoyance about the Iraq problem and about American motives, and explains their rejection of the US-led war based on this clairvoyance and also on a conception of international relations and a world view opposite to Bush's—and in continuity with the Gaullist legacy claimed by Chirac and heralded by Villepin.[7] They were, they argue, defending multilateralism and rejecting

4

the use of force except as a last resort while trying to prevent a so-called clash of civilizations. Yet some have contested this narrative as well, starting of course with the American and British leaders of the time. French policy, the detractors object, was in fact aimed at protecting a regime with which Paris had long had close relations, if not at defending France's mercantile interests. In this view, French opposition to the war was fed primarily by an atavistic anti-Americanism and by the desire to create a *Europe-puissance*—a "Europe-power"—in order to balance America's "hyperpower" while fostering a "multipolar" world.[8] It was also aimed, some critics suspect, at shielding French society from the fallout of a conflict that might feed the rancor of its increasing population of Arab or Muslim origins. Others claim that French policy throughout the 2002–3 Iraq crisis reflected France's perennial obsession with its "rank" and "grandeur." In short, these critics argue, the French instrumentalized this crisis for domestic purposes.[9]

Finally, much speculation persists about Iraq itself, its leaders, and their motivations. Many shadowy areas persist here as well, starting again with WMD: Why did Saddam Hussein's regime, which effectively had destroyed its WMD arsenal in the aftermath of the Gulf War (although it had done so without notifying the UN inspectors), then play cat-and-mouse with the UN throughout the 1990s and show no hurry in 2002–3 to prove its good faith and thereby spare itself a new war? Did Saddam Hussein want to preserve a WMD capability that could be relaunched later if necessary? Did he want to maintain uncertainty about the fate of the Iraqi arsenal, in order to preserve a deterrent capability against adversaries like Iran and to ensure his regime's capacity to intimidate internal opponents? Or did Iraq simply demonstrate the incoherence of a hard-pressed power that was incapable of transparency? The issue remains open, even though the objectives, modus operandi, and mental maps of the Baathist dictatorship have become the subject of serious academic research based on the regime's archives and on interviews with its former leaders.[10]

Thus, more than a decade after the Iraq war, questions are not lacking. This book intends to contribute some possible answers by addressing these events through the particular role of France and through the prism of Franco-American relations. To do this, I was able to gain access to the relevant official archives, namely those of the French presidency (the Élysée) and the French Ministry of Foreign Affairs (the Quai d'Orsay), which allowed me to review thousands of pages of once confidential or secret documents. In addition, some former actors were willing to entrust me with their personal papers. I also was able to conduct more than seventy personal interviews with former officials, mostly French and American.[11] Completing the wealth of documents already available on the American (and British) side, this evidence allowed me to enter into the heart of decision-making and to view the behind-the-scenes relations between nations and their leaders, starting with the French and American presidents.

The choice to look at events through the prism of Franco-American relations is justified by the centrality of these relations to the Iraq question. Indeed, Iraq had long been a decisive issue in relations between France and the United States, sometimes as a subject of convergence but more often as a bone of contention. In the 1970s, in light of the Cold War and the ongoing transformations in the Middle East, France had developed close relations with Iraq, a country that had long been a British preserve.[12] In line with General de Gaulle's policies, France under presidents Georges Pompidou (1969–74) and Valéry Giscard d'Estaing (1974–81) tried to assert itself within the Arab world. At the same time, the United States saw Iraq—mostly because of its closeness to the Soviet Union and its hostility to Israel—as a regional nuisance. Things changed in the 1980s when Saddam Hussein's regime, having started a war against Iran in the wake of that country's Islamic revolution of 1979, was supported by the Western powers as a rampart against the threat of Shi'a extremism. These events brought Paris and Washington to agree on the need to support Saddam Hussein, with Paris in the front line owing to its status as a major arms supplier of Iraq. This Franco-American convergence was confirmed at the end of the decade, but this time in the face of a new Iraqi challenge. Indeed Washington and Paris were in unison in condemning Iraq's surprise invasion of Kuwait in August 1990, and France chose from the start to participate in the international coalition assembled by the United States and to fully take part in the war alongside the Americans and British in January and February 1991.

The 1990s were a prelude to the 2002–3 Iraq crisis; it is impossible to understand the crisis without observing this period. Here again, the Franco-American relationship occupied a central place. In the years immediately following the Gulf War, France and the United States remained side by side when faced with a defeated Saddam Hussein who nonetheless refused to fall into line. At first, the French and the Americans were in full agreement on how to solve the Iraqi issue, starting with the necessary disarmament of Iraq. But starting in the mid-1990s, Paris and Washington began to diverge on the proper conduct faced with what was then turning into a latent crisis that would durably remain high on the international agenda. The United States, under President Bill Clinton, wanted to maintain sanctions against Baghdad indefinitely in order to "contain" a country that it had characterized a "rogue state," and it was already contemplating a policy of "regime change" in Iraq. By contrast, France under Jacques Chirac advocated applying UN resolutions strictly and not excluding a "rehabilitation" of Iraq if it fulfilled its obligations, beginning with disarmament. At the time, the Iraq issue did not lead to Franco-American confrontation, but it did grow into a source of permanent friction between the two countries.

The disagreement over Iraq in this period reflected a growing divergence between France and the United States over the very nature of the international system and America's role in the world. For the French, from the second half of the 1990s on, American policy toward Iraq became emblematic of the rising tendency to unilateralism that in their view had come to characterize US foreign policy after the Cold War. Far from the "new world order" organized around the UN that George H. W. Bush had announced in the immediate aftermath of the Gulf War, America—now the sole superpower after the disappearance of the Soviet Union, and in search of a world mission after the Cold War—was indeed increasingly willing to free itself from the constraints that limited its international choices and simply to impose these choices, even on its allies. This unilateral tendency was further encouraged by US domestic politics, in particular by the growing influence of a Republican-controlled Congress whose international options were becoming increasingly radical. Seen from Paris, US unilateralism took many forms: Washington's defiance of the UN; the unilateral, or even extraterritorial, imposition of sanctions on countries such as Cuba, Iran, or Libya; the nonratification of international treaties that might limit the US international margin of maneuver, such as the Comprehensive Nuclear-Test-Ban Treaty, the Kyoto Protocol on greenhouse gas emissions, or the treaty establishing an International Criminal Court; and an increasing temptation to resort to military force, not to mention the usual commercial conflicts between Europe and the United States and Washington's perennial hegemonic penchant within the Atlantic alliance.

French policy tried to temper these tendencies—which were especially manifest in the crises in the former Yugoslavia, from Bosnia to Kosovo—by arguing the need for a "multipolar" world and for a more regulated globalization; Chirac also called for the emergence of a *Europe-puissance* that would be a counterweight to the United States within the framework of a rebalanced transatlantic relationship. Throughout the 1990s, Paris and Washington continued to grow apart on a series of topics, with Iraq (and more generally Middle East issues, starting with the Israel-Palestine conflict) in the foreground. By the end of the decade, against the backdrop of the rise of the "indispensable nation" (in the words of Bill Clinton on the eve of his second term in January 1997) or the "hyperpower" (in the words of French foreign minister Hubert Védrine), the rift between France—and Europe—and the United States was increasing. But even though the two countries had thus far been able to manage these divergences without drama—although an all-powerful America was already visibly resentful of France's standing in its way—the arrival of George W. Bush in the White House in January 2001 and the September 11 attacks quickly transformed their differences into an open crisis, with Iraq once again in the spotlight.[13]

Franco-American relations soon became central in the Iraq crisis of 2002–3. After 9/11, America was determined to act forcefully in order to solve the Iraqi problem once and for all, and Bush's decision in September 2002 to "go down the UN route" confirmed the centrality of these relations. The ensuing negotiation of UN Security Council Resolution 1441—which gave Saddam Hussein a "last opportunity" to comply—was played out largely between Paris and Washington, and it was concluded in November by Secretary of State Colin Powell and Foreign Minister Dominique de Villepin. The result was a compromise between French objectives and American ones—or rather, as will be seen, a papering-over of the persistent differences between the two capitals. The centrality of the relationship was again demonstrated when the crisis turned into a confrontation starting in January 2003. Although France was not alone in opposing the United States, it was indeed the obvious leader of the "peace camp," as was confirmed by National Security Advisor Condoleezza Rice's *bon mot* after the war: "Punish France, forgive Russia, and ignore Germany."[14] In short, the international crisis over Iraq throughout 2003 was above all a Franco-American crisis, and the relation between France and the United States is therefore a useful angle for understanding it.

* * *

Since any explanation of events lies in their narrative, it is up to the reader to discover what this book brings to historical understanding. It may nevertheless be useful to supply a preview of its main findings. The first relates to the central question: why did this war take place? The answer lies in the tale of the ten years leading from the Gulf War in 1991 to the events of 2001, a critical period in which the French perspective helps to decode American policy. It was in this decade that Iraq and Saddam Hussein, through their own actions but also because of Washington's policies, became a veritable American obsession, embodying by the end of the decade a challenge out of all proportion with the danger it really represented and laying the ground for the events of 2002–3.[15] What had been in the 1990s but a limited matter—one, at any rate, that did not justify war, despite the occasional use of force against Baghdad—changed radically after 9/11. The attacks led American leaders, now haunted by the possible conjunction (the "nexus") between terrorist groups and states developing WMD, to see Iraq as a primary objective for the "global war on terror," although one that was deferred until after success in Afghanistan. The US decision to take on Saddam Hussein and his regime was thus "strategic" in the full meaning of the term (that this decision was erroneous is not the issue here), and it derived from a fundamental choice made in the context of trauma and the discovery of the new vulnerability of the United States, albeit combined with hubris and a belief in America's unlimited power. This choice involved reacting to the events of 9/11 through a response that would not only prevent future attacks but also transform the Middle East and the international system as a whole: a program that would begin with the removal of Saddam Hussein, who had now become the intolerable embodiment of resistance to American power. In many ways, it was a war meant as an example, in which US oil interests or the complex relation between the two presidents Bush were but secondary factors. The influence of neoconservatism should not be overestimated, either; although George W. Bush would adopt the "democratic" and "transformational" justification of the war advanced by the "neocons," the choice for war clearly arose first and foremost from a logic of national security.[16]

So was it primarily a matter of manipulation, or one of conviction? The two interpretations are not mutually exclusive. There is hardly any doubt today that American (and British) leaders did want, through "spin," exaggeration, and even mystification—about WMD and hypothetical links between Baghdad and the September 11 attacks—to "sell" American public opinion and the international community on the notion of an imminent threat that would justify a preventive war. But this does not mean that they did not truly see, through the magnifying glass of 9/11, Iraq and Saddam Hussein's regime as a major challenge, if not an intolerable danger that would justify regime change even at the cost of war. In fact, only a handful of those in the intelligence and decision-making communities believed that the Iraqi WMD arsenal did not actually exist. Although it would be naive not to see the extent to which the American decision to attack Iraq resulted from the dissembling of an administration for which the ends clearly justified the means, it would be just as simplistic to reduce that decision to pure deception. Yet even today, the US choice for war and the decision-making that led to it retain shadowy aspects that only access to the American archives may one day illuminate. (Perhaps not even then, since the Bush administration's dysfunctional decision-making casts doubts on the ability of future historians to find certainty in its archival documents.) When did Bush—for he was indeed at the heart of the decision—make the effective and irrevocable choice for war? What was the influence of his personality, starting with his religiosity? What was the exact role of his entourage, first and foremost Vice President Dick Cheney's? What were the proportions of error and manipulation in the evaluation of the Iraqi threat? How can one explain the disastrous preparation and then management of the postconflict phase, and the grossly mistaken overall expectations of the consequences of the war? All these open questions demonstrate that this unparalleled story, on the American side, has not yet been definitively written. Until it becomes possible to do so, I believe that the Franco-American dimension offers an important contribution to reconstructing the narrative.[17]

The French attitude presents fewer unknowns regarding both its policy toward Iraq and its motivations regarding the United States, as well as the internal determinants of its attitude. As with the American policy and in symmetry with it, the years 1991–2001 are decisive for understanding the French attitude in 2002–3. The conviction that the Iraq question might be solved peacefully and within the strict framework of the UN resolutions was, in that period, the guiding principle of a policy that was already in conflict with American policy, though one that had not given way to major clashes. For France, as for the United States, oil and commercial interests were not decisive, contrary to what some in Washington asserted by pointing to alleged French misconduct (particularly with regard to sanctions), an accusation that predictably resurfaced at the height of the crisis.[18] At that time, the French believed—at least until the withdrawal of the UN inspectors from Iraq in 1998, which helped open the way to the 2002–3 crisis—that the WMD question was by and large under control, if not settled; and, as mentioned earlier, they saw the Iraq situation as a textbook case of the increasing unilateralism of American policy. So it is hardly surprising that the French decision-makers, Chirac first and foremost, approached the 2002–3 crisis in the light of what had preceded it. Their experience and knowledge of a dossier with which they were long familiar explain the dual conviction that framed their attitude from the start: first, that Iraq did not represent a threat of a nature or magnitude to justify a preventive war (even if the French, it must be underlined, did not entirely exonerate the regime on the issue of WMD, and constantly maintained pressure on Baghdad to disarm fully and verifiably); and second, that the geopolitical consequences of a conflict—apart from its dismal human consequences—would be catastrophic both for Iraq and for the entire Middle East. The French feared that Iraq would splinter and further destabilize not only the Middle East but also relations between the West and the Arab and Muslim worlds, which after 9/11 could well give way to a "clash of civilizations."

Even though it is not possible to decode the Iraqi attitude through the French prism alone, the French perspective can provide a better understanding of some of its key aspects. The Americans tended to interpret the regime's behavior in terms of "rational" strategic calculations and to exaggerate its actual WMD capabilities, whereas the French (correctly) proved more skeptical on both scores. Having integrated into their analyses the psychology of Saddam Hussein, the characteristics of Iraq's political system, and the cultural and economic situation of Iraq and the region, the French did not believe that the regime had massively reconstituted its WMD arsenal, and they refrained from exaggerating the regime's potential danger—external, at least, since its internal brutality was not in doubt—even as they questioned its willingness or ability to cooperate in full. As a result, what the Americans dismissed as French complacency now appears as relative foresightedness: Iraq, as it turned out, was a weakened country equipped with a brutal, inward-looking regime, led by a dictator who was barely open to the external world, incapable of correctly judging power relations, and surrounded with people who out of fear kept the truth from him, and who therefore was prone, as Chirac would often deplore, "to make the wrong choices." As war approached in 2002, the Iraqi attitude of both bravado and resignation rather than the required cooperation seemed to confirm this perspective. Although it would be a mistake to assert that the French were totally correct in their assessment of the Iraq issue—they never, as shall be seen, entirely excluded the existence of WMD remnants in Iraq—their assessment was nevertheless less removed from reality than that of the Americans.[19]

Be that as it may, the French wanted to approach the Iraq crisis on its own merits. Contrary to the interpretation made by American leaders, for whom it was always tempting to reduce French policy to a Pavlovian expression of anti-Americanism, France's attitude was not systematically motivated by an instinctive desire to oppose the United States or by the idea of using the Iraq crisis to promote the concepts of *Europe-puissance* or a "multipolar world."[20] From the start of the crisis in the autumn of 2002, French decision-makers, in fact, faced an agonizing choice between defending a certain view of the international system and preserving Franco-American relations, which remained a vital aspect of French foreign policy after the Cold War. They went to great lengths to avoid a confrontation with Washington, just as they tried to turn the page as quickly as possible once the crisis was over. If the confrontation took place anyway, it was because the US attitude (Washington's choice for war clearly had been settled in advance) and the state of play within the Security Council (the British wanted to obtain a new UN resolution to justify the war) led the French to brandish the "absolute" weapon of a veto in the hope of not having to use it—though, ultimately, with the same effect as if they *had* used it.[21] At this stage, a clash had become inevitable. French leaders dealt with it without qualms, since what was at stake now far outstripped the Iraq crisis: a certain conception of world order and a determination (shared with others, starting with Germany) to reject American unilateralism, especially when it came to war and peace. The legacy of Gaullism doubtless played a part, as did the massive support of public opinion in France, within Europe, and even elsewhere in the world, on which French leaders could capitalize in their face-off with the United States, giving French diplomacy its hour of glory at the UN. It was difficult at that point for them not to be carried away by the wave, as illustrated by Villepin's UN speech. But while Villepin drew the spotlight, it was in fact Chirac who firmly set the course, in accordance with the presidential dominance that characterizes foreign policy making under the Fifth Republic. Chirac based his determinations on two considerations from which he did not depart throughout the crisis: an extreme reluctance to consider any French involvement in what he saw as a military adventure in Iraq, and the refusal to legitimize a military intervention except as a last resort and within a UN framework.[22] At the end of a long career of many turns and jolts, Jacques Chirac—a politician with a reputation for versatility and a mixed record as president, yet one who was "egoless," according to those close to him—would thus leave his mark in history by an attitude that derived first and foremost from his personal experience and convictions. Personalities do count in international politics.[23]

This book seeks to offer a dispassionate reading of a major international crisis that has now become history. The military adventure and subsequent fiasco of the war in Iraq were hardly an inevitable response to the challenge of the September 11 attacks, yet they cannot simply be reduced to a plot or manipulation. They must be understood for what they were: a strategic mistake of monumental proportions, which can only be explained by the impact of the 9/11 trauma on an America that was torn between an unprecedented feeling of vulnerability and the unfailing certainty of its superiority but also was convinced that it had finally found a "mission" after the Cold War. Likewise, the French attitude, far from simply mirroring the Gaullist stereotype of the French quest for "grandeur" or being attributable to sheer anti-Americanism, reflected the dilemma of a medium but still influential power that found itself caught between its strategic interests and its vision of world order. And yet the international and transatlantic crisis—and in particular, the Franco-American crisis—over Iraq cannot be interpreted as a "perfect storm" whose magnitude was caused by the improbable, unfortunate conjuncture of factors, as some believe.[24] Nor was it "just another major crisis" in a long series that periodically have shaken Franco-American and Euro-American relations since the creation of the Atlantic alliance.[25] To believe so would be tantamount to neglecting its deep-seated causes: the tectonic shifts at work in the international system and in American policy from the end of the Cold War to the aftermath of 9/11—shifts for which the Iraq crisis served as the seismograph, until the final earthquake of the war.[26]

Prologue
Faced with a Hyperpower

On November 26, 1997, former US president George H. W. Bush visited French president Jacques Chirac at the Élysée. The two men maintained a relationship of trust comparable to the one that had prevailed between Bush and Chirac's predecessor, the late François Mitterrand, with whom Bush recalled having had "very frequent" contact. Chirac opened the conversation by describing the state of Franco-American relations: they were "good," he said, but "complicated" by Congress. Bush agreed, lambasting Congress's hostility to China, its desire to disengage from Europe, and its refusal to pay its share of the United Nations budget. He reproached his successor, President Bill Clinton, for not being "truly interested" in the European continent at a time when it was facing major challenges, specifically in achieving peace in the Balkans and the coming launch of the single European currency. The current Franco-American disagreements, Bush concluded, were not France's fault. Chirac replied that in his eyes there was no "Franco-American problem," although he conceded that "from time to time" both sides might take umbrage with each other. The "real question," he said, was "the image of the United States in the world," which was deteriorating. The United States wanted to "command," he went on, but it was doing so badly. It should avoid humiliating others, such as by ceasing to adopt sanctions that affected third countries, a practice that many nations rejected. The United States should also change its policy in the Middle East and, as Bush had done in his time, put pressure on Israel. The situation there was very dangerous, Chirac stressed, since

Palestine Liberation Organization leader Yasser Arafat might "disappear" and the United States was doing nothing to prevent this from happening. When Bush approved these statements, Chirac hammered home the message that the "evolution of the world" should encourage Washington to "change [its] attitude" and adapt to a multipolarity that had become economically and politically unstoppable.

However, when the conversation moved on to Iraq, over which yet another crisis was then unfolding—provoked by Baghdad's refusal to let the UN disarmament inspectors do their work—the exchange between Bush and Chirac became markedly less consensual. Although he had just acknowledged as a general rule that the United States should "do more diplomacy," Bush stressed that "no concession should be made to Saddam Hussein." Chirac reassured him on that score by explaining the French position, which was not one of leniency toward the Baghdad regime, but he also emphasized that in his view the US embargo on Iraq should be lifted gradually if the inspectors concluded that Iraq no longer possessed weapons of mass destruction. The United States, Chirac deplored, refused to consider removing the sanctions until Saddam Hussein was "eliminated." At that point in the conversation, Bush came back to the 1991 Gulf War. He wanted to justify the choices that he had made at the time: many would have wished for Operation Desert Storm to finish the job by going to Baghdad, he said, but this option had been ruled out. "The coalition would not have held," he explained, and American forces would have been transformed into "troops of occupation in an Arab country." Chirac did not react to this mention of the past, preferring to return to the charge about sanctions: the "Iraqi people should not be held hostage," he insisted, because the regime was not affected by the embargo but the Iraqi population was in a "disastrous" humanitarian situation. Bush objected, stating that Iraq had ignored many UN resolutions and that Baghdad should respect all of them. Yes, Chirac retorted, but if the regime finally complied and if the UN inspectors' reports became "positive," then it would be necessary to "move toward a lifting of sanctions." Bush ended up conceding that if the disarmament reports were truly conclusive, then in effect it would be "difficult" for the United States to oppose the lifting of sanctions. But, he repeated once more, this outcome had to be conditional on the resolutions being "truly respected." Before Bush left, he confided to Chirac that he had intentionally come to speak to him that day without being accompanied by the US ambassador—a Democrat—for he wished to have "a frank and straight talk" with the French president. He then concluded the conversation with a political and family confidence: if his son George W. Bush won reelection as governor of Texas the following year, he might well decide to launch into the race for the Republican Party nomination for the presidential elections in 2000.[1]

The conversation between Bush and Chirac that day perfectly summarized the situation of Franco-American relations in the second half of the 1990s and in the post–Cold War era. Relations between the two countries were good, but the Iraq question, against the backdrop of the increasing unilateralism of the "hyperpower," was one of the growing irritants that complicated relations between Paris and Washington, though it had not degenerated into an open crisis. The two men obviously could not foresee that their conversation would assume its full meaning after George W. Bush was indeed elected US president three years later—nor how the events that had occurred from "Bush 41" to "Bush 43" would change the course of history.

Chapter 1
From One War to Another: 1991–2001

To understand why Iraq was involved in three major wars in less than a quarter of a century, we have to go back to the latter half of the Cold War. Starting in the 1970s, sitting on its gigantic oil resources, Iraq found itself at the nexus of decisive economic and strategic stakes, both regionally and globally. In this context, the leaders of Iraq—with Saddam Hussein rising to prominence in that period—were determined to build up their country into a key actor in the Middle East, first and foremost from a military standpoint. Iraq's steady growth in power throughout the 1970s culminated in its leaders' decision in 1980 to unleash a war against Iran, where an Islamic revolution had taken place the previous year. When this devastating conflict ended in 1988, Saddam Hussein did not relent. By the end of the decade, Iraq was already an international problem of prime importance. Iraq's surprise invasion of Kuwait in August 1990, which occurred against the background of the end of the East-West conflict, came as a dramatic confirmation that the world was tipping into a new era.

The outcome of the Gulf War, which took place in the first weeks of 1991, could have settled the Iraq problem. Yet it did nothing of the kind: Saddam Hussein remained in power and adopted a defiant attitude in spite of his humiliating defeat, and as a result the Iraq problem became more durably entrenched—with the question of weapons of mass destruction (WMD) at its heart. During the following years, Iraq thus became the focus of what turned into a permanent, if latent, international crisis. Although France and the United States had acted in unison in the 1991 Gulf War and its aftermath, their positions diverged more and more in the latter half of the 1990s. To be sure, the Iraq question was then only one subject of friction among others in the Franco-American relationship, but the prologue to what would occur between 2002 and 2003 was already in place.

"The Mother of All Battles"

Iraq had become a British mandate after the collapse of the Ottoman Empire in World War I, and in the 1950s it was still an important ally of both Great Britain and the United States in the Middle East. Everything changed in 1958 when the pro-Western monarchy of King Faisal II was overthrown by a coup by "progressive" military officers under General Abd al-Karim Qasim. The new regime rapidly began to approach the Soviet Union. This move was confirmed in the 1960s with the conquest of power by the socialist-leaning Baath Party, which definitively took control in 1968 under the leadership of General Ahmed Hassan al-Bakr. In 1972, Iraq signed a friendship and cooperation treaty with Moscow; from then on, it became a major Soviet client state. The Soviet Union emerged as Iraq's foremost arms supplier, and as a result, Iraq saw its relations with the United States deteriorate significantly. As the Cold War intensified in the Middle East in the 1960s and 1970s, the rapprochement between Iraq and the Soviet Union was a matter of increasing concern for Washington. This concern was compounded by Baghdad's hostility to Israel, and diplomatic relations between the United States and Iraq were broken off after the June 1967 Six-Day War. Meanwhile, during the 1970s Iran became the prime regional ally of the United States and the guarantor, along with Saudi Arabia, of America's strategic and oil interests in the Middle East. Iraq observed with apprehension the ascent of its long-time Persian rival. Considering that Baghdad, after the 1978 Camp David Accords between Egypt and Israel, took the lead in a "rejection front" of Arab nations against peace with Israel, one can understand how the combination of East-West tensions and regional factors had made Iraq the *bête noire* of the United States by the end of the 1970s.[1]

Meanwhile, Baghdad had become Paris's privileged partner in the Middle East.[2] Here, too, the Six-Day War had marked a turning point. President Charles de Gaulle's condemnation of the Israeli decision to take a preventive offensive against Egypt won France immense prestige in the Arab world.

Thanks to de Gaulle's quarrel with the "Anglo-Saxons" and his willingness to reach out to the Third World, France was now seen as the champion of anti-imperialism. De Gaulle was driven mostly by considerations of regional and global balance, as well as by a search for international "status." His successor at the Élysée, Georges Pompidou, who came to power following de Gaulle's resignation in April 1969, was willing to go further and reinvent France's traditional "Arab policy" by restoring its once-privileged ties with the Arab world, which had been ruined by decolonization and the Algerian War (1954–62). Although the return of French influence in the Middle East enhanced French prestige, the reinvention of France's Arab policy also derived from economic and strategic objectives: its aim was to guarantee (especially after the 1973 oil crisis) energy supplies and to open up markets for French exports.

At the start of the 1970s, France saw Iraq as an ideal partner in that regard. Baathism, a variant of secular Arab nationalism harboring vast ambitions in terms of political and economic modernization, claimed to be inspired by the French "republican" model. In addition, Iraqi leaders saw a close partnership with France as a corrective, if not a complete alternative, to an overly exclusive dependence on the Soviet Union. French diplomacy, in turn, was prone to see Iraqi aspirations as exemplifying a sort of Arab "Gaullism," echoing de Gaulle and his successors' refusal to adhere to the bloc system that divided the world along superpower lines. Thus, a close relationship between France and a former British preserve was formed, allowing the French—whose regional ambitions and influence had long been overshadowed by first the British and then the Americans—to take a kind of revenge on their "Anglo-Saxon" rivals.

A milestone was reached in 1972 when Baghdad nationalized Iraqi oil and gave French companies preferential contracts for exploiting its deposits: a coup for France in the face of their Western competitors. Reputed to hold the world's second-largest petroleum reserves (after Saudi Arabia), Iraq seemed to be a future El Dorado for oil. At the same time, France was becoming one of the prime exporters to Iraq. At first, major civil contracts dominated Franco-Iraqi exchanges, but weapons contracts occupied a growing place throughout the 1970s. These arms exports helped finance the development of French defense programs, the cornerstone of France's policy of "independence." The same pattern held true for nuclear power: at the end of the decade, France delivered to Iraq the research reactor "Osirak," a controversial decision in light of the risk that Baghdad could apply this cooperation to military use—which led Israel to destroy the Osirak reactor in an air raid in June 1981.

21

By the mid-1970s, Iraq had become a French passion, mingling ideals and economic interests, involving politicians and businessmen, combining civil contracts and arms exports. An Iraqi lobby was formed in France at the intersection of these different milieus. More than President Georges Pompidou or his successor Valéry Giscard d'Estaing (1974–81), it was Jacques Chirac (prime minister from 1974 to 1976) who became identified with this policy toward Iraq. After a visit to Iraq in October 1974, Chirac welcomed Saddam Hussein (then second in command) to France in September 1975. "The Iraqi leader, who enjoyed great popularity in the Arab world, was not then a pariah," Chirac noted later, recognizing that "the man appeared intelligent, not without humor, and even rather sympathetic" and that their relations were tinged with "great cordiality."[3] A quarter-century later, some in Washington would use this episode to discredit French policy.

Unlike the 1970s, the 1980s were marked by convergence between France and the United States over Iraq. Following the Islamic revolution and the fall of the shah in 1979, Iran became for the Americans the principal threat to the region's stability, which became even more at risk after the Soviet invasion of Afghanistan in December of that year. With the "new" Cold War—a surge in East-West tensions that resulted from US and Western perceptions of the Soviet Union's growing expansionism starting in the latter half of the 1970s—in full swing, the Middle East was a strategic priority for the United States, now concerned about containing the Islamic revolution while checking Soviet expansionism. In the eyes of the Americans, the most expedient way to achieve this dual goal was to support Iraq. Baghdad had triggered a merciless war against Tehran in September 1980 in the hope of winning an old contest over the sovereignty of the Shatt al-Arab waterway and preventing Ayatollah Ruhollah Khomeini from spreading his Islamic revolution to Iraq. Saddam Hussein feared in particular that Khomeini might be tempted to make use of Iraq's Shi'a minority as a destabilizing force against the Sunni-dominated regime.

France, under the socialist President François Mitterrand, played a prime role in the West's aid to Iraq. When Mitterrand entered the Élysée in 1981, he was hardly sympathetic to the regime of Saddam Hussein, who in 1979 had assumed full power through a bloody purge at the top of the Baath Party. Moreover, Mitterrand initially was inclined to reexamine French policy on arms exports. Yet as of the summer of 1981, he chose to continue arms deliveries to Baghdad. In 1982, 40 percent of French arms exports went to Iraq, and the geopolitical stakes in the Middle East made France provide decisive support to Iraq. (Paris, like Washington, feared Shiite expansionism, which it saw a threat to the stability of the Middle East and the Persian Gulf.) By 1983, French support would even approach a situation of cobelligerence, as Paris "lent" Baghdad Super-Étendard fighter-bomber planes equipped with Exocet missiles for its war against Iran.

The United States supported and even encouraged French policy. Behind the façade of US neutrality in the Iran-Iraq conflict, Washington in reality took Iraq's part, and in 1982 it began to make overtures to Baghdad. The symbol of this policy came in December 1983, when Donald Rumsfeld, President Ronald Reagan's envoy in the region, shook hands with Saddam Hussein—an act that also would provoke much commentary later on. For the time being, Washington granted Baghdad credit after credit, struck Iraq from the list of terrorist states, and passed along useful military information. Even though it did not directly sell arms to Iraq, it encouraged other countries (starting with France) to do so. In 1984, relations between Baghdad and Washington were officially reestablished. The Americans were convinced that Iraq under Saddam Hussein was the best bulwark against Ayatollah Khomeini's Iran; in addition, they reckoned that by supporting Iraq, the Western powers could bring it to distance itself from Moscow.

Of course, there was already a looming Iraqi "problem." The regime's brutality did not abate, and the war with Iran even exacerbated it: between eliminating opponents and repressing minorities, the gravity of human rights violations in Iraq in the 1980s was not in doubt. But realpolitik led Western governments to avert their gaze. The most glaring illustration of this attitude came toward the end of the Iran-Iraq conflict, in March 1988, when the Iraqi regime did not hesitate to use chemical weapons against its own population— specifically, the Kurds of northern Iraq, whom Saddam Hussein suspected of colluding with Iran—killing several thousand people in the city of Halabja. Western reactions, including America's, were moderate to say the least; the Reagan administration decided against imposing sanctions on Iraq.[4]

Halabja confirmed another alarming characteristic of the Iraq regime: its determination to acquire WMD. It evidently had already done so with chemical ones, since Baghdad had used such weapons several times against Iran, starting in 1983, before doing so against the Kurds. Iraq's ballistic capabilities were also quite real, as witnessed in 1988 by the "war of the cities," the last phase of the conflict during which improved Soviet Scud missiles were launched against Iran. But Iraq was also suspected of possessing biological capabilities, as well as attempting to build a nuclear weapon, an objective that Saddam Hussein had openly proclaimed in the late 1970s despite the supposedly civilian nature of the Iraqi nuclear program. All the same, in the 1980s the danger of WMD proliferation remained obscured by the centrality of the East-West conflict. Whether for developing countries in general or Iraq in particular, only in the wake of the 1991 Gulf War would WMD proliferation truly be perceived as a serious danger and the Iraq problem appear in its true dimension, outside the norm. Yet by allowing Iraq to acquire massive amounts of equipment and sensitive technologies throughout the 1970s and 1980s, the West—out of naivety or laxness, cynicism or interest—had largely contributed to this growing threat.[5]

For the time being, the West chose to downplay the concerns that the Iraqi regime might legitimately have raised. To be sure, at the end of the 1980s human rights organizations routinely denounced the regime's abuses, and its activities with respect to WMD worried the West's intelligence services. But in the aftermath of the Iran-Iraq conflict, which ended in the summer of 1988, Western governments preferred to wager on Saddam Hussein's "moderation." They hoped that Iraq, exhausted by eight years of a war that it had instigated and almost lost, damaged by heavy debt, and facing immense resource needs for reconstruction, would prove a reasonable partner and would incline to the status quo. Paris and Washington essentially shared this analysis.

Coming from very different positions, France and the United States arrived at a sort of convergence on the Iraq issue by the end of the 1980s. On the French side, a more balanced relation with Baghdad was sought. Combined with the normalization of relations with Iran, the problem of Iraq's debt to France (which by then had risen to 30 billion francs) led to reduced French arms sales to Baghdad—even if some, like Defense Minister Jean-Pierre Chevènement, continued to push for their continuation. On the American side, inversely, George H. W. Bush, who succeeded Reagan as president in January 1989, tried to consolidate US ties with Iraq. Although the Cold War was now in its terminal phase, the United States was still concerned with countering Soviet influence in the Middle East; in addition, US decision-makers believed that Iraq remained the best bulwark against Iran, and that from now on it might contribute to regional stability by adopting a moderate position on Israel. Further engagement with Iraq, of course, also offered significant commercial openings, a prospect dangled by Washington's Iraq lobby, which by then had become quite active.[6]

Yet far from settling down, Saddam Hussein demonstrated a disquieting revival of aggressiveness in the first months of 1990. While continuing Iraq's military buildup, he vocally denounced both the United States, which he accused of conducting a policy of occupation in the Middle East, and Israel, which he threatened to wipe off the map. Perhaps even more ominously, he now put Kuwait—with which Iraq had an old territorial dispute—in the crosshairs. Unable to persuade Kuwait (and Saudi Arabia) to erase the huge debt that Iraq had accumulated during the war with Iran, he accused Kuwait of trying to strangle Iraq financially by provoking a drop in oil prices, and in the summer of 1990 he threatened military action. The West, at that juncture, gravely underestimated Saddam Hussein's intentions. On July 25, American ambassador April Glaspie—following the instructions that she had received from Washington—met with Saddam Hussein and indicated to him that in spite of "concerns" about Baghdad's attitude, the United States "took no position" on the border issue. Glaspie left the meeting secure in the idea that Iraq would refrain from invading Kuwait.[7] Meanwhile, her French counterpart, Maurice Courage, was categorical: "I exclude a priori some military adventure," he wrote at the end of July.[8] Yet on August 2, almost 150,000 Iraqi soldiers and 2,000 Iraqi tanks invaded Kuwait.

The invasion of Kuwait was like a clap of thunder in a serene sky. Combined with German reunification, which would occur just two months later, the invasion signaled with resounding publicity the end of the Cold War. The bipolar confrontation had fed conflicts in the developing world, but it had also put a lid on regional crises. "This is the first test of the post [Cold] War system," Deputy Secretary of State Lawrence Eagleburger aptly commented after the invasion. "If [Saddam Hussein] succeeds, others might well try to imitate him."[9] From the start, it was indeed clear that the fait accompli of the invasion and subsequent annexation of Kuwait would be unacceptable to the international community, all the more so because there was no certainty that Saddam Hussein would stop there. Might not Saudi Arabia be his next prey? The stakes in the crisis—whether regional or global, economic or geopolitical, petroleum or something else—were colossal. As early as August 3, Mitterrand and Bush concurred in the view that it was impossible to let Saddam Hussein "secure his hegemony over the Arab world." One way or another, the Iraqi dictator would have to end up withdrawing his troops: this aggression "will not stand," Bush famously declared on August 5.[10]

But how to achieve this was another matter. From the beginning, American policy aimed to gather as large a coalition as possible, which implied that it would have to seek legitimacy from the United Nations (UN)—a resolutely multilateral approach, and one on which George W. Bush would turn his back twelve years later. On August 6, UN Security Council Resolution 661 imposed severe sanctions on Iraq. Neither Moscow nor Beijing blocked the resolution with a veto—a sign that the Cold War was well and truly over—yet soon it appeared that the embargo alone would not make Saddam Hussein yield. At the end of October, Bush doubled the US military personnel already on the ground to defend Saudi Arabia as part of Operation Desert Shield; on November 29, the Security Council adopted Resolution 678, which authorized member-states to use "all necessary means" to obtain an Iraqi withdrawal. The resolution invoked Chapter VII of the UN Charter, the provision that authorized the use of force to restore or maintain international security, for the first time since the start of the Korean War in 1950. January 15, 1991, was the date of the ultimatum for Iraq's withdrawal, yet any remaining hope of a peaceful solution quickly evaporated. Saddam Hussein, who by all the evidence underestimated American determination and incorrectly evaluated the situation (as he habitually would do), dug in his heels; Washington, meanwhile, left very little room for negotiation and in fact discouraged any initiative in this direction. On January 9, 1991, Secretary of State James A. Baker III met with his Iraqi counterpart Tariq Aziz in Geneva, but to no avail. On January 16, the aerial phase of Desert Storm was launched in the form of a massive bombing campaign.[11]

France was engaged alongside the United States from the start. Its former support for Saddam Hussein's Iraq was irrevocably reversed. "I am quite unforgiving about his behavior, [which is] very bellicose," Mitterrand had confided to West German chancellor Helmut Kohl in early July 1990, less than a month before the invasion of Kuwait.[12] Once the invasion had occurred, Mitterrand ruled out the possibility that France would shirk its responsibilities as a permanent member of the Security Council. Although he was conscious of getting involved in a "logic of war" that was being denounced by some in France (including Chevènement, who would resign shortly after operations started), he was not ready to shy away from Western solidarity. No doubt he believed—at the risk of misunderstandings with Washington—that he ought to do everything to give peace a chance, hence the official and unofficial attempts undertaken by France to reach a negotiated solution in the weeks preceding the ultimatum. Yet in reality, Mitterrand had few illusions about the success of these attempts, and his efforts did not contradict France's fundamental choice to participate in the coalition and, if necessary, in military operations. "Bush does not have a nuanced attitude," he conceded to Kohl at the start of December, but added, "We cannot remain outside the coming war.

. . . Saddam Hussein has had the time to reflect."[13] Despite the doubts that some American leaders had expressed in the preceding weeks, France's commitment proved to be clear-cut, even though it was limited in means. (France and Great Britain were the only two European countries to contribute both land and air forces to the coalition, but the French division, named "Daguet," comprised only fifty-some aircraft and about 11,000 troops, significantly less than the British contribution.) France's armed forces, organized as they had been throughout the Cold War around nuclear deterrence, were scarcely prepared for expeditionary interventions. Moreover, irrespective of the military contribution, there was a wish to project an image of French participation that was not overly aligned with the United States.[14]

What, in France's view, were the war's objectives? According to the letter of the Security Council resolutions, they should aim at reestablishing the status quo ante, neither more nor less. Mitterrand's approach was legalistic: "If the war objectives are limited to the liberation of Kuwait, then we are consistent," he stressed a few weeks before the ultimatum, though he noted that others had "war objectives that go beyond the resolutions."[15] In fact, it was clear by then that the United States was trying to use the opportunity to get rid of the threat that Iraq represented for the region, which at a minimum implied taking advantage of the coming war to destroy its military potential. Yet Mitterrand had no qualms about the legitimacy of using military force on a large scale; questioned by Kohl in mid-February 1991 on the efficacy of four weeks of air strikes, he observed that their effects had been "considerable": Iraq's air force was now "nonexistent," "about a third of its tanks [had been] destroyed, [and so had been] the navy, the chemical, [and] the nuclear." But, he added just a few days before the start of ground operations, "the delicate moment will be the day Kuwait is evacuated by force. There will be divergent views of what is suitable to do then. It will be wise to stop there."[16]

The ground offensive, which began on February 24, was stunning. The coalition's encircling maneuver by means of a "left hook," in which allied forces deeply penetrated Iraqi territory, proved a success. By the 27th, the Americans estimated that the Iraqi forces, caught in the trap, largely had been destroyed; the "mother of all battles," as Saddam Hussein had declared it would be, turned into a debacle for his troops. From a military point of view, at least, it therefore seemed perfectly possible to pursue the Iraqi army as far as Baghdad in order to put an end to the regime. For Bush, though, there was no question of doing so. Many reasons contributed to his decision to reject this option: the absence of a UN mandate authorizing such an objective; the refusal of the allies (illustrated by Mitterrand's earlier commentary) to envisage it; the prospect of an uncertain occupation of the country; and especially the fear of Iraq's fragmentation and the regionally destabilizing potential consequences of a breakup, such as the secession of Iraq's Kurdish population or the rallying of Iraqi Shiites to Iran. When he was informed that a large portion of the regime's elite Republican Guard had been destroyed, and warned of the risk that the destruction of Iraqi forces retreating along the infamous "highway of death" would turn into a massacre, Bush took the advice of Joint Chiefs of Staff chairman General Colin Powell and Operation Desert Storm commander General Norman Schwartzkopf and decided to cease operations on February 28—barely a hundred hours after they began. This decision bore heavy consequences and would haunt American leaders for a long time to come.[17]

"The mother of all resolutions"

In spite of his blatant defeat, Saddam Hussein remained in power for more than a decade after the events of early 1991. His continued presence would weigh on the fate of his country and make the Iraq question a durable headache for the international community. "Saddam Hussein [is] still here," a disillusioned Bush noted just after the conflict. That had not been the expected outcome: another reason for the American decision not to "go to Baghdad" was the near-certainty among those in charge in Washington—including the intelligence community—that Saddam Hussein would not be able to survive a humiliating defeat. The favorite hypothesis in Washington was that there would be a military coup. In fact, on February 15, Bush had called on the Iraqis (foremost, the military) "to take matters into their own hands," no doubt in the hope of avoiding a costly ground operation.[18]

But the opposite scenario occurred. Of course, Iraq paid a high price for the war, both economic (almost $200 billion in war damages) and human (up to 35,000 civilians and 100,000 soldiers killed, as opposed to 350 for the coalition). But the losses inflicted on its military potential, including the WMD arsenal, were in the end more limited than the American generals had believed. As for the Republican Guard, Bush's decision to put a quick end to operations had prevented it from being annihilated. Saddam Hussein thus conserved a portion of his resources.[19] Worse still, the American decisions in the critical weeks at the end of the winter of 1991 enabled the regime to consolidate its hold, at the cost of additional suffering for a portion of Iraq's population. Bush's call for the Iraqis to take matters into their own hands, relayed inside the country by the Central Intelligence Agency (CIA), was received as encouragement for an uprising. In the first days of March, during the rout of the Iraqi armies, the Shiites started a rebellion in the south; the Kurds in the north followed suit a few days later. But the Americans, still fearing a possible splintering of the country, in reality had no intention of actively aiding rebels to overthrow the regime. This lack of support, in effect, gave a green light to the bloody repression that Baghdad quickly undertook—an episode that would long haunt the consciences of US decision-makers. In those critical days, Schwartzkopf even allowed the Iraqi military to use their helicopters for "logistic" and "humanitarian" reasons, thereby permitting the regime to regain control. The result of these events was not only to help the regime quickly put a stop to the revolts, but also to contribute to its survival. Indeed, even if the military coup that Washington was trying to arouse soon after the war appeared to be imminent, the uprisings in the south and in the north reversed the situation. Fearing the consequences of these rebellions (and in particular the success of a Shiite uprising) as much as Saddam Hussein did, the Iraqi generals gave up on their project to depose Saddam Hussein and stuck with the dictator. The support of his generals strengthened Saddam Hussein to the point that the shame of defeat was quickly forgotten. The surprising resilience of the Iraq regime and of Saddam Hussein himself would be a constant in the decade to come.[20]

It was in this context that the Security Council, in the aftermath of the conflict, laid the basis for a settlement of the Iraq question. The principal elements of this settlement were the object of a consensus among Western powers. Anglo-American relations were then particularly close, and so the diplomatic game was played out mostly between Washington and London, with France having a more limited role. But to the extent that cooperation between France and Britain in the Security Council traditionally was positive, and Paris and Washington had trusting relations in this period, consensus was formed first within the "P3" (France, the United Kingdom, and the United States, the Security Council's three permanent Western members) before being enlarged to the "P5" (adding the Soviet Union—later Russia—and China, the other two permanent members) and then to all fifteen Security Council members.[21]

The key elements of a settlement were laid out in Resolution 687, which was adopted by the Security Council on April 3. Drafted mainly by the Americans and the British, Resolution 687 contained a series of measures that gave the UN a central role in settling issues, ranging from Iraq's acceptance of liability for war damages to the demarcation of its border with Kuwait—hence its nickname, "the mother of all resolutions." Yet two aspects bore a particular importance for later on.

The first concerned sanctions. Sanctions were not lifted automatically after the liberation of Kuwait, for Resolution 687 stated that this would happen only when Iraq had fulfilled all of its obligations, including disarmament. Yet because a new resolution was necessary to lift the sanctions, any permanent Security Council member now held a veto over the decision. The United States would not fail to make use of this mechanism: over the years, the transformation of temporary sanctions into de facto permanent sanctions would become a subject of friction and a major issue with regard to Iraq.[22]

The second aspect, inseparable from the first, concerned disarmament. Resolution 687 had put in place a mechanism whose strictures were meant to respond to long-standing worries about Iraq's WMD ambitions. The goals were to definitively eliminate these weapons and their corresponding programs, and to make it impossible for Iraq to reconstitute them, all in a verifiable manner and under international control. The resolution created the United Nations Special Commission (UNSCOM) to oversee the disarmament, which would involve verifying Iraq's declarations concerning its WMD armaments or programs; conducting inspections of declared sites; and arranging for the destruction, removal, or neutralization of any weapons found. For nuclear issues in particular, UNSCOM would be supplemented by the International Atomic Energy Agency (IAEA). A follow-up system of ongoing monitoring and verification (OMV) of Iraq's disarmament was to be put in place to guarantee that Iraq would not resume its activities. Here again, the initiative for this mechanism came first and foremost from London and Washington. In the aftermath of the Iraqi defeat, there was nevertheless complete consensus in the West on the necessity of disarming Iraq. The French had no objections, as they were fully convinced of the risks entailed by WMD proliferation. (In 1992, in the wake of the conflict, France became party to the 1968 Nuclear Non-Proliferation Treaty, which it had not originally signed during the Cold War years.) Moreover, as it appeared unlikely that Baghdad would dare to oppose the international community, most actors and observers at the time thought that the disarmament would be carried out rapidly. Iraq had been severely defeated and its arsenal was largely destroyed; it seemed to have a clear interest in ensuring that sanctions would be lifted as fast as possible so it could devote itself to reconstruction. But this way of reasoning did not anticipate the attitude of defiance that Saddam Hussein would adopt right from the start.[23]

In addition to sanctions and disarmament, no-fly zones were established above a large part of Iraqi territory. This decision was the result of the humanitarian concerns raised by the violent repression of the Kurds and the Shiites in the aftermath of the conflict. Inspired by France (under the influence of François Mitterrand's wife Danielle, an advocate of the Kurdish cause) and Belgium and supported by the United States and Great Britain, Resolution 688, adopted on April 5, 1991, opened the way to Operation Provide Comfort, conducted a few days later by the United States, France, and Great Britain to protect Kurdish refugees. To implement this operation, the three countries created a no-fly zone north of the 36th parallel; it was completed in August 1992 by a similar zone south of the 32nd ("Southern Watch"), motivated by the need to protect the Shiites. Although these operations initially were the object of a thorough entente among the three countries, they—and, more generally, the issue of the use of force by means of aerial strikes against Iraq—would later become an apple of discord among them.[24]

There was another source of potential Franco-American disagreement: the fate of Saddam Hussein. From the start, the United States believed that there was nothing to be expected from Saddam Hussein and that only his departure from power would normalize the situation. "Saddam [cannot] be redeemed,"[25] Lawrence Eagleburger had declared in May 1991. Washington had already hinted that the sanctions should remain in place as long as he was in power; it also was studying the possibility of getting rid of him through covert actions, even though it did not overly believe in their effectiveness or, arguably, in the desirability of the outcome. The events of the end of winter 1991 had showed Saddam Hussein's capacity for resistance. In addition, such a scenario could cause Iraq to break apart, which remained the Westerners' nightmare. Overall, as later explained by Richard Haass, who at the time was in charge of the Iraq issue at the National Security Council (NSC), Washington in effect chose to put in place a policy of "containment." Much as in the case with the communist bloc during the Cold War, the United States' principal objective was to limit Iraq's ability to be a nuisance, and its secondary objective was to foster a possible regime change. For the time being, the latter was but a long-term objective: in 1992, the consensus of Washington's intelligence community was that Saddam Hussein was "likely to hang on." Yet the question of regime change would, in time, divide the French and the Americans.[26]

31

Still, for now the Western nations were united in their desire to implement Resolution 687 regardless of Iraq's defiant attitude. Indeed, Baghdad quickly adopted a posture of noncooperation, even provocation, which led the Americans, British, and French to join together to hold a firm line, especially over the question of disarmament. Far from playing the game, the Iraq regime seemed intent on multiplying obstacles, even demonstrating a desire for obstruction, thereby preventing any chance of a quick settlement. At the same time, it had also become clear that the breadth and sophistication of the Iraqi WMD programs very much exceeded what was thought to be in place before the hostilities, and that the scale of destruction that the coalition's air campaign had inflicted on Iraqi capabilities had been vastly overestimated.[27]

The magnitude of UNSCOM's task became clear at the start of the inspections in the spring and summer of 1991, when UN inspectors could measure the (largely unsuspected) extent of the programs, facilities, and armaments they would have to dismantle. The surprise did not come from chemical or ballistic weapons, whose existence had been known ever since the Iraqis had used them against Iran and also against their own population in the 1980s. Even if many aspects of these two areas (most notably for chemical weapons) were still unknown at that time because of Iraq's noncooperation, the start of UNSCOM inspections essentially confirmed the extent of their presence. As for the biological area, Iraqi activities in that realm were poorly known by intelligence services before the conflict, and it was only later that their actual scope would begin to be suspected and then proven. So it was in the nuclear domain that the first discoveries made by the UN inspectors came as a major surprise: as of the summer of 1991, it appeared clear that Iraq's nuclear capabilities were much more advanced than Western intelligence had anticipated before the war. Not only did the inspectors uncover a capacity to produce fissile material for military purposes—corroborated by the discovery of plutonium and of highly enriched uranium—but thanks to information furnished by defectors, they laid hands on items that demonstrated that Iraq had made progress toward an operational nuclear military capacity. All these advances had happened over the previous years without the IAEA—charged with watching over nuclear activities in any country that had signed the Nuclear Non-Proliferation Treaty—being able to detect these activities.[28]

Another bad surprise at the start of the inspections concerned Baghdad's obstructionism. It took various forms, often laughable, sometimes dramatic, but all of which tended to limit the efficacy of a process whose validity Iraq would never thoroughly accept. It included incomplete declarations aiming to hide the existence of entire weapons programs (the first such declaration, dated April 18, 1991, failed to mention either the nuclear or the biological program); attempts to hide equipment (like the famous "calutrons" designed for uranium enrichment and moved at the approach of an inspection in June 1991); efforts to block the inspectors from accessing sensitive documentation or sites (as in the "parking lot" incident at the end of September 1991, when a team remained blockaded for four days before being able to remove documents relating to Iraq's nuclear program that had been found in a building); and measures of intimidation, harassment, and even threats (on one occasion, inspectors were shot at). Thus began a veritable UNSCOM "saga" that would last more than seven years.[29]

Whether these obstructive tactics stemmed from the regime's desire to preserve some hope of reconstituting its capabilities once the outside controls were lifted, or out of its visceral rejection of an intrusive mechanism that impugned its sovereignty, or simply because of its unwillingness to recognize the reality of its own disarmament in the face of its external enemies (above all, Iran) and internal opponents, Iraq once again underestimated the determination of the international community, which swiftly demonstrated its firmness and cohesion. In the summer and autumn of 1991, two new Security Council resolutions (707 and 715) were added in order to strengthen Resolution 687. These resolutions required that Iraq issue a "full, final and complete disclosure" of its existing programs, and imposed an OMV mechanism that was both intrusive and of unlimited duration in order to prevent any resumption of Iraq's WMD activities. Above all, the Security Council several times condemned Iraq's attitude, stressing in some cases that it constituted a "material breach" of existing resolutions—a phrase that, when associated with the threat of "serious consequences," opened the way to use of force. This threatened action ended up occurring in January 1993, after several weeks of a standoff stemming from Baghdad's denying the inspectors access to sites and its repeated violations of the no-fly zones. When Iraq decided to forbid UN inspectors from using its own aircraft above Iraqi territory, the United States, France, and Great Britain launched air raids to show their resolve. Baghdad finally yielded.[30]

The beginning of UNSCOM was a critical period for what came after. A recurrent pattern emerged: Iraqi obstruction led to a threat of force (or the actual use of it), thus bringing Iraq to compliance, at least up to a certain point . . . and until the next crisis. But there was a paradox here. On the one hand, it was clear that Baghdad was not playing the game. The first UNSCOM report from the fall of 1991 pointed out that Iraq's "concealment" and "lack of cooperation" "have not created any trust" in its intentions and had "engendered an atmosphere of profound skepticism."[31] This skepticism remained in March 1992 when Baghdad, while acknowledging that it had not initially declared the existence of certain chemical and ballistic weapons, affirmed that it had destroyed them the previous summer. Retrospectively, this move was a major turning point for the regime, for in deciding in July 1991 to destroy a large part of its WMD capabilities under cover of secrecy, it had shot itself in the foot. Had the Iraqis realized the determination of the inspectors, which they had underestimated until then? Was it an attempt to cut their losses, or a desire to avoid the humiliating spectacle of destructions imposed by foreigners? Whatever the case, not only was this decision a new violation of Resolution 687, which had made UNSCOM the supervising body for the elimination of WMD, but in the years to come Baghdad as a result would prove incapable (whether out of bad faith or incompetence) of supplying convincing evidence of the exact scope of these destructions conducted without witnesses. UNSCOM thus had to undertake a veritable archeological effort to verify Baghdad's statements; in the end, doubts about their veracity never vanished, a point that would count heavily in 2003. Saddam Hussein himself would recognize much later that his decision to destroy his arsenal unilaterally had been a mistake.[32]

Nonetheless, real progress was achieved in this first period despite Iraq's negative attitude. Caught in the wrong by UNSCOM, Baghdad was forced to start shedding light on its capabilities, and to deliver to inspectors vast quantities of weapons and disclose entire areas of its programs. In the summer of 1992, the commission began to destroy many chemical weapons and facilities as well as ballistic missiles. In the nuclear domain, not only was all sensitive material removed from Iraq, but by mid-1992 the inspectors felt that most of Iraq's previous activities had been exposed. Finally, in the biological domain, after having initially denied its existence altogether, in the summer of 1991 Baghdad admitted having pursued research in that area, and then in the spring of 1992 acknowledged that it had undertaken a full-fledged program. The result was paradoxical: if disarmament was proving to be problematic as a process, the progress was nonetheless significant on substance. This dichotomy would be crucial later. For the time being, in the summer of 1992, US defense secretary Dick Cheney was ready to acknowledge the progress. "The inspections have worked well; they've uncovered a lot of new information . . . , destroyed a lot of facilities," he declared, though he added that one would have to wait and see if the UN "is indeed up to its task." (Baghdad, at the time, was again busy hampering an inspection.) Of course, nobody then could have foretold the role that Cheney would play ten years later.[33]

Western cohesion was unfailing in this period. In the two years following the end of the conflict—a time in which President George H. W. Bush had announced the advent of a "new world order," with the UN as its cornerstone—Franco-American relations remained on track on the Iraq issue. Meeting Bush in March 1991, Mitterrand had mentioned "a euphoric period of friendship between our two countries," while Bush had congratulated the French for the "total camaraderie" that had characterized Franco-American relations during the war.[34] This cohesion had led Paris, London, and Washington, first in the autumn of 1991 and then in the summer of 1992, to envisage the use of force to secure Saddam Hussein's compliance—and even to resort to it in January 1993. Yet the triumph of the Gulf War had been replaced by a political rout for Bush himself, who had not been able to gain enough of a profit from his military victory to ensure his reelection in November 1992. Within a few days of the January air strikes, Bush had given way to Bill Clinton in the White House. But Saddam Hussein was still there.[35]

"A 'toothache' that we [can] live with"

It was during Bill Clinton's first term, from 1993 to 1997, that the Iraq question gradually would become entrenched in international politics. "Iraq is a 'toothache' that we [can] live with," the new Secretary of State Colin Powell said in February 1993.[36] The image is appropriate, and it would be verified in the following years. Admittedly, the responsibility for the stalemate fell above all on Baghdad, which continued periodically to defy the UN and thereby prevented a definitive solution. Yet US policy, as shall be seen, was also an important factor. The international community had trouble maintaining its earlier cohesion: the West, oscillating between the carrot and the stick, increasingly was divided over the proper course of action. Paris and Washington, in particular, began to diverge significantly.

The Clinton administration excluded two opposite approaches to Iraq from the start. The first was reengaging with Iraq in the event that Saddam Hussein changed his attitude. Clinton had appeared to contemplate this prospect when, a few days before arriving in the White House, he said that he believed in the possibility of Saddam Hussein's "conversion." But the possibility of reengaging Iraq all but vanished when a plot to assassinate former President Bush, imputed to the Iraqi intelligence services (and scheduled to take place during Bush's forthcoming visit to Kuwait), was foiled in the spring of 1993. This episode, still somewhat enigmatic today,[37] led the White House to launch a salvo of cruise missiles against Baghdad in June. For Clinton, just as for Bush, it had become clear that the Iraqi dictator could not be "redeemed." Yet the administration did not wish to take the opposite approach and launch a major confrontation with Iraq. Clinton was reluctant to use force—all the more so when faced with a country that did not appear to threaten US vital interests—and he did not want to make Iraq a defining issue in his foreign policy. So between an unlikely reengagement and an unwished-for confrontation, the pursuit of containment stood out as the best available option. (The strategy was now described as one of "dual containment," as the Clinton administration included Iran, the other "rogue state" in the region, in the concept.) In fact, Clinton's containment of Iraq essentially continued the Bush approach: it included pursuing inspections and maintaining sanctions, launching occasional airstrikes in no-fly zones, and (as Bush had done) waging covert actions aimed at possibly overthrowing the regime. Although US decision-makers now described the containment of Iraq as "aggressive," in practice it would prove more or less so depending on whether hawks or doves prevailed in Washington.[38]

Clinton's policy, however, kept the abscess festering. Starting in the second half of 1993, Baghdad finally seemed to be heading for better cooperation in the hope of rapidly reaching the end of sanctions, but Washington was reluctant to have UNSCOM recognize possible progress in disarmament, precisely because the United States wanted to maintain the embargo as the centerpiece of its containment of Iraq. This attitude, understandably, was unlikely to bring Iraq to engage in unlimited cooperation, and the stalemate that occurred only increased the risk of confrontation, as illustrated by the sequence of events in 1993–94. In the fall of 1993, after having rejected it for two years, Baghdad finally accepted (at least in principle) a very intrusive OMV plan that included regular inspections of sensitive facilities and multiple means of detection. Disarmament seemed to be on the right path. In the spring of 1994, UNSCOM completed the destruction of chemical weapons and equipment that it had begun two years previously, and that summer it recognized that the regime now appeared ready to cooperate, stressing the progress achieved. In the autumn, UN secretary-general Boutros Boutros-Ghali even declared that UNSCOM was "approaching a full understanding of past weapons programs."[39] Better still, Swedish diplomat Rolf Ekéus, UNSCOM's executive chairman, had been saying, at least in private, that he thought that

36

the disarmament of Iraq was now practically achieved.[40] And yet, starting in October 1994, things again began to deteriorate. Baghdad, which wanted to end sanctions as quickly as possible, went back to its erring ways: the regime demanded that UNSCOM recognize immediately that the OMV system was fully operational, threatening otherwise to cease cooperation. Such recognition, which would have been a decisive step toward lifting the embargo, was met with American opposition, and Saddam Hussein responded by concentrating his troops on the Kuwait border. Once more, the dictator had gone too far, strengthening the advocates of a hard-line policy. Washington flexed its military muscle in the Gulf, and in mid-October secured a fresh Security Council resolution (949) that required the withdrawal of Iraqi forces. For the resolution, the United States obtained the support of countries like Russia and France, which previously had wanted to send encouraging signals to Baghdad. Again, an American demonstration of force paid off: in the following months, Iraq resumed a more cooperative attitude.[41]

Starting in 1994–95, the Iraq issue settled in for the long haul, as was increasingly clear in the sanctions dossier. The sanctions originally had been intended for a limited period, and maintaining them over the years was problematic: Iraq's humanitarian situation, already catastrophic in the aftermath of the Gulf War, could only deteriorate as a result of the embargo, even if humanitarian goods were exempt from it. The extended embargo was in fact increasingly criticized by a major part of the international community, particularly in the Security Council, where Russia, France, and China, believing that disarmament was progressing, thought it desirable to contemplate at least a gradual lifting of the restrictions. Washington therefore had to accept a certain loosening of the sanctions in the hope of preserving their legitimacy and durability. To that end, Resolution 986 (creating a so-called "Oil-for-Food Programme"), passed in April 1995, allowed Iraq to purchase and distribute humanitarian goods with the income from oil exports as authorized by the Security Council. Yet Iraq viewed its sovereignty as still unduly restricted under the Oil-for-Food Programme, and believed that the new arrangement's main purpose was to allow the United States to maintain sanctions *sine die*. Baghdad, as a result, rejected the program's implementation for months before finally accepting it in the spring of 1996 under international pressure, in particular from Paris. As Washington had wished, the program indeed helped to establish sanctions in the long term; with some adaptations, and a gradual raising of the ceiling on oil exports, they would remain in place until the fall of the regime in 2003. Yet the arrangement quickly proved counterproductive, because the distribution of humanitarian aid ensured the regime's greater control over the people while allowing it to profit from the lucrative black market. "Oil for food," in effect, reinforced Saddam Hussein's rule without alleviating the population's suffering. Most important, it opened up considerable financial revenue for the regime thanks to a system of commissions on imports of goods and surtaxes on oil exports. All of these abuses would be exposed a few years later when the "Oil for Food" scandal broke out.[42]

Meanwhile, disarmament arguably had reached an impasse. UNSCOM had continued to make progress; after the crisis of autumn 1994, the Iraqis proved more cooperative. In the spring and summer of 1995, UNSCOM confronted Baghdad with evidence obtained after the defection of the head of the Iraqi intelligence service. The regime was forced to acknowledge that it had in the past produced vast quantities of the dangerous nerve agent VX and conducted an offensive biological weapon program—without having proceeded to its actual militarization, it nonetheless asserted—even though it still claimed to have destroyed everything in 1991. But if these belated admissions once again highlighted the regime's propensity to dissimulate its past activities, they were also a breakthrough for the inspectors, who had until then neglected the biological area. By mid-1995, UNSCOM and the IAEA reckoned that they had made decisive progress in identifying and destroying Iraqi WMD capabilities. UNSCOM chairman Rolf Ekéus now believed that any possible remnants of prohibited programs would be exposed eventually and dealt with if necessary through the OMV mechanism, which finally had been declared operational that spring.[43]

However, in August 1995 this optimism would run up against a new and bizarre event: the defection of Hussein Kamel, Saddam Hussein's son-in-law and the highest official in charge of the Iraqi military-industrial complex. The episode at first allowed the inspectors to make even more progress. On top of the new evidence that a regime in panic now felt obliged to communicate to the inspectors, Hussein Kamel's testimony revealed certain heretofore unknown aspects of Iraq's past efforts—including the fact that there had indeed been militarization of biological material and that a crash program of uranium enrichment had been set up in 1990—while confirming that the bulk of its WMD capabilities actually had been destroyed in the summer of 1991. True, the impression prevailing among inspectors was that the Iraqis had performed these destructions reluctantly, and perhaps had tried to keep the capacity to relaunch some programs at a later date by hiding certain documents or equipment or by maintaining dual-capacity installations. This suspicion was subsequently never completely abandoned. And yet the following months were marked by an unprecedented cooperation on Baghdad's part, as it furnished a wealth of fresh documents to the inspectors. (In the wake of this episode, the regime, now on the defensive, also finally agreed to the implementation of the "Oil for Food" plan). Accordingly, the December 1995 UNSCOM report mentioned that there had been a "great step forward . . . in uncovering, subject to verification still, the remaining elements of Iraq's programmes"—although it stressed that many aspects still needed to be clarified.[44]

Yet even with this progress, the Hussein Kamel affair ended up bogging down the disarmament issue, since it revealed once more the scope of the lies of which Iraqi authorities were capable. The regime even tried to impute to Hussein Kamel its own misdeeds by making available to the inspectors thousands of pages of documents that it claimed, implausibly, that Hussein Kamel had hidden on a chicken farm he owned. (As for Hussein Kamel himself, he would commit the fatal error of going back to Iraq a few months later.) The affair thus produced even greater distrust, not only from UNSCOM but also among the Security Council members, starting with the United States. As a result, in autumn 1995 Ekéus and his team decided to conduct more intrusive inspections. These inspections, which started in the spring of 1996, specifically targeted sites linked to the leaders and those close to the regime and had the priority objective of searching for documents that the regime might have hidden. The result of this more offensive approach was not long in coming: for three years, the inspectors had been able to gain access to sites without major obstruction, but once again incidents multiplied. Even though the Iraqis had negotiated an agreement with UNSCOM (to Washington's dismay) in June 1996 concerning access to certain "sensitive" sites, in the fall they tried again to limit access on the pretext that the inspectors were infringing Iraq's security and sovereignty. Baghdad's attitude only heightened the inspectors' suspicions: they were more and more convinced that the Iraqis were trying to hide something, even if they could not be sure it was weapons as such. (We now know this was not the case, as neither UNSCOM nor the successor UN Monitoring, Verification and Inspection Commission [UNMOVIC] ever discovered hidden WMD, at least in significant quantities.) So Iraq's disarmament entered a vicious circle, opening the way to the events of 2002–3, when warmongers would have an easy time discrediting inspections by explaining that Iraqi dissimulations were responsible for the absence of incriminating discoveries—the proverbial "smoking guns."[45]

Meanwhile, the United States failed to solve the Iraq problem by more expeditious means. In the spring of 1995, Saddam Hussein foiled an operation to overthrow the regime, conducted from Kurdistan. Washington itself had interrupted the operation, which had been supported by CIA agents who had not warned the White House about their activities. In the summer of 1996, Saddam Hussein thwarted another coup attempt; profiting from a division among Kurdish factions, he pushed his advantage by having his forces enter the Kurdish town of Erbil, the advance base of exiled opponents of the US-sponsored Iraqi National Congress (INC). This was a lightning operation: once the regime's opponents had been liquidated, the Iraqi units withdrew swiftly, removing any justification for a large-scale Western intervention. The US reaction was limited to the launch of Cruise missiles from US warships into the south of Iraq, as Turkey and Saudi Arabia had denied the Americans the use of their bases. The episode had not turned to Washington's advantage. The United States had appeared hesitant, while once more Saddam Hussein had demonstrated surprising resilience.[46]

By the end of Clinton's first term, containment already seemed a position that would be increasingly difficult to hold. The Republicans, who had been dominant in Congress since 1994, so far had supported a policy that was in line with that of Clinton's predecessor. But some hawks—like Paul Wolfowitz, a former Pentagon official under Bush, who had criticized the decision not to "go to Baghdad" in 1991—now started to advocate a more offensive strategy aimed at getting rid of Saddam Hussein once and for all.[47] At the same time, however, public opinion was growing sensitive to the humanitarian consequences of containment, while some international partners, particularly Russia and France, were increasingly critical of a policy that they considered uselessly harsh. "The repeated confrontations with Saddam Hussein's regime . . . have led to containment fatigue within the international community," the State Department summarized at the end of 1996, concluding that during Clinton's second term the administration would have to choose whether to do more to "accelerate Saddam's departure," to "consolidate the coalition," or to seriously give thought to "beginning Iraq's rehabilitation."[48] This last option had little chance of being chosen in Washington, however: henceforth, the divergence with Paris could only be accentuated.

The French approach, sketched in 1993–94 and confirmed by Jacques Chirac in the wake of his election as president in May 1995, differed markedly from that which prevailed in Washington. It consisted precisely of trying to rehabilitate Iraq. "France," Chirac declared to Secretary-General Boutros-

Ghali in January 1996, "is prepared to reintegrate Iraq into the international community."[49] Iraq's rehabilitation would of course be conditional on its respect for the Security Council resolutions. "These resolutions, and they alone," Chirac stressed a few months later in a speech at the University of Cairo, "should be applied by Iraq, but also by the Security Council and the international community."[50] Chirac's line was clear: if Baghdad complied with the UN requirements, starting with disarmament—which, considering the scope of its ongoing cooperation, was no longer an implausible scenario—then the Security Council (first and foremost, the United States) ought to vote to lift sanctions. For Paris, reintegrating Iraq into the international community and strictly implementing resolutions were two sides of the same coin. The French, in other words, privileged the "reengagement" of Iraq and rejected the logic of containment. The same was true for Iran, with which the French and the Europeans also wanted to reengage.

By 1994, France had already begun to reestablish bilateral contact with Iraq, with which it had broken off diplomatic relations in the leadup to the Gulf War. In September 1994, Foreign Minister Alain Juppé met with Iraqi deputy prime minister Tariq Aziz in New York at the UN General Assembly, and again a few weeks later in Paris. The polished and presentable embodiment of the regime, Aziz would be a regular visitor to the French capital over the next three or four years. At the start of 1995, Paris opened an "interests section" in Baghdad—the embryo of an embassy—and entrusted it at first to a middle-ranking diplomat.[51] This resumption of contact remained low key until Chirac intensified it in early 1997 with the appointment to Baghdad of the more senior diplomat Yves Aubin de La Messuzière. Obviously, this policy was disliked in Washington, which was trying to keep Iraq banished from the international community. It also raised doubts in some sectors in Paris. The diplomatic service was split: the Quai d'Orsay's Middle East directorate was in favor of reengaging with Iraq (as part of Chirac's ambition for a new "Arab policy"); others worried that France was risking appearing to support a brutal regime and being identified with defense of the status quo in the Middle East.[52] But for the time being, the Élysée had no qualms about its difference of approach with Washington.

The French and the Americans diverged, first of all, on the interrelated issues of sanctions and disarmament. Paris was hostile to the prospect of indefinitely maintaining the former, judging that they hurt the Iraqi people most and in fact helped strengthen the regime. The French argued for softening the sanctions as disarmament progressed and thought it necessary to assert that sanctions would be lifted once Iraq conformed to its obligations. Not taking this path, they argued, would be counterproductive, since the regime would not be encouraged to fulfill its obligations. "I say clearly that if Iraq has applied all the resolutions," Chirac declared publicly in the spring of 1996, "then the sanctions ought to be lifted."[53] As for disarmament, the French separated themselves from the Americans not over the goal itself—indeed, they affirmed in plain language the need for Iraq to disarm without restrictions, and they fully supported UNSCOM in its task—but on the way of achieving it. Hence in the spring of 1995, the French representative at the UN, like UNSCOM chairman Rolf Ekéus, thought that any remaining uncertainties about previous Iraqi WMD programs might be dissipated through ongoing monitoring once the actual disarmament phase was declared over. But Washington rejected this position, which implied that sanctions eventually would be lifted.[54]

Paris also increasingly differentiated itself from Washington on the use of force. After the January 1993 airstrikes, France was more and more skeptical about the periodic US and British raids. In June 1993, the French refrained from recognizing a justification for the strikes that Washington had launched in retaliation for the purported plot against former President Bush. (The Americans had not informed them about the strikes in advance.) Then, in the fall of 1994, Paris had been content with only symbolic participation in the demonstration of force mounted by Washington after the Iraqi regime had deployed its army on the border with Kuwait. But it was mostly starting in the summer of 1996 that Paris began to distance itself systematically from Washington's and London's propensity—a propensity that the French judged excessive—to launch airstrikes against Iraq. France disapproved of the raids performed in response to the incursion of Iraqi forces into Kurdistan in August 1996, stressing that the choice of targets in the south bore no relation to the incursion. At the same time, Paris distanced itself from the Anglo-American decision to extend the no-fly zone under Operation Southern Watch from the 32nd to the 33rd parallel—almost the latitude of Baghdad—and it decided to keep the 32nd parallel as the patrol boundary for French airplanes. In December, the French stopped participating in the northern no-fly zone (renamed Operation Northern Watch), whose utility was no longer clear to them. Although Franco-American divergences over Iraq until then had been rather muffled, they were becoming public and were discussed in the press. On the French side, some commentators suspected electoral motives among the Americans: two months away from the November 1996 presidential election, Clinton, they sensed, wanted to appear firm in the face of the Republicans. Conversely, the American side stigmatized the French attitude as primarily motivated by a concern to protect commercial interests in Iraq. Mutual recriminations, from then on, would only intensify.[55]

In the years that followed, French "dissidence" over Iraq would give periodic rise in the United States to petty accusations about its supposed motivations. The US denunciations culminated in 2003 when, at the worst point in the Franco-American crisis, some in Washington entertained the rumor of collusion between the Iraq regime and French officials at the highest level. The accusation was hardly credible: whatever their relations had been in the past, Chirac had ceased contact with Saddam Hussein after the invasion of Kuwait in 1990; he had clearly condemned the invasion through his support for French participation in the coalition; and since then he had kept the dictator and his regime, for which he no longer showed any sympathy, at a distance. (The Élysée was also careful to keep at bay all kinds of intermediaries from the pro-Iraqi lobby that had regained strength in the mid-1990s; some of them did not hesitate in Baghdad to claim to be the French president's representatives.)[56] As for the accusations of mercantilism in French policy toward Iraq, they were a caricature. Of course, the Iraqis clearly hoped to be able to influence Paris's positions—starting with the issue of sanctions—by assuring French companies of substantial benefits as part of "Oil for Food" and dangling the granting of important contracts once the embargo was lifted. It is also undeniable that major French firms, petroleum and other, were waiting impatiently for sanctions to be lifted in order to regain their presence in Iraq, and that the government was hoping to see France one day resume its former position as Iraq's foremost Western supplier. But both the Élysée and the Quai d'Orsay were very prudent: while Paris was openly in favor of lifting sanctions when the situation permitted, there was no question of being caught red-handed before they actually were lifted. Clear warnings to that effect were sent to major French companies, especially the communications equipment company Alcatel and the oil firms Elf and Total, that were tempted to sign conditional contracts with a view toward resuming activity in Iraq after sanctions were lifted. (Elf and Total coveted two gigantic oil fields, Majnoon and Nahr Umr, whose future exploitation rights the Iraqis were promising.) For the French government, there was no question of contradicting the letter or even the spirit of UN resolutions, and such an initiative would only create serious difficulties with the United States. "Even if we have to prepare for the

43

future," the Élysée and the Quai d'Orsay recognized at the end of 1995, "we have to be vigilant" and not be accused of "going it alone."[57]

The motivations that pushed Chirac's France to separate itself from the United States over the Iraq issue were, in fact, political. First, there was the realization that the American approach—starting with the embargo issue—was counterproductive. "Saddam Hussein's regime has never been so strong," Chirac told UN secretary-general Kofi Annan in March 1997. "The economy has taken off again, the rich live well; only the people are in misery." (This judgment went beyond the case of Iraq alone: in general, Chirac's diplomacy proved critical of American policies toward "rogue states" and judged that the US utilization of sanctions as a weapon against them was both abusive and ineffective.) Then there was the conviction that the US approach was harmful to the region and could only aggravate the division between the West and the Arab and Muslim world—all the more so because it took place against the backdrop of a US policy toward the Israel-Palestine conflict that was judged increasingly uneven in favor of Israel. For Chirac, whose speech in Cairo in April 1996 had marked the launch of a new "Arab policy," the American approach was potentially disastrous: "The result of the embargo," he told Clinton's secretary of state, Madeleine Albright, in February 1997, "[is] an accumulation of hatred and frustration in Iraq—and well beyond it in the Arab world." Finally, Chirac's more vocal critique of US policy toward Iraq stemmed from a growing Franco-American disagreement on the very nature of the international order. "Some day," Albright had replied to Chirac during their February 1997 conversation, the French and the Americans ought to make "a thorough assessment" of the efficacy of the instruments at their disposal in order to deal with cases like Iraq, namely "negotiation, economic pressure, and war."[58] Albright could not have expressed better what lay at the core of the Franco-American disagreement over Iraq: their differing opinions over key features of the international system—multilateralism, sanctions, and the use of force—in the second half of the 1990s explained the growing distance between Paris and Washington over Iraq, in the face of the increasing unilateralism of the US "hyperpower."

"The Americans still want to strike"

The critical period in the growing disagreement was 1997–98, and it resulted in December 1998 in a major crisis that to a large extent opened the way to what would happen in 2002–3. Clinton's second term marked a shift in foreign policy in general and over Iraq in particular. To be sure, the Americans continued to reject a possible opening to Baghdad, though they also wanted to avoid a major confrontation. There was nevertheless a hardening of US policy, explained by the play of personalities and by domestic policy. Previously, the doves had carried the day, but the hawks were now dominant. Albright, who had been UN ambassador during Clinton's first term and was now secretary of state, was among them: the United States was the "indispensable nation," she once famously claimed, using a formula that Clinton had coined in his second inaugural address. "We do not agree with the nations who argue that if Iraq complies with its obligations concerning weapons of mass destruction, sanctions should be lifted," she declared in March 1997—thus making explicit what American leaders formerly had left implicit, namely that only Saddam Hussein's departure would allow a definitive settlement of the Iraq issue.[59]

Meanwhile, the Republicans were becoming more vocal in the Iraq dossier. Although Paul Wolfowitz had until then seemed a lone voice, a whole group—including other neoconservatives like him—was now advocating a much more offensive approach, which quickly became the party line. Judging that Clinton's attitude was too lax, and entertaining ties with Iraqi opponents in exile like INC founder Ahmed Chalabi (with whom Wolfowitz was in close contact), the group stood for an active policy of regime change. It actively canvassed Congress and public opinion through think tanks like the new Project for the New American Century (PNAC), run by noted neoconservative William Kristol. In January 1998, eighteen personalities under the PNAC aegis sent an open letter on Iraq to Clinton. (There would be six more such letters over the following years.) The gist of the PNAC letter was that containment was no longer viable and that the Iraqi regime was profiting from the status quo to rebuild its arsenal. Washington, therefore, should abandon the UN route and concentrate its efforts on evicting Saddam Hussein by combining diplomatic, political, and, if necessary, military means. Although it would be wrong to see this message as the start of a linear process leading to the invasion of Iraq five years later—in 1998 there was no question of such a scenario, even from the most bellicose hawks—the PNAC letter marked the launch of a Republican offensive over Iraq.[60]

Meanwhile, there was a parallel hardening by UNSCOM. The discovery of the magnitude of Iraq's pattern of dissimulation had led to more aggressive inspections starting in the spring of 1996, but Ekéus's replacement in July 1997, after six years as head of the commission, by the Australian diplomat

Richard Butler further accentuated this change. In his final report in April 1997, Ekéus had written that "not much is unknown" about Iraq's capabilities, though he also recognized that "what is still not accounted for cannot be neglected."[61] Yet Butler quickly adopted a more confrontational approach to UNSCOM's relations with Iraq. Butler's inflammatory style quickly made him the *bête noire* of Baghdad (and soon of Moscow and Paris, where he was considered "Francophobic and obtuse"), all the more so because he did not refrain from proclaiming his proximity with Washington: "Butler did, indeed, become very close to the US administration—sometimes too close," his deputy Charles Duelfer later acknowledged. This proximity fed the suspicion, not only among the Iraqis, that the CIA was using UNSCOM to gather intelligence about Saddam Hussein and the regime—suspicions that Ekéus later recognized as justified.[62] The inevitable result came in September 1997: by launching inspections whose proclaimed objective was to "saturate" Baghdad's capacity to thwart the work of the inspectors, Butler furnished the Iraqis with the pretext for a series of incidents, including refusing inspectors' access to sites and concealing documents from the commission.[63]

The subsequent skirmishes were the most serious since 1991. Denouncing Washington's grip over UNSCOM, at the end of October 1997 Baghdad required the withdrawal of American inspectors as well as the end of U-2 reconnaissance flights, which led Butler in mid-November to withdraw his teams of inspectors from Iraq while Washington threatened to resort to force. Confrontation ultimately was avoided when Russian foreign minister Yevgeny Primakov got Baghdad to let the inspectors return. Although tensions relaxed, the episode revealed the growing differences between France and Russia on the one hand and the United States and Great Britain on the other. To be sure, Clinton and Chirac congratulated themselves on their bilateral relations throughout the crisis; it had permitted, said Clinton, the allies to pursue a "determined" diplomacy supported by a "credible" threat of the use of force.[64] But the two did not read the episode in the same way. For the Americans, the crisis had resulted from divisions in the international community: for the first time since 1991, Paris, Moscow, and Beijing had all abstained during the late October vote on a Security Council resolution (1134) threatening Baghdad with new sanctions if it pursued its obstruction. Seen from Washington— where the French "defection" was viewed severely—this attitude had only made Baghdad bolder. For the French, by contrast, it was American extremism that explained Iraq's behavior, particularly because Washington clearly advanced the objective of evicting Saddam Hussein, which obviously would not encourage Baghdad to cooperate. "Our feeling [is] that the United States would not in fact accept the lifting of sanctions until Saddam Hussein was eliminated," Chirac said to former president Bush at the end of November.[65]

Barely one month later, Iraq announced its refusal to open its "presidential" sites for reasons of security and sovereignty. The issue of the use of force was now central, and it divided Paris and Washington. If the obstruction persisted, Clinton told Chirac, a "strong message" would have to be sent, without excluding the use of force. Chirac agreed that the Iraqis had to comply and announced that Paris and Moscow would put pressure on them, but if Baghdad played the game and if UNSCOM registered progress, he said, it should be made clear that such positive behavior would be taken into account and that sanctions would be lifted as soon as the various disarmament issues were closed. If, however, the regime persisted in its obstructions, then measures of retaliation would need to be considered, including imposing restrictions on the movements of Iraqi dignitaries. But Paris, Chirac emphasized, was "completely hostile" to strikes: "This would be the best way to strengthen Saddam Hussein's position, because he could use it to build up the consensus of his people," he said, and added that the sanctions had made the humanitarian situation in Iraq "dramatic."[66] Chirac was not optimistic. "The Americans still want to strike," he confided to King Hassan of Morocco a few days later, adding to his perplexed interlocutor: "They are like that. They are very clumsy."[67]

The crisis flared again at the end of January 1998, when Baghdad confirmed its refusal to give UNSCOM access to eight "presidential" sites. The United States was ready to strike hard: by February, its forces in the area would total 45,000 troops, 35 ships, and 350 planes, not counting the resources of its allies, first and foremost Great Britain. Aware of the pivotal role of the French in the P5—a favorable vote from Paris, they thought, could rally Moscow and Beijing—the Americans put pressure on them, arguing that only the threat of force could bring Iraq to yield. The United States wanted a resolution that would declare Iraq to be in "material breach" of previous resolutions, which in the event of Iraqi persistence would give the Americans ipso facto the right to strike without having to obtain a new resolution. But the French, along with the Russians and the Chinese, did not want to concede any "automaticity" in the possibility of resorting to force, a position that prefigured the 2002–3 debates.

Chirac at that point decided to become intensely involved in the crisis in the hope of facilitating a peaceful outcome. Yet he faced a recurring dilemma: how to avoid giving carte blanche to the Americans to resort to force, while also avoiding divisions within the Security Council in order not to weaken the message being sent to the Iraqis (which might tempt them to prevaricate, and therefore ultimately lead to a confrontation). Clinton asked for Chirac's help for a "tough" resolution: this was the "most serious challenge to UNSCOM since 1991," he declared, stressing that Saddam Hussein wanted "to play games with us" in order to obtain a "premature" lifting of sanctions and to preserve its WMD programs. Chirac again expressed his reservations: a strike would be counterproductive, he said, since it would allow Saddam Hussein to "expel UNSCOM" and to "rally his people around him," while Washington would alienate Arab and world opinion. Chirac then proposed acting in two directions: one, to lead the Iraqis—by making them realize the gravity of the threat to which they were exposed—to accept a solution that would satisfy UNSCOM but would allow Iraq to avoid "losing face"; and two, to rally Moscow and Beijing to a sufficiently "firm" resolution to make Baghdad withdraw. Clinton resigned himself to attempting the maneuver that Chirac suggested; as he told Chirac, Saddam Hussein might be convinced if it were explained to him that "Clinton is half crazy and ready to strike."[68]

Over the following weeks, Washington and Paris engaged in an implicit sharing of roles: the threat of strikes on one side, and active diplomacy on the other. On February 3, Bertrand Dufourcq, the secretary-general of the Quai d'Orsay, brought Saddam Hussein a firm letter from Chirac, warning him of the seriousness of the American threats and proposing a formula for the inspection of presidential sites: the UNSCOM inspectors would be accompanied by diplomats when accessing them. The proposed formula was crafted so as to allow the Iraqis to save face without compromising UNSCOM prerogatives, yet for two weeks Baghdad refused to budge on the matter. On the 17th, Chirac, with some hesitation, agreed to receive Iraqi foreign minister Mohammed Saeed al-Sahhaf. Feeling that the Iraqis were now starting to move, Chirac blew hot and cold: in case of strikes, he warned al-Sahhaf, Saddam Hussein would be "beaten, humiliated, rejected," and he stressed (as the future would verify) that UNSCOM would then be forced to leave the country, which would make Americans further suspect that Baghdad was seeking to produce or keep prohibited weapons. However, said Chirac—playing on the dictator's psychology—if Saddam Hussein accepted the French proposals, this would signify that the Americans had "backed down," and would offer him a successful exit from the impasse.

At this juncture, the hopes for a peaceful outcome rested on the trip that Kofi Annan, encouraged by Paris and Moscow, decided to take to try to get Baghdad's agreement for an acceptable formula concerning the presidential sites. Passing through Paris on February 19, Annan received Chirac's "complete support" as well as some advice about the right way to approach Saddam Hussein: a "rather sentimental man" with whom one must establish a "personal rapport," Chirac knowingly whispered. The tangible sign of Chirac's support was a French government Falcon 900 plane, put at Annan's disposal to take him to Baghdad.[69]

Annan undertook his mission under terrific pressure. The US administration, itself under Republican surveillance, suspected him of being ready to give the Iraqis concessions that were unacceptable. On February 23, after three days, Annan nevertheless managed to extract an agreement: Baghdad recognized once more the prerogatives of UNSCOM and the principle of unrestricted inspections, while the commission promised to respect Iraq's "security," "sovereignty," and "dignity" by establishing a special procedure for "presidential" sites. Washington bowed to this arrangement. Clinton was personally relieved to have avoided a military confrontation, but it was a climbdown with respect to the hawks' desire to strike. On March 3, the Security Council passed Resolution 1154, which adopted the terms of the agreement signed by Annan. Meanwhile, Annan had stopped in Paris on his way back, where Chirac congratulated him for the "extraordinary work" he had done, saluting "a victory for the United Nations and its secretary general."[70]

Now that it had brokered a solution to the crisis, French diplomacy would try for several months to bring the Iraq issue out of its impasse, first and foremost by ensuring that the new agreement was implemented effectively. This involved passing very firm messages to Baghdad: Saddam Hussein had no "way out" and had to cooperate without fail, Chirac told Crown Prince Abdullah of Saudi Arabia. Without total compliance with the resolutions, Iraq would be fated to "war and desolation."[71] In early March, Bertrand Dufourcq went to Iraq again to carry the same message. But Chirac wanted to go beyond the successful management of the crisis by trying to reengage Baghdad. Discussing the matter with Yves Aubin de La Messuzière, he stressed that priority should be given to a "perfect implementation" of the agreement but that he was ready, under this condition, to receive Tariq Aziz and even to consider formally reestablishing diplomatic relations with Iraq.[72] A few weeks later, when the implementation of the agreement was judged to be satisfactory, Aziz went to Paris. Chirac wanted to project into the future: France wished for the "reintegration of Iraq into the international community," he repeated, on condition that Baghdad adopted "another approach." Pointing out that France had found herself isolated in the search for a political solution and that he had "taken some risks," he warned that in the future Iraq had to avoid "shooting itself again in the foot." Aziz tried to push forward, invoking the "former relations among the leaders" of the two countries—a transparent allusion to the relations between Chirac and Saddam Hussein in the 1970s. He also stressed that France was Iraq's first commercial partner in the "Oil for Food" framework, a way of dangling the economic prospects available if the embargo was lifted. But Chirac remained cautious. Although he confirmed to Aziz his agreement for a normalization of diplomatic relations before the end of the year, it was on strict condition that Baghdad's attitude remained "satisfactory" between now and then, and he required the plan to remain confidential for the time being. As for accusations that UNSCOM was being used by Washington—which Aziz reiterated while assuring Chirac that Baghdad was ready to work "day and night" to advance disarmament—Chirac was content to stress that Iraq should be "realistic" and that Paris was planning to be more involved in UNSCOM, while affirming that sanctions would be lifted some day.[73]

In the spring of 1998, Chirac thus wanted to capitalize on his personal success in solving the presidential sites crisis. This outcome presupposed that Iraq would renounce its policy of defiance and that the United States would agree to demonstrate more flexibility, in particular on the issue of sanctions. (The same was true for Great Britain, whose attitude Chirac considered "incomprehensible" and even more intransigent than that of the United States, as he said bluntly to Prime Minister Tony Blair after the crisis, prefiguring the sharp Franco-British confrontation that would take place in 2003.) Paris, in essence, advocated a "light at the end of the tunnel" policy intended to make the Iraqis understand that it was in their interest to cooperate. Annan, who visited the Élysée in mid-May, shared this approach; he believed that the Iraqis were "going to play the game," and confided that he had just explained to Madeleine Albright that there would be a serious new crisis if the international community did not manage to "encourage Iraq to make progress" or if Baghdad was "provoked."[74]

At this juncture, Washington's choices were indeed crucial. American diplomats seemed eager to get out of the apparent impasse. As Martin Indyk, the US assistant secretary of state for Near East affairs, conveyed in May to Jean de Gliniasty, the head of the UN directorate at the Quai d'Orsay, Washington wanted to be "forthcoming" and to recognize that the Iraqis "had achieved progress" in disarmament. Some differences remained: Paris considered that it was now possible to close the nuclear file and move on to OMV in that area, but Washington had not reached the same conclusions.

Still, there was an impression that their positions were not that far apart. Two months later, though, the atmosphere had changed. When de Gliniasty visited former UN ambassador and Under Secretary of State for Political Affairs Tom Pickering—the principal author of Resolution 687—he met with a diatribe: Saddam Hussein, argued Pickering, was "not redeemable," and lifting sanctions was therefore "out of the question." There was a "deep divergence" with Paris, Pickering added; France seemed to be "doing everything" to be able to "rapidly resume its privileged relations" with Baghdad, which created "a risk of tension" with the United States. When de Gliniasty rejected the usual accusations of mercantilism and reiterated the disarmament imperative, Pickering became more diplomatic. The American refusal to trust Saddam Hussein was leading Washington to favor one interpretation of Resolution 687, he said—whereas Paris, by estimating that Iraq must recover its place in the international community, had another interpretation. This, Pickering concluded, was a "difference of perspective" that could have "important consequences" for relations between France and the United States. The growing disagreement between the two nations over the Iraq question could not have been better summarized.[75]

By the summer of 1998, Washington effectively had rejected the scenario of a negotiated outcome to the Iraq issue that Paris favored. In the spring, Iraq had sent a signal of openness: Saddam Hussein's immediate entourage had conveyed to the White House through Duelfer that if the United States accepted dialogue, then all the points of contention (including WMD) might be solved.[76] Yet Baghdad received no response: American policy, in great part under pressure from the Republicans, was now on another path. Washington was now engaged in a virulent and already disproportionate denunciation of the Iraq danger. In November 1997, Defense Secretary William Cohen had brandished on television a bag of sugar and a small vial full of liquid to illustrate the dangers of the anthrax and of the VX that Iraq was suspected of having produced, and perhaps still possessed. Then, in February 1998, Clinton himself had sounded the alarm. After being briefed at the Pentagon on the strikes being prepared, the president had spoken publicly to justify a possible military action. Heralding the combined risks of proliferation and terrorism—denouncing the "nexus" constituted by these two threats would later become the mantra of the Bush administration—he emphasized that Baghdad was endangering regional stability and US security. Iraq, Clinton said, was a test case: "If we fail to respond today, Saddam and all those who would follow in his footsteps will be emboldened tomorrow by the knowledge that they can act with impunity."[77] To be sure, such statements did reflect the assessment of future threats that was now prevailing in Washington in light of a rising terrorist danger and growing worries that terrorist groups might manage one day to obtain WMD. (These concerns were already associated with Osama bin Laden, who came into the public eye after the simultaneous truck bombings of the American embassies in Kenya and Tanzania in August 1998.)[78] Yet there was also a large dose of alarmism, because inspections and sanctions meant that the danger represented by Iraq was, in effect, under control: in light of the looming crisis over presidential sites, these statements clearly aimed at mobilizing public opinion, which was hesitant about any military intervention. But in doing so, the Clinton administration was playing into the hands of the Republicans, who were ever more virulent in denouncing the danger from Iraq and the "appeasement" policy allegedly pursued by the UN with the US government's consent. The Republicans were now clearly determined to advance a policy of regime change, if necessary by force.[79]

Annan's prediction about the inevitability of a new crisis was soon confirmed. The crisis burst out in the fall of 1998 after new frictions had occurred between Baghdad and UNSCOM. Some members of the latter now appeared to be increasingly maximalist, and in this instance the issue of VX served as trigger. In May and June 1998, analyses of missile warhead fragments found in Iraq had revealed possible traces of the toxic agent. These findings contradicted Baghdad's assertions that it had not managed to militarize VX, assertions that were all the more suspicious because Iraq previously had denied even having produced it. The affair was leaked to the press by the American inspector Scott Ritter, who was anxious to galvanize Washington's shaky (as Ritter saw it) support for UNSCOM's new aggressive approach. But the conclusions of the various chemical analyses made on the warhead fragments were ambivalent; a French laboratory, in particular, differed from its American equivalent. As for the Iraqis, they rejected the analyses altogether.[80] Whatever the truth of the matter, Baghdad saw the findings as American manipulation intended to prevent UNSCOM from closing the chemical file and thus to justify the indefinite maintenance of sanctions. (The Iraqis may have drawn the same conclusion from the American refusal to let the IAEA close the nuclear file, although the agency was heading in that direction in the autumn of 1997.) Another incident occurred after USNCOM in July discovered in the Iraqi air force archives a document implying that Baghdad had not given the exact number of chemical bombs used during the war against Iran, refreshing uncertainty about what had happened to a large quantity of them; the affair led to a new clash during a visit by Butler to Baghdad in early August 1998. "You promised me the work would be done honestly and quickly," Tariq Aziz told Butler accusingly, but "UNSCOM has been neither quick nor honest." UNSCOM, Aziz charged, was constantly prolonging the process artificially: "You must answer two questions: Are there weapons [of mass destruction] in Iraq? Is there a capability to produce weapons?"[81]

Aziz thus put his finger on the central issue that the Americans would use in 2002–3 to advance their goals: the burden of proof. The letter of UNSCOM's mandate, as stipulated in Resolution 687, was *not* to comb the length and breadth of Iraq in order to determine whether it had effectively disarmed, but to certify (or not) that it had done so by ensuring that the WMD capabilities that had been identified, in particular on the basis of Iraqi declarations, had been destroyed. But the Iraqis stressed that this was an impossible task, since it was a matter of proving the nonexistence of something and thus of "verifying the unverifiable." This was not an unvalid argument, but it overlooked the fact that this situation resulted above all from the Iraqis' own misdeeds. "The Iraqis had provided so many explanations over the years," Duelfer later summarized, "that it became impossible for them to recreate a completely consistent and verifiable accounting of their WMD material. Given the track record of past concealment and their reluctant admission of key program elements, UNSCOM had no reason to give Iraq the benefit of the doubt." Duelfer, who after the 2003 American intervention became responsible for tracking presumed Iraqi armaments, later offered a possible explanation of Iraqi behavior: Baghdad, in the summer of 1998, had concluded that the Americans knew the truth about the status of their WMD but would not acknowledge this publicly in order to keep sanctions in place. As a result, Duelfer believed, the Iraqis had concluded that, all things considered, it was preferable to have "sanctions without inspections" rather than "sanctions with inspectors."[82]

On August 5, Tariq Aziz announced to Richard Butler that Iraq was suspending its cooperation with UNSCOM except for long-term monitoring, thereby opening a new crisis. For several weeks, Annan tried to put the process back on track by proposing a "comprehensive review" to identify the remaining stages to be completed before it might become possible to close the disarmament process and lift sanctions. The Americans were skeptical of Annan's plan; Chirac considered it to be "lucid, realistic, and courageous."[83] But the Iraqi regime now seemed to have decided to finish with inspections once and for all, believing that UNSCOM would never agree to certify Iraq's disarmament. On October 31, Baghdad announced that it was putting an end to all UNSCOM activities in Iraq, including long-term verification. This time the Iraqis were going too far, even for the French. Chirac, who had been very much involved over the previous months in promoting a settlement, saw this decision as inexcusable and decided to suspend any "high level" contact with Baghdad: there would be no more "carrots" held out to Saddam Hussein, he conceded to Clinton. But he nevertheless remained hesitant to wield the stick. Security Council Resolution 1205, adopted on November 5, did not include any explicit authorization to resort to force if Baghdad persisted in its refusal to comply.[84]

This time, Washington wanted to act with or without the explicit authorization of the Security Council. The domestic context was conducive. In October, the Republican-controlled Congress had passed the Iraq Liberation Act, which made regime change the official goal of the United States. Clinton had signed the law on October 31; on that same day, Iraq announced the end of its cooperation with UNSCOM. True, the administration moved only sluggishly in the direction of regime change, despite Congress's granting $97 million to support the Iraq opposition, including Ahmed Chalabi's INC. Still, the president had less and less margin for maneuver over Iraq because the Republicans could exploit any softness on his part. And the Monica Lewinsky affair, then at its height, further complicated the situation: if Clinton renounced the use of force, he could be accused of being too weak to make even those decisions necessary for the nation's security, whereas resorting to force would expose him to the reproach of using it as a distraction from the sex scandal at home. Within the administration, the hawks (Albright and Vice President Al Gore first and foremost) advocated a forceful response. On November 14, Clinton ordered widespread air strikes—and then recalled the planes at the last minute, when Tariq Aziz *in extremis* had declared that Iraq was ready to resume cooperation. This was a new vexation for those who wanted to play hardball: they deplored the fact that Clinton had failed to go all the way in demonstrating force by "punishing" Saddam Hussein. Chirac—who might perhaps have condoned a strike if Baghdad had not retracted—understood the situation that prevailed in Washington. Clinton "was more and more isolated," he told Annan, because many in the administration wanted a military intervention and were seeking "a new pretext" via UNSCOM. He deplored the "denigration" with which his own "balanced" approach was met in the United States: "We are not in favor of Saddam Hussein," he said; "we are in favor of respect for international law."[85]

Subsequent events confirmed Chirac's intuition. On December 15, Richard Butler transmitted to the Security Council a report concluding that Baghdad's cooperation still was not satisfactory. Then, without consulting any Security Council members except for the United States and Great Britain, he ordered the withdrawal of all UNSCOM personnel in anticipation of an Anglo-American attack. Butler's move was manifestly coordinated with Washington: the administration had had knowledge of his report before it had been circulated to the Security Council. The report, in essence, served as a trigger for a unilateral Anglo-American operation, and the other Security Council members were faced with a fait accompli: on December 16, while the council was meeting to discuss the issue, Washington and London launched Operation Desert Fox. Those four days of intensive air strikes would be a major turning point that opened the way to the events of 2002–3.[86]

Desert Fox—and After?

With 650 air sorties and 415 Cruise missile shots, Operation Desert Fox was the largest military operation against Iraq since Desert Storm. Some had advocated an action of even greater scope, aiming to make the regime fall by removing its command capabilities and destroying the units in charge of its safety. But the operation eventually proved more limited in intensity and duration: Clinton once again had showed himself hesitant to use massive force. Desert Fox did not aim to make Baghdad change its attitude, something Washington no longer believed possible: rather, the goal was to make the regime pay for having stood up to the United States. It was, in a sense, a punitive operation. But although Desert Fox seemed to have destabilized Saddam Hussein for a while, the dictator quickly got back on his feet: French intelligence soon determined that the consequences of the strikes appeared "limited" and that the regime had not been "profoundly shaken."[87] In short, Saddam Hussein was still there.

Desert Fox nevertheless marked the beginning of a new phase in American policy. For a few months, the administration seemed to actively pursue regime change. With the passing of the Iraq Liberation Act the previous autumn, regime change had in effect become US official policy, with Albright appointing a "special coordinator for transition in Iraq" whose task was to unite the various opposition groups. Regime change, however, soon appeared impracticable. The CIA was increasingly skeptical about the possibility of conducting effective actions in Iraq and distrusted Chalabi and the INC. For its part, the Pentagon did not believe in the possibility of regime change in the absence of a ground operation, which was then out of question. All these factors led the administration to implicitly give up this objective. Meanwhile, the Iraq issue passed into the background with the Kosovo crisis in the spring of 1999. In short, Iraq was no longer a US priority at the end of the Clinton presidency. Even though the rhetoric, driven by Republican pressure, remained oriented to regime change, the operational reality was quite different.[88]

Washington, as a result, was now pulling back to a policy of "muscular" containment. In the absence of inspectors, which the Americans had essentially written off after Operation Desert Fox, Washington and London relied on sanctions and strict surveillance of no-fly zones to contain Iraq, not hesitating to strike periodically in order to keep up the pressure on the regime and to further diminish its military capabilities, which were already blunted by sanctions. A sort of a low-intensity war with Iraq was starting to settle in. By the spring of 1999, the French judged that this approach was unlikely to be abandoned, whatever the international disapproval provoked by the combined effects of sanctions and strikes. US domestic politics had indeed become a preponderant factor, the French observed: one year before the US presidential elections, the administration wanted to avoid accusations of weakness in the Iraq issue, knowing that the pressure on Baghdad already appeared "insufficient" to an "overwhelming majority" of congressmen, both Democrats and Republicans.[89]

Admittedly, the French had refrained from loudly condemning Desert Fox: "Nothing should weaken the Security Council," Chirac had been content to declare at the start of January 1999. At most, they decided to suspend (at least temporarily) French participation in Operation Southern Watch in order to demarcate themselves from the Americans and British. But Paris had a very negative assessment of Desert Fox: "The strikes have solved nothing and the departure of the inspectors has left Iraq without surveillance," the Élysée regretted, having anticipated this latter and crucial point for months. True, Chirac's diplomacy did not contest the fact that Saddam Hussein bore the bulk of the responsibility for this "spiral"; as Chirac's entourage recognized, everyone was "unanimously" against the Iraqi dictator, including within the Arab world. But more than ever, there was total disagreement with Washington over the path to follow: "We will not create the conditions for a political change by letting the country collapse from an economical and humanitarian point of view," said the French, who wanted "a real solution for Iraq."[90]

Chirac, having spent his credit in vain to reach a solution to the crisis in the spring of 1998, did not want to be in the limelight again. He had broken

56

contact with Baghdad in the previous autumn, and if anything had remained of his past relations with Iraqi leaders before the crisis, it was now definitely a thing of the past. Yet French diplomacy could not be disinterested in what remained a major international issue. In January 1999, the Quai d'Orsay put on the table a plan for an overall solution that would establish a reinforced long-term monitoring program, one that would take into account the still-unresolved disarmament questions. In exchange for continued monitoring, the program would lift sanctions in the civilian domain (e.g., ending the embargo on oil exports, authorizing nonmilitary imports) while maintaining close financial and economic surveillance (e.g., maintaining the ban on importing military equipment, requiring prior authorization for the import of dual-purpose goods) to ensure that Iraq would not use its resources for military purposes. These ideas did not amount to giving up on controlling Iraq—far from it, in fact—but unsurprisingly, the Americans and British criticized the French plan as too lax.[91]

Whatever reservations the United States had with regard to the French plan, it was clear that the status quo was untenable. In the early weeks of 1999, the Security Council began to work on a new resolution with a view, if possible, to reach consensus on a new approach. Yet the negotiation proved laborious, as so many points of view remained distant from each other, and it took no less than the whole year to reach Resolution 1284, adopted on December 17, 1999—one year after Operation Desert Fox. At the core of the arrangement was the creation of a new commission: the UN Monitoring, Verification and Inspection Commission. This was a success for the French and the Russians; they wanted to replace UNSCOM, which had been discredited in their eyes by excessive politicization and the lack of professionalism demonstrated under Butler's leadership. Hans Blix, a Swedish diplomat who had been IAEA director-general from 1981 to 1997, was appointed UNMOVIC chairman at the start of 2000. His priority task, in accordance with Resolution 1284, was to prepare for a resumption of the inspections. Yet in spite of this success, France had not been able to carry forward all the ideas that were contained in the January 1999 plan; the Americans and British had been reluctant to make concessions during the negotiations. Whereas Paris initially had advocated the prospect of lifting civilian sanctions if Iraq cooperated, Resolution 1284 foresaw only their possible suspension—but without clearly specifying what would constitute satisfactory cooperation. So the French, like the Russians and Chinese, abstained when the Americans and the British put the text to a vote in December 1999. In the absence of a consensus, Paris, Moscow, and Beijing considered the vote to be premature. The Security Council thus remained divided. As for Iraq, it dug in its heels, criticizing (though not formally rejecting) the resolution while refusing to cooperate and most of all to permit the return of inspectors, more than ever suspecting that the United States would never lift the sanctions. The impasse continued.[92]

Ten years after the invasion of Kuwait, the Iraq issue as seen from Paris seemed a huge mess. The situation in the country was continually deteriorating as a result of sanctions, despite the implementation of "Oil for Food" and the gradual rising of export ceilings. Visiting Iraq at the end of 1999, a delegation from the Quai d'Orsay discovered a "devastated" economy and a country "on the road to under-development," in which a "minority of profiteers from the embargo" dominated while the state was being transformed into into a "contraband network." This was all the more the case since the embargo was being "ostentatiously violated" with the complicity of neighboring countries: oil was exported from Iraq by tanker trucks, while manufactured products were imported, escaping controls.[93] One year later, the Quai d'Orsay confirmed this observation. Iraq—which exported as much oil in 2000 as in 1990—was engaged in a policy "of eroding the embargo" and "illegally reconquering its sovereignty." These illicit activities were bearing fruit: Iraq's isolation had become "very relative," as attested by the success of the Baghdad Fair, which was attended by a growing number of European companies—some of which, especially German and Italian ones, did not hesitate to respond favorably to Iraqi demands to circumvent sanctions, notably by paying surtaxes on the purchase of oil. In addition, Baghdad was engaged in "active lobbying" for sanctions to be lifted by dangling promises of future commercial deals while trying to win Western public opinion over to its cause by eliciting sympathy for the condition of Iraqi children. (UNICEF, for instance, regularly denounced the effects of sanctions.) The regime, in sum, was clearly betting that time was in its favor and that it would ultimately free itself of the embargo.[94] This view was also held in Washington, where the Clinton administration was aware of the sinking efficacy and legitimacy of sanctions even though sanctions continued to be the central pillar of the containment policy.[95]

Disarmament was also stuck in the sand. The chasm between the procedure and the substance of disarmament was larger than ever, prefiguring the events of 2002–3. Even before Desert Fox, UNSCOM's mandate appeared more and more illusory, given the difficulty (owing to past Iraqi concealments and failings, starting with the unilateral destructions back in 1991) of verifiably accounting for both the WMD programs and their effective neutralization.

Baghdad's predictable refusal to have inspections resume after the December 1998 strikes prevented any hope of further progress; later on, this situation would strongly accredit the suspicion that Iraq might have relaunched its programs. For the time being, the crises of 1997–98 overshadowed the progress that had been achieved since 1991. And yet that progress had been quite real: even before Desert Fox, the disarmament of Iraq was plausibly very advanced. Such was the conclusion, in the spring of 1999, of Brazil's UN representative Celso Amorim, who had been charged by the Security Council with presiding over a commission whose mandate was to examine the various aspects of the Iraq issue and to propose solutions to break the impasse. "In spite of well-known difficult circumstances, UNSCOM and IAEA have been effective in uncovering and destroying many elements of Iraq's proscribed weapons programmes," concluded the March 1999 Amorim Report, adding that "although important elements still have to be resolved, the bulk of Iraq's proscribed weapons programmes has been eliminated." The report stressed that although the members of the Security Council diverged over the remaining questions, it may be impossible in any case to achieve "100% of verification." In short, there was "some uncertainty," which could be assessed only through a "policy judgment."[96]

The principal actors, including the Americans and French, nonetheless agreed on the objective success of the work accomplished by the inspectors before Desert Fox. "In seven years UNSCOM destroyed more weapons than during the Gulf War," Chirac insisted at the time of the crisis over presidential sites in 1998, adding that the ballistic and nuclear issues were "almost solved."[97] This view was in fact shared by the Americans, at least in private: the United States, Kofi Annan confided to Chirac at the time, recognized that the inspectors had destroyed more weapons than the bombing was ever able to do.[98] The Desert Fox raids, paradoxically, had confirmed this finding: though their official aim was to destroy suspected weapons capabilities, only eleven of the ninety-seven objectives involved presumed WMD facilities, for lack of precise intelligence. "By 1999, the Americans and the British, like the French, knew that few things remained to be accomplished with respect to disarmament," a senior official at the White House knowledgeable about intelligence later confided, adding: "In public they discussed accounting, of course, but in private everybody recognized that nothing much remained."[99]

But this objective realization did not prevent more subjective differences over the nature of the "important elements" (in the words of the Amorim Report) that still had to be "resolved," as well as over the threat that these same elements, particularly the chemical and biological ones, might represent. For some, at worst it was a matter of residual elements of old programs; for others, it was a matter of capabilities that were, if not operational, then at least quickly recoverable. A conversation between French foreign minister Hubert Védrine and his British counterpart Robin Cook soon after Desert Fox illustrates this divergence of opinion. "We believe," Védrine said, that Saddam Hussein "no longer poses a threat." Of course, he could "become dangerous again," but one had to "keep a sense of proportion." Remarking that "there will always be some uncertainty," Védrine asserted that the Iraqi "potential" had been destroyed by the Gulf War, by UNSCOM, and by Desert Fox. He concluded: "The inspection of disarmament is not completed, but it will give nothing more than what the Special Commission has obtained in seven years, unless we want to occupy the country." "We do not have the same perception of the threat," Cook replied, pointing to "very significant chemical and biological programs"—he cited VX and anthrax—and affirming that the UNSCOM experts "are rather unanimous about the chemical and biological capabilities still present in Iraq."[100] Cook's latter formulation was debatable; the inspectors were not affirming that these programs and capabilities *did* exist, but only that they *might* exist to the extent that their elimination could not be verified. Such sliding of uncertainties into suspicions, and then of suspicions into certainties, would be at the heart of the controversy over Iraq's alleged WMD four years later.

The UNSCOM withdrawal accentuated these divergent views. Once an end was put to inspections—which until that point had been the best source of information on Iraq's WMD programs—suppositions about the possible capabilities that might have escaped UNSCOM's discovery or might have been reconstituted after its departure intensified, as French leaders had predicted before the strikes. A discussion between Clinton and Chirac in June 1999 illustrates this. Denying that the United States was "obsessed" with Iraq, Clinton took up the theme that he had been developing for several months and that George W. Bush would adopt after 9/11: "In ten or twenty years," he declared, the Americans and the Europeans "might be faced with the threat of terrorist groups possessing miniature nuclear, chemical, or biological weapons given to them by nations like Iraq." Chirac, who had warned against this predictable consequence of strikes beforehand, did not reject Clinton's premise. "The absence of inspection of Iraq's armaments is indeed worrying," he admitted, since Saddam Hussein had the necessary financial means to be in a position to "reconstitute his forces." Yet he did not share Clinton's conclusion. The withdrawal of the inspectors, Chirac said, had been a "grave mistake" for which Butler was responsible—this was a diplomatic way of not explicitly attributing responsibility to the Americans, of which Chirac was undoubtedly convinced—and he added that existing suspicions about the intentions of the Iraq regime made it all the more indispensable to "restore the inspections."[101] The conversation exposed the growing split between the increasing American concern about the long-term danger of proliferation posed by an Iraq freed of all constraint, and the French feeling that only the resumption of inspections might solve this problem. It revealed the opposing sides of the debate that the French and Americans would engage in slightly more than three years later.

At the end of the Clinton administration, as 2000 turned into 2001, the Iraqi issue was at an impasse as seen from both Washington and Paris. Admittedly, as Madeleine Albright endlessly repeated, Saddam Hussein was "in his box." Since Desert Fox and the end of inspections (which the Americans thought had reached the end of their effectiveness anyway), containment now relied solely on sanctions combined with periodic air strikes. In the background was an ostensible though rather uncertain policy of regime change. This policy mix was enough to prevent Iraq from doing damage: despite alarmist rhetoric about the long-term "threat," the Iraqi danger was in fact limited and under control, and so containment remained "the right approach," at least for the time being.[102] At the end of the Clinton administration, some in Washington nevertheless believed that containment was not sustainable in the long run, if only because sanctions were increasingly contested internationally and because Iraq, as mentioned earlier, was managing to get around them. Some were beginning to think about possible "smart sanctions," which would allow some civilian imports but continue to restrict other forms of trade, in order to recover the efficacy of the embargo and make it last longer. Yet it was now becoming clear that the containment policy could not be maintained forever. For the doves, the moment had come to abandon an approach that generated useless international friction, and move to a policy of deterrence. A weakened Iraq could be placed under electronic and satellite surveillance at a distance, they reasoned, and if the threat reemerged, the United States had the military means to tackle it. For the hawks, on the contrary, it was necessary at present to implement a genuine policy of regime change and not merely a "cosmetic" one, as the Clinton administration had done. In short, after nine years of a containment policy that had run out of steam, the time for hard choices was approaching.[103]

On the French side, there were no more reasons to be satisfied. The "reha-bilitation" of Iraq, on which Paris had bet for a while, had clearly failed by the fall of 1998; since then, not only had Baghdad continued to defy the international community, but the Saddam Hussein regime could now hope to escape isolation purely and simply by circumventing the UN. Paris's position remained fundamentally unchanged (i.e., the resolutions and nothing but the resolutions), and it still diverged with Washington's on key aspects (e.g., the need for a political solution, rejection of regime change as a policy goal, disapproval of quasi-permanent air strikes), but the failed attempt to promote a settlement in 1998 had scalded Chirac's diplomacy and it was now in a back seat when it came to Iraq. In the wake of the adoption of Resolution 1284, some in Paris envisaged a resumption of relations with Baghdad. "I think the time has come to renew dialogue cautiously," pleaded Yves Aubin de La Messuzière, now head of the Middle East directorate at the Quai d'Orsay, at the start of 2000. His plea was motivated by the hope of using France's influence to bring Iraq to resume cooperation with the UN, but also by a defense of French interests. Other countries, including some European ones, were not hesitating to plant a commercial foot in Iraq—some by getting around UN rules—and so France, La Messuzière argued, risked finding itself supplanted.[104] But even though Hubert Védrine met with Tariq Aziz in New York in September 2000 during the UN General Assembly, nothing came of it. Paris's margin of maneuver was limited. The French were under surveillance: the Americans were proving more ready than ever to denounce France's supposed complacency about the regime. When in the summer of 2000, US under secretary of state for political affairs Tom Pickering shared with his French counterpart Gérard Errera "rumors" that Paris—just like Moscow and Beijing—was sponsoring Baghdad's planned "campaign" to "escape sanctions," Errera characterized this "accusation" as "unacceptable and inappropriate."[105] (In truth, the pro-Iraq lobby once again was quite active in Paris, which blurred the French official position; this was all the more the case since some of the lobby's representatives presented themselves—wrongly, but profiting from a negligent attitude on the part of official authorities—as authorized intermediaries between Paris and Baghdad.)[106] The usual accusations of mercantilism and suspicions about anti-American motivations in French policy were again surging in Washington, notably in the press: during the 2000 presidential campaign, it was tempting for the Democrats to target French policy to foil Republican attacks over the Iraq issue.[107] In these conditions, it was difficult to "relaunch" Franco-Iraqi relations. Baghdad, at any rate, was now less eager to do so: the French position disappointed the Iraqis, who considered it overly aligned with the "Anglo-Saxons." Iraq barely concealed its blackmail attempt to make Total sign the contracts it had negotiated by insinuating that the Majnoon and Nahr Umr oil fields might not be awarded to the French operator after all—a vain ploy, since Paris obviously was not ready to fall into the trap by infringing sanctions. At the end of the 1990s, the French could only observe that the privileged commercial position that had been theirs after the establishment of "Oil for Food" had eroded rapidly to the benefit of Russia and other nations that were disposed to play the game of getting around sanctions. By 2001, Iraq held only a marginal place in French foreign trade—0.2 percent of imports and 0.3 percent of exports—giving the lie to American accusations. At the dawn of the new decade, there was little left of the privileged relation that had existed in the past between France and Iraq.[108]

As the November 2000 US presidential elections approached, the Iraq issue was no longer at the forefront internationally. It remained latent, and might at any moment degenerate into an open crisis, but it did not seem to be a major hazard for regional stability—the failure of the Israeli-Palestinian peace process at Camp David in July 2000 was more worrying—and still less so for international security. If for years it had been a bone of contention in Franco-American relations, it was only one "irritant" among many others, which Paris and Washington had learned to manage as best they could despite periodic frictions. Of course, the two capitals still had discordant views on this issue, which largely reflected divergent international options, but overall the stakes were limited.

Yet in retrospect, the forerunners of the 2002–3 crisis were already present and its parameters were fixed: in many respects, the coming war was played out during the decade from the 1991 Gulf conflict to September 11, 2001. Whatever the actuality of its stakes in that decade—foremost, WMD—the Iraqi issue and the figure of Saddam Hussein had become an "American obsession," which concentrated all the paradoxes and contradictions of the unequaled, uncounterbalanced American power while illustrating the considerable influence of domestic politics on US foreign policy. Whereas Clinton, hesitant to use massive force, had been able to keep a sense of proportion, others after him would not necessarily have the same attitude. This was all the more so because Clinton's rhetorical concessions to the hawks and the ongoing reassessment of potential threats to America had, however involuntarily, prepared the ground for a more offensive approach—one that appeared tempting for Republicans as they reconquered the White House in the 2000 elections. George W. Bush's ascent to the presidency in January 2001 would turn out to be a game changer . . . even if it would take an event that nobody could then imagine for the Iraq issue to result, finally, in a new conflict.

Chapter 2
Bush 43 and September 11:
January–December 2001

The arrival of a Republican in the White House in January 2001 did not seem at first to signal a major break in US foreign policy. Because George W. Bush had been declared the winner of the November 2000 presidential election as a result of a dysfunctional electoral process followed by a Supreme Court ruling, it was widely expected that, wanting to make people forget that the election had been badly flawed, he would pursue middle-of-the-road policies. Many observers believed that he would follow in the footsteps of his father, former president George H. W. Bush, who ten years earlier had peacefully ended the Cold War and called for the emergence of a "new world order" organized around the United Nations. The George W. Bush administration soon belied these expectations, revealing itself as much too unilateralist—even isolationist—for European taste. But the administration was profoundly divided, and six months into his presidency, "Bush 43" was still in search of a foreign policy.

Everything changed on September 11, 2001. Aghast, the world witnessed the collapse of the World Trade Center's Twin Towers on live television and discovered the existence of al-Qaeda leader Osama bin Laden, who hitherto

---

"Bush 43" is used here as an abbreviation for George W. Bush, the forty-third president of the United States, to distinguish him from his father George H.W. Bush, the forty-first president.

had been unknown to the general public. Everyone waited anxiously for the American response: would there be an isolationist withdrawal or a new international engagement? Unilateral retaliation or multilateral action? Would the response be targeted or global? The answers to these questions would not be long in coming: by declaring a "global war on terror" in which Afghanistan and the ruling Taliban were only the first theater, the United States made a choice whose consequences would prove tectonic. Having remained in the background of the administration's priorities in its first months, Iraq suddenly was back in the crosshairs.

Bush 43 in the White House

Although he did not carry the popular vote in what had been a very close race, Bush was finally declared victor in the November 2000 US presidential election on December 12, 2000. The electoral process had taken more than a month, with numerous recounts and procedural maneuvers that had culminated in a Supreme Court decision over the disputed Florida vote, and it made Bush a president with contested legitimacy. This controversy immediately raised speculation about what type of presidency—consensual or partisan—he would adopt, and it was paired with uncertainty about his international orientations. Although foreign policy, a subject over which he had poor mastery, had not occupied a central place during the campaign, Bush had been critical of Clinton's policies. This seemed to presage a reorientation, but in what direction? On the one hand, Bush had defended a more modest diplomacy. In accordance with his proclaimed "compassionate conservatism," he favored a "humble" attitude on the international scene; the United States, he argued, was enjoying unprecedented power that might provoke opposition on the world stage, a rhetoric that seemed to herald a certain isolationist propensity. On the other hand, he had berated Clinton for his wobbly leadership of the allies and declared himself in favor of a fierce defense of the national interest, presaging a unilateralist, even hegemonic policy justified by America's "exceptionalism." Yet after the election, nobody could say which of these two options would carry the day.[1]

The personality of George W. Bush, moreover, was an unknown quantity. True, "Bush 43" was the eldest son of a former president who still enjoyed a widespread image of moderation and competence. But as a candidate he had displayed (no doubt at least partly by design) a lack of sophistication, if not a certain intellectual simplicity, stressing his "instinct" and "values." During the

66

campaign, he had appeared badly prepared for the international aspects of the presidential office, making gaffes and stumbles. Rare were there Europeans who thought highly of him; still, in the wake of the presidential election, the French ambassador in Washington, François Bujon de l'Estang, warned his authorities that "[Bush] should by no means be under-estimated," adding that "history is not written in advance." Bujon even ventured a daring comparison: "From Truman to Reagan," he wrote, American history "has included many presidents who, upon contact with supreme responsibility, have managed to show unsuspected dimensions."[2] From a certain standpoint, this was a premonition.

The French president was the first Western leader to be able to gauge "W." A few days after the dénouement of the election, on December 18, Jacques Chirac—who, as current EU chairman, had come to Washington for a final meeting with Clinton—met with the US president-elect at the French ambassador's residence. Bujon had organized the informal meeting through Condoleezza Rice, whom Bush had just named as national security advisor. It was a diplomatic "coup" for Chirac. Bush tried to be reassuring: he wanted to establish a "strong partnership" with America's allies, he told Chirac, and he would not try to "impose" US views. He wanted to draw lessons from the election and to extend a hand to the Democrats: "The past month," he said, would make him "a better president." For his part, Chirac wanted to pose as Bush's privileged interlocutor. He wanted to see this meeting as a "gesture" that augured well. The president-elect, he said, forcing the tone a bit, benefited from a "favorable prejudice" and would be welcomed in Europe, where people were convinced that his administration would maintain "good transatlantic cooperation." Bringing up his own experience of "cohabitation" with a legislature controlled by the opposite party, Chirac encouraged Bush "to resolutely take the bipartisan path," and he affirmed his wish for relations "as good and as close" as those he had formed with Clinton and with George H. W. Bush (whose friendship he valued very much, he emphasized). Even if he judged the son's personality less outstanding than the father's, Chirac left the meeting satisfied and thinking—wrongly—that he and Bush had started off on a good footing. In fact, without knowing it, Chirac had touched a sensitive chord: Bush's relationship with his father.[3]

In the first weeks of 2001, while the administration was taking its first steps, this initial good impression nevertheless seemed to be confirmed. Bush's choice of principals (the administration's key members for national security) was appreciated in Paris, starting with the appointment of Colin Powell as secretary of state. Most observers saw this as a guarantee of moderation and, like the appointment of Rice, a former National Security Council member under George H. W. Bush, as evidence of continuity with Bush 41. Such continuity also seemed evident by the choice of Vice President Dick Cheney, who had been the elder Bush's secretary of defense, even though Cheney had the reputation of being an uncompromising conservative. As for Secretary of Defense Donald Rumsfeld, he too was seen as a hard-core Republican, but his long experience gave him an undisputable credibility; once a rival of the elder Bush, he was almost seventy years old and had already headed the Pentagon under President Gerald Ford twenty-five years before. The overall impression was of a team of "heavyweights" that would be able to compensate for the inexperience of a president who said that he wanted to rely on them. If there were differences of sensibility—Powell appeared measured and in favor of a multilateral approach, while Cheney and Rumsfeld were classified as "hawks" and unilateralists—the idea prevailed that a balance would set in. After all, Bush had proclaimed his wish to govern in the manner of a corporation president who knew how to delegate while setting the course.

Granted, from the outset public opinion in Europe was allergic to the personality and rough style of "W." But governments were reassured by the new team. The French, Chirac confided during his first telephone conversation with Bush a few days after his inauguration, were "favorably impressed" by his appointments. Bush confirmed this impression: he assured his counterpart of his wish for close cooperation and said that he wanted to defuse possible misunderstandings about questions like missile defense. (This was a matter of concern for the Europeans because of its potential consequences for strategic equilibrium.) The two presidents then ended the conversation by agreeing on the utility of "direct and informal" contacts for discussing any question "that might pose a problem."[4] Consequently, in spite of the well-identified potential issues, a Euro- or Franco-American confrontation was not inevitable at the start of the Bush administration. On the most critical subject of friction, European defense, the new US administration even seemed to be relatively open. Some in Washington, particularly at the Pentagon, were still dead-set against it, but the White House considered that the Clinton administration had proved too "rigid" and that it was desirable to find grounds for agreement, most notably with the French. At a time when the Americans wanted to reduce their presence in Europe—first of all, in the Balkans—as Bush had hinted during the campaign, a militarily more autonomous European Union seemed to be in Washington's interest.[5]

Yet the French soon started to fear that things might get more complicated. Coming to Washington at the end of March for his first contact with the new administration, French foreign minister Hubert Védrine wanted to encourage its apparently good dispositions. Paris wished for "de-dramatized" relations, he said, denying the "widespread idea" that France "takes malicious pleasure" in opposing the United States. This message seemed to be well received, in particular with regard to European defense, over which Védrine discerned a positive evolution in US thinking.[6] Yet he did not leave Washington entirely reassured. Despite this apparently favorable first contact, Védrine had the feeling that on priority subjects the new administration would prove a difficult partner and fight tooth and nail for narrowly defined American interests, adopting positions that would be the opposite of European preferences. This apprehension was verified in the following weeks. Whether on missile defense (in June, Washington withdrew from the 1972 Anti-Ballistic Missile Treaty, a pillar of the strategic stability inherited from the Cold War), on climate change (in March, Condoleezza Rice declared bluntly that the Kyoto Protocol was "dead"), on international justice (in May, Bush withdrew the US signature from the treaty establishing the International Criminal Court), or on disarmament (the administration reaffirmed its opposition to the Comprehensive Nuclear-Test-Ban Treaty), the Bush team started in the spring of 2001 to confirm European fears about Washington's growing unilateralism. Paris was particularly concerned about plans for missile defense; as for climate change, Chirac (for whom this was a major issue) did not conceal his "serious concern" from Colin Powell when he received Powell at the Élysée in mid-April. But although Powell was seen as the moderate in the Bush team, he stuck to the administration's stance that the Kyoto Protocol was well and truly "dead" while nevertheless regretting the lack of consultation with allies on the subject.[7]

Another subject of preoccupation for the French and Europeans was the Middle East peace process. The Bush administration wanted to disengage from negotiations that it said ought to depend primarily on the will of the two parties; here, too, Bush's desire to break with Clinton was clear. Yet as seen from Paris, this attitude barely disguised a pro-Israeli bias; against the background of a new intifada and a surge of violence that had spelled the failure of the 2000 Camp David summit, followed by the election of the right-wing Ariel Sharon as Israeli prime minister in February 2001, this was a matter of serious concern. Chirac, who telephoned Bush at the end of April to discuss the subject, did not mince words. The situation risked "getting out of any control" and even leading to an "explosion," he stressed, adding that there was no military solution and that the principle of exchanging land for peace must remain "the key to everything." Bush merely objected that the Europeans had a "false perception" of American policy; the United States remained "involved" and disposed to work with both parties, he claimed.[8] The situation did improve somewhat in the following weeks as the Americans started to reengage with the region. CIA head George Tenet, who had continued in his post in the Bush administration, was sent to the Middle East to help implement a cease-fire. But UN secretary-general Kofi Annan, speaking on the phone with Chirac, nevertheless deplored that Sharon remained "very tough."[9]

As the summer of 2001 approached, the Europeans felt some relief. Although the first steps of the new administration had confirmed their fear of a more assertive US unilateralism, they also detected a more reassuring priority in Washington, namely establishing stable relations with the other major geopolitical entities, starting with America's strategic "competitors." This priority was demonstrated by the peaceful end to an aerial incident that had taken place at the end of March between a Chinese plane and an American plane over the China Sea; while the hawks had wanted to demonstrate force, Powell—whose moderating influence appeared to have been strengthened as a result—had led a negotiation with Beijing to end the crisis. Another positive sign was the personal rapport that had been established between Bush and Russian president Vladimir Putin during their first meeting in mid-June, although Bush's subsequent comment about Putin ("I looked the man in the eye [and] I was able to get a sense of his soul") only confirmed European malaise about the American president's religiosity. The US-EU summit that took place a few days later in Gothenburg, Sweden, went quite well, although Bush deliberately had avoided stopovers in Paris and Berlin for this first trip to Europe, instead visiting Madrid, Warsaw, and Ljubljana. While public opinion clearly was reserved—the European press now routinely depicted the American president as a "cowboy"—Bush, without renouncing his positions (first and foremost on the Kyoto Protocol) proved patient and affable despite the fastidious format of the meeting with the EU's fifteen leaders. The latter, in fact, came away rather charmed by him; Chirac even found Bush "cooperative," a compliment that he swiftly conveyed . . . to the president's father.[10]

So what about Iraq? If the French and Europeans in the summer of 2001 were somewhat reassured about Bush's foreign policy orientations, this was largely because this subject apparently was not a priority in Washington and the options under consideration within the administration seemed moderate. Many observers had expected that regime change would figure among Bush's priorities, whether in order to "finish the job" of 1991 or to "avenge" his father for the 1993 alleged plot against him. Yet during the campaign, Bush had stuck to approving the Iraq Liberation Act of 1998 and calling for strengthened sanctions against Iraq. When Chirac had met him in Washington in mid-December 2000, Bush had not even mentioned Iraq; similarly, when Donald Rumsfeld had visited Bush in Texas to discuss his nomination to the Pentagon a few days later, the subject had not been raised either. Dick Cheney, whose interest in this matter was well known, had insisted that Bush receive a briefing on Iraq before he took office; the briefing had occurred on January 10 in the presence of the outgoing secretary of defense, William Cohen, but Bush had not seemed very interested in the subject. Three days later, when Tenet had briefed him on the threats that the United States was facing, Iraq had not even been mentioned.[11]

But on February 16, Iraq suddenly found itself once again on Washington's radar screen. On that day, five Iraqi sites were hit in Anglo-American strikes, the harshest raid since Operation Desert Fox. The reason given was that Baghdad was about to deploy a fiber-optic system (supplied by China, said Washington) to improve its air defenses; the raid, which targeted that system, was thus presented as a preventive operation to allow for the continued enforcement of the no-fly zones. Yet it was also, no doubt, designed to show that Washington had no intention of relaxing military pressure on Baghdad.[12] The Quai d'Orsay diplomats were left to speculate about the significance of the strikes and more generally about the new administration's approach.[13] From the start, the Bush team, as seen from Paris, seemed divided between partisans of a coercive approach and proponents of a moderate policy. Unsurprisingly, the new under secretary of defense, Paul Wolfowitz—who had well-known views on the matter—was identified as the leader of the hawks. Wolfowitz had called publicly for the overthrow of Saddam Hussein as early as February, and during the early months of the administration he continued to advocate regime change through a strategy that would rely on air strikes as well as increased support for the Iraqi opposition, starting with Ahmed Chalabi's Iraqi National Congress. Wolfowitz's principal ally inside the administration was Lewis "Scooter" Libby, his former assistant at the Pentagon in the early 1990s and now Cheney's national security advisor. Wolfowitz and a few others, an observer later wrote, formed in this period a "band" that developed an "almost obsessive fixation" on getting rid of Saddam Hussein and his regime. But in this initial phase, they were far from having the upper hand.[14]

Predictably, at the other end of the spectrum of policy options, Powell embodied moderation and defended an extension of the containment policy that had been pursued for ten years. Along with his friend Richard Armitage (a former Navy officer who had distinguished himself in Vietnam), the under secretary of state, Powell could count on the support of the State Department, which was resistant to any adventure in Iraq. Assuring Kofi Annan of his wish to work within a UN framework, Powell from the start advanced the goal of adapting the sanctions. Although he judged that the sanctions had worked well and that Iraq no longer posed a threat, he nevertheless thought it necessary to improve their effectiveness (which had been weakened as the embargo was increasingly circumvented) and their legitimacy (which had been weakened by their humanitarian consequences). Powell's proposed approach was consistent with reflections that had been initiated at the end of Clinton's second term: it was about devising "smart" sanctions that would permit increasing civilian imports to benefit the Iraqi population while drying up backdoor funding schemes that profited the regime and its probable desire to relaunch its weapons programs. Powell obtained Bush's green light, and on March 1, the NSC asked the State Department to elaborate on the new approach and then to defend it at the UN. Powell asked the State Department's Policy Planning Staff, directed by Richard Haass—a former NSC staff member under George H. W. Bush and a moderate on Iraq—to take on the task of refining the new approach.[15]

In Washington, bureaucratic victories are never definitive. Although the CIA agreed with the Powell line—having become skeptical over the years that regime change could be achieved by supporting opponents—Powell soon realized that Pentagon higher-ups were still willing to promote a harder line. Relations between State and Defense were fast turning into a bureaucratic guerrilla war. Powell observed that Rumsfeld, who pointed to US planes being attacked in the no-fly zones and to Iraqi imports of suspect materiel, had a tendency to exaggerate the Iraqi danger, though for the time being, Powell also noted, Rumsfeld was content to deplore the lack of "clarity" in US policy.[16] It was Wolfowitz who appeared to be the most activist. When between May and July 2001, Rice's deputy Stephen Hadley gathered the deputies (the principals' assistants) to discuss Iraq policy, Wolfowitz came back to the charge. He now defended an "enclave strategy": occupying the oil fields in southern Iraq and from that base helping opponents to trigger an uprising to topple the regime. "This is lunacy," said Powell, encouraging Bush not to "let [himself] get pushed" into such a scheme.[17]

By the summer of 2001, Powell was carrying the day with an Iraq policy that essentially continued Clinton's. On August 1, a top-secret document presented to NSC members the conclusions of the Hadley group, which advocated a strategy of pressure on Baghdad by means of sanctions, no-fly zones, and support for the opposition. This was by no means an offensive policy of regime change by military means—contrary to the later legend of an administration that had been planning a war from the start. The overall impression was that Powell was setting foreign policy in general and Iraq policy in particular. For those close to him, it was clear in the summer of 2001 that the Iraq issue simply was not a priority for the Bush administration. When a new Anglo-American raid was launched on August 10, it did not even make the front page: pinprick attacks had long since become routine.[18]

The Europeans were reassured, even if they knew that the hawks were fighting against Powell's approach. The French were inclined to support a policy that coincided with their own orientations: to alleviate the suffering of the Iraqi people while keeping the regime's activities under surveillance. Smart sanctions, in fact, were an echo of their own proposals of 1999. Hubert Védrine therefore declared France's backing for the US policy while conveying to Washington (where many people were still suspicious of French policy) the message that Paris was not willing to defend either the status quo or the regime.[19] The French also sent a warning to the Iraqis against continuing to procrastinate, as they had done persistently since 1999. Whatever Baghdad thought of the success of its strategy to erode sanctions, the French declared, any solution would necessarily "come through the United Nations." This, in turn, presupposed Iraqi acceptance of Resolution 1284, knowing that some aspects of it might be clarified—starting with the conditions for suspending the embargo after inspections resumed—and that Paris would be ready to contribute to this clarification in order to help to break the impasse. The French were all the more eager to counsel flexibility to Baghdad, since they understood that Powell's moderate approach might not last forever.[20]

Six months after the start of his presidency, Bush's foreign policy remained a subject of speculation. Would he manage to make his mark? Which orientation would prevail within an administration that evidently was split between proponents of a pragmatic multilateralism like Powell, defenders of the national interest like Cheney and Rumsfeld, and neoconservative ideologues like Wolfowitz? What would be the place of Europe, with which a number of differences had cropped up in the preceding months? And last but not least, what were the Bush administration's priorities: realist management of the status quo, preservation of power relations with strategic "competitors," or else promotion of democratic values? In hindsight, one thing at least is clear:

the terrorist threat, which over the years had become a serious worry for the Clinton administration with the rise of Osama bin Laden's network, was not a priority for the new administration on the eve of September 11—although signs of a probable terrorist action of major proportions had been accumulating all summer.[21]

"The Pearl Harbor of the twenty-first century"

On the morning of September 11, 2001, when Bush was told that an airliner had struck one of the two World Trade Center towers while he was visiting an elementary school in Sarasota, Florida, he did not immediately comprehend the scope of the event, thinking it was an accident. A few minutes later, when a second plane hit the other tower, there was no longer any doubt: "America is under attack," his chief of staff Andrew Card murmured to Bush, who was attending a second-graders' reading class. Choosing not to interrupt the class, Bush made a statement a few minutes later. "Terrorism against our nation will not stand," he declared, paraphrasing his father's 1990 statement—his subconscious was speaking, he later explained. One hour later, the tone was no longer the same: "We're at war," he told Cheney, whom he reached by telephone from Air Force One. (Bush would make two additional brief stops at air force bases away from Washington at the request of the Secret Service, who wanted to shelter him from a further attack that was perceived as likely.) Meanwhile, a third plane had struck the Pentagon, and a fourth, plausibly aimed at the White House or the Capitol building, had crashed in the Pennsylvania countryside.

Returning to Washington at the end of the day, Bush solemnly addressed the country. It was now clear that the attacks were the work of al-Qaeda. Wishing above all to be reassuring, he abstained that night from referring to the attacks as acts of war, but he pronounced a phrase with major implications: "We will make no distinction between the terrorists who committed these acts and those who harbor them," he said, laying the foundation for what would become the "Bush Doctrine." After the speech, Bush chaired a formal NSC meeting, followed by a smaller gathering of his key national security advisers in the underground shelter of the White House (the danger was far from over, it was thought). The discussions were confused, since there were so many open questions, but for Bush, who had refused to sleep in the shelter despite Secret Service insistence, one thing was clear at the end of that day of fright and chaos. "The Pearl Harbor of the 21st century took place today," he wrote that evening in his diary. Justified or not, a whole sequence of events would flow from this historic parallel. America was at war.[22]

Once the initial shock subsided, the attacks' first effect was immense compassion expressed throughout the world. In the face of an event thought at first to have caused almost ten thousand deaths (the final count was slightly under three thousand), the editor-in-chief of the French daily *Le Monde* voiced this sympathy the next day: "We are all Americans," wrote Jean-Marie Colombani in an editorial that entered into posterity. France did not hold back on manifestations of sympathy. "The whole French people are alongside the American people," declared Chirac the same day, assuring Bush of his "total support." When he reached Bush the next day by telephone, Chirac used the personal touch he liked to employ: "I am your friend," he told Bush. Flags were lowered to half-mast at the Élysée, where a ceremony took place in the presence of the US ambassador on September 14 (decreed, as elsewhere in the EU, a national day of mourning). Chirac had stated the day before on CNN that "France would be at the side of the United States . . . to punish this murderous madness," thereby implying that it might participate in military operations. Rarely had Franco-American friendship been so prominent; 96 percent of the French felt solidarity with Americans.[23]

A sense of "absolute" solidarity is how British prime minister Tony Blair remembered his conversations with his European equivalents—not only Chirac and Putin, but also German chancellor Gerhard Schröder and Italian prime minister Silvio Berlusconi—in the hours following the attacks.[24] This solidarity translated the next day into political action. On September 12 in New York, the UN Security Council unanimously adopted Resolution 1368. France held the rotating chair of the council for the month of September, and the French representative, Jean-David Levitte, had drafted the text; he had taken the initiative without instructions, since he had not been able to communicate with Paris in the hours following the terrorist attacks. The attacks were "unequivocally" condemned as a threat to "peace and security," and the Security Council declared "its readiness to take all necessary steps."[25] Strictly speaking, Resolution 1368 had no legal scope, since it did not refer to article 51 of the UN Charter (which justified individual or collective self-defense against an armed attack) and did not contain a "decision" made by the council. Yet from a political standpoint, it was a forceful statement that amounted to supporting in advance the American response. Having witnessed from his office the crumbling of the Twin Towers, Levitte (who knew Chirac well, having been his diplomatic adviser before taking up the UN post) had thus taken it upon himself to send a signal of total solidarity, for which Chirac would congratulate him.[26] A similar scenario occurred on the same day in Brussels, where NATO secretary-general Lord Robertson, encouraged by the US representative Nicholas Burns, was able to get the North Atlantic Council to adopt a text invoking article 5 of the Washington Treaty—NATO's own collective defense clause—thereby legitimating the probable US reprisal. Never before had the Atlantic alliance invoked article 5, and now it was doing so for the sake of the American protector—a once-inconceivable situation. To be sure, Robertson's initiative was to a large extent a response to the Atlantic uncertainties that had prevailed even before 9/11 as a result of the Bush administration's limited interest in NATO; in time, this initiative would have a boomerang effect. Be that as it may, the French clearly had associated themselves with a strong signal of solidarity at NATO, even though other nations had proved more reticent to do so.[27]

At the Élysée, the historic magnitude of the September 11 events was realized immediately. The strike at the "hyperpower" and the coming US response were bound to affect the world situation in major ways. "The Americans have discovered that their country is vulnerable. The very heart of American power has been hit," wrote Chirac's diplomatic adviser Jean-Marc de La Sablière (who had replaced Levitte a few months earlier) in an analysis written three days later; "what has happened," he continued, "is a major event that raises many fundamental questions." It was, first of all, a "test" for Bush, who visibly was "very emotional" but also "determined," La Sablière observed, adding that Bush possessed an advantage since "as always in any ordeal, the Americans rally around their president." But the principal questions revolved around the nature of the reprisal. "What will the American reaction be?" La Sablière wondered; "clearly it will be forceful, involving the allies, but going how far?" The United States, he ventured, will strike not only the bin Laden network and its Afghan protectors, but also exert "strong pressure" on Saudi Arabia and Pakistan: fifteen out of the nineteen terrorists of 9/11 were nationals of the former, and the latter was the principal external support of the Taliban. "Will Iraq also be targeted?" he then wondered, confirming the uncertainties that still prevailed in this matter despite the apparent victory of the Powell "line." Overall, La Sablière concluded, all of American foreign policy was suddenly in question, in the Middle East and well beyond. "The struggle against terrorism will become the great priority," he added, "and we can already guess the risks of simplification and the problems we are going to encounter." Hence the decisive question: "What consequences will this event have for the organization of international society? Are the Americans going to further develop their isolationist or unilateralist tendencies? Or are they going to understand that a collective management of globalization is indispensable?"[28]

Behind these questions was a French reading of events that was already very different from the American one. On September 13, France's external intelligence agency, the DGSE (Direction Générale de la Sécurité Extérieure; General Directorate for External Security) issued a memo signed by the head of security intelligence, Alain Chouet, offering a preliminary analysis of what had happened on 9/11. Although the DGSE did not doubt that the bin Laden network was responsible, Chouet stressed that the attacks, whatever their "magnitude" and their "spectacular" character as well as their "media" effects, were first and foremost the culmination of a sequence that included the August 1998 attacks on the American embassies in Kenya and Tanzania and the October 2000 attack on the USS *Cole* in Yemen. Furthermore, without excluding the possibility of other attacks against American or Western interests, especially in Europe, the DGSE reckoned that the bin Laden network had put all its strength into this one attack: given the probable US reaction, there was little chance of its being successfully followed by another operation of a comparable scale. As for the "especially terrifying," even "apocalyptic" character of the attacks, it evidently aimed to arouse a massive reaction from America and to trigger a conflict between it (and the West as a whole) and the Muslim world. Overall, without minimizing the intrinsic horror of the attacks or their consequences in light of the probable American reaction, French intelligence did not see the events of September 11 as a radical rupture per se: they marked neither the start of an offensive (which had begun a few years before) nor the eruption of a "hyper-terrorist" phenomenon that was truly new in terms of means or modus operandi—it was, rather, a case of an unprecedented use of the old technique of hijacking airplanes. With their long experience of terrorism, French political leaders no doubt shared this reading of 9/11: the Franco-American misunderstanding of the following months and years started there.[29]

Chirac had an early opportunity to gauge his American counterpart and perhaps obtain initial answers to his questions when he traveled to Washington barely one week after 9/11. By a chance of the calendar, a bilateral meeting had been fixed for September 18: Chirac was scheduled to participate in a UN summit on children's rights in New York, and he had wanted to use this opportunity to pay a visit to Bush. The UN summit had been canceled as a result of 9/11, but the question of whether to keep his visit to the American capital surfaced. "Given the circumstances, I would understand if my trip were postponed," Chirac said when he called Bush the day after the attacks. But Bush would not hear of it: "It is not up to terrorists to dictate the agenda of democracies," he answered, adding, "Do come as planned." Rice confirmed separately to La Sablière and Bujon de l'Estang that "during traumatic periods, people need to see friends. We are counting on you for the 18th." Thus, Chirac became the first foreign head of state to travel to the United States after the tragedy.[30]

Although Chirac's goal was to reaffirm French solidarity and to learn more about the American response, he was also willing to convey some messages, as suggested in the preparatory notes he took with him. His first message concerned France's possible military involvement alongside the United States; here, Chirac wanted to be all the more clear with Bush, because after the attacks he had immediately expressed a solidarity which, in his view, could not amount to France's being drawn into "any action whatever." A choice had to be made, the Élysée thought: "Either the Americans act alone, which we could perfectly understand in the present circumstances, or they wish to act with allies, and in that case French participation could not be automatic [and] we ought to be involved in the planning of the operation and in the subsequent decisions." Hence the second message: the reprisal should be balanced, and an operation against Afghanistan would be legitimate, but precautions should be taken against collateral damage, whether by causing "innocent victims" or by creating "confusion between terrorism and Islam." Most especially, one had to avoid giving the impression that the sole response to terrorism was a military one. Faced with a "new type of threat that globalization makes more effective than ever," Chirac's entourage stressed the need to mobilize intelligence agencies and to use the relevant international bodies, starting with the UN and the G8, all of which had to be done within the framework of international law. As for the third message, it bore more generally on US policy: the world needed a "strong America" but the United States "also needed the world," the French thought. Washington, therefore, should resist the temptations of both unilateralism (particularly on the issue of missile defense, for which 9/11 might serve as a justification) and isolationism (particularly in the Middle East, where American reengagement should be confirmed in order to avoid fueling "amalgams" after the attacks).[31] Behind the cautious language that French authorities were willing to use was a noticeable worry about the nature of the choices that the Americans might make. Thanks to the "climate of friendship" that held sway after 9/11, Chirac hoped "to make President Bush reflect on the position of the United States in the world" while also making the "opinion of Europeans" heard. Events over the coming months would show that this hope was illusory; for the time being, the Élysée was aware that it was a "difficult exercise" and a "risky visit."[32]

Yet the Bush-Chirac meeting at the White House in the afternoon and evening of September 18 came as a relief. Flanked by Rice, Cheney, Rumsfeld, and Powell, Bush wanted to be reassuring. Thanking Chirac several times for France's support, he expressed his "satisfaction" at seeing the two countries side by side in the ordeal; the United States "had no interest in acting alone," he asserted. "We are angry," Bush conceded, but he immediately added that "our strategy will not be dictated by anger but by determination." The United States wanted to weigh carefully the "consequences of the decisions" it was making, he said, laying out the line he intended to follow in Afghanistan: to require that Osama bin Laden be turned over to the American authorities and to make the Taliban understand that if they did not accept, "there would be consequences" that might bring about "the end of their regime." True, a cold anger arose several times when Bush mentioned bin Laden and his "accomplices": Bush's favorite style—that of the rough Texan—took the upper hand. "We're gonna get them," he told Chirac, adding, "We'll have to smoke them out of their holes." But for the rest, the American president made statements that must have sounded reasonable to his French counterpart.

Chirac's reply nevertheless expressed a concern that would remain constant in the following months. He was worried about a possible "clash of civilizations" that would result from lumping together Islam and terrorism, which would only play into bin Laden's hands, and he therefore suggested that Bush put pressure on the Israelis and Palestinians to come back to the negotiating table with the goal of avoiding an "escalation" that in turn could only feed fundamentalisms. Bush agreed entirely, emphasizing to Chirac that he had just made a "very clear" declaration to the press on the first point; as for the Middle East, he said, the United States intended to remain "very involved."[33] The same consensual tone characterized the survey of the international situation that the two presidents then conducted. Of course, some issues continued to divide French and Americans. One such issue was missile defense, which Bush believed was not at all invalidated by the events of September 11; it was necessary, he said, "to do everything" to have the wherewithal tomorrow if faced with terrorists "possessing missiles or nuclear weapons." This theme of the "nexus" between terrorism and WMD would dominate the discourse of the Bush administration in the months to come and serve as justification for the Iraq adventure, but things were not there yet. As for Iraq, it was Chirac himself who mentioned it by stressing that Powell's proposals on smart sanctions were "interesting," garnering Powell's warm thanks for the "vigorous" French support over this issue. Although one member of the French delegation thought that she heard Rice express herself in a more threatening way over dinner, the impression that the French drew from the discussion—wrongly, as we shall see—was that Iraq, at that juncture, was not in the White House's crosshairs.[34]

Overall, Chirac and his team left Washington rather reassured, though there were also one or two shadows. First, despite Chirac's pressing interrogations about the exact nature of the military reprisal being prepared, Bush did not show his hand at all. A French participant would later remember that Bush had remained "totally enigmatic" on the subject, which already suggested that an American-only operation might be in the works. Then, a divergence was revealed when Chirac, speaking with the press after the meeting, said that he was reluctant to use the expression "war on terror." What at the time may have seemed to be but a semantic nuance in fact already heralded the basic disagreement that soon would emerge between the two countries. Indeed, during his meeting with Chirac, Bush had repeated constantly that this was a "war," stressing that new attacks could occur "at any moment" ("these terrorists want to destroy us—and destroy you," he added), whereas Chirac had insisted on a plurality of responses by mentioning police and legal cooperation, intelligence, and the struggle against financing terrorist networks. Still, overall the French delegation took away a good impression of the meeting. Chirac judged that he had successfully transmitted France's testimony of "friendship and compassion" to Bush, and he had the feeling that the American reaction to 9/11 would be thought through and controlled. President Bush, he even wrote later, appeared to him that day as "extraordinarily calm, mastering himself as if inhabited by a cold and determined awareness of the duty and mission that were incumbent on him."[35]

The next day, Chirac made a stop in New York. A meeting was planned with Mayor Rudy Giuliani, who had emerged as a heroic figure thanks to the energy he displayed after 9/11. Giuliani proposed flying over Ground Zero in a helicopter, and so Chirac was the first foreign dignitary to discover *in situ* the scope of the tragedy. Then he met with Kofi Annan, with whom (noted Levitte) there was an "exceptional convergence of analysis and objectives." Chirac reported that Bush had appeared "calm, determined, perfectly aware of the need to avoid making an amalgam between terrorism and Islam or the Arab world." Annan, who had spoken to Bush at length on the telephone after the attacks, shared Chirac's sentiment; the United States wanted to avoid "indiscriminate punishment," he believed. The two men had no trouble agreeing on the need for a multilateral and UN response to the September 11 attacks: the struggle against terrorism, said Chirac, called for a "long-term" and "global" strategy that required strengthening states' means of action but also putting "new means" at the UN's disposal. Chirac confided to Annan that Bush was aware of the need for "increased effort" to relaunch the peace process in the Middle East; Hubert Védrine, who attended the luncheon, said that the "shock of 9/11 might give Powell the opportunity to conduct the policy he wanted." Annan replied that Bush understood "perfectly" that in order to "eradicate" terrorism, one had to deal with "deep causes," starting with the Middle East conflict and with poverty.[36]

In retrospect, Chirac and Annan were mistaken in their optimism, as later events would show. Yet their conversation reflects a feeling that was widespread in the days and weeks following the attacks—namely, that the United States would be eager to respond in a thoughtful and collective manner, and that a presidency initially tempted by unilateralism and isolationism might be persuaded of the need for multilateral engagement in the face of the complex, protean nature of terrorism. Three days after the attacks, George H. W. Bush had even declared that 9/11, just like Pearl Harbor sixty years before, contradicted "the concept . . . that America can somehow go it alone."[37]

The historic parallel was irresistible; but would "W" listen to his father? The speech he gave to Congress on September 20 already augured an answer. Delivered in an atmosphere of patriotic fervor in the presence of Tony Blair— who from that day on played the unfailing ally—the speech was interrupted by many standing ovations. "On September the 11th, the enemies of freedom committed an act of war against our country," Bush declared, warning that "our war on terror starts with al-Qaeda but it does not end there." He added, "Every nation . . . now has a decision to make. Either you are with us, or you are with the terrorists. From this day forward, any nation that continues to harbor or support terrorism will be regarded by the United States as a hostile regime."[38] Two days after Chirac's visit, the tone was set: the United States was indeed launching a "global war on terror" with vast, even open-ended objectives, a war that had the potential to transform the international system on the basis of an opposition between the forces of "good" and "evil" and that, domestically, presupposed the nation's unity and unfailing patriotism. Bush now had carte blanche, as Congress had voted by an overwhelming majority on September 14 for a resolution that gave the president the power "to use all necessary and appropriate force against those nations, organizations, or persons he determines planned, authorized, committed, or aided the terrorist attacks that occurred on September 11, 2001, or harbored such organizations or persons."[39] The passage of the Patriot Act the following month, with its strengthened security controls and plans for increased levels of public surveillance, soon confirmed this promise.

"In this war, the mission will define the coalition"

The international community now anxiously awaited the operation that the United States was preparing to launch against Afghanistan. Everybody was aware that it would define the American response to 9/11: would the United States conduct the campaign alone or with the support of its allies? And would those allies be involved in decision-making? Although Chirac had not obtained an answer to these two questions on September 18, the doubt would not last much longer. The Americans had decided to conduct a reprisal that was foremost national, and they did not intend to grant other nations any *droit de regard* over forthcoming operations. Even though many in the administration—at the State Department first and foremost, with Colin Powell in the lead—wanted to assemble as large a coalition as possible, the Pentagon had other views. Its civilian leaders, starting with Donald Rumsfeld, wanted to avoid at all costs any conditions being imposed by other nations. At the end of September, the defense secretary pronounced a maxim that would go down in history: "In this war, the mission will define the coalition—not the other way around," Rumsfeld said, seemingly questioning the very principle of a multilateral alliance like NATO.[40]

The Americans in effect quickly swept aside any NATO role in the coming military operation: less than a week after article 5 was invoked, Paul Wolfowitz declared in plain language that there was no question of such an involvement.[41] This reflected the Pentagon's civilians' blatant disregard for NATO, an attitude that had existed prior to the attacks but was exacerbated by 9/11. As for the US military, it wanted to have a free hand in preparing the operation in Afghanistan, which to a large extent was improvised in the absence of any preexisting plan. (The US military also had been scalded by the precedent of Kosovo, when the NATO allies, starting with the French, had wanted to have a say in the choice of targets to be struck.) Even though the Americans had installed a "coalition village" at CENTCOM (the US military command for the Middle East and the Gulf, headquartered in Tampa, Florida, and in charge of operations in Afghanistan) where liaison missions were sent, most of the allies—except for the British—were soon confronted with the slowness and even reluctance of the US military and especially the Pentagon civilians to accept their offers of help. As a result, most allies quickly concluded that the Americans, by and large, wanted to go it alone.[42]

Paris came to terms with Washington's willingness to conduct a mostly American-only operation. "The Americans clearly intend to act alone, which I fully understand,"[43] Chirac said at the beginning of October. In truth, the French were hesitant about a heavy engagement in Afghanistan. Chirac, of course, had announced France's military solidarity in the aftermath of 9/11, which implied at least some form of engagement alongside the Americans; France's nonparticipation would be unthinkable, given the gravity of the attacks and the legitimacy of a reprisal under Security Council Resolution 1368. France also wanted to avoid appearing to lag behind other European allies, particularly Great Britain. But Chirac still hoped that this engagement would be limited: from the start, he was skeptical about major involvement in Afghanistan, a terrain that was remote from France's traditional sphere of military action. And then there was the "cohabitation" factor: Prime Minister Lionel Jospin and the socialist government were even less eager than Chirac to consider a large-scale commitment. With the presidential election scheduled for the spring of 2002 and the campaign looming, divergences between the Élysée and Matignon (the prime minister's office) were likely to be exacerbated. Chirac wanted to assert his prerogatives as commander-in-chief, while Jospin wanted the government to exercise oversight. The American attitude did not help: it was expected that Washington would transmit its demands at the very last moment and not divulge in advance the precise mission it would assign to allied forces, which complicated decision-making in allied capitals. If one adds the technical constraints affecting the French military in a context of budgetary restrictions—France's only aircraft carrier, the *Charles de Gaulle*, was under repair in the fall of 2001—one understands why, according to a former French general, France's engagement in Afghanistan would prove, at least at first, "very difficult" if not "extremely laborious."[44]

As could be predicted, the Taliban rejected Washington's ultimatum to hand over Osama bin Laden, and so less than a month after the September 11 attacks, Washington launched Operation Enduring Freedom. When air strikes began on October 7—Bush had informed Chirac only one hour in advance—France's participation was symbolic, limited to authorizing over-flight of its territory by the US Air Force and to sending a frigate and a supply ship to the Indian Ocean. By contrast, Britain was vastly engaged, as a number of its forces were already in the Gulf for maneuvers that had been planned for a long time, facilitating early British involvement. Paris remained ignorant of American plans despite the presence of a French general in Tampa, and it was only in mid-October, more than a week after the start of the operation, that the Americans extended precise requests, including requests for special forces, a medical unit, and air support involving twenty-some Mirages. These requests were well received on the French side; on October 25, Chirac announced that France was sending naval and air reinforcements and was studying the sending of special forces. The next day, Bush called to thank him for this manifestation of "friendship and support," to praise the cooperation underway between the military commands of the two nations, and to reassure Chirac that the cam-paign was progressing "satisfactorily" (although, Bush said, the approach of the Muslim holiday of Ramadan might complicate things.)[45]

Less than two weeks later, on November 6, Chirac was again at the White House. He wanted to discuss the ongoing operations and the international situation. Two months after the attacks and one month after the start of the offensive in Afghanistan, the context had changed considerably in compari-son to the preceding visit. The operations, which combined air strikes alter-nating with ground offensives by groups of opponents, were slowing down, complicated by difficult political and military circumstances. Although the Americans were relying on the Uzbek and Tadjik combatants of the Northern Alliance (the anti-Taliban front in Afghanistan), they wanted to preserve the future ethnic equilibrium inside the country, which led them to measure their support to them carefully in order not to alienate the Pashtuns in the south. Moreover, while CIA operatives had been active in the coun-try early on to establish contact with opponents, the deployment of US military units (with special forces having a key role in guiding air strikes) ran up against logistical difficulties. Added to these problems was the deli-cate handover of control from the CIA to the Pentagon; the latter did not have the upper hand over operations until the end of October. Although Operation Enduring Freedom had begun with a fanfare, one month later the impression was spreading that Afghanistan might become a quagmire for the Americans—if not a "graveyard of empires" as it once was for the British and then for the Soviets.[46]

The Élysée was pessimistic. As his visit to Washington approached, Chirac's entourage judged the situation "barely encouraging." The Taliban were resisting; the Northern Alliance was not progressing; and collateral damages, even if limited, were starting to disturb public opinion internationally. To be sure, the French knew that they were hardly in a position to criticize the conduct of operations. At that time, their participation remained minimal: Paris had agreed to send thirty aircraft to participate in air strikes in response to American demands in mid-October, but it had not been able to obtain the agreement of countries in the region, which prevented the deployment and delayed the operation. As for the dispatch of special forces, it was still being discussed by the French and American military chiefs of staff. Thus, when Chirac returned to Washington at the start of November, French engagement was still symbolic. Still, the Élysée thought it necessary to have a "frank conversation" "between friends" and to make the Americans sensitive to the "political consequences" of their choices, starting with the prevailing "distress" in public opinion about the prolonged conflict and its civilian casualties. The French also wanted to advance a number of demands: to establish within the coalition a "true exchange" about strategy, which until then had been nonexistent; to warn about a coming "humanitarian catastrophe" in Afghanistan with the arrival of winter; to intensify the search for a "political solution" in the country; and finally, to not lose sight of the need to relaunch the Middle East peace process, whose blockage—aggravated by the intensification of Israeli operations in Palestinian territories—could only feed fanaticism and complicate keeping the coalition together. In short, it was a matter of reminding the Americans that the fight against terror belonged to a "global combat" that would be "long-lasting" and for which the UN should serve as the framework.[47]

Evidently, two months after the attacks, the French were not trying to hide their worries about the turn taken by the American response to 9/11. The Israel-Palestine situation was central in their preoccupation, considering what they saw as Ariel Sharon's brinkmanship and Washington's misplaced support. The meeting on November 6, as a result, took place in an atmosphere that was very different from that of September 18. Of course, Chirac began by again assuring Bush that France remained in "total solidarity," which Bush saluted by expressing his "gratitude." But then Chirac sounded an alarm bell. If public opinion in the United States naturally supported the operations in Afghanistan, he pointed out, things were otherwise in Europe, which had not been attacked and did not feel as threatened. The Europeans, he said, had until then "almost blindly" followed their leaders, but now they wished to "fully understand the purpose of the action undertaken." And opinion in Muslim countries was reacting negatively. "All this must be handled with extreme caution," Chirac pleaded, adding that there was a need to "act very quickly" to respond to the "anxiety" that was starting to be manifest, in particular by intensifying humanitarian aid to the Afghan population. The "corrosive" effect of the images broadcast by the Al Jazeera television channel—which could only weaken the coalition—had to be countered, he said. Bush agreed with Chirac; stressing that Powell was preparing an international conference on the reconstruction of Afghanistan, he said that he concurred with Chirac's suggestion that Annan should designate someone to be responsible for humanitarian aid. Yet Bush also pleaded for patience in the face of "a new type of war;" and he remained evasive about subsequent operations, declaring that he had no idea how much more time was needed before Kabul would fall to the coalition forces. Then the conversation slid to the Middle East situation, about which Chirac expressed "very great worry," pointing to the "unacceptable" attitude of the Israeli government, which had gone "much too far" with its incursions into Palestinian territories, its desire to eliminate Palestine Liberation Organization leader Yasser Arafat, and targeted assassinations, all of which threatened to feed "new terrorist vocations." This represented a "very great danger" for regional stability and for the coalition, Chirac lamented, calling on Bush to influence Israeli choices. But Bush remained impassive, not hiding his reluctance to put pressure, at least openly, on Sharon.[48]

After the November 6 meeting, the French were once again struck by Bush's determination. To them, he appeared to be concentrated on his objectives in Afghanistan—"we will be cautious, but we will be tough," he had said—and realistic about the possibility of attaining them in short order. But they also noticed an attitude that was impervious to the stakes of the situation in the Middle East, which were crucial in the eyes of the French. This was no doubt the beginning of the Franco-American divorce after 9/11. This divorce was political, and perhaps also personal; as the French would later learn, Bush had been annoyed by Chirac, who perhaps had been wrong to launch into a long exposition about the fragile balance in the region, an exposition that his counterpart had found "pontificating."[49]

The situation on the ground, though, would completely change in a matter of days. On November 10, the city of Mazar-i-Sharif fell into the hands of the Northern Alliance, followed by Kabul on the 13th. One month later, Kandahar in the south was abandoned by the Taliban. Of course, Osama bin Laden was still at large, since the Americans had committed the error—with heavy consequences—of relying on the local militia to chase him. But Operation Enduring Freedom, which had seemed bogged down, was transformed almost overnight into a triumph for the United States. The victory in Afghanistan, even if the stabilizing phase was only beginning, had been rapid and sparing of American forces, validating the "new type of war" that Rumsfeld wanted to promote. Meanwhile, the Americans had begun to focus on the postconflict phase, on which they were now working with the opposition forces and regional actors in conjunction with the UN. On November 27, an international conference opened in Bonn, and would lead to the designation of Hamid Karzai to direct the "transition" in Afghanistan; on December 20, the Security Council adopted Resolution 1386 authorizing the creation and deployment of the International Security Assistance Force (ISAF) to maintain Afghanistan's security.

In the same period, French involvement in Afghanistan was strengthened. After the fall of Kabul, the Élysée—though Matignon was still reluctant—had decided to make up for the French delay, notably in relation to Great Britain. True, this plan was not without complications. Although Paris finally had not agreed to send special forces, as French control over how they would be used was judged insufficient, it had decided in mid-November to deploy 250 marine infantry personnel to demonstrate French presence. But the logistical difficulties remained considerable, and it was only in early December that the marines reached Mazar-i-Sharif, after their transit had been blocked for three weeks by Uzbekistan. (A hundred more French soldiers would arrive in Kabul in January to secure the airport as part of ISAF, which was placed under British command.) And while the *Charles de Gaulle* aircraft carrier was finally in the Gulf area and operational at the end of December alongside the American carriers, it was not until the end of February 2002 that the Mirage fighters, deployed from the Manas base in Kyrgyzstan, were able to go into action. Still, at the start of 2002, French participation in Enduring Freedom clearly had become more consequential than at the start of the operation.[50]

Overall, three months after 9/11, Franco-American relations, against the background of the nascent "global war" on terror, were good. Admittedly, the French military engagement in Afghanistan remained constrained by logistical and operational factors as well as political circumstances related to cohabitation on the domestic political scene. The American choice of a primarily US operation that excluded the allies' right to have a say in its execution also meant that France did not want to sign a blank check. Still, even though

French military engagement was not without limits, Paris did not question the legitimacy of the American reprisal. Cooperation between the two countries, moreover, could not be closer in another domain that was vital for the struggle against terrorism: intelligence. In the summer of 2001, French intelligence, persuaded like the other Western agencies that a large-scale terrorist operation was in preparation, had alerted their American counterparts to the danger of a French national, Zacharias Moussaoui, who had been training as an airline pilot in the United States. The Federal Bureau of Investigation had arrested Moussaoui in mid-August but could not search his belongings for want of sufficient evidence; it became clear with hindsight that he probably was meant to be the twentieth terrorist on 9/11, and the episode would later be at the heart of controversies about the malfunctioning of US intelligence agencies.[51] US-French intelligence cooperation further intensified after the attacks in New York and Washington, resulting at the end of September 2001 in the dismantling of the terrorist network led by the Franco-Algerian Djamel Beghal, who was suspected of planning an attack on the US embassy in Paris. This increased cooperation was welcomed on both sides: a former CIA official even judged later that the French intelligence services, particularly experienced as they were in antiterrorism, had cooperated with the Americans "more than any other country" in Europe.[52]

Yet this close cooperation did not prevent the French intelligence services from detecting among their American counterparts what they considered to be a sudden aberration. In the autumn of 2001, the American press had echoed CIA director George Tenet in anticipating a new wave of terrorist attacks, one at Thanksgiving and another at Christmas. This declaration astonished the French, who did not possess any evidence pointing in that direction and who thought that this information did not reflect what American intelligence previously had shared with them. One fact was becoming clear to the French: American intelligence services were giving a systematically alarmist twist to their assessment of the terrorist threat, based on the precautionary principle. Unlike the French analysis, their implicit postulate was that the attacks on New York and Washington, as Tenet would later write, "were not the end of anything. They were the beginning."[53] This postulate, in the weeks and months following 9/11, would serve as a compass for American leaders and profoundly influence their decisions. As Bush later wrote, "We believed more attacks were coming, but we didn't know when, where, or from whom."[54]

In this context, the beginning of a detachment between France and the United States was already perceptible, starting with Chirac's second visit to

Washington in early November. It would be confirmed in the following weeks. Two months after the attacks, it was clear that the Bush administration's once-anticipated "conversion" to multilateralism, required by the terrorist challenge, had not taken place, and that the American response to 9/11 was taking a turn very remote from what the French—and, no doubt, a majority of Europeans—had been hoping for. As seen from Paris, the US-only conduct of the campaign in Afghanistan and the already patent choice of a primarily military response (heralded by the very concept of a "global war on terror"), combined with maintaining in the Israeli-Palestinian conflict a line favorable to Sharon's policy, were the troubling and premonitory signs of the difficulties to come. America, at the pinnacle of its power and at the same time aware of its vulnerability, seemed more determined than ever to break free of any constraint. This prospect could only worry French leaders; as Chirac later wrote, "My conviction was that the worst reaction faced with fanaticism would be to feed the hatred and rejection of the other [and] to adopt an attitude just as radical, violent, and impassioned."[55] Granted, Franco-American divergences in the last weeks of 2001 remained muffled, as solidarity with the United States and the legitimacy of its reprisal remained the key words. Most of all, the fall of the Taliban prevented Afghanistan from being transformed—for the time being—into a transatlantic abscess. But it was increasingly clear that Operation Enduring Freedom was merely the first phase of the global war on terror.

"We are not going to take care of Iraq now"

We still have to explain how and why Iraq soon found itself back in America's crosshairs. Of course, Saddam Hussein himself reminded Washington of his existence by declaring shortly afterward that the attacks were merely the result of the "abject" policy of the United States. Iraqi television further proclaimed that the "American cowboy" was reaping the "fruits of his crimes against humanity." Yet these Baghdad declarations, ill-advised as they were to say the least, were not needed for observers to anticipate that Iraq would rapidly return to the top of the Bush administration's priorities in the aftermath of 9/11. On September 14, as mentioned earlier, the Élysée was already wondering whether Iraq would be "targeted." The *New York Times*, commenting on alleged statements by Paul Wolfowitz about "ending states who sponsor terrorism," stated in an editorial the next day, "We trust he does not have in mind invading and occupying Iraq."[56]

Yet that is indeed what Bush and others already had in mind. As early as the afternoon of 9/11, Donald Rumsfeld wondered in front of his staff whether Saddam Hussein should be hit at the same time as Osama bin Laden; he asked the question again the next day in the presence of Bush during a meeting at the Pentagon. During a NSC meeting on September 13, it was the president himself who raised the issue by wondering about the possible involvement of Baghdad in the attacks and about its possible links with al-Qaeda, to which George Tenet responded that the CIA was looking into the subject. (The previous evening, Bush had already posed the same question, to the great astonishment of Richard Clarke, who had been the NSC counterterrorism czar under Bill Clinton and had stayed in the post for the first months of the Bush administration.) Then, when Rumsfeld mentioned Iraq once more, Bush asked if an action against it might be conducted at the same time as one aimed at Afghanistan—which General Hugh Shelton, chairman of the Joint Chiefs of Staff, confirmed. But it was above all during the weekend of September 15–16 at Camp David, where Bush assembled the NSC to elaborate a strategy in response to the attacks, that Iraq was put in the spotlight. Charged with framing the debates that Saturday, Condoleezza Rice mentioned three possible scenarios: a reprisal against al-Qaeda, a reprisal against al-Qaeda *and* the Taliban if they refused to deliver bin Laden, and a reprisal that would also extend to Iraq. At this time, no heavyweight defended the idea of attacking Saddam Hussein—at least not immediately. Without excluding this option for later on, Dick Cheney said that the United States risked tarnishing its image as a "good guy" that it had enjoyed since the attacks; as for Rumsfeld, he did not pronounce in favor of such an operation at this stage. Colin Powell, of course, was resolutely hostile: he said that an attack on Saddam Hussein would have no justification in the absence of an established link between Baghdad and the attacks, and it would compromise the international support from which Washington had benefited since 9/11. Tenet also expressed his disagreement, judging that the priority should be al-Qaeda. Overall, only Wolfowitz defended—as he had done relentlessly over the preceding days—the idea of attacking the Baghdad regime at the same time as the Taliban, but Bush did not appear convinced by his arguments. The next day, Bush made his decision: the first theater of operations would be Afghanistan, he told the NSC. But that Sunday, he spoke his mind to Rice. She was the first to know his deeper thoughts. "We won't do Iraq now," he said, "we're putting Iraq off." All the same, he added, "But eventually we'll have to return to that question."[57]

As mentioned earlier, when Chirac visited Bush on September 18, he was not taken into confidence about the discussions of the preceding days. Things went differently for Tony Blair during his visit two days later. Iraq was not an immediate problem, Bush confided to him, and said that even if some on his team had other views it was up to him alone to make the decision.[58] A schema was thus established, to be confirmed in the following months: Bush would open up—to some extent—to the British, but he would not show his hand to others, including the French. This does not mean that Paris was ignorant of the debates over Iraq that were agitating the administration. On September 20, the day of Blair's visit and Bush's speech to Congress, the *New York Times* published a long article that largely echoed the discussions at Camp David. Eight days after the attacks, it was publicly known that two camps confronted each other within the administration over a possible action against Iraq, even if it appeared that the proponents of caution had won the day for now. The French, although concerned that this option might resurface, were reassured for the time being: for the Élysée, action against Iraq seemed to be ruled out, at least as long as the operation in Afghanistan was pursued. The Bush-Chirac meeting of November 6 appeared to confirm this assessment. Bush, noted François Bujon de l'Estang after the meeting, "at no moment gave the impression of envisaging conducting any military operation outside Afghanistan."[59]

Yet it was during these critical weeks that the logic that would lead to war a little more than a year later was put in place. So, why Iraq? Although it remains impossible to answer this question definitively for lack of archival evidence, the existing testimony permits us to discern what was at play in this period in people's minds. Mentioning his state of mind after the attacks, Bush would later write that "as long as I held office, I could never forget what happened to America," adding that "I would pour my heart and soul into protecting the country, whatever it took."[60] Here we discern some of the emotions that dominated the countries' leaders at the time, starting with the president himself. First, there was an (unavowed, to a large extent) sense of culpability: for the Bush team, the knowledge that they had not been able to anticipate the attacks despite the warning signs—even if these signs had not been specific enough for American leaders to be able to prevent them—must have haunted them after 9/11 and influenced their decisions. Then there was a feeling of anger (perceptible, for instance, in the statements that Bush made to Chirac on September 18), which must have weighed heavily in these decisive moments. But there was also fear about a new attack, which explained the bioterror psychosis that was unleashed in late September and early October 2001 when five deaths were caused by letters that contained anthrax. In 2010, the FBI revealed that the anthrax letters were the work of an American scientist who probably was mentally disturbed, but Bush reported in his memoirs that at the time, "one of the best intelligence services in Europe" had suspected that Iraq was involved. It is difficult to assess the credibility of this information and its impact on US decision-makers, but it is not absurd to think that in the post-9/11 context this episode must have fed the propensity to make Iraq a target.[61] Guilt, anger, and fear: as the historian Melvyn Leffler rightly emphasizes, these were the emotions that animated American leaders immediately after 9/11, and they should be kept in mind when reconstructing and trying to explain their decisions.[62]

Yet these decisions did not reveal emotional factors alone. They also, and perhaps more importantly, derived from rational schemas. The possibility of taking military action against Iraq was indeed envisaged from the first days following 9/11 in terms that were intended to be "strategic." The impulse came from Bush himself: by declaring as he did on the day after the attacks an all-out "war on terror" and by targeting in advance the regimes that sponsor it, Bush in essence was calling for a response going well beyond the immediate target constituted by al-Qaeda and the Taliban. The hawks then built on this call by stating that the response could not be limited to reprisals against the authors of the September 11 attacks, but should aim to prevent or dissuade new ones by means of a resolutely offensive strategy that should aim at all those, whether states or organizations, that supported terrorism and might be tempted to wager on the weakness of America. A response that was limited to the bin Laden network and to Afghanistan—a state without real military means—would risk, said Rumsfeld on September 14, being a mere stab in the water, a "hollow" reprisal that might prove "embarrassing." The underlying argument was clear: by taking on a country that was suspected of trying to equip itself with WMD and of encouraging terrorism while possessing a long record of violating UN resolutions and routinely attacking the United States (namely, in the no-fly zones), America would set an example that would have a dissuasive value. In short, after 9/11 Iraq—which had defied America for so many years—appeared to be a ready-made target for "phase two" of the war on terror, and for that matter an easy target, given Iraq's military weakness and America's strength. The Bush administration after 9/11, Richard Haass wrote later, had become "the proverbial hammer looking for a nail," and "Iraq became that nail."[63] By deciding that the "war against terror" would be conducted in an "offensive" way and that Afghanistan would be only the first front, Bush all but condoned the hawks' line of argument. And even though he later claimed to have wanted to avoid resorting to a military conflict to settle the Iraqi question—notably by obtaining in Afghanistan an overwhelming success that would make Saddam Hussein think twice—a logic of war therefore was clearly in existence from the start.[64]

What was left was the play of personal equations, calculations, and biases. Colin Powell thought that some people in the administration were trying to instrumentalize the September 11 attacks to promote their own "policy obsessions" and to "settle old scores": the neoconservatives, he noted, had constructed their careers on the idea that the "mistake" of 1991 had to be "corrected."[65] In fact, on September 20, William Kristol's Project for the New American Century published a new open letter in which forty-some signatories proclaimed that "any strategy aiming at the eradication of terrorism and its sponsors must include a determined effort to remove Saddam Hussein from power."[66] The neocons were evidently oiling the engine to advance the cause of a regime change in Baghdad, which had been their obsession since the second half of the 1990s; within the administration, Paul Wolfowitz was their standard-bearer. Bush's defenders would, of course, staunchly deny that the president was trying—consciously or not—to surpass his father or else "avenge him" for the suspected assassination plot of 1993 by envisaging going after Iraq from the day after the attacks.[67] Yet the psychological factor cannot be eliminated altogether: Bush himself confided his desire to seize the opportunity of 9/11 to "achieve big goals." To do something striking was, no doubt, the profound wellspring of his decision to take on Saddam Hussein in the wake of the attacks.[68]

One question remains: could Iraq at the time objectively present a pressing threat in the eyes of American leaders? Hardly so. On September 21, Bush received a first response from the CIA to his question about possible ties between Baghdad and al-Qaeda: there was no sign of Iraqi involvement in the attacks or convincing evidence of links between Baghdad and al-Qaeda. (This was also the conclusion of French intelligence.) Such a hypothesis was judged highly unlikely in light of the secular and nationalist orientations of the Iraqi regime, whatever the Iraqi support in the past for other forms of terrorism, especially Palestinian.[69] As for WMD, the *hypothesis* that Iraq had been trying to reconstitute its capabilities since the departure of inspectors in 1998 was of course commonly accepted by Western intelligence, the CIA first of all.[70] Yet when 9/11 occurred, the presumed Iraqi potential was *not* perceived as an urgent threat. George Tenet, in fact, would remember later that at Camp David, the advocates of military action against Iraq—first and foremost Paul Wolfowitz—had not advanced this argument. They preferred instead to put forward the supposed links between Baghdad and al-Qaeda, a notion from which Wolfowitz had not budged for a long time despite the CIA's opinion.[71] Therefore, when Iraq became a potential target for the United States in the days following the attacks, it was *not* due to the danger that it represented *presently*. (As will be seen, this would not prevent a manipulative administration in the months to come from trying all the same to give credit to this idea by depicting an imminent Iraqi threat.) Rather, the partisans of an operation against Iraq advocated a preventive action against a *potential* threat, a concept that would enter into US strategic doctrine a few months later. "No one in the administration doubted that the terrorists would have gladly killed ten or a hundred times the number killed on 9/11," Rumsfeld would later argue, adding that "their potential acquisition of WMD represented a major strategic danger."[72] This fear seemed to be corroborated in the following weeks by information that al-Qaeda allegedly was interested in procuring such weapons, including nuclear ones. Such a risk, even if it was minimal, was now at the heart of American thinking: even if there were only a 1 percent chance of its being verified, it had to be treated "as a certainty," Dick Cheney declared at the end of November, thereby formulating what was handed to posterity as the "one percent doctrine."[73]

Formerly rather theoretical, the fear of a nexus between WMD and terrorism was thus erected into a strategic dogma after 9/11. This dogma justified a reevaluation of the threat posed by states suspected of developing such programs: was there not a risk of seeing one of them transformed into a purveyor of WMD to terrorist networks? Hence Iraq's case was quickly set, whatever the tenuous character of suspicions about its arsenal and of its putative links with the bin Laden network: "Iraq was portrayed as the most dangerous thing in national security," Richard Clarke would later remember. "It was an idée fixe."[74] Leaving Saddam Hussein in power would mean risking that Iraq could eventually turn out to have nuclear or biological arms and could therefore cooperate with terrorist groups; such was the reasoning propelled by the hawks.[75] Because this line of reasoning was about extrapolating a danger that was still virtual, it inevitably opened the way to exaggeration in the evaluation of threats and to excess in how they were presented to the public, particularly since American officials were haunted by their failure to anticipate 9/11 and by dread of a new wave of attacks. Bush manifestly took this line of reasoning at face value. "Before 9/11, Saddam was a problem America might have been able to manage," he later wrote, "[but] through the lens of the post-9/11 world, my view changed." He concluded, "The lesson of 9/11 was that if we waited for a danger to fully materialize, we would have waited too long."[76] "Had 9/11 not happened," Tenet later observed, "the argument to go to war in Iraq undoubtedly would have been much harder to make."[77]

The favorable turn taken by the campaign in Afghanistan after mid-November led to an acceleration of the Iraq calendar. On November 21, Bush asked Rumsfeld to start to focus on a possible Iraq operation and to review existing war plans. (The most recent plans went back to 1998, and Rumsfeld considered them obsolete.) He wanted Rumsfeld to keep this out of sight as long as possible, as he was worried about arousing speculation in the United States and abroad, and he wanted to hide his hand as much as he could.[78] With the war in Afghanistan still going on, the top brass were stunned by Bush's request, but Rumsfeld was determined to fulfill his task with his usual zeal. Success in Afghanistan came at the right moment: although several days previously the press had mentioned that the campaign was a mess, the Taliban regime fell almost effortlessly. Unsurprisingly, American leaders (Rumsfeld first and foremost) were prompt to see this turnaround in the situation as confirmation of the unequaled possibilities of US military power. Surely, the recipe applied so successfully in Afghanistan could be applied in Iraq. Hence the leaders felt that the preparations for "phase two" might be undertaken even if "phase one" was not yet complete—and that this could be done along the lines of the emerging "Rumsfeld Doctrine." The Rumsfeld Doctrine derived from the so-called "revolution in military affairs" and aimed at reducing ground forces by using the multiplier effect of high technology in terms of firepower, target acquisition, communications, and the like. It was also intended by its author to be the opposite of the "Powell Doctrine" of using "overwhelming force," which had been applied against Iraq in 1991 and which continued to characterize the Pentagon's existing plans.[79]

Does this mean that in effect a war was decided upon in the fall of 2001? Bush would always deny this. "Unless I received definitive evidence tying Saddam Hussein to the 9/11 plot, I would work to resolve the Iraq problem diplomatically," he later said. Bush described the two parts of the "coercive diplomacy" he intended to conduct in parallel: to "rally a coalition" to put pressure on Saddam Hussein, and to "develop a credible military option" in case he refused to hear reason. Today, it is still impossible to confirm or invalidate this version: the moment when the war was *effectively* decided remains the principal question mark over this history. At most, one can note with what determination and what promptness Bush decided to put into effect—and in the greatest secrecy—the "coercive" part.[80]

Be that as it may, the tone of American leaders hardened noticeably around late November. On the 26th, Bush announced to the press that Saddam Hussein must let the inspectors come back to Iraq to "prove to the world that he's not developing weapons of mass destruction." When asked what would be the consequences if Saddam did not comply, Bush answered, "He'll find out."[81] At the same time, the administration ramped up what appeared to be a campaign to convince Americans of the gravity, if not the imminence, of the Iraqi "threat," even if this meant twisting the facts. During a television interview on December 9, Cheney revived speculation about Baghdad's ties with al-Qaeda by giving credence to allegations that a meeting had taken place in Prague a few months before 9/11 between Mohamed Atta—the hijacker-pilot of the first plane that struck the World Trade Center—and an Iraqi agent. Although both the CIA and the FBI had cast doubt on this Czech information (rightly so, the 9/11 Commission would later conclude), Cheney would continue to assert the veracity of the rumor tooth and nail, thereby helping plant in American public opinion the idea that there was in fact Iraqi involvement in 9/11.[82] As for WMD, *New York Times* reporter Judith Miller shortly afterward published a story—manifestly inspired by sources within the US administration—in which she made public the testimony of an Iraqi defector who claimed to have been personally involved in the renovation of installations for the production of biological, chemical, and nuclear weapons. (This was the first in a long series of similar stories by Miller, whose questionable character would be discovered later.)[83]

It was not happenstance that at the same time, the Iraq issue returned to the forefront at the UN. In the autumn, Powell's initiative in favor of "smart" sanctions had remained stuck in the Security Council due to Russian objections; Moscow feared an arrangement less favorable to its fruitful trade with Baghdad. For its part, France supported the Powell initiative, as Chirac had confirmed to Bush on September 18. As seen from Paris, 9/11 indeed changed the Iraq issue: a failure by Powell at the UN, the French understood, could only play into the hands of the hawks.[84] Yet the Iraqis did not appear to realize that the world had changed. Coming to meet Kofi Annan in New York in mid-November, Iraqi foreign minister Naji Sabri condemned terrorism "in all its forms" and denied any link between Baghdad and 9/11—but he placed Iraq among its victims by pointing the finger at American bombing. And although he said that he was open to resuming dialogue with the

UN as Annan was asking, he added that cooperation would be difficult as long as the American bombing continued.[85] Baghdad did not seem ready to budge despite the storm clouds that were accumulating. In this context, an unexpected development occurred. Washington submitted a draft resolution to the Security Council reaffirming the need for a "comprehensive" solution that would include a "clarification" of Resolution 1284. This seemed to be a major concession, since Iraq had previously argued that the vagueness of the conditions for a possible lifting of sanctions as defined in Resolution 1284 was its reason for refusing to resume cooperation with the UN. The apparent American softening was warmly welcomed by the Security Council: on November 29, 2001, Resolution 1382 was adopted unanimously.[86]

Yet Jean-David Levitte had no doubts that the American evolution aimed to prepare the ground for a possible intervention. The French UN representative imagined the following scenario: with Washington ready to engage in a discussion on the "clarification" of Resolution 1284, Annan would receive a mandate to resume dialogue with Baghdad on this basis. Then, either Saddam Hussein would accept the return of inspectors, or else the United States would benefit from the Security Council's "comprehension," if not its "support," for tough action. Levitte's Russian colleague Sergey Lavrov shared this analysis, seeing in the sudden American flexibility "an ultimately formidable threat" for Iraq.[87] In short, it was the UN part of the Bush strategy of "coercive diplomacy" that was being put in place by Washington in the last weeks of 2001.

Was the maneuver an expression of the sincere desire to solve the Iraq problem peacefully, or was it merely the prelude to a war already decided upon? With hindsight, the secrecy that for many months would continue to surround the "coercive" part of the Bush strategy (that is, the military preparations for a possible Iraq invasion) argues for the latter interpretation. If the threat of an intervention was supposed to convince Iraq to yield, why hide the preparations? Yet at the end of 2001, the advocates of a peaceful approach—France included—had no better option than to bank on the former interpretation. France, Levitte recommended, should promote a "reasonable" solution before the "obstinacy and bad calculations" of Iraqi leaders led to "drastic" US actions, and argued that Paris should contribute to a settlement based on the "clarification" of Resolution 1284 that would enable Annan to obtain the return of inspectors. This presupposed using a "language of truth" with Baghdad, he emphasized.[88]

Paris thus returned to trying to pass messages to the Iraqis. In mid-December, André Janier, head of the French interests section in Baghdad, met with

Naji Sabri to insist that the "context" had changed—an understatement implying that Iraq was now in American sights—and that the status quo was no
longer an option. Baghdad, Janier warned, "had to make the right choice." This
message was received at least partially: Sabri confirmed that he was ready to
have a "political dialogue" with Annan, although he still ruled out the return of
inspectors as long as the bombing continued. Janier was moderately optimistic:
"The Iraqis have perhaps understood that the moment [has] come for them to
budge" and give up their tactic of "refusal and defiance," he told Paris.[89] A week
later, Janier even heard Tariq Aziz praise Iraq's "good relations" with France,
even though several months earlier the regime had accused France of all kinds
of evil. Janier was not fooled by Aziz's flattery: as he saw it, the Iraqis, who
previously had thought that they had broken their isolation and were able to
stand up to the United States, were beginning to realize that the situation had
been transformed since 9/11.[90] Meanwhile, Annan, too, wanted the Iraqis to
open their eyes. Although it "would be ill-advised to attack Iraq now" since this
could only "exacerbate the situation and increase tensions in a region already in
turmoil," he declared publicly, Baghdad nevertheless needed "to start answer-
ing the Security Council's questions" and to accept the return of inspectors.[91]

At the end of 2001, the French embassy in Washington tried to decipher
American intentions. Anti-Iraq circles had been "remobilized" by 9/11 and
"galvanized" by the pace of the offensive in Afghanistan, French diplomats
assessed, and they now wanted to finish with the regime: the proponents of
a "phase two" (now extending beyond neoconservative circles) were on the
offensive. Still, the administration was divided; as a result, without a deliberate provocation from Baghdad, the United States would not attack Iraq in
the short term. Bush, while adopting a threatening rhetoric, was sticking to
Powell's policy. But, they continued, while the White House still hesitated on
the method and the pace, it was probably preparing for a gradual hardening
between then and the spring. French authorities, the Washington embassy
believed, therefore had an obvious interest in supporting Powell to allow him
to show that the multilateral approach was the "least bad." But Paris should
not have too many illusions: all this presupposed that Baghdad would behave,
which to say the least was not a sure thing. Overall, they concluded rather
lucidly, "the chances of finding an exit with the help of Bagdad are thin. But
without such help, chances are nil." They then added that "as long as Baghdad
gives the impression of seeking only to escape its obligations, the Americans
will be geared toward a strike against Iraq—and sooner or later we will find
ourselves with our backs to the wall."[92]

By the end of 2001, French diplomacy was thus fully aware that a dynamic was in motion that would be hard to stop, and therefore it expected probable difficulties between Paris and Washington. Yet the French were ignorant of how advanced military preparations were. When on December 28 General Tommy Franks, the head of CENTCOM, came to brief Bush at his ranch in Crawford, Texas, the subject on top of the agenda was not (as officially indicated) the Afghanistan campaign, but the state of the still-secret plans concerning Iraq. The plans still remained to be finalized, explained Franks. He gave a general outline: whereas preceding plans included the deployment of a force of 400,000 men through a six-month buildup, the plans now being developed involved at first only 100,000 troops, rising to 200,000 in the following weeks, deployable on short deadlines. Preparations—including the sending of force components to Kuwait—would have to be started shortly, Franks said, but initially they could be kept discreet since they would pass for normal force rotations in the context of operations underway in Afghanistan, thus permitting a better surprise effect when the time came. Franks took care to specify that his work still had to be refined and that preparing such an operation would take time. Bush said that he understood this. But although he had revealed nothing of his intentions during the briefing, he took away from it that there existed an "option" to meet the Iraqi "threat."[93]

Chapter 3
The Axis of Evil: January–September 2002

When George W. Bush gave the annual State of the Union address to the joint houses of Congress on January 29, 2002, the ambiance was very much the same as it had been on September 20: bursts of applause came in waves during the fifty-some minutes of a speech that was full of references to the heroism of Americans in the "war on terrorism." Yet while four months previously he had been speaking to a disoriented country in shock, this time Bush offered a first review of accomplishments. "In four short months, our nation has comforted the victims, begun to rebuild New York and the Pentagon, rallied a great coalition, captured, arrested, and rid the world of thousands of terrorists, destroyed Afghanistan's terrorist training camps, saved a people from starvation, and freed a country from brutal oppression," he declared in the presence of Hamid Karzai, now chairman of the Afghan Interim Administration, the post-Taliban government of Afghanistan.

The essential message, however, lay elsewhere. Bush used his address to announce his objective beyond this "first phase" of the war: namely, "to prevent regimes that sponsor terror from threatening America or our friends and allies with weapons of mass destruction." Among these regimes, he named North Korea, Iran, and especially Iraq, which he accused of having sought secretly for more than a decade to procure anthrax, nerve gas, and nuclear weapons. "States like these, and their terrorist allies, constitute an axis of evil, arming to threaten the peace of the world," Bush proclaimed, warning that "I will not wait on events, while dangers gather. I will not stand by, as peril draws closer and closer. The United States of America will not permit the world's most dangerous regimes to threaten us with the world's most destructive weapons."[1]

"This is fucking serious"

Bush's speech, in retrospect, clearly marked the launch of phase two of the war on terror. The phrase "axis of evil" was designed to focus minds. Karl Rove, Bush's political strategist, had supplied this striking formula, which displayed the religiosity and the "moral clarity" that Bush had proclaimed, even at the risk of his seeming Manichean. And of course it echoed the "evil empire" famously denounced by Ronald Reagan in 1983, thus underlining the political legacy to which Bush laid claim. It was the signal that the United States had finally found its mission in the post–Cold War era, as the rationale for this "axis of evil" lay in the famous "nexus" formed by terrorism and the proliferation of weapons of mass destruction, which the hawks had been advancing since 9/11.

Of course, Bush's advisers wanted to avoid anything that might seem akin to an implicit declaration of war on Iraq. To attenuate this possibility, they added Iran and North Korea, two states that allegedly were active in matters of terrorism and WMD, to the agenda. This precaution was necessary to avoid giving credit to the idea already circulating in Washington that an operation against Iraq was only a matter of time. Yet the media were not fooled: even if the White House swiftly specified that a military intervention was not imminent, many people saw these three countries as a list of the future objectives of the war on terrorism, and Iraq was at the top of that list. Charles Krauthammer, an influential columnist with neoconservative credentials, called the speech "an astonishingly bold address" and characterized it as "just short of a declaration of war" on Iraq. As for international reactions, they were, unsurprisingly, mostly alarmed. Only Baghdad, once again, set itself apart by calling Bush's speech "stupid." Yet Bush had achieved his goal: to harden his position without explicitly pointing to the Iraqi target, thus permitting preparations to be pursued under the greatest discretion.[2]

These preparations advanced at a sustained pace in the first weeks and months of 2002. After the briefing at the Crawford ranch on December 28, Donald Rumsfeld had asked General Tommy Franks to prepare very quickly a full-fledged plan of operation that Bush could order implemented if he decided to do so. During the first half of January, Rumsfeld—always eager to assert his preeminence over the top brass—had put pressure on his generals in order to steer the preparations in the direction he wished: toward an operation as rapid and economical with troops as possible, and one which would provide a startling demonstration of the effective "transformation" of American military force. Franks had presented Rumsfeld with the latest stage of his work on January 17, and Rumsfeld, anxious to hasten the pace, had asked him to come back to see Bush within three weeks. Thus on February 7, eight days after the State of the Union address, Franks again appeared before Bush and his war cabinet in the White House situation room. He said that he was in a position to start operations as soon as October or November 2002, though he preferred to use a "window" in December, January, or February 2003. Questioned by Bush, Franks made it clear that it would still be possible to intervene after this date despite the less-favorable climatic circumstances. But he also stressed that significant preparations—in particular, obtaining the support of countries in the region—remained to be carried out. Overall, Franks had the feeling that Bush was well aware of the scope of the problems raised by such an operation, and that he would have the time to prepare it.

While the preparations were intensifying in the first months of 2002, they took place in the greatest secrecy as required by presidential directives. Certainly the heavyweights in the administration were informed, including Colin Powell, who had direct personal contact with Franks. (Powell was concerned that the operation might deviate too much from the "canons" of the doctrine that bore his name, which required using "overwhelming force.") At least among those in the loop, it thus was evident from the end of the winter that a logic of war was being put in place. The top military, in particular, were soon convinced of the probability of an operation against Iraq. Shortly after the February 7 briefing, CENTCOM's plans began to circulate in the Pentagon; exercises were conducted to test certain aspects. At the end of March, Franks himself broached the issue with the chiefs of the various branches of the US military—army, air force, navy, and Marines—gathered at the Ramstein base in Germany. The message was clear: The war will take place, he warned his generals. On the occasion of another meeting with them a little later, Franks—known for his blunt language—was even more direct: "This is fucking serious. You know, if you guys think this is not going to happen, you're wrong. You need to get off your ass."[3]

Officially, however, none of this existed. For the time being, the official line remained that the administration had no bellicose plan concerning

Iraq. Appearing before a Senate committee on February 12, five days after the briefing by Franks at the White House, Powell reminded the legislators that American policy since 1998 had aimed to change the regime in Baghdad and declared that the administration was "looking at a variety of options that would bring that about," but stated that the president "ha[d] no plan on his desk right now to begin a war with any nation." American leaders would repeat this phrase ad nauseam in the following months, even if this meant that public opinion and the international community were deliberately misled. Bush used it at the start of April when he received Tony Blair at Crawford: "I have no plans to attack on my desk," he stated in a television interview, repeating that "Saddam needs to go." (He would say the same thing in Berlin and Paris at the end of May.) Franks, too, made equally deceptive statements, and went even farther: questioned during a press conference on May 21 about the number of troops and amount of time that would be necessary to conduct an operation in Iraq, he answered, "That's a great question and one for which I don't have an answer because my boss has not yet asked me to put together a plan to do that." Yet Franks would soon have two brigades deployed in Kuwait and equipment in position for four more brigades.[4]

Around the same time, the administration was beginning to seek the cooperation of key countries. In mid-March 2002, Dick Cheney undertook a tour of Middle Eastern countries—Egypt, Turkey, Jordan, Israel, Yemen, Saudi Arabia, and other Gulf states like Qatar, Bahrain, and the United Arab Emirates—that the Pentagon considered likely to occupy a place in the arrangements when the time came. Before his departure, Franks and Rumsfeld briefed him on the contributions being sought, whether active (e.g., intelligence, aviation, even ground troops) or passive (e.g., air space, transit, bases). In fact, the goal at this time was less to obtain firm and precise commitments from the leaders concerned than to transmit a message about American determination and to sound out their attitudes. The result of Cheney's tour was mixed. Although the Americans expected that Arab leaders would prove prudent in their public statements about a possible military intervention, they had been anticipating that in private they would be favorable. Yet Cheney heard it said more than once that the United States ought first to try to restart the Israeli-Palestinian peace process and put pressure on Israel to stop the Israeli Defense Forces' incursions into the occupied territories.[5]

Crown Prince Abdullah of Saudi Arabia delivered a similar message during his visit to Crawford at the end of April 2002. Meanwhile, the Israeli-Palestinian situation had deteriorated further. In response to a series of murderous suicide attacks on Israeli territory, at the end of March Israel had launched Operation Defensive Shield, the largest military operation waged in the West Bank since 1967, besieging Yasser Arafat in Ramallah. Vexed by American disinterest in a by-now moribund peace process and furious at Bush's unconditional support for Israeli prime minister Ariel Sharon—whom Bush had described as a "man of peace," which the prince saw as a provocation—Abdullah was close to leaving the ranch early, and only the intervention of Powell prevented a clash. Coming after Cheney's tour a month earlier, Abdullah's visit was a warning for the administration: an operation against Iraq would be hard to accept in the region without real progress on the Israel-Palestine issue. This warning would lead Bush, under pressure from Powell, to give a speech at the end of June in which he said that he was favorable to a solution that included two states. Yet the speech remained short of the expectations of those for whom US involvement in the peace process remained the top priority. Nor did it convince those who rejected the theory that a war against Iraq—by transforming the whole Middle East in a democratic direction—would contribute to a resolution of the Israel-Palestine problem.[6]

At this time, a major factor for Bush was confirmed: the support of Tony Blair. The British prime minister, determined that his country should stand alongside the United States in the face of the post-9/11 challenges, was certain that sooner or later the Americans would want to "take care of" Iraq. Believing that the once-manageable Iraqi problem had changed in nature as a result of the terrorist attacks, he resolved that Great Britain would have to participate in a military operation if such an operation proved inevitable. Certainly Blair admitted that it was less the threat itself than the evaluation of the "risk" that had evolved: "The WMD problems don't seem obviously worse than three years ago," he confided to an adviser in the middle of March 2002.[7] Faithful to the doctrine of humanitarian intervention that he had laid out in his landmark speech in Chicago in 1999, Blair was nonetheless convinced that the very nature of the regime sufficed morally to justify an operation—though he also recognized that the humanitarian justification probably was not acceptable under existing international law, and that only Baghdad's lack of respect for UN resolutions could serve as a legal pretext for an intervention.[8]

Still, Blair's prime motivation in throwing his weight behind Bush was no doubt the preservation of the sacrosanct Anglo-American "special relationship." The alliance with the United States was of "vital strategic interest" for Great Britain, he later wrote, adding, "When they had need of us, were we really going to refuse?"[9] It is difficult, with hindsight, not to see this statement as confirmation of Blair's fundamental choice: to stick to the United States whatever happened. In the years to come, Blair constantly would claim that his attitude aimed to influence American decisions in the direction of taking into account the stakes he judged most decisive—starting with the Israel-Palestine issue—and to act so that the United States made the choice of multilateralism. Yet this approach was vulnerable to the risk of circular thinking: to not let the United States commit errors and act alone, one had to stand by its side, Blair seemed to think. The choice, Blair would later testify, was "clear and simple": the United States had decided to "tackle the issue" and there was no doubt that they could "do it unilaterally," but in his view it was preferable that they do it "multilaterally."[10]

At Crawford on April 5–7, 2002—a mostly tête-à-tête meeting—Blair, at any rate, seems to have promised Bush that Great Britain would bring its support to an American military operation aiming at a change of regime in Iraq, at least if certain conditions were fulfilled.[11] Did Bush then accept these conditions, starting with the necessary passage of the decision through the United Nations? This is not certain: "I didn't have a lot of faith in the U.N.," Bush would later write, "but I agreed to consider his idea."[12] Yet Bush's lack of a firm commitment did not prevent Blair from deciding that his country would henceforth participate closely in American military planning, a decision that Blair would later justify by claiming that the British needed to be informed about the preparations. True, he insisted, this decision did not mean that war was "certain," yet he also recognized that Britain's participation in US planning did imply that London "had to be, at least in principle, open to being part of the action."[13]

The first half of 2002 retrospectively appears as a decisive period in the march to war. In the months following the "axis of evil" speech, a mechanism, no doubt, was launched. Of course, it is difficult to say whether Bush had already made his decision, but everything now occurred as if the military option were in fact prioritized, despite the White House's systematic denials. In the first months of 2002, Deputy National Security Advisor Steve Hadley began to gather the "deputies" to discuss preparations systematically on the occasion of twice-weekly lunches in the White House situation room. These ultra-confidential discussions were restricted to one or two representatives per department or agency. Richard Armitage and Paul Wolfowitz were flanked respectively by Marc Grossman and Douglas Feith, the third-ranking officials at State and the Pentagon; CIA deputy director John McLaughlin; Scooter Libby; and one or two generals. The goal of these discussions was not to debate the rationale for but rather the modes of a possible war. The central hypothesis was implicit: nobody, Feith later wrote, contested (at least openly) that "Iraq must be disarmed"; nobody asserted that disarmament "could be achieved without a regime change"; and nobody maintained that Saddam Hussein "could be removed from power without military action."[14] This situation inspired in Armitage and Grossman a feeling of "unreality," since no formal decision had been taken in favor of war. This perspective might explain why Powell and those close to him did not take the exercise seriously, no doubt underestimating the determination of the hawks—and of Bush.[15]

Whatever the case, a major factor—the absence of resolute opposition within the administration—was already perceptible. To be sure, the Bush team was notoriously divided between partisans of a muscular approach, namely Cheney, Rumsfeld, and Condoleezza Rice, and those who were reticent, starting with Powell and Armitage. Yet in these critical months, the latter did not openly oppose the logic of an intervention. Was this precisely because they underestimated the determination of the hawks? Or, as his adversaries would reproach him, because Powell privileged a "win-win" posture that allowed him to be critical without breaking with the president? Regardless, the objections that he expressed in the internal debates pertained less to the principle of an intervention than to its modalities, and notably to the choice of timing and the international context. For Powell, priority should be given to consolidation in Afghanistan, to setting up a coalition, and only then—perhaps at the start of Bush's second term—to an intervention in Iraq. This approach would lead Powell to make himself, like Blair, the advocate of "going through the UN" but not make him clearly reject the military option. This may explain why his foreign partners—foremost the French—appear to have overestimated his capacity or his will to prevent a war.[16]

So how did French decision-makers read American intentions in the first half of 2002? In contrast to the British, the French were not privy to the details of the discussions within the administration, and they were mostly ignorant of how advanced the military planning was. Although they were aware of the direction taken in the weeks following Bush's State of the Union address, French diplomats probably at first overestimated the degree of openness of the American game: "The administration knows what it wants [i.e., regime change]," wrote Ambassador François Bujon de l'Estang in mid-February, but it "has not yet decided between various ways of getting there." He added, "Despite the racket kept up here by the warmongers, many in Washington harbor serious doubts about the wisdom of military action." French diplomats were encouraged in this analysis by their American colleagues, who themselves overestimated (no doubt in good faith) how open Bush's choices actually were. "The debate continues within the administration between those who want to 'finish the job' begun under Bush senior and those who are worried about the consequences," confided Elizabeth Jones, the under secretary of state for Europe, during a meeting with British, French, and German colleagues in London on February 19.[17]

Starting in the spring of 2002, however, the French reading of American intentions became more precise. In mid-April, Hubert Védrine gathered the principals at the Quai d'Orsay to discuss the subject. All agreed that the White House, despite the reservations of Arab countries, wanted to proceed to action in Iraq after the midterm elections in November, and that only a resumption of inspections would be likely to delay things, although the administration was divided on the possible role of new inspections. "The general opinion," Védrine summed up that day, "is that the United States has made its decision" and that any remaining obstacles "will not make it pull back."[18] In a telegram written from Washington a few days later, Bujon de l'Estang specified what the calendar might be. He confirmed that Bush had decided to "get rid" of the Iraqi regime, but he thought it unlikely that there would be an operation in the short term. The White House, he explained, knew that it was supported by a majority of American public opinion and it was convinced that hesitant allies "would applaud to bring the house down" when the job "was done," but action against Iraq was not "urgent" in its eyes: the operation in Afghanistan was far from complete, and due to the climate conditions the Pentagon did not want a quick opening of a "second front." In addition, Bujon wrote, the Arab countries were balking because of the collapsed Israeli-Palestinian peace process, and right now there was no credible alternative power in Iraq. Most important, the UN process was still ongoing, and the White House knew that a military intervention would be easier to manage if it was done under the UN aegis; therefore, the United States wanted to give itself the possibility of exploring "all avenues of a multinational solution" before "deciding on a unilateral intervention if necessary." Bujon concluded that there was "little chance that operations would be launched before the coming autumn or winter," and they might even be pushed back to the winter of 2003–4 if the operation in Afghanistan stalled or if the Israeli-Palestinian crisis deteriorated.[19]

"Simplistic" and "vapors"

The first months of 2002 were marked by a cooling of Franco-American relations. Gone was the unanimity proclaimed after 9/11, as witnessed by the name-calling in which Hubert Védrine and Colin Powell indulged after the "axis of evil" speech. The speech did not go down well in Paris: the French disliked the messianic character of the phrase and considered it reductive to place Iraq, Iran, and North Korea in the same category. "We were sincerely and deeply in solidarity over the tragedy of September 11," Védrine declared, but "today we are threatened by a new simplistic approach that brings all the problems in the world down to the struggle against terrorism."[20] In fact, Védrine was not the only one to express reservations: his German equivalent, Joschka Fischer, complained that the allies were treated as "satellites," and the European Commissioner for External Relations, the British politician Chris Patten, warned the United States against the temptation to act alone. This hue and cry brought Powell to answer vigorously; Védrine was "getting the vapors," he flung back. "A virile exchange between friends," Védrine commented, in the hope of putting a stop to the skirmish.[21]

Yet the weeks and months that followed merely confirmed the Franco-American disagreement. The 2002 French presidential election was a turning point in French politics. The first round of the election on April 21 saw the far-right National Front candidate Jean-Marie Le Pen advance to the second round by beating the Socialist candidate Lionel Jospin. That event would later influence Chirac's determination to oppose Bush's policy in the name of rejecting a "clash of civilizations": in Chirac's view, Le Pen's strong showing revealed the fractures that existed in French society and which 9/11 had only aggravated. In the short term, though, the French presidential election somewhat eased the strained atmosphere between Paris and Washington. Chirac's massive victory against Le Pen in the second round on May 5, with over 82 percent of the popular vote, put an end to five years of a forced "cohabitation" with a Socialist government. As a result, Chirac could recover undivided authority with respect to foreign policy. The team he appointed wanted to strengthen Franco-American relations and turn the page on the frictions of recent months. The new prime minister, Jean-Pierre Raffarin, belonged to the Atlanticist center-right; as for Dominique de Villepin, the minister of foreign affairs, he was a career diplomat close to Chirac (having been Chirac's chief of staff at the Élysée during his first term) and was considered familiar with Washington, where he had been in post in the mid- to late

1980s. Villepin presented himself as pro-American: shortly after his arrival at the Quai d'Orsay, he sent a message to Colin Powell via Powell's associate Richard Haass, promising that he would do nothing to embarrass the secretary of state. Should he have disagreements over American policy, he said, he would express them in private. Villepin then went to Washington bearing the same message in July.[22]

Bush's visit to Paris on May 26 nevertheless confirmed the growing divergences between France and the United States. It had taken fourteen months for the American president—who had stopped in Berlin before coming to Paris—to visit the major European capitals. The context was tense, as illustrated by the demonstrations that took place in Germany in advance of Bush's visit. The Paris ambiance was different from what it had been between Bush and Chirac in Washington six months previously: during their joint news conference, the two presidents could scarcely hide the distance between them, even a degree of mutual irritation. Bush added to the problem by playing the Texan cowboy who did not care for the rest of the world, rebuffing an American journalist for asking him a question in French. Bush and Chirac were scheduled to go to Normandy the next day—Memorial Day in the United States—for a ceremony of remembrance of the D-Day landings, but even though Bush declared that "there's a heck of a lot more that unites us than divides us," the impression of a Euro-American fracture was only confirmed. The American press was severe toward Bush: if his goal was to calm the worries about American unilateralism, his performance was judged mixed at best.[23]

Discussions between Chirac and Bush—accompanied by Powell and Rice—indicated the growing distance between the French and the Americans. Agreement was total with regard to the immediate response to 9/11, starting with the operation in Afghanistan, where both men deplored that the operation was dragging on against the backdrop of the difficult stabilization of the country. As for the antiterrorist struggle, it continued to produce intense cooperation. Chirac saw "no divergence" in this domain, and Bush thanked France for its contribution with respect to intelligence. There was relative consensus on other subjects like relations with Russia, with which the United States had just signed a strategic weapons disarmament treaty; while Chirac reiterated his conviction that one should avoid "humiliating" Russia, Bush assured him that Moscow now accepted the new enlargement of NATO that Washington was defending. But the two presidents could not dissimulate the persistence of subjects of discord that had been appearing in recent months between Europe and the United States, in particular over environmental issues. Chirac again said that he was "concerned" about the environment and once more affirmed his conviction that the Kyoto Protocol had to be implemented—to which Bush replied that he "had not changed his opinion" on this subject and that he was not willing to "ruin" the American economy by implementing Kyoto.

Unsurprisingly, the discussion became tenser when it focused on the Middle East. True, on the Israeli-Palestinian conflict, the tone was civil. Bush said that he was aware of the gravity of the problem and asserted that he wanted to continue his efforts to remedy it. Although he denounced an "ineffective and corrupt" Palestinian Authority that he thought should be reformed, he recognized that Yasser Arafat must remain a key actor, thereby differentiating himself from Ariel Sharon's perspective on the situation. Insisting on the need to support moderate Arab countries, Bush admitted that Crown Prince Abdullah's visit to Crawford had been very difficult: the Saudi prince had been "close to packing his bags," he said. Chirac, for his part, agreed that Arafat was a difficult interlocutor and had committed a "grave error" two years earlier in rejecting an agreement with Sharon's predecessor Ehud Barak, but in his view Arafat nevertheless remained "irreplaceable." Expressing his "very deep concern," Chirac said that only the United States could influence Israel, and repeated that only an international conference could respond to such a "threatening" situation.

But then Bush and Chirac turned to Iraq. Chirac was forthright: it would be a serious mistake to think that attacking Iraq would improve the situation in the Middle East, he stated, warning Bush against a military intervention. "The Arab world will not accept it," he said, because it already thought that the West was doing nothing to resolve the Israel-Palestine problem; in the event of an attack on Iraq, he added, "no Arab head of state would be able to survive." Bush did not concede anything. "They will survive," he blustered, reiterating yet again that there was "no plan on his desk today for a military attack." And, he added in the same breath, Saddam Hussein constituted a "threat"—what would the French say "if he developed a missile capable of being aimed against France?" Chirac responded that the European position was "not to undertake anything without the formal authorization of the Security Council." Recognizing that Saddam Hussein had "resumed his efforts" and that he was profiting from contraband money, Chirac stressed that nobody knew what was happening in Iraq and that therefore the most urgent thing was to obtain the return of inspectors—who, he emphasized, had got "results" before 1998—once again attributing responsibility for their departure to former UNSCOM director Richard Butler. "The only alternative," he concluded, was a war that carried "many grave dangers."[24] The stage was set for the confrontations of the coming months.

The American hardening toward Iraq in the first weeks of 2002 placed France in a dilemma from which it would not escape until a year later—and at the cost of an unprecedented crisis with the United States. On the one hand, the French wanted to avoid an American military adventure because of its grave regional and international consequences, and doubtless also because of possible domestic repercussions against the backdrop of intercommunity and religious tensions that had been fed by 9/11. For some time, French authorities had been concerned by a new wave of anti-Jewish sentiment in certain fringes of the population of Muslim background, and it was feared that the Israeli-Palestinian conflict would be imported into France. On the other hand, Paris understood that direct opposition would have no effect on Washington's determination and would damage Franco-American relations. The French, in addition, could not dismiss the necessity of solving the Iraqi problem; after all, they had never denied its existence, although they did not share the United States' appreciation of its gravity. What was required, therefore, was a middle path that extended the "legalistic" approach that Paris had defended for years: to enable the UN process to follow its course in the hope of avoiding a war. But there was a problem: since this process could be "hijacked" by the proponents of an intervention, how could Paris make sure that playing the UN game would not in effect reinforce the hand of the war-mongers? This concern was, and in the coming months would remain, the central problem of French policy.

All the same, from the start of 2002 French diplomacy had to adapt its UN approach to take into account the evolution of the American position. Until then, Paris had stuck to the logic of Resolution 1382, adopted in November 2001, which was supposed to lead to establishing the "smart sanctions" proposed by Powell. At the same time, the French wanted "clarification" of Resolution 1284—in other words, specifying the conditions for suspending and then lifting sanctions after the return of inspectors—in the hope of bringing Baghdad to cooperate.[25] But now, the "axis of evil" speech and the growing possibility of an American operation against Iraq changed the situation. "The Iraq issue is at a turning point, and we must be prepared for it," judged the Quai d'Orsay. The Quai's reasoning was simple: the previous approach of advocating the suspension of sanctions in exchange for Baghdad's resumption of cooperation was out of date, because such a quid pro quo would lose its attraction if "smart sanctions" were put in place. Thus the only lever that remained was fear of the "serious consequences" for the Iraqi regime from the United States if the former refused to cooperate. In short, only Baghdad's unconditional acceptance of the return of UN inspectors was capable of "arresting the spiral" and returning the Iraqi issue to a cooperative framework.[26]

There ensued a marked hardening in the Paris position in the first weeks of 2002, with the French switching to a more robust approach toward Iraq. At the end of February, the political director at the Quai d'Orsay, Gérard Errera, suggested to his colleagues in the "quad" group (France, Germany, Great Britain, and the United States) that the members of the P5 might ask Kofi Annan to express in their name to Baghdad the exigency of an unconditional return of the inspectors. (Errera took the precaution of underlining that his authorities, while considering the return of inspectors "essential" to the political solution of the Iraq problem, remained opposed to military action.) The Americans replied that they were in agreement with the basis of the French proposal, and the British applauded vigorously.[27]

French hardening derived from a simple calculation: only the UN path might permit American decisions to be steered from military intervention, which in return implied harboring the greatest firmness with respect to Iraq. But should the prime objective of French diplomacy be to avoid American intervention, or to channel it through the UN process? The two approaches were not contradictory—and the second might serve as a backup, in case the first failed—but they denoted perceptible nuances among French diplomats, both in terms of analysis (had the American decision been definitively taken?) and of objectives (should France seek actively to oppose a war?). For Ambassador Bujon, who believed that there was a slight chance of preventing the debates inside the US administration from spiraling toward war, it was desirable to "offer the Americans an approach that would enable either avoiding" an operation or else putting such an operation "in phase with international legality." The administration, he argued, was not "completely indifferent" to international opinion. If it found that opinion "divided and hesitant," then it would feel "encouraged to take unilateral action" to solve the Iraq problem and make this a "textbook case." If, on the other hand, "it saw a consensus in favor of a reasonable option, it would not necessarily decline to follow it, while reserving the right to come back to a unilateral option." Bujon stressed that personalities like Powell were worried about the consequences of a unilateral option. "Let us endeavor to put them in our camp," he concluded, "which implies avoiding being accused of weakness or leniency toward Baghdad."[28] France's UN envoy,

Jean-David Levitte—who would not deviate from this line in the months to come—clearly privileged the second approach. Since Washington had all but decided "to go ahead no matter what," he reasoned, the goal should be "to build a scenario that would strongly reduce the unilateral character" of this probable operation, for a "purely unilateral" intervention would have serious consequences because of reactions in the Arab and Muslim world. Hence, it was necessary to enjoin Iraq to accept unconditionally the inspectors' return. "If Baghdad refused," he went on, "the international community would no doubt be led to better accept an American initiative."[29] Levitte was, in essence, defending a line close to Tony Blair's: the goal in his view was more to avoid a *unilateral* American action than to try to prevent a war.

Yet between these two approaches, it was only a matter of nuances. Neither approach at this stage called for directly opposing American choices, and both affirmed the need for great firmness with respect to Iraq—starting with exhorting an unconditional return of inspectors—which alone would enable France to influence events. For French diplomacy, there was hardly any other option at this juncture than to try to weigh on the United States by accompanying the Americans in their determination to solve the Iraq problem, as long as they took the UN path. This, of course, was a gamble: what if at a later stage Washington should free itself from multilateral constraints in order to engage in a unilateral adventure in Iraq? The dilemma, in other words, was only postponed; although for the time being there were nuances between the two possible approaches, one day France might be faced with an agonizing choice. Bujon was well aware of this: to make his proposed approach credible, it would be necessary "to give Washington solid political assurances on the sequel, which might include expressing our determination to officially acknowledge possible Iraqi breaches at the Security Council, and to do so in terms that would be equivalent to a green light."[30] One could not better pose the terms of an equation that French diplomacy would be faced with a few months later.

The chances of success of the French approach depended foremost on Iraqi cooperation, which was far from guaranteed. After Bush's State of the Union address, Baghdad still did not seem in a hurry to act. Since February 2001, Kofi Annan's attempts to revive "dialogue" with Iraq were at an impasse: Iraq continued to reject Resolution 1284 and to refuse to allow the inspectors to return. The Iraqis did seem willing to discuss things with the UN, but there was still no question of letting UNMOVIC do its work in Iraq. Bad memories of UNSCOM might help explain this attitude, conceded the

French chargé d'affaires, who nonetheless was astonished—given the clarity of American threats—by Baghdad's "abnormally firm" tone, which "did not augur any great flexibility."[31] Still, the following month the Iraqis agreed to discuss the inspectors' return with the UN secretary-general. A delegation led by Naji Sabri went to New York on March 7, but confined itself to asking questions—no less than nineteen of them—about a possible resumption of inspections. Annan nevertheless thought this was "a good start," although he kept "absolutely prudent" about the expected results. Meanwhile, the permanent members of the Security Council refrained from arguing among themselves, so as not to compromise the process. Hans Blix, who participated in the discussions, would later remember that the Iraqis seemed "aggrieved," adding that "I did not have an impression of a lack of sincerity, rather of people living in another world of thinking."[32]

The debate agitating Washington in the spring of 2002 could hardly lift the Iraqis' spirits. True, the State Department was clearly betting on the UN in accordance with a line elaborated by Haass that consisted of demanding the unconditional return of inspectors. But Bush at this stage was still far from having opted for the UN road. The hawks were hopping mad; their goal was to discredit inspections in advance. Rumsfeld held forth in the press to argue that most of what the UNSCOM inspectors had found in Iraq before 1998 had been located only because of the testimony of defectors. Newspapers reported that at the start of 2002, Wolfowitz had charged the CIA with enquiring into Blix's record as director-general of the International Atomic Energy Agency between 1981 and 1997 in the hope of finding elements to discredit UNMOVIC. By all the evidence, the partisans of a muscular approach feared that a resumption of inspections would compromise their plans. Their nightmare was that inspections conducted without results—meaning without an incriminating discovery, the proverbial "smoking gun," being found—would lead to lifting sanctions and preventing an intervention.[33]

A new "round" of the "dialogue" in New York from May 1 through 3 marked slight progress. It still did not result in Baghdad's accepting the resumption of inspections, but Blix was able to converse with Iraqi experts and answer the questions raised by them during the preceding meeting. As for IAEA director-general Mohamed ElBaradei, he confirmed that the nuclear file might be closed quickly if the IAEA, once allowed back in Iraq, could determine that the situation had not evolved since 1998. Annan called the meetings "frank and useful," and a third "round" of the "dialogue" was scheduled before the summer. The French delegation at the UN observed that Annan had been "deliberately positive," Blix was "firm," and ElBaradei "encouraging": a division of roles that would be confirmed later. As for the members of the Security Council, the French diplomats noted that none of them, not even the Americans, had asked for an end to the exercise.[34]

The meetings nevertheless showed that the Iraqis were still far from having understood that the game had changed—or perhaps that they understood this all too well. They were still trying to obtain improbable concessions in exchange for the return of inspectors—starting with the assurance that a military operation would not be unleashed—or trying to limit the brief of the latter. Blix, who from the start adopted a legalistic line from which he would not depart, had to admonish them that it was up to Baghdad to demonstrate that it no longer held WMD. Iraqi behavior left everyone perplexed. Present in New York, Jacques Baute, a French nuclear physicist who directed the IAEA's "Iraq Action Team," even described as "surreal" the conversation between ElBaradei and Jafar Dhia Jafar, one of those most responsible for the Iraqi nuclear program. Although the IAEA evidence showed that, pending verification by inspectors, the nuclear problem was "practically settled," Baute recounted that Jafar—manifestly tested by the long journey from Baghdad and by various forms of harassment such as searches and visa issues—had spent his time making dialogue "impossible" while reproaching the IAEA for not having closed the file back in 1998. (The Iraqis habitually would demonstrate such counterproductive behavior in the following months.) French diplomats were already barely optimistic: Iraq, they noted, was stalling for time, and yet concrete results (in other words, the return of inspectors) must be achieved soon. The Iraqis had obtained another two-month reprieve, but it would be surprising, French diplomats thought, if the United States would prolong it "indefinitely."[35]

"The president has already made up his mind"

As the summer of 2002 approached, the administration was getting ready to blow the whistle to end the game. On June 1, a new milestone was laid: four months after the State of the Union address had pointed out the "threat," Bush gave a speech that aimed to lay out the "method" he intended to use to deal with it. At the West Point military academy—a telling choice of venue—Bush unveiled what would appear three months later in the form of a very official "national security strategy." The gist of his speech was the need to neutralize threats before they became concrete. "If we wait for threats to fully materialize, we will have waited too long," he theorized; "the war on terror will not be won on the defensive. We must take the battle to the enemy, disrupt his plans, and confront the worst threats before they emerge. In the world we have entered, the only path to safety is the path of action. And this nation will act."[36]

Iraq was not mentioned in the speech, but there was no doubt in anybody's mind that it was in the background. Preparations for a possible operation, meanwhile, were progressing. Rumsfeld and Franks were busy refining military planning, obsessed with reducing even more the volume of forces as well as the time delay between a presidential decision, if (or when) it was made, and its implementation. This combination of reduced forces and tightened action times produced a mounting worry among many military leaders who questioned the soundness of an operation against Iraq—which in their eyes amounted to a diversion from the fight against al-Qaeda and terrorist networks—as well the modes of such an intervention. The Rumsfeld Doctrine, they feared, might lead to minimizing dangerously the necessary forces, particularly the army. Rumsfeld and Franks were scarcely bothered by such concerns. On June 19, Franks presented to Bush a plan that called for a considerably reduced time scale thanks to the prepositioning of troops, which was already underway in the Gulf; as for the volume of forces, it would be possible to launch the intervention with only 50,000 troops, to be reinforced by the same number within three weeks. In July, Bush agreed to commit some $700 million to execute American infrastructure improvements in Kuwait. The keyword continued to be secrecy, so as not to give the impression of a programmed war, but it was increasingly difficult to hide the reality: on July 28 and 29, the *New York Times* and the *Washington Post* respectively ran top stories on the ongoing military planning. On August 5, Franks again briefed the president and the complete NSC. By early August, the preparations had reached interagency level. Rice and Hadley charged Frank Miller, the NSC point person for defense policy, with setting up an Executive Steering Group to ensure coordination among the various sectors of the administration—an urgent task, given the crying lack of cooperation between different government departments and the military services, including within the Pentagon itself.[37]

It was also during the summer that the administration's rhetoric changed markedly. Although the Iraq "problem" had until then been presented as a long-term danger, the tendency was now to talk in much more disturbing terms, even as a threat to be dealt with as quickly as possible. As a result, the gap began to grow significantly between public declarations and the intelligence actually possessed by the administration—which, as we shall see, was much less categorical than that implied by political leaders—leading some members of the intelligence community to suspect the existence of a systematic campaign of distortion. It was also in July 2002 that Sir Richard Dearlove, the head of British intelligence agency MI6, came back from Washington with the impression that "the intelligence and facts were fixed around the policy." This phrase, extracted from a note written by a close adviser to Blair (the famous "Downing Street memo," which was leaked to the British press in 2005), would lead to much ink spilled later over the ambiguity of the expression "fixed around the policy," which could point to a deliberate manipulation of the content of intelligence or else simply to a tendentious presentation—in short, to strong "spin." Dearlove later would reject the former interpretation of his own words, though he recognized that Washington's use of intelligence—in particular among the vice president's entourage—at the very least was loose. (The disagreement revolved less around WMD—about which the British and American intelligence agency assessments were close—than about Baghdad's supposed links with terrorist networks, of which Libby had stubbornly defended the existence to Dearlove during his July 2002 Washington visit.)[38]

By the summer of 2002, clairvoyant observers, foremost among them the top brass, had begun to understand that a war was probably inevitable. The day after Bush's West Point speech, Air Force Major General Victor Renuart, Franks' assistant, realized that the plan on which he had been working for months might effectively be put into operation. Similarly, when he became head of the First Marine Division at the beginning of August, Major General James Mattis—a Marine Corps officer known for his perspicacity and judgment—put his staff on alert for a probable operation in Iraq, based not on confidential information but on his personal analysis of the situation. (Later events would prove him right: Mattis and his division would participate in the invasion of Iraq in the spring of 2003.)[39]

Powell and his entourage had to face the evidence that the wind was not blowing in their direction. Richard Haass was among them. For some time, he and his team had had the feeling that their opposite numbers at the Pentagon, at the NSC, and in the vice president's office were gaining the upper hand on Iraq. Haass decided to open up to Rice in July: "Are you really sure you want to make Iraq the centerpiece of the administration's foreign policy?" he asked his former NSC colleague. Rice's answer stunned him: "You can save your breath, Richard. The President has already made up his mind on Iraq." Haass later wrote that this conversation should not be interpreted as evidence that a *formal* decision to launch a war had been taken in the summer of 2002 and then kept secret; but for him, Rice's statement did confirm that Bush had already concluded that it was necessary to eliminate Saddam Hussein and that he was ready to do what was necessary to achieve this—knowing that this would "almost certainly" necessitate the use of force.[40]

The same impression of a programmed war was being confirmed among the British military leaders, who were now in the "loop" of American preparations. On his return from Washington in July, Dearlove reported that a military intervention was now considered "inevitable" and that "Bush wanted to remove Saddam, through military action, justified by the conjunction of terrorism and WMD." Of the same opinion was General Sir Mike Boyce, the British chief of defense staff, who told Blair during a meeting at the end of July that, except for a turnaround, Bush had indeed decided to conduct a military action. Minister of Defense Geoff Hoon detailed the variants of these actions during the same meeting. (Blair later maintained, somewhat incredibly, that at the time he still had the conviction that Bush had not yet decided to unleash a war.)[41]

In this context, the Iraqi attitude remained enigmatic. During a new round of the discussions that took place in Vienna at the start of July, the Iraqis, in spite of the sound of marching boots in Washington, still did not appear disposed to budge. They continued to pose conditions on the modes of inspections, which Blix rejected. Even if it was agreed to maintain contact, no date was set for a fresh meeting. "The Iraqi stance was puzzling," Blix later noted, recalling that the *New York Times* that very day had published its umpteenth article on the Pentagon's plans and that the delegations were well aware of it. He wondered, "Was Saddam not well informed or was the Iraqi conduct simply a piece of hard bargaining in the bazaar?"[42]

Long doubtful about the existence of a spiral to war, Powell finally became aware in the middle of the summer that things were taking a bad turn. From briefing to briefing, he realized that the military preparations were progressing without the question of the justification for an operation ever being raised. Despite his aura, Powell had to face the fact that his influence on the president was limited, for want of having been able to develop a close relation with him. So at the start of August, he decided to sound an alarm bell: he asked, through the intermediary of Rice, for a tête-à-tête meeting with Bush. The talk took place on August 5, just after the Franks briefing, during a dinner in the president's private quarters, followed by a conversation in his office—all in the presence of Rice.[43]

Powell was well prepared: he had brought with him three or four pages of handwritten notes aimed to make Bush aware of the risks of a conflict. A war, Powell warned, might shake up friendly Arab regimes, starting with Saudi Arabia, Egypt, and Jordan; it might destablize the oil market; and it would be conducted to the detriment of the priority fight against terrorism. Most critically, it would lead the United States to take charge of Iraq for an unforeseeable period of time. "You are going to be the proud owner of 25 million people," Powell said. "You will own all their hopes, aspirations, and problems." Powell wanted to make Bush understand what he and Richard Armitage called between themselves "the Pottery Barn rule": "You break it, you own it." And he added that a war would "suck the oxygen out of everything," swallowing the whole American foreign policy. "This will become the first term," he said, stressing the electoral risk of defining his presidency in this way.

For Powell, it was even more important to make Bush understand that such an operation could not be conducted by the United States alone. It would require bases, facilities, and access—in other words, allies. But most nations at the time were hostile to a war. "It's nice to say we can do it unilaterally, except you can't," he said. "If you think it's just a matter of picking up the phone and blowing a whistle and it goes—no, you need allies," he then exclaimed, explaining to Bush that the focus should not be on military planning alone. But Powell understood that he could not be content with formulating warnings; he also had to make proposals. "What should I do?" Bush asked him in effect. "You can still make a pitch for a coalition or UN action to do what needs to be done," Powell answered, but warned, "If you take it to the UN, you've got to recognize that they might be able to solve it. In which case there's no war. That could mean a solution that is not as clean as just going in and taking the guy out." In short, Powell concluded, trying to obtain an international "cover" might well change the situation entirely.

Powell left the White House with the feeling of having said what he had to say and of having been heard. But this was only partly the case; the next day, Rice congratulated him for his very convincing plea for building a coalition. But Powell's intended message, of course, went beyond that: he had wanted to make Bush understand to what extent the enterprise in itself was risky. And yet Powell had not explicitly advised Bush against an attack on Iraq. As a good soldier, he would not dispute orders—only how they were implemented. This, in effect, is what Bush had retained from the meeting; on that day, he would confide to journalist Bob Woodward sixteen months later, Powell had discussed *tactics*. It was up to him as president to be *strategic*, and the "strategy," Bush stressed, was in his mind dictated by the "solemn duty to protect America" and beyond that to "improve the world." In short, he said—inherently confirming the messianic dimension of his enterprise—his intent was to "achieve big goals." Moreover, Bush added, if Powell indeed believed in the necessity of going through the UN, others in the administration were more than skeptical on this point.

Powell nevertheless thought that he had won the first round of the formidable struggle of influence that was being played out inside the administration starting in mid-August. On the 14th, the NSC gathered around Rice. (Bush was absent, having gone to Crawford.) At the top of the agenda was discussion of a draft presidential directive concerning Iraq. The document under discussion postulated that the United States should act in coalition "if possible," but "alone if necessary." Powell tried to push his case: even the British, he argued, would not support the United States in the absence of a UN cover, and the search for a peaceful solution was a prior condition without which it would be unthinkable to launch a war. Bush, he went on, should seize the opportunity of his next speech to the General Assembly to tackle the Iraq issue. Rice rallied to this approach, but Cheney unsurprisingly was hostile. If in the end he accepted the idea that Bush might discuss Iraq at the UN, the president's speech, Cheney said, should include a formal demand: after years of prevarication, the UN would have to settle the Iraq problem once and for all, or else be discredited. Bush ratified this line two days later during a subsequent NSC meeting in which he participated by videoconference.[44] At that point, of course, everything would depend on the precise content of the speech: between a formal demand to the UN and a declaration of war on Iraq, the boundary was thin.

Powell received strong support. In the *Wall Street Journal* of August 15, Brent Scowcroft, the former national security advisor to George H.W. Bush, published an op-ed piece titled "Don't Attack Saddam." Worried by insistent rumors about a war that he was convinced would be a serious mistake, Scowcroft, a prominent Washington figure who was vastly respected for his sound judgment, vigorously argued for a UN approach that would include the resumption of effective inspections. Of course, everybody in Washington knew that Scowcroft was very close to the senior Bush, and so all presumed (justly) that he would not have taken the initiative for the article without submitting it to him. This stand won Scowcroft the gratitude of Powell—and the reprimand of Rice, his former NSC colleague. Rice told Scowcroft that the president was unhappy with his taking a stand that might appear as an attempt by the forty-first president to force the hand of the forty-third. Once again, the father/son relationship was central.[45]

Another leader who took a position in favor of going through the UN was British foreign secretary Jack Straw, who at Blair's request came a few days later to meet Powell discreetly on Long Island, where he was vacationing. Sensing the wind turning, the British prime minister wanted to be assured that, in line with what he had pleaded for with Bush at Crawford a few months earlier, the American administration would indeed take the UN route. The message delivered by Straw was clear: if the Americans seriously envisaged a war and they expected to count on the British, then they should go through the UN. Straw's message made Powell happy, since it strengthened his hand.[46]

At the end of August, the secretary of state had the feeling that the trend was favorable to him. But this impression did not reckon with Cheney: cautious after 9/11, the vice president was now a declared advocate of an intervention in Iraq, and in his view going through the UN could only slow things down or even get them stuck in endless procedures. As for Rumsfeld and his entourage, they continued to lead the charge against inspections, which were accused of being a sham, since the Iraqis had long since proved masters of dissimulation. Cheney had now firmly decided to throw all his weight into the balance—all the more so since James Baker, the former secretary of state under the elder Bush, had (like Scowcroft) taken a position against unilateral action, further strengthening the moderate camp. Realizing that the administration had not until then announced the official line, Cheney wanted to fill the void: he shared with Bush his intention to give a speech on Iraq, even before Bush was to speak to the UN on September 12. Cheney's idea met with no objection; better still, Bush did not request advance knowledge of the content of his speech.

A suitable occasion was soon found: Cheney was to speak on August 26 in Nashville at the national convention of the Veterans of Foreign Wars (VFW). The speech, centered on Iraq, was blunt. "A return of inspectors," Cheney asserted, "would provide no assurance whatsoever of [Saddam's] compliance with U.N. resolutions"; on the contrary, "there is a great danger that it would provide false comfort that Saddam was somehow 'back in the box.'" Cheney gave his own evaluation of the threat: the Iraqi regime had made big efforts to "enhance its capabilities in the field of chemical and biological agents," he said, and the Iraqis "continue to pursue the nuclear program they began so many years ago." "Many of us are convinced that Saddam Hussein will acquire nuclear weapons fairly soon," he declared, and nothing so far, whether inspections or air strikes, had been able to stop him. The result, Cheney averred, was clear: "There is no doubt that Saddam Hussein now has weapons of mass destruction." "Time is not on our side," Cheney concluded, warning that "the risks of inaction are far greater than the risk of action."[47]

The importance of Cheney's speech did not escape anybody: the administration "has just made it known that the fun and games are finished and that it's time to start class," summed up the French embassy. Was the vice president forcing the president's hand by "preempting" the military option? Certain witnesses, who have since maintained that Bush had been surprised by the content of a speech that, once given, could only commit him, believe that this was the case. The fact that Cheney's speech had not been cleared beforehand speaks volumes, in any case, about the closeness of ties between the two men, and by the same token about the extraordinary influence that Cheney seemed to exert. Whatever the case, it was a decisive moment. Cheney's speech, Haass later wrote, "accomplished what the vice-president and most others in the administration sought, which was to reestablish the march to war."[48]

Cheney's statement also confirmed and even amplified the gap that now existed between the public declarations of the nation's highest leaders and the information held by the intelligence services. "The vice-president's speech," wrote Haass, "badly overstated the Iraqi threat."[49] General Anthony Zinni, a retired Marine Corps general who had a long record of dealing with Iraq and was present at the VFW convention, was extremely surprised by it. As CENTCOM commander until 2000, he had seen no intelligence that would allow such assertions. George Tenet, too, was astonished by the tenor of the speech that, contrary to custom, had not been transmitted to the CIA in advance for validation. The speech, he later wrote, "went well beyond what our analyses could support."[50] Nevertheless, Cheney had set the tone: the administration's declarations in the weeks and months to follow invariably would be categorical and alarmist about the Iraqi threat. As will be seen, the administration's alarmist tone, in turn, would rub off on the analyses produced by the intelligence agencies themselves, contributing to distortions in their assessments. August 26, 2002, marked the point of departure for a process that would lead to a war conducted on distorted premises.[51]

"Movement, initiative, and expression"

The acceleration of events in Washington placed the rest of the international community before a choice. Paris had to position itself vis-à-vis an increasingly likely American offensive. By a chance of the calendar, Cheney's speech took place on the eve of an annual ambassadors' conference that assembled the upper crust of French diplomacy. Profiting from the occasion, on August 27 Villepin held a meeting on Iraq in the presence of the principals at the Quai d'Orsay and the ambassadors concerned. The American position was "dynamic," and thus France's position should be dynamic too, he said. Villepin laid down its parameters: "There should be no intervention outside the UN framework, but no option should be excluded within this framework," he said, knowing that the language used toward Iraq should be "firm." The tone was set. All scenarios, including a military intervention, could be envisaged as long as they were part of a UN process. Because the French attitude had previously been hostile to the use of force, the shift—which conceivably was prompted, at least in part, by Cheney's speech—was notable.

Villepin and those present then went around the table on the questions under examination. What were the American intentions? What was the exact nature of the Iraqi danger? What position should France adopt? As ambassador to Washington, François Bujon de l'Estang spoke first. A debate was raging within the US administration, he stressed, and Bush had not made his decision. There were divergences on the costs and benefits of a military operation, he went on, but there was consensus on the goal of regime change, and American public opinion was open to an intervention. "The war will take place, but not immediately," he said, adding that the "firing window" was situated between January and April 2003, or in 2004. This assertion was not contradicted by anyone around the table: French diplomacy converged on the hypothesis of a probable American offensive in Iraq in the short or medium term.

A second question was debated: the state of the "threat." Although he did not possess "concrete elements" to support his position, André Janier, France's chargé d'affaires in Baghdad, said that he was "convinced" that Iraq had "never ceased developing WMDs." Yves Aubin de La Messuzière, his predecessor in Baghdad, shaded this statement somewhat but thought, too, that the Iraqis had kept a "secret garden" of chemical and biological materials and that at least there was a risk at the regional level. This evaluation by and large was shared by the DGSE representative, for whom there was no "major threat" at the level of the international community for the time being but rather a "threat in the local theater." Overall, the roundtable expressed a sentiment that was now widespread among most French decision-makers: there was a general conviction that Iraq had not renounced its WMD ambitions, even if its operational capacities remained for the time limited to a local threat, but there was no evidence-based certainty. This consensus led Villepin to stress the need to obtain "credible" information in a realm where one could not be content with "intuitions."

So what position should France adopt? Should it keep its distance from Washington by stressing that the priority was not military action but rather a resumption of inspections? Or, on the contrary, should Paris play the game of "coercive diplomacy" in order to obtain Iraq's cooperation in the hope that the war logic would be defused as a result? At the end of August 2002, French diplomacy, under Villepin's impetus, clearly opted for the second approach, which led to a perceptible hardening of its stance on Iraq. France, Villepin stated once more, should announce its "determination" and "not exclude any option." Levitte went further: one had "to build a coalition" to constrain Baghdad to accept the return of inspectors, since the more the United States proved "ready to strike," the more the Iraqis would be "close to ceding." This gambit, he added, presupposed that Paris should "hint that it would be on the side of the coalition if Iraq did not cooperate," a logic that Levitte would defend with constancy later on. Villepin concluded the meeting by advocating "initiative, movement, and expression," a slogan in line with the activism he had displayed since his arrival at the Quai d'Orsay a few weeks earlier. In this new phase of the Iraq crisis, Villepin wanted French diplomacy—and no doubt himself—to play one of the main roles, and for the time being this ambition took the form of a search for credibility with regard to Washington. This credibility, in turn, implied the need for Paris to harbor the utmost firmness toward Iraq.[52]

The speech that Villepin gave the same day to the opening of the ambassadors' conference confirmed this push for firmness. "The international community," he said, is confronted with a "regime that for years has defied international rules . . . , takes its people hostage, and poses a threat to security, especially of its neighbors. Such an attitude is not acceptable." Of course, Villepin added, "the measures to be taken should be decided by the international community according to a collective process and in respect for procedures." But he hinted implicitly at a possible use of force, albeit one framed by the UN: "In this spirit, no military action can be conducted without a decision by the Security Council." Villepin's message was all the more clear as a result of Paris's simultaneous rejection of Tariq Aziz's request to meet with Jacques Chirac, on the grounds that the Iraqis had still not accepted the unconditional resumption of inspections. Returning to Baghdad a few days later, André Janier did not mince words: by acting as they did, he told Naji Sabri, the Iraqis risked playing the game of the Americans, adding that in this case the Europeans would not be able to do anything for Iraq. Aziz replied without hiding the mood that dominated in Baghdad: why accept the return of inspectors, he wondered (without closing the door entirely), if the ultimate American goal was to "destroy the regime"?[53]

Under the Fifth Republic, it was up to the president in the Élysée to decide the major outlines of foreign policy. So if Villepin was active on the diplomatic scene, it was Chirac who fixed the "line," especially since the crisis involved the question—regal as it was—of war and peace. (Chirac, moreover, had a long history of dealing with Iraq.) Presidential preeminence in foreign policy decision-making would thus apply from start to finish in France's management of the 2002–3 Iraq crisis. Yet the proximity between Chirac and Villepin was real, and in the coming months the French position would result largely from the sometimes exclusive interaction between the two men and their close entourages. Of course, as we shall see, this proximity did not prevent differences in style or a certain sharing of roles from appearing occasionally. This differentiation was already on display at the end of summer 2002: while Villepin wanted to adopt a rather hawkish position—explained by a wish to give the United States promises of firmness in order to lend credibility to the "diplomatic path"—Chirac wanted to distance himself from what he perceived as the coming war. At the start of August, his personal military chief of staff, General Henri Bentégeat, had alerted him to the possibility of a US military operation within a few months, based on his reading of the American military buildup in the Gulf region. "The prospect of an armed conflict did not seem to me excluded, even if I refused publicly to mention it," Chirac later remembered. Chirac's reluctance to openly envisage a military intervention was confirmed in the speech he gave on August 29 at the closing of the ambassadors' conference. Pointing a finger at the "temptation to legitimize the unilateral and preventive use of force," he stressed that "if Bagdad obstinately refuses the unconditional return of inspectors, then the Security Council— and it alone—is qualified to decide on the measures to take" (measures that he refrained from specifying). The contrast between Chirac's statements and those that Villepin had made two days earlier did not go unnoticed in Baghdad.[54]

Chirac's statements, though, went beyond the case of Iraq: it was also a matter of rejecting a new American doctrine that in his view broke with the international order issuing from the UN Charter. At the start of September, the White House was indeed about to make public the national security strategy document on which the NSC had been working since the West Point speech in June. This strategy, the French embassy in Washington believed, would make the idea of preemptive strikes official, yet behind the notion of preemption (which was not so new) lay a much more radical one: preventive war. "We are witnessing the premises of a fundamental strategic rupture," the embassy stated, adding that this doctrine would render "obsolete" the idea of deterrence while challenging the role of the Security Council as the ultimate guarantor of the legitimacy of the use of force. From the Élysée's perspective, this prospect was simply unacceptable. Chirac's diplomatic adviser, Jean-Marc de La Sablière, wrote in a note to him that this analysis "confirmed the fears we had," adding, "It was important for you to express early on, as you have done in the speech to the ambassadors, your apprehensions and reservations.[55]

It was in this state of mind that Chirac tackled a telephone conversation that Bush requested in order to inform him—like the principal allies and partners of the United States—of his current thinking on the Iraq issue before his UN speech on September 12. The context was both uncertain and rapidly evolving. Despite Bush's programmed speech, the French embassy in Washington warned, the proponents of multilateralism would be wrong to claim victory, for it remained to be seen what precise role the US president wanted to assign to the UN: inspections combined with exorbitant conditions might suit the hawks, because the least lapse would justify an intervention. And, the embassy concluded with a grain of salt, "By accepting the return of inspectors, Baghdad leaders would thus be collaborating in their own elimination. This is perhaps too much to ask of them."[56]

Before speaking to Bush on September 6, Chirac had two important conversations that day, starting with Kofi Annan, whom he received at the Élysée. The two men were more in unison than ever. The UN secretary-general, who had just met Tariq Aziz on the margins of the World Summit on Sustainable Development in Johannesburg, said that he was very worried about the prospect of an intervention. He thought that the Iraqis were not ready to accept the return of inspectors rapidly because the United States seemed determined to intervene in any case, and he considered the new American doctrine "particularly dangerous" and a threat to the Security Council's authority. Chirac said that he was entirely in agreement with Annan, and he reiterated the French position: only the council should decide. He was convinced that the Americans had indeed decided "to go," which he considered a "folly." The Bush administration, he added, wanted to drag along the international community, which he would not accept.[57]

Then Chirac spoke by telephone with Blair, who wanted to consult with him before meeting Bush the next day at Camp David. During the conversation, Chirac did not hide his reservations. Although he shared with Blair an aversion to the Iraqi regime, "engaging in steps to war" would be "heavy with consequences," he said, adding that the current situation had "nothing to do" with the 1991 Gulf War or with the action against Afghanistan in 2001, on which "the whole world agreed." Chirac recalled the historical background: one should not forget that UNSCOM and Richard Butler had been responsible, at least in part, for the withdrawal of inspectors in 1998. Whatever the case, he conceded, the regime since then had "recovered a certain margin of maneuver," and it was likely that it was trying to reconstitute some part of its arsenal. As a result, Chirac said, the inspectors should be able to resume their work without restriction, and indicated that he was ready to discuss a resolution in that direction. (This was a major point for Blair before his meeting with Bush the next day.) If Baghdad continued to oppose the return of the inspectors, Chirac went on, then there were two alternatives: either the United States would engage in a unilateral action, with which France could not be associated; or, if the matter was referred to the Security Council once again, then Paris would be ready to discuss the measures to take, knowing that France alone (an important qualification, as will be seen later) "would not oppose a possible intervention with its veto." If the Security Council gave a "green light," he added, then "we will see what we will do." Chirac did not conceal his pessimism: "for fifteen years," he observed, Saddam Hussein has "systematically taken bad decisions."[58]

Bush, as agreed, called Chirac after the phone call with Blair. The conversation was brief. As his UN speech approached, Bush advanced "his desire to inform a certain number of friendly leaders" and assured him that, contrary to "speculations," no decision had yet been taken. He was aware of "differences" with Chirac, but he thought that they had two points of agreement: Saddam Hussein constituted a "threat" and was stubbornly "defying" the international community. Chirac answered that he was "open to debate" on the path to follow. Without denying the "danger" that Iraq was posing for "the region and the world" and the need to obtain the unconditional return of inspectors, he said that he hoped that Baghdad would listen to reason, because an intervention would prove to be "a difficult and dangerous adventure." But as with Blair, Chirac did not hide his pessimism about Saddam Hussein's attitude. To conclude, he repeated that he was "open to conversation," to which Bush replied that he was looking forward to "pursuing his dialogue" with Chirac after his UN speech.[59]

Two days later, Chirac granted the *New York Times* a long interview that would appear in print on September 9. At this stage, the French approach had been refined by Chirac and Villepin and their respective aides, Jean-Marc de La Sablière and Villepin's chief of staff Pierre Vimont. It could be summarized as a "two-step" approach: the Security Council should by means of a first resolution require the unconditional return of inspectors; and in case Iraq did not cooperate, it would be up to the council to decide what measures to take via a second resolution, without excluding any option a priori, including a military one.[60] For Chirac, the *Times* interview was a good occasion to cross the t's and dot the i's on his position. He began by reiterating his attachment to the United States—for him, this had become something of a ritual statement—"a country that I love, that I admire, that I respect." But once that was out of the way, he did not hold back on the criticism. Condemning the Baghdad regime and calling for a "democratic and humane" Iraqi government that had good relations with neighboring countries, he tartly rejected the "preventive" doctrine and declared himself "totally against unilateralism," in passing taking a dig at the American vice president: "what M. Cheney says does not interest me." Saying that he was "very worried" about the consequences of an intervention, he stressed that the goal of the international community could not be to impose regime change, for "a few principles and a little order are needed to run the affairs of the world." "The issue today is to know whether there are any weapons of mass destruction," he continued, "and to know it, one should go to see. And to see it, the inspectors must be free, without any restrictions or conditions, to visit." Then Chirac explained his two-step approach: if the inspectors could not go back, it would require a second resolution "to say if there should be or not an intervention," and "following the second resolution, France will definitely give its position." "I have a tendency to trust M. Bush," he concluded. "I am awaiting his speech calmly."[61]

Chirac's interview was well received in Washington. Despite the criticism, the French president's statements were perceived as confirming a change of attitude: there were harsh words for the regime in Baghdad, and he had not closed the door on the use of force even if he had advanced strict conditions for it and reserved his decision. In doing so, Chirac had clearly differentiated himself from German chancellor Gerhard Schröder, who—amid an electoral campaign in which he was seeking reelection—had declared himself opposed to the use of force in any circumstances, even with the prior approval of the Security Council. Chirac could hope to weigh on Bush's choice; would not a more reluctant attitude have played into the hawks' hands, since they wanted to demonstrate the uselessness of the UN? The adopted line, the French hoped, might at least help strengthen the proponents of the multilateral route.

But nothing was certain. The fierce struggle for influence being played out in Washington would last until the very day of Bush's speech, with an alternation, sometimes from hour to hour, between the unilateral option and the multilateral option. Although it was understood that the American president would present his "strategy" before the General Assembly, nothing had been decided about what exactly he would announce there or what the substantive role of the UN would be in his approach. Should the United States try to obtain a resolution and, if so, what should be its terms? The hawks had seemed to score a decisive point with Cheney's VFW speech, which had created the impression that the UN would be allotted only a backseat role, that of a mere podium from which the president of the United States would launch an ultimatum to Saddam Hussein. But Bush had let his vice president know that he did not intend to have his hand forced, and Cheney had somewhat moderated his public statements over the following days. On September 1, Powell had again asked for a meeting with Bush on his return from Crawford, and Bush had reassured his secretary of state that his intention was indeed to go to the UN to ask for a resolution imposing the return of inspectors. At the start of September, Cheney's offensive seemed to have been curbed.

Not so. On the evening of the 6th, the "principals" met at Camp David in Bush's absence to discuss the speech. Cheney was very tough, fighting tooth and nail against a new resolution that for him risked tying the president's hands. Bush, he argued, should denounce Iraq's multiple violations of previous resolutions and say that he was prepared to act. Powell once again stood his ground: it was impossible, he said in substance, to require the UN to rally to a declaration of war. The only way of involving it would be to obtain a new resolution, he said, and he warned that a unilateral action with unpredictable consequences would risk unleashing a worldwide hostile reaction. The next day, September 7, the NSC gathered in the presence of Bush. Powell repeated that there was no other path than the return of inspectors, which implied a new resolution, and Cheney retorted that the latter might demonstrate weakness and result in no clear conclusion, which would only complicate the US objective, namely to eliminate Saddam Hussein. Bush did not close the debate, but promised to reflect on it.[62]

Afterward, Bush met with Blair, who had come to Camp David for a few hours. The objective of the prime minister, who had sent Bush a note before traveling, was to get the United States to agree to take the multilateral path and to accept a resolution in advance of any action against Iraq—a condition sine qua non of British involvement. The discussion was crucial for what followed. Blair would keep a memory of a meeting that had been a "little tense," but at the end of which he tore from Bush his promise to take the UN route. For his part, Bush did not hide from his guest that the probable outcome of this process would be war, and he got from him, in private, the promise of British military involvement if necessary. "I am with you," Blair is said to have assured him. "Your man has got *cojones*," Bush declared to Alastair Campbell, Blair's spin doctor and confidant.[63]

This was not the end of the story, though. In the following days, the drafting of the speech—of which no less than twenty-four versions circulated—was the subject of new arguments between Cheney and Rumsfeld on one side and Powell on the other. Until the last day, Powell was not assured of having prevailed. On the eve of his appearance at the UN, Bush confirmed to Rice that he would ask the Security Council to work up a resolution and asked that a sentence in this sense be added to the text he would read. But the suspense would last literally until the last minute: while Powell, seated in the UN chamber alongside Rice, listened to Bush give his speech, he saw that the crucial few words did not figure in the written version he had before his eyes—probably due to an editing mistake. Perceiving the error, Bush corrected himself, adding a sentence: "We will work with the UN Security Council for the necessary resolutions," he declared, while warning that without this, the UN would become "irrelevant." It was a close call: without the sentence in question, the speech no doubt would have put the matter in a quite different light.[64]

An editing mistake, or a Freudian slip? In any event, the incident showed how much the debates between the two camps had been both tense and indecisive, with Bush himself hesitating between the two approaches before deciding under the combined influence of Powell and Blair. If the French position had counted, it was only marginal: it was by far more important for Bush to be able to rely on British support, and if it came to that, on British participation in a military operation. For this, the price to pay was to take the UN route. Yet it remained to be seen if Bush's choice in favor of the latter—taking the risk of getting bogged down in long palavers in the Security Council and then in the uncertain inspections process—had been a choice of adroitness or of sincerity, a tactical or a strategic decision. For the world could no longer have any illusions: the objective of the American president was regime change in Iraq, and achieving it had a high chance of entailing the strong-arm option. The UN process—not merely the deliberations in the Security Council, but also the inspections—promised to be extremely unpredictable. Would this be the opportunity to put on track a peaceful solution to the Iraq problem, or would it be a shortcut to war?

Chapter 4
The Negotiations:
September–December 2002

George W. Bush's speech in New York on September 12 had reassured the proponents of multilateralism. At least for a while, Bush's choice of the "UN road" had removed the prospect of an intervention, especially when, on September 16, Baghdad finally accepted the unconditional return of inspectors. But this did not mark the end of the debate that had raged for several months within the American administration. The negotiations that began at the end of September in the Security Council, with a view to adopting the resolution demanded by Bush to demonstrate that the United Nations remained "relevant," were everything except assured of success. At the end of a protracted negotiation conducted essentially between Paris and Washington, however, it resulted on November 8 in the unanimous adoption of Resolution 1441, a text that gave Iraq a "final opportunity" to fulfill its obligations.

Would this diplomatic success, for which Colin Powell and Dominique de Villepin deserve most of the credit, permit the international community to keep the multilateral process on track, or did it merely postpone an inevitable confrontation? At the end of 2002, it seemed that a peaceful solution was still possible, if only because unencumbered inspections had resumed in Iraq following the adoption of the new resolution. But the American administration, while ostensibly playing the game of Resolution 1441, had in reality lost nothing of its bellicose determination. On the eve of 2003, Bush, deep inside, in all likelihood had already made his decision.

"The mother of all resolutions"—Take 2

Bush's choice to "go through" the UN shifted the debate that had divided Washington for months: the question was no longer "if" but "how" the UN ought to solve the Iraqi problem, or else risk dwindling into insignificance. From the day after Bush's speech, the two camps began to skirmish over the content of the resolution to be negotiated in New York. For Powell, it should aim at enabling a peaceful solution and, failing that, offer the legitimacy necessary for military action; so it should be a text that was capable of bringing Iraq to compliance but also permitted the largest possible international consensus. For Dick Cheney and Donald Rumsfeld and their respective entourages, on the contrary, the resolution should give every latitude to the United States so that it could impose disarmament on Iraq by force if it decided to do so and, furthermore, enable the regime change that remained the true objective; as a result, it should be a deliberately one-sided text aimed at Iraq and with no concessions to the points of view of other Security Council members. It did not matter in their eyes if a proposed American resolution along these lines (ideally, a pure and simple ultimatum) was rejected by Iraq or by the rest of the international community, since that rejection would in itself constitute the perfect pretext for American action.

Leading the negotiations on the American side fell foremost to Powell and to Washington's UN representative, John Negroponte, a career diplomat with a reputation for being "tough." But prior to the negotiation in New York, determining the US position was the subject of intense bargaining in Washington. The Pentagon—and also the vice president's staff—not only had a voice but even managed to propose language for the resolution. Powell, in other words, was not alone in calling the tune, and he knew that he was under close surveillance by the hawks. True, the notion (defended by the hawks) of a resolution that would aim not only at weapons of mass destruction but also at the very nature of the Iraqi regime and its supposed links with terrorist networks was quickly set aside, as this approach seemed most unlikely to obtain the necessary Security Council support. Still, the Americans placed the bar very high: the resolution, in their view, should call for "strengthened" inspections, and it should state that Iraq was already in "material breach" of previous resolutions and warn Baghdad that unless it complied it was exposing itself to "serious consequences." The latter combination of terms, in UN parlance, was synonymous with a possible recourse to force. The bottom line was clear: the only acceptable text was one that would authorize Washington to unleash an operation if it decided to do so.[1]

Although the French were pleased that President Bush was committed to working within the UN framework—at least for the time being—they had been expecting an intransigent position from the Americans and their British allies. At the UN, French representative Jean-David Levitte was able to confirm this intransigence on September 18 during a conversation with his British colleague, Sir Jeremy Greenstock. Washington and London, Greenstock told Levitte, wanted to insert into the draft resolution an "automatic" clause that assured them that it would be possible to unleash an operation without any further pronouncement from the Security Council. This aim, of course, ran counter to the requirement advanced by Chirac of having the council decide (or not) on an intervention in the event Iraq defaulted, which would require a second resolution.[2]

Washington's hawkish position placed the French in a dilemma. On the one hand, letting a text of this nature pass—by abstaining during a vote—would be contrary to the principles promoted by French leaders. Faced with the US "preventive" strategy, what was at issue, for Paris, was a certain conception of the international order. Letting such a resolution be adopted, moreover, would ensure Saddam Hussein's refusal to cooperate—why would he cooperate, if a war was authorized in advance?—and consequently would open the way to a unilateral American operation. But on the other hand, it was hard at that stage for the French diplomatic apparatus to conceive of a hypothetical French veto to a planned American resolution. "It is the absolute weapon," but "in appearance only," warned Levitte, stating that "nobody imagines that France alone would veto" a text whose stakes the Americans considered to be decisive, and for which neither the Russians nor the Chinese appeared to be willing to go beyond abstention.[3] Villepin's entourage shared this argument: a French veto "would conform to our principles" but would "contradict our strategic interest," warned his adviser Bruno Le Maire, a young career diplomat. The risk, Le Maire pointed out, was one of "breaking the strategic link" with the United States, of "blurring the message" on the risks of proliferation, of appearing to protect an arbitrary regime, and—in the probable absence of Russian and Chinese vetoes—of seeming to divide the Security Council. This attitude, he concluded, "would be all the more ineffective because it would not prevent the United States from striking," and moreover, this would even play into the hawks' hands "by showing the 'irrelevant' character" of the UN.[4]

This dilemma would remain at the heart of French policy in the coming months. The only solution for the time being was to try to escape it at the cost of a compromise. Engaging in negotiation, Levitte cautioned, meant seeking a formula "that would go short of the American requirement" of automaticity but also "of our requirement of a Security Council decision." Whatever happened, he wrote, the compromise "would not give total satisfaction" to Paris. Levitte then posed the alternatives. Either the text was unacceptable and abstention was an option, in which case Iraq could conclude that the international community was divided, giving Baghdad an incentive to lie low and thereby providing Washington with the pretext for war; or the French managed to "tear from the Americans an acceptable text," in which case it would be desirable to vote for the resolution and thus contribute to unanimity within the Security Council in order to convince Baghdad to play along. Levitte clearly preferred the second scenario, but warned that "the game that is starting will be extremely difficult."[5]

Levitte's warning was confirmed the next day. On September 26, the British transmitted to the French the text of a draft resolution that the Americans had refined with their help. The draft—which Powell himself judged "maximalist"—bore the signature of the hawks. Not only did it call for "coercive" inspections in which the inspectors would be escorted by a military force (a concept recently promoted by the Carnegie Endowment for International Peace, a Washington think tank), but it included nothing less than a blank check for an intervention. According to the draft, Iraq was already considered in "material breach," and any false declaration or omission in the declaration it was required to present concerning its WMD or any failure in its obligations would constitute a further breach permitting "the use of all necessary means." Such language was unacceptable to the French: it amounted to dispossessing the Security Council of its prerogatives, since it would permit the United States alone to declare such a possible breach—and to respond to it by force if necessary. For Paris, this was a nonstarter; two days later, Chirac signaled to Kofi Annan that it was likely that France would veto such a text.[6]

But this disagreement did not mean that there could be no dialogue. On September 27, Marc Grossman, the State Department's under secretary of state for political affairs, went to Paris. Bush had called Chirac beforehand: Washington wished to consult with Paris, Bush said. He justified the harshness of the draft by the need to make Saddam Hussein bend, and implied that the

United States would be ready to intervene with a few other countries in the event a resolution failed. Thanking Bush for having sent Grossman, Chirac said that he was open to dialogue but did not hide his rejection of the logic inherent in the Anglo-American project. Although he agreed with the notion of not making "the least concession" to Baghdad, and said that he was ready to contemplate a certain hardening of the inspections—at least to the extent that Hans Blix himself thought desirable—he pointed to a "fundamental" divergence on the question of authorizing the use of force, and reiterated that his support required a two-step approach that respected the prerogatives of the Security Council. This was a "serious" affair, Chirac said, since it was a matter of "deciding on going to war," and he offered the "most extreme reservations" to a clause involving "automatic" recourse to force. Each side thus maintained its "red line" while committing to the pursuit of cooperation.[7]

Although the meetings that Grossman had with Villepin and then Jean-Marc de La Sablière were rather tough, they confirmed this willingness for dialogue. The meetings made clear that the coming negotiations essentially would take place between France and the United States, with the British playing the role of honest brokers. Grossman admitted that the Anglo-American text was "ferocious," which he justified by the need for a credible enough threat to make Saddam Hussein bend, but he expressed Washington's wish to negotiate with Paris. A draft resolution that brought France and the United States together would be "irresistible," he argued. This barely veiled appeal did not leave French diplomats indifferent: beyond the "politeness" of the statement, they thought, the argument advanced by Grossman seemed difficult to challenge.[8] Even if it promised to be very closely fought, the game could now start.

On September 30, Powell (to whom Grossman had reported on his Paris meetings after a stopover in Moscow) called Villepin. Washington, Powell said, was ready to take into account French and Russian reservations. He proposed two separate negotiations: one between UN representatives on the modalities of the inspections, and one between ministers on the question of the use of force. Villepin said that he was open to this proposal.[9] This was the first of a series of about twenty telephone conversations between the two men, who in the latter phase of the negotiations would be speaking to each other at least once a day—including during the wedding of Powell's daughter. Of course, the negotiations over the resolution were not exclusively Franco-American. Although the Chinese remained aloof, the British and Russians participated actively, and there were numerous phone calls between Villepin and his British and Russian counterparts, Jack Straw and Igor Ivanov. Although, properly speaking, the nonpermanent members of the Security Council did not take part in the negotiation, their votes, of course, mattered. Still, it was ultimately between Paris and Washington that most of the game took place. The British essentially were aligned with the Americans, and the Russians—who played their own game and certainly weighed in—had positions close to the French.

The Franco-American contacts during these few weeks were particularly close. While Chirac and Bush in this period had only two telephone conversations, they followed the negotiations closely. On the French side, contact was continual between the president and the foreign minister, either directly or through the intermediary of their advisers. On the American side, Bush arbitrated the American position as drafts were submitted to him at key moments in the negotiations. The atmosphere between Paris and Washington was very good: in mid-October, Powell confided to Ambassador François Bujon de l'Estang that the relationship between Villepin and himself was "very amicable." A few days later, this time to former French prime minister Alain Juppé (who was visiting Washington), Powell praised the "excellent" working relations and the "dense" discussions he had with Villepin. The secretary of state, noted Bujon, seemed decidedly "well disposed."[10]

This close contact did not signify that agreement would be easy—far from it. The inspections were not the principal difficulty: as Chirac said again to Bush during their second telephone conversation on October 9, Paris was ready to strengthen the inspection process on the condition that it would not "provoke" Iraq, which could serve as pretext for an intervention. Thus it was the question of the use of force that was at the heart of the negotiation. From the start, discussions focused on the French demand for a two-step approach, inspiring a subtle diplomatic ballet throughout most of October. On the American side, initially the game was to persuade Paris that such an approach was not necessary. In the event of a new material breach on the part of Baghdad, Bush assured Chirac on October 9, "the United States would coordinate with France" as "one of its principal allies." Yet this assurance was seen in Paris as a "false opening," La Sablière would remember later. Chirac stuck to his guns: in the event of Iraqi noncooperation, he declared, the Security Council "ought to meet to decide the measures to take."[11]

The central issue, as a result, soon became the possible link between the two "steps." In the face of the French demand for such a double sequence, the Americans and British tried to obtain a commitment about the French attitude should this "second step" occur. Clearly acting under orders, Jack

Straw raised the subject with Villepin on October 4. The Americans would accept two steps, Straw said, on the condition that they felt the French would not oppose a potential decision to use force, if it came to that point.[12] Faced with this approach, the French game consisted of hinting at an open attitude when examining a further resolution, though without tying their hands in advance. True, both men in charge of negotiations on the French side were visibly tempted to give tokens of flexibility to obtain satisfaction on the two steps. On October 7, Villepin told Powell that in the event of an Iraqi violation, Paris "would not oppose a Security Council that manifested firm determination"—a formula that might be interpreted as a commitment that France *alone* would not block with its veto a majority that was favorable to an intervention, as Chirac had assured Blair at the start of September. On the eve of the October 9 telephone conversation with Bush, Jean-David Levitte even suggested to Chirac that he should promise that he would pose no obstacle to the use of force in such a situation. But Chirac, who judged that his former diplomatic adviser was too quick to compromise—either "by fatigue or out of conviction," he would later write—was wary of following him onto this terrain. "No option is excluded, including the use of force," he merely repeated to Bush that day.[13]

Two weeks after the Americans had transmitted their draft, things had not advanced. "The key variable," said Straw to Villepin, was "the degree of trust between the French and the Americans." That indeed was the rub. "We should not be hostages of the internal debate in Washington," Villepin replied to Straw, adding that "current American policy" might prove to be "dangerous."[14] The current "internal debate" in the United States, for that matter, could scarcely incline France to give the Bush administration a blank check. Of course, Powell multiplied the assurances that nothing was decided about an intervention. "I know what my president thinks," he solemnly asserted to Alain Juppé on October 23.[15] Yet the administration maintained its menacing rhetoric. In a speech in Cincinnati on October 7, Bush, denouncing an "urgent danger" that "only grows worse in time," seemed to threaten to bypass the Security Council if the resolution failed. "Saddam Hussein must disarm," he declared, "or we will lead a coalition to disarm him."[16] Washington, meanwhile, continued to increase its military pressure by intensifying its buildup: almost 60,000 American soldiers were now in the region, the French embassy in Washington reckoned at the end of October. Even more ominously, on October 10 and 11 the White House had obtained a vote in both houses of Congress on a resolution authorizing the president to use armed force against

Iraq "as he determines to be necessary." The resolution passed by a comfortable majority of 296 to 133 in the House and 77 to 23 in the Senate, which amounted to far more votes than George H. W. Bush had won on the eve of Operation Desert Storm in 1991. In a political climate still marked by the shock of 9/11 and its domestic instrumentalization by the White House, few Democrats—with exceptions like Senator Ted Kennedy—were ready to take the risk of appearing weak in the face of a national security threat. The vote on the congressional resolution naturally relativized the importance of a possible UN resolution, and it made clear that Washington might even bypass the UN altogether if necessary. The White House's deliberate choice to obtain such a congressional blank check, even before the UN negotiations had concluded, was the inverse of the approach taken by the George H. W. Bush administration in 1990–91.[17]

In these conditions, it is not surprising that negotiations remained at an impasse. The French maintained their requirement for a procedure that would give the last word to the Security Council; the Americans stuck to a façade of concessions. Yet the situation would evolve after mid-October. The French side began to fear that the majority of countries that opposed the American text might crumble, which would permit the United States to push its resolution through; and the American side started to worry about getting stuck and to fear that a failure in negotiations might be politically costly. Both sides were now ready to compromise.[18]

The opening came from Washington, and in the following three weeks it would give rise to fierce bargaining. On October 16, the Americans began a slight movement in the direction of the French demand: they proposed that in the event of a new Iraqi failure to comply, the IAEA and UNMOVIC would report to the Security Council, which would then "consider the situation." For Paris, this was progress, but was still insufficient. Although this wording (which was part of the crucial paragraph 4 of the future resolution) seemed to foreshadow the required "two steps," since it called for a new Security Council meeting, nothing in this language made it plain that it was up to the council to characterize such a failure as a "material breach," let alone to decide on the possible use of force. Meanwhile, the rest of the text was unchanged. Not only did paragraph 1 already declare Iraq in "material breach," but the United States kept total latitude to unilaterally denounce a new "material breach" and in its wake to launch an intervention. The "two steps" and "automaticity" still coexisted, which remained unacceptable for Paris.[19] Discussions went in circles for ten days; then the Americans started again to move in measured steps. Powell was now clearly eager to wrap up the negotiation with the French while isolating the more intransigent Russians, and so on October 31 he sent a new proposal to Villepin. The proposal included a new advance, inspired by the British, specifying that even though Iraq was already in "material breach," a "final opportunity" would nevertheless be granted for it to fulfill its obligations. This position was a sort of "firewall" to reassure Paris that paragraph 1 would not serve in itself to justify an operation. Powell accompanied his proposal, sent by fax, with a handwritten note that was friendly but pressing: "Dear Dominique. . . . Please call me soon so we can close on this."[20]

This time, the French indeed felt that a result had to be achieved, though not without still battling over paragraph 4. On November 4, they demanded that the draft resolution specify that any possible new failure to comply be reported to the Security Council "for assessment." It was a matter of balancing the statement that such a failure would ipso facto constitute a new material breach—a statement on which the Americans insisted—with a stipulation that the Security Council officially would be the one to categorize the violation. Washington accepted this demand on November 5. The French had a final request: they wanted this categorization to be based on an inspectors' report and not solely on a report to the Security Council from a member-state. This point implied that paragraph 4 would have to relate to *both* paragraph 11 (which called for the IAEA and UNMOVIC to report to the council on any Iraqi infraction) *and* paragraph 12 (which called for the council to consider the situation), and not merely to paragraphs 11 *or* 12. (Admittedly, it was a subtle difference.) On the evening of November 7, Powell called Villepin to give his agreement. In passing, Powell also said that he accepted Moscow's wish to replace, at the end of the text, the word "restore" with the word "secure" with regard to international peace, a formula that the Russians thought implied less "automaticity."[21]

The Franco-American accord permitted the Security Council to unanimously adopt Resolution 1441 on November 8. This had been a major objective for Paris: only such a manifestation of unity would be an incentive for the Iraqis to cooperate, while at the same time cutting the ground from under the feet of the hawks. France had contributed largely to this unanimity. Not only had it managed a compromise with the United States, but it had rallied Russia thanks to a telephone conversation between Chirac and Putin on November 6, and in doing so it secured China's support. Even more important, France had convinced Syria, the only Arab country then sitting on the Security Council, to vote for the resolution, an outcome that initially had seemed very unlikely. (Chirac, who had met Syrian president Bashar al-Assad in Damascus two weeks earlier and thought it possible to convince him by advancing the risk of Syrian isolation, managed to win him over in a telephone conversation just three hours before the vote.) This important success, which echoed Syria's participation in the 1991 coalition, allowed the Security Council to present a display of full support from the Arab world.[22] So it was not surprising that French diplomats felt pleased with themselves. On November 8, Villepin sent a message to all French diplomatic posts: The negotiations "have been conducted with tenacity, rigor, and pragmatism," he wrote, adding that "our result reinforces the stature of France in the world." Clearly less euphoric, Chirac—whose advisers had to convince him that the terms of the "deal" were acceptable—judged the accord merely "reasonable." Chirac was skeptical. "It remained to be verified," he later wrote, "what interpretation the United States, firmly decided in any case to take on Iraq, would make of this resolution, which fixed certain limits without the Americans' feeling necessarily bound to respect them."[23]

Although the French had some measure of satisfaction, they knew that they had not obtained everything they wanted. To be sure, the resolution no longer bore much resemblance to the initial American draft. The inspections were strengthened, since the inspectors were granted "immediate, unconditional and unrestricted" access to all sites, including the "sensitive" ones (the so-called presidential sites); but the most stringent American demands, like "coercive" inspections, had been abandoned. In addition, the most flagrant "automatic" elements or "triggers"—which might have served as justification for a discretionary intervention—had been removed from the text. The resolution clearly established a "two-step" sequence, one that if necessary would involve a new referral to the Security Council. Yet the Quai d'Orsay was obliged to recognize that "ambiguities" remained: the resolution did not exclude an interpretation that Iraq was at all times incurring "serious consequences" since it was already in "material breach." Moreover, paragraph 4 enabled any member-state to condemn the least Iraqi infraction—including any "false statements" or "omissions" in the declaration that Baghdad was to submit within thirty days—as a new "material breach." This condemnation would involve a report from the inspectors and a Security Council meeting, but it would not prevent the condemning states from acting unilaterally, as had been the case in December 1998. Overall, French diplomats considered that Resolution 1441 made it "difficult" but "not impossible" for a pretext for military intervention to be "fabricated," and it made "the council move very clearly in the direction of legitimation of the use of force," which might take place on the basis of a violation by Iraq that would be evaluated with a very low "threshold of tolerance."[24]

That outcome, indeed, was what the Americans were prone to emphasize. The White House also considered that the outcome of the negotiation was "a triumph"—albeit one for US diplomacy. After having undergone two months of intensive shelling from the hawks, Powell came out strengthened against Cheney and Rumsfeld, with Bush in the end having given his blessing to the negotiations. Despite the concessions he had made in New York—at the cost of continuous guerrilla warfare in Washington—Powell could point out that he had made the French and the international community as a whole accept a very firm resolution that committed them for the future, and therefore he could hope that Iraq would cooperate and be disarmed by peaceful means or, failing that, that the problem would be solved by force but in a multilateral framework. Yet the hawks could (and did) argue that a certain interpretation of the resolution allowed the United States to take action regardless of what happened, especially if Baghdad did not demonstrate perfect cooperation, which, given its past behavior and the level of exigencies imposed on it, was more than plausible. In short, Resolution 1441 had masked a number of divergences—notably Franco-American—that had every chance of reappearing as events unfolded, especially considering two factors: Iraqi behavior and American intentions. Indeed, nothing ensured that the former would facilitate things; as for the latter, Bush's first comment after the resolution was adopted spoke volumes. "The United States has accepted to discuss any material breach with the Security Council," he told the press, "but without jeopardizing our freedom of action to defend our country."[25] "The path to peaceful disarmament no doubt exists, but how narrow it is!" commented the French embassy in Washington, adding that "we still hear the sound of drumbeats."[26]

"The issue on which everybody agrees"

After Cheney's August 26 speech, the administration had further hardened the public tone on the issue of Iraqi WMDs. On September 8, Condoleezza Rice had even raised the specter of a "mushroom cloud," suggesting that Iraq was dangerously close to mastering a nuclear device. A few days later, Rumsfeld asserted that there was no doubt about the fact that Iraq was maintaining active WMD programs. At the same time, the press echoed alarmist information, with the *New York Times* publishing a new series of articles under Judith Miller's byline. Bush's choice of the "UN path" on September 12 had established the issue of WMD at the heart of the debate. It was on their presumed existence and the threat they represented—more so than the nature of the Iraqi regime, which was unlikely to justify an intervention in the eyes of the international community, or than on Iraq's supposed links with terrorist networks, which were more difficult to demonstrate—that the war, or at least its justification, would be played out.

To this day, the most controversial question is what sort of intelligence American leaders really possessed at the time. US leaders, of course, said that they were relying on solid data: those who doubt the reality of the threat, Dick Cheney had declared at the beginning of September, have not "seen all the intelligence that we have seen."[27] Yet Iraqi WMDs had not previously been at the top of the preoccupations of the US intelligence community. Giving an overview of the existing threats before the Senate Select Committee on Intelligence in February 2002, CIA director George Tenet had touched on Iraq in only three paragraphs on page ten of an eighteen-page presentation. The National Intelligence Estimate (NIE) that Tenet commissioned in mid-September 2002 at the request of this same Senate committee changed things utterly. The committee wanted the CIA to produce an NIE before Congress voted on the resolution authorizing the use of force at the beginning of October. As a result, the document was written in less than three weeks—whereas most NIEs, which are supposed to reflect the consensus of the intelligence community, typically are the result of months of meticulous work.[28]

Entitled "Iraq's Continuing Programs for Weapons of Mass Destruction," the top-secret ninety-two-page document was adopted at the start of October 2002. From the outset, the tone was set: "We judge that Iraq has continued its weapons of mass destruction (WMD) programs. . . . Baghdad has chemical and biological weapons as well as missiles with ranges in excess of UN restrictions; if left unchecked, it probably will have a nuclear weapon during this decade." Pointing to the Iraqi regime's systematic effort to dissimulate, the NIE warned that the available intelligence did not permit more than a small part of the real situation to be known, and it stressed the lack of precise information on many aspects. Despite this caveat, the document asserted that since 1998 Iraq had continued its efforts in the chemical area, relaunched its ballistic program, and invested massively in the biological domain. Most of all, it stressed that according to most US intelligence agencies, Baghdad was in the process of reconstituting its nuclear program. This was the document's most spectacular conclusion, and the most alarming one. "Although we assess that Saddam does not *yet* have nuclear weapons," the NIE asserted, with emphasis, "he remains intent on acquiring them." The report conjectured that Iraq would not succeed in its efforts until 2007 or 2009, unless it managed to procure a sufficient quantity of fissile material, in which case it might refine a nuclear weapon "within several months to a year."[29]

With its tenor and assertive tone, the October 2002 NIE marked a clear escalation in the evaluation by US intelligence agencies of Iraqi WMD, starting with the nuclear component. True, it did not corroborate the most alarmist statements made by Cheney and others in preceding weeks, which tended to give credit to a feeling of imminent menace. Yet the conclusions were much more alarmist than those the CIA had been able to advance until then, since it had never before categorically asserted that Iraq *effectively held* WMD. The preceding NIE devoted to Iraq, completed two years previously, had concluded only that Baghdad kept a reduced stock of chemical agents, and not weapons properly speaking. With regard to biological weapons, the earlier report considered that Iraq was continuing to work on them but did not actually possess them. Overall, in 2000 the CIA had admitted that it did "not have any direct evidence" that Iraq had resumed its WMD programs since Operation Desert Fox in 1998, although it stressed that such activities ought to be considered as "likely" in light of Iraq's previous behavior.[30]

It is not surprising, then, that the October 2002 NIE would later find itself at the heart of debates, especially when it became evident after the invasion that WMD would not be found in Iraq. The Iraq Intelligence Commission, a panel established at Bush's request in early 2004 to investigate US intelligence failures regarding Iraqi WMD, not only stressed that the 2002 NIE estimates had proved "wrong" but also pointed to "serious shortcomings in the way these assessments were made and communicated to policymakers."[31] How then can such a fiasco be explained? The various inquiries—not since Pearl Harbor has an intelligence failure been so thoroughly investigated—give us some ideas, although shadowy areas still remain.[32]

A full examination of the intelligence failure must distinguish between three levels of information. The first is that of "raw" material: the concrete information possessed by the US intelligence agencies. As we have seen, the withdrawal of UNSCOM in 1998 had dried up the most reliable source of information on Iraqi WMD. Because the US intelligence agencies had invested only scarce resources in Iraq since 1998, they had very limited on-the-ground capacity for collecting "human intelligence" (often known as HUMINT) and so most of the data were gathered from a distance through satellite imagery and electronic interception. As a result, what little information was collected after 1998 would prove to be weak—some of it was actually erroneous—and yet alarmist estimates regarding the resumption of Iraqi programs would later rely on it. In some cases, the evidence simply was not compelling or was ambivalent; this was the case with photos from the spring of 2002 that seemed to show truck movements around storage sites suspected of stocking chemical material, on the basis of which the NIE deduced that Iraq had resumed the actual production of chemical *weapons*, not just agents. The same ambivalence, or lack of compelling evidence, prevailed in the case of Iraq-bound aluminum tubes that were intercepted starting in the spring of 2001, which would serve as the main evidence to justify the NIE's conclusion that Baghdad had resumed a uranium enrichment program.

Other pieces of raw intelligence mentioned in the 2002 NIE would be revealed purely and simply as false. Two of them in particular would remain topics of contention in later debates. The first, communicated in 2001 by a foreign intelligence service—apparently Italy's Military Intelligence Service (Servizio per le Informazioni e la Sicurezza Militare; SISMI)—concerned the allegation that Iraq had sought in previous years to procure from Niger some 500 tons of partially processed uranium ore, or yellowcake. Granted, the NIE did not assert that this attempt was successful, and it did not present this piece of information as part of the evidence that allowed it to conclude that the nuclear program was in fact resumed. (Iraq already possessed an equivalent stock of yellowcake, a nonrefined material that would need many subsequent steps of processing, not least actual enrichment, before being usable in a nuclear program.) Sent to Niger by the CIA in February 2002 to investigate this allegation, the former US ambassador Joseph Wilson had expressed doubts on the reliability of this piece of intelligence upon his return—an episode that later precipitated a political scandal when some in the Bush administration tried to discredit Wilson by revealing that his wife, Valerie Plame, was a covert CIA operative. Yet despite the dubious character of the yellowcake intelligence (in which British intelligence seemed to believe), it did appear in the NIE, though not in its foreground. In the following months, it would contribute strongly to the justification for war, before it was established that it derived from an intelligence forgery.[33] A second piece of false intelligence bore on the existence of so-called mobile laboratories for manufacturing biological weapons, a piece of information from 2000 that would be the source of the NIE's assertion that Iraq possessed biological weapons and would reinforce presumptions concerning the existence of chemical weapons as well. This intelligence would prove just as fictitious: it came from a single source, namely an informant to Germany's Federal Intelligence Service (Bundesnachrichtendienst; BND) who ironically was code-named "Curveball." The source proved to be toxic, since "Curveball" was later revealed to have made up the mobile laboratories story.[34]

The second level of intelligence information relates to *analysis*. The colossal intelligence failure culminating in the 2002 NIE resulted not only from the inadequate collection of raw information, but also from extrapolations by intelligence analysts (and to a certain extent, as we have seen, by disarmament inspectors) that had been perceptible starting in 1998 and had become nothing short of systematic by 2002. The meager concrete information that the intelligence agencies possessed led them to rely more than ever on the postulate that Iraq *was* continuing to try to obtain WMDs and to dissimulate its activities accordingly. To be sure, this line of reasoning was fed by some objective facts, such as the regime's use of WMDs before 1991, Baghdad's repeated dissimulations or refusals to explain its actions, and finally the Iraqis' refusal to let the inspectors return after Operation Desert Fox. Still, the notion that Iraq was actively seeking WMD ultimately was a mere hypothesis. As the Iraq Intelligence Commission would later stress, while "this hypothesis was not unreasonable . . . the problem was that, over time, it hardened into a presumption." It had hardened to the point, arguably, of fostering biased interpretations of brute facts: this error happened in particular with the aluminum tubes, as numerous analyses systematically discounted the possibility that they might serve purposes other than building centrifuges for uranium enrichment—for instance, as parts for building artillery rockets. (The NIE, however, did note reservations—which later would prove entirely justified—in the State Department's Bureau of Intelligence and Research, which believed that it did not have convincing proof of Iraq's systematic and coherent effort to obtain nuclear weapons.)[35]

It was rare to find those who were ready to defend the reverse hypothesis, i.e., that Iraq no longer held WMD—an hypothesis that would *not* have been unreasonable in light of the work conducted by UNSCOM before 1998 and the probable embargo-related difficulties that Baghdad would have encountered if it had effectively attempted to reconstitute its arsenal. Stressing that he had never seen any intelligence supporting the existence of WMD, General Anthony Zinni, the commander of CENTCOM at the time of Operation Desert Fox, was among the few skeptics. "There are no weapons of mass destruction programs in Iraq," he stated in the autumn of 2002; "there may be some isolated weapons, though I doubt even that, but no programs."[36] Yet within the intelligence community, almost nobody was ready to take a strong position against the dominant belief that Iraq was continuing its efforts. "At best, intelligence could have said that there was no firm evidence that Saddam had stockpiles of chemical and biological weapons and was actually pursuing nuclear bombs," a prominent intelligence specialist wrote later, but "it could not have said that he had ceased its efforts."[37] And yet to stress the absence of such firm evidence while at the same time advancing strong suspicions— which French intelligence would do, as shall be seen—would have better fit the reality and would have put intelligence assessments in quite another light. As George Tenet later recognized, "We should have said, in effect, that the intelligence was not sufficient to prove beyond a reasonable doubt that Saddam had WMD."[38]

This, then, is the third level of intelligence information: the manner in which intelligence assessments were *presented*, both to policymakers and to the general public. The peculiarity of the 2002 NIE was its affirmative tone: in it, assessments that the services had previously called "probabilities" now appeared as "certainties." This tone was accentuated by the fact that the "Key Judgments"—a short summary placed at the head of the document, which often is the only section that the decision-makers read—clearly went beyond the more circumspect tone of the analyses developed in the body of the document itself. Even worse, it seemed that the information presented to Bush in his Presidential Daily Briefs during this period was even more peremptory, to the point of erasing any trace of skepticism or questions about the Iraqi arsenal estimates. The same was true of presentations designed for the general public. The CIA, pressed by Congress to publish a declassified document in the wake of the NIE, produced (in haste, Tenet would later plead) in October an even more categorical text that was based on the "Key Judgments" but was purged of phrases such as "we judge" or "we assess" that gave nuance to its statements. The result was a tone that was even more assertive than the NIE itself. Its tone also resembled that of the White Paper that the British government had published a month earlier—the infamous "September Dossier," which gave credence to the yellowcake affair and maintained that some Iraqi WMD might be made operational in forty-five minutes, an assertion that would remain at the heart of subsequent polemics about intelligence and the decision-making that led to the war.[39]

So was the WMD intelligence fiasco a mistake or manipulation? Even today, the question remains hard to decide. For some, the affair arose from serious dysfunction, but it did not challenge the integrity of the intelligence community: this is the consensus of the various inquiries conducted later.[40] In fact, many objective factors might help explain the fiasco. In 2002, the CIA was far from having recovered from the crisis into which it had plunged at the end of the Cold War, a crisis that affected a profession that was more and more tempted to abandon in-depth analysis in favor of the search for a "scoop" in order to meet decision-makers' priorities. Added to this crisis, the trauma of 9/11 led to a lowering, consciously or not, of the "threshold" of proof. This state of mind in turn fed a phenomenon of "groupthink" on an issue that increasingly had become the subject of false certainties, thereby diminishing the necessary critical thinking. Finally, the haste in which the NIE was assembled—or rather, cobbled together—obviously must have contributed to the fiasco, on top of undeniable and inexcusable breaches of professionalism.[41] In short, as Tenet later admitted, the "intelligence process" was revealed as "flawed" but not "disingenuous."[42]

Yet for others like Tyler Drumheller, at the time chief of the European division in the CIA's Directorate of Operations, mistakes and negligence, even incompetence, do not explain everything. The intelligence community and its leaders, in his view, clearly were reduced to mere instruments of the executive power.[43] Admittedly, the allegation that the CIA made itself the willing auxiliary of political power by producing, at the administration's request, intelligence that conformed to the administration's wishes regarding Iraqi WMD appears to be refuted by the CIA's attitude on two other issues. First, it was deeply skeptical about the alleged links between Iraq and al-Qaeda, even though the Cheney and Rumsfeld entourages blatantly wanted to influence its analyses in this direction. (A Pentagon office led by close associates of Under Secretary of Defense for Policy Douglas Feith had been devoted since 9/11 to the search for evidence that such links existed.) Second, it constantly warned decision-makers about the negative consequences of a possible military intervention and occupation. And yet there is no doubt about the existence, at the very least, of a bias in the CIA's assessment of the Iraq WMD issue. Starting in the autumn of 2002, the US intelligence community tended systematically to espouse the administration's line in this issue. "There was a natural bias in favor of intelligence production that supported, rather than undermined, policies already set,"[44] Paul Pillar, a senior CIA official, later acknowledged. Indeed, the US intelligence community did not escape the war fever that gripped Washington in this period. Cheney's August 26 speech to the Veterans of Foreign Wars had marked a turning point; while many analysts had until then remained skeptical on the subject, the certainties proclaimed at the top had an effect. "Well, who are we to argue?" many of them must have wondered, since the country's highest authorities—at least, this is what Cheney insinuated—seemed to possess information to which they did not have access. The growing awareness that a war might already have been decided upon made people feel fatalistic: what was the point of resisting political leaders, knowing that an underestimation of the danger might have grave consequences for American forces, which might find themselves in harm's way? Better to cover oneself at the risk of producing excessively alarmist estimates, even if this meant lending faith to dubious sources (like "Curveball") or to hazardous information (like that concerning the yellowcake purchase), or setting aside contrary clues or opinions, if not sidelining those who advanced them (as seems to have been the case in the aluminum tubes affair.) This tendency was consciously espoused by those in charge at the CIA; as its deputy director, John McLaughlin, argued, the agency should advance clear-cut rather than equivocal estimates, even at the risk of being wrong. Most were convinced, in any case, that "something" eventually would be found.[45]

Should one go farther and speak of a politicization of the intelligence agencies? Drumheller later would do so by pointing the finger at Tenet, not for having deliberately lied but for not having been able to establish the "necessary professional distance" from the Bush White House.[46] A Democrat initially appointed by Bill Clinton in 1997, Tenet owed Bush for having maintained him in his job in 2001, and he had developed very close relations with the president—perhaps to the point of letting the White House hear what it wanted to hear. Even though Tenet defended his decisions, he later regretted not having sounded the alarm after Cheney's August 26 speech. "I should have told the vice-president privately that, in my view, his VFW speech had gone too far," he later wrote. (Six weeks after Cheney's speech, by contrast, Tenet warned the White House that the CIA was skeptical about the Niger uranium affair—or at least that it could not certify it—which led it to be withdrawn from Bush's Cincinnati speech on October 7.)[47] Did those responsible at the CIA, as some have maintained, go farther in deliberately discounting information that pointed to the WMD file being almost empty? Such information allegedly included testimony to that effect from Naji Sabri, shared by the French services after they had secretly "debriefed" him in September 2002. This affair remains controversial today, although as a senior French intelligence official would later judge, it is not necessarily significant, since Sabri was not in the inner circle of those around Saddam Hussein.[48]

Whether or not the intelligence was politicized, the Bush administration unsurprisingly would later make the CIA a scapegoat to justify the Iraqi adventure after the fact. Of course, this overlooks the essential fact that the WMD issue was far from being the sole or even the main reason for the war—even though, as we have seen, it was indeed one of the factors explaining the route that led from 9/11 to Iraq. As Paul Wolfowitz himself publicly recognized after the invasion in the spring of 2003, WMD were "the one issue that everyone could agree on" within the administration.[49] Be that as it may, with Bush's choice of the UN route, the WMD issue did become central to the justification for an intervention, and so the NIE became a major element in the rationale for war. Until it was issued, among decision-makers (and even more so in public opinion) there was only a mere notion that Iraq probably possessed capabilities in this domain, although these capabilities were poorly defined. By contrast, the NIE effectively established the idea that a proven threat did exist, influencing even those who were not in favor of war. It reinforced the "certainty" that Iraq possessed WMD, wrote Richard Haass, "which at least made the war a reasonable option even to those of us who would have preferred that we not go down that path." The alarmist rhetoric inaugurated by Cheney, previously not supported by intelligence, found itself confirmed by both the NIE and by the unclassified documents published first by the British government and then by the CIA. Bush's speech in Cincinnati on October 7 further confirmed these assessments, conveying as it did the most worrying (and, retrospectively, the most stupefying) estimates, even exaggerating them. "If the Iraqi regime is able to [obtain] an amount of highly enriched uranium a little larger than a single softball, it could have a nuclear weapon in less than a year," Bush declared in his speech.[50]

Did American leaders, Bush foremost, consciously mislead the American public and the international community by falsifying intelligence concerning Iraqi WMD? Even witnesses that would be least likely to sympathize with the Bush administration do not affirm this assertion. "Those who wanted the war the most sought to exaggerate the threat in order to justify it," Drumheller wrote, though he conceded that they might well "have believed their own hype." "I know of no attempt to falsify intelligence by anyone within the US government," Haass would later testify, adding: "It was more a case of people selecting ('cherry-picking') reports that supported a certain position and going with them despite questions about their accuracy."[51] In short, it was a matter of "spin" rather than lying, and yet the line between the two was a thin one indeed. The bottom line is that the bellicose plans of the Bush administration were facilitated by the erring ways of the intelligence agencies, which opened the way to an unscrupulous policy of conditioning, if not manipulating, the public—a policy which, in the autumn of 2002, was only beginning.[52] The first success of this policy came on October 10 and 11, with the passing of the congressional resolution authorizing military action against Iraq, which arguably was the main purpose of Bush's Cincinnati speech and of a subsequent briefing for senators based on the NIE and its "Key Judgments." Less than a month later, the administration comfortably won the November 2002 midterm elections. This victory was a sign that Karl Rove's strategy to unashamedly use the "war on terror" for domestic policy purposes was indeed bearing fruit.[53]

"I have not yet seen these proofs"

What evaluation did Paris make in autumn 2002 of the question of Iraqi WMD, and what role did this issue play in determining the French position? Former American and British leaders later would assert that the evaluations of key countries opposed to intervention in Iraq—starting with France, Germany, and Russia—were similar to those of the United States and Great Britain. "The conclusion that Saddam had WMD was nearly a universal consensus," Bush would write. "Intelligence agencies in Germany, France, Great Britain, Russia, China, and Egypt believed it." This assertion was widely taken at face value in later investigations. But what was the real situation?[54]

When the Iraqi problem came back to the foreground at the end of summer 2002, Paris obviously considered that the question of evaluating WMD would be a determining factor. But the available information appeared weak, as shown at the August 27 meeting convened by Villepin. The dominant sentiment in Paris was that Iraq had probably not renounced its ambitions and perhaps had reconstituted capabilities that might constitute a local or at most a regional threat, notably in the biological and chemical domains, but the concrete evidence was meager. This finding posed a problem: "We cannot be content with intuitions about this when it comes to legitimizing an intervention . . . or, inversely, expressing reservations against it,"[55] the Quai d'Orsay noted in mid-September.

So the authorities naturally turned to the intelligence services. Even if their means were clearly inferior to those of their American equivalents, the French services—the DGSE for foreign intelligence, the DST (Direction de la Surveillance du Territoire; Directorate of Territorial Surveillance) for counterespionage, and the DRM (Direction du Renseignement Militaire; Directorate of Military Intelligence) for technological intelligence—possessed solid expertise. "We did have credibility," the former boss of one of them would say later, adding that "of course, we were not at the same level as the Americans (if not the British) but we were in the picture, we were not nil." "They did good work even if they were under-resourced," judged a former French senior official and long-time user of intelligence. The French "had very good services," a former senior CIA official confirmed, while acknowledging that the American intelligence agencies could at times prove "disdainful" about others, except perhaps the British.[56]

Of course, by the fall of 2002 the French services had a long record of monitoring the issue of Iraq's WMD. Yet the decision-makers felt a need to reexamine all available elements in order to take a position on the information advanced by the United States and Great Britain. Jean-Claude Mallet, the head of the Secrétariat Général de la Défense Nationale (Secretariat-General for National Defense [SGDN], the interagency coordinating body for defense and security under France's prime minister) was given a mandate to produce a synthesis of the available information in his capacity as chairman of the Comité Interministériel du Renseignement (an interagency board placed under the SGDN and in charge of coordinating work of the intelligence agencies). Mallet was recognized for his high competence and meticulousness. The task took the form of regular meetings during which representatives of the agencies concerned, including the Quai d'Orsay, the Ministry of Defense, and the Atomic Energy Commission (Commissariat à l'Énergie Atomique; CEA), pooled their information under Mallet's mediation. Meanwhile, the intelligence services continued to transmit their evaluations directly to decision-makers, foremost to the Élysée.[57]

So what did the French intelligence services have to say, and to what extent did they agree with their American and British colleagues? Here, too, one must distinguish between three levels, starting with the raw material. In this respect, the data held by the French services were not significantly different from those of their equivalents. Like the Americans and the British, the French had indications, such as orders of sensitive material from abroad and satellite photos of suspect sites, that *might* have implied that Iraq had possibly resumed prohibited activities after the departure of UNSCOM in 1998. Of course, part of this data was of American or British origin, since intelligence agencies routinely exchange information—although frequently without revealing their sources, which may pose problems of evaluation and even create a phenomenon of circularity in the information. But the French also had their own clues that ran in the same direction.

As a matter of fact, the French services did not diverge categorically from their American or British colleagues regarding the information that later would become especially controversial, beginning with the alleged mobile laboratories and aluminum tubes. Regarding the former, they were simply not in a position to either challenge or confirm the veracity of the information concerning the alleged existence of these laboratories. French services had not received a clear warning from their German colleagues about the questionable reliability of "Curveball," and they did not know that the latter was the only source of this particular piece of intelligence. As for the aluminum tubes (of which the DST had obtained a sample that had been tested by French laboratories), the same divergences among experts appeared in Paris as in Washington. Some thought that they were no doubt components for centrifuges, while others believed that this was unlikely, given what was known about prior Iraqi programs (Iraq already had moved beyond the stage of needing aluminum to manufacture centrifuges). There was one exception, however, and it concerned the alleged Iraqi purchase of yellowcake from Niger. The French did not find the yellowcake intelligence to be a reliable piece of information. Niger was a former French colony whose uranium production was a preserve of the French firm Areva, and following in-country verifications performed in 2001, French intelligence had swiftly concluded that such a transaction simply was not credible, especially since its real utility for Iraq appeared doubtful. To complicate matters, though, the French services seem to have been very cautious in how they formulated their rejection of this alleged piece of information—the whole affair remains something of an enigma—which may well have falsely given credit to the idea that they did not entirely refute it or, more generally, that they subscribed to the American assessments concerning Iraqi WMD.[58]

When it came to the *evaluation* of Iraqi WMD (in contrast to the raw information), however, the French services did differentiate themselves from the American and British agencies. To be sure, they shared a similar line of reasoning: since the Iraqis possessed a clear expertise in WMD and a well-known capacity for dissimulation, and since they probably had never given up their ambitions in that respect, then the withdrawal of inspectors in 1998, combined with the decreasing efficacy of the embargo, could well have led them to seek to resume their activities. "Taking into account the Iraqi 'track record,' there was enormous suspicion," a former French senior official confirmed.[59] Nevertheless, the French services differed from their American and

British colleagues on the conclusions to be drawn. The Americans and British tended to see the issues that had not been previously resolved by UNSCOM—especially those that stemmed from UNSCOM's lack of evidence of alleged unilateral Iraqi destructions—as the almost certain signs of Iraqi dissimulation, whereas the French were less categorical in that regard. And while the American and British agencies tended to interpret in a systematically alarmist sense the evidence gathered since 1998, the French services were more cautious. Although they considered it *plausible* that the Iraqis might have preserved previous stocks of prohibited material and even relaunched WMD programs after 1998, they judged that they were not *certain* of it: "We did not deny this possibility," a French official recalled, "but we had no proof whatsoever, no 'smoking gun.' . . . We could not dismiss the possibility that there existed residual stocks or a small-scale resumption, but this was absolutely not proved."[60]

Moreover, the French services diverged from the Americans and British from both quantitative and qualitative standpoints. First was the quantitative position: in the French view, supposing that the suspicions of WMD existence were confirmed, the stocks or weapons that the Iraqis actually possessed could only be limited, given the state of the country and the maintenance of the embargo, however imperfect. "We thought that this was nothing compared with what existed before 1991, that [whatever existed now] was not at all on the same scale," the same French official added. And then there was the qualitative position: although they were worried about the chemical and biological dimensions of Iraq's potential WMD, the French services did *not* believe that the Iraqis had resumed their activities in the nuclear domain, and they were divided over the possibility that the Iraqis had significantly increased their ballistic capabilities, notably by obtaining missiles of a range clearly superior to the 150-kilometer range permitted by Security Council Resolution 687. "We were rather definite on these two points," he went on; "no resumption of nuclear activity and no real capability to fire projectiles beyond the borders of Iraq."[61]

Finally, and most importantly, the French services diverged on the assessment of the Iraq WMD situation in terms of the "threat" that the Americans and British were brandishing from the autumn of 2002, as in the famous phrase about "45 minutes" that figured in the British "September Dossier." In French eyes, there was no evidence that Iraq had turned its possible resumption of certain WMD activities into operational capabilities; they thought that to the extent there was a "threat," it would be local, or regional at most, but certainly not global. In fact, a French intelligence official recalled, "We never used the term 'threat'; at the most, we were talking about 'potential.'" Another senior French official would later confirm this point: between the suspicion that some activities had been resumed to the existence of a known military threat, he said, "there was a step we did not take [because] there was no proof that they had the military means."[62]

Overall, then, it is wrong to assert that the French services—and this is no doubt true of other European services, especially the German and Russian—shared an assessment identical to that of American intelligence about the WMD issue in 2002–3. It may have been shared, with nuances, until 2001. But when the American assessments—in particular after 9/11—took a clear turn to the categorical and the alarmist, culminating in the October 2002 NIE, then the divergences could only become accentuated. The French services did not follow their Anglo-American colleagues down that path. Granted, one French official said, there was "some common ground" with the Americans and the British with regard to Iraq WMD intelligence, but it was in fact limited to strong suspicions about the existence of residual stocks and a possible resumption of some activities.[63]

Yet it would be equally mistaken to believe that the French had reached conclusions opposite to those of the Americans or British, namely that Iraq no longer possessed WMD. "We did not completely exclude this," a former senior French intelligence officer remembered, "but the idea that Saddam Hussein was no longer doing anything was difficult [to sustain]." "There was no positive evidence, but no negative evidence either," another summed up. True, some may have been intimately convinced of the negligibility (if not the complete nonexistence) of Iraqi WMD, as was later confirmed by a former senior CIA official who at the time was in close contact with his French colleagues: "I think that they simply did not believe [in their existence]," he confided. Yet for lack of irrefutable evidence, French intelligence services—inclined toward caution like most intelligence services, and perhaps averse to taking the risk of contradicting their American colleagues—were not and arguably *could not* be categorical in denying the existence of Iraqi WMD. As Villepin's adviser Bruno Le Maire later wrote, the French intelligence services did not furnish "black-and-white evidence." They refrained, in essence, from going too far in either direction.[64]

This restraint might explain why the spectrum of opinions among French decision-makers was rather wide. Intelligence reports, especially when they are not fully conclusive, typically are interpreted according to institutional or personal factors, such as the report writers' position in the state apparatus or the availability of other sources of information. Thus at the Quai d'Orsay, regional specialists were convinced that Iraqi WMD could not credibly represent the kind of threat denounced by the Americans, whereas strategy and proliferation specialists were not ready to dismiss the possibility that programs had been resumed. The latter view, by and large, was shared by the Ministry of Defense and the SGDN. "We over-evaluated," one participant in the report synthesis work later recognized. "It is probable that the evaluation was somewhat inflated in relation to what we actually knew. But this was out of good faith, unlike the Americans."[65]

Others went farther, like Thérèse Delpech, CEA director of strategic affairs and the French UNMOVIC commissioner. Considered to be one of the foremost French experts on WMD proliferation and known for her forceful character, Delpech was an influential figure in the state apparatus, perhaps even to the point of influencing evaluations with her alarmist analyses and information, which echoed those that were circulating in Washington. "Self-persuasion, the indefatigable support for the Americans, the wish to get rid of Saddam, or simply naïveté have misled many," Le Maire later commented, while also pointing to the role of "ideology."[66] Should we see Delpech's influence in some official declarations? This is quite possible: early on, Villepin himself—perhaps wanting to make the French position credible in the eyes of the Americans—advanced views that arguably were not substantiated by the available evidence. In early October 2002, for instance, he wrote in *Le Monde* that while Iraq "does not yet possess nuclear means, all indications converge on the idea that it has reconstituted biological and chemical capabilities."[67]

On the whole, however, the consensus among French decision-makers was to stress the existence of suspicions rather than the absence of proofs. In other words, it was about seeing the glass as half full, rather than half empty. Was this a reflex of precaution with regard to both a possible Iraqi danger and the American ally? "We thought that everything [that Iraq was suspected of doing] was plausible," remembered a French senior official, adding that "nobody exonerated Iraq."[68] An illustration of this mindset may be found in the public language that the Quai d'Orsay wanted to refine in September 2002 in the light of the evaluations provided by the intelligence agencies: "There are strong suspicions that Iraq has kept some chemical and biological weapons and continues clandestinely its WMD and missile programs. . . . Iraq threatens the security of its neighbors by making the specter of chemical and biological proliferation hang over us. Worrying indications point in this direction. Therefore the return of inspectors is necessary to shed light on Iraqi activities and to put an end to worries about it."⁶⁹ There was no mention of the nuclear component, but there were "strong suspicions" and "worrying indications" in other domains, evoking risk on a regional scale: although such language was far from the most categorical American assertions, the French tone was firm about the Iraqi danger, no doubt reflecting the prevailing opinion inside the French state apparatus at the time.

There was one notable exception, however, and it was Chirac himself. From the start, Chirac's tone was different. "They are always talking about proofs, but I have not yet seen these proofs," he declared in his September 2002 *New York Times* interview. Was this a reflection of Chirac's perspicacity, or of his longtime familiarity with the Iraq dossier—or was it the result of a bias that derived from his opposition to the war? Whatever the case, from start to finish the French president proved much more skeptical than many others about the issue of Iraqi WMD, though at the same time he refrained from asserting publicly that they did not exist.

So what was the state of mind among French decision-makers in the autumn of 2002 regarding a possible military intervention? Since the end of the summer, the official position was not to reject a priori the use of force, a point that distinguished France from Germany. Chirac later wrote that "for my part I never excluded France's being engaged alongside the United States" should an intervention prove "legitimate."⁷⁰ He would not depart from this assertion at the height of the Franco-American crisis, insisting on the fact that his opposition to the war did not arise from principled pacifism. According to some, Chirac's France in the fall of 2002 was even close to "going." So what really were French intentions? Was French military intervention alongside the United States envisaged, if not effectively prepared?

To be sure, the position adopted by the French government was not to reject in advance a possible French military participation. Because France, as a permanent member of the Security Council, maintained that it was up to the council to decide on the use of force, it would have been difficult for Paris to reject this possibility from the start without losing its credibility with the Americans. Down the road, such a loss of credibility would have played into the hands of the Washington proponents of unilateral war. The French position "did not hold the use of force as ineluctable, but it did not exclude it" if Saddam Hussein refused to cooperate, Chirac later wrote.⁷¹ Yet Chirac proved noticeably reluctant to *effectively* envisage such a scenario, and he would not deviate from this attitude in the following weeks, advancing his refusal to use force *except as a last resort and with the approval of the Security Council.*

At the start of September, Chirac had once again conveyed to both Blair and Bush his reservations about an intervention (as he had done with the latter in the spring), especially if it were conducted unilaterally. "We must avoid playing with fire and creating a situation that we cannot control," he told Bush on September 27, adding during their conversation on October 9 that the Western nations "were in the process of inciting a massive rejection [on the part of the Arab and Muslim world] which may prove very costly."[72] The seizure of power by the Shiites in Iraq, the destabilization of a Middle East already rendered fragile by the Israel-Palestine issue, and the aggravation of the split between the West and Islam and therefore of the terrorist danger—these were the many risks that Chirac advanced in order to repel the war scenario. Chirac's analysis was fed by his contacts with Arab leaders: when he met with Egyptian president Hosni Mubarak in Alexandria in mid-October, Mubarak confided to him that the American policy was in his eyes "marked by a total absence of knowledge of the region" and was likely to provoke destabilization and radicalization.[73]

Chirac took advantage of a fresh meeting with Bush on November 21, on the occasion of a NATO summit in Prague, to bring up Iraq once again. (This turned out to be their last face-to-face conversation prior to the conflict the following spring.) Two weeks after the adoption of Resolution 1441, Chirac warned Bush of the consequences of war in no uncertain terms. "We are not afraid of war because we are pacifists," he said, "but we fear a war because its consequences would be very serious." Stressing the ethnic and religious complexity of Iraq, as well as its lack of democracy and its long tradition of political violence, Chirac implicitly underlined the United States' lack of experience in this region. "Once you are there," he stated, "you are going to have to stay there for years, and you run the risk of creating battalions of little Bin Ladens." Although Bush did not comment on the substance of Chirac's statement and merely thanked him for his "frankness," he clearly felt that he had been lectured to by his French counterpart. But Bush could not be mistaken about his colleague's state of mind. "Chirac gave Bush an extraordinary lesson about the consequences of the war. . . . Bush listened with a slightly disdainful air," a witness remembered, adding that Chirac "had exceptional knowledge of the region and he was convinced that [this war] was an enormous mistake."[74]

Nobody was more privy to Chirac's thinking than the French top military. From the start of the UN phase in the autumn of 2002, French generals—as was their role—were beginning to consider the possibility of a military action and what France's role might be. "We were anxious to know what Chirac thought about this," one of them remembered; "we wanted to present him with the consequences of his choices. Whether we participated or opposed [a military intervention], there would be major consequences on Franco-American relations, on NATO, and on European defense." It did not take the generals long to realize that the president was hesitant to take a position on this terrain. "Chirac listened to us and said absolutely nothing," he went on, adding that in his view it was clear from this moment that Chirac did not envisage French participation in an intervention. An unmistakable sign of this thinking was that in this period, no Defense Council was convened at the Élysée. Such a council—a formal meeting of the president, the prime minister, the relevant ministers (beginning with foreign affairs and defense), and the military chiefs—had been convened for the war in Afghanistan, but it was not forthcoming for Iraq.[75]

The military, however, did want to discuss the issue, and so pressed the point. The official French position, after all, was not to exclude any options; might it not be possible that an unforeseen event—perhaps an attempt by Baghdad to obstruct the inspections, or the revelation that a WMD threat of an unsuspected scope really existed—could tip the balance in the direction of intervention? In such a case, they pointed out, French forces should be ready to intervene as soon as possible. This implied a minimum of preparations, especially since French forces might then have to find some space within the existing American force deployments. General Henri Bentégeat, Chirac's military chief of staff at the Élysée, and General Jean-Louis Georgelin, Bentégeat's soon-to-be successor, therefore insisted that Chirac receive the incumbent chief of staff of the armed forces, General Jean-Pierre Kelche. (Kelche was nearing the end of his term, and would be replaced by Bentégeat at the end of October.) Kelche wished to offer Chirac possible options in case of a decision to intervene. Chirac agreed, though without enthusiasm. In late October 2002, a few days before his departure, Kelche unfolded his maps on the table in the Élysée's Pompadour Room and presented Chirac with a possible vision of the French participation: an expeditionary corps roughly the equivalent of "Daguet," the French division-size contingent deployed in the 1991 Gulf War.[76]

Though he listened to Kelche's presentation with polite interest, Chirac proved extremely reticent. The generals interpreted his reaction as "Have no illusions; I don't intend to go there." The generals pointed out to Chirac that some unforeseen event might change the situation, and that in such a case a French intervention could not be conducted without prior preparation.

"If you should tell me in mid-February that we are going, we would not be able to," Bentégeat explained to Chirac. Realizing the military's desire to be ready whatever happened, Chirac authorized them to undertake the preparations they thought necessary, but on two conditions: first, that nothing filter through to the public, and second, that there be no joint planning with the Americans and British. The first condition aimed to avoid a contradiction between visible military preparations and an official discourse that stressed a peaceful solution. The second condition was designed to prevent being pulled into an intervention through French participation in US planning, from which it would be difficult to disengage. A few weeks later, Bentégeat, now chief of staff of the armed forces, confirmed this position with Le Maire: "[The president] does not wish for the French armies to participate in planning on Iraq with the Americans because it is a slippery slope," he confided. "Once we are there, there will be no way of getting out." "And," he added, "there's no way we could get him to change his mind."[77]

The French military could only implement the presidential instructions, so for the time being they confined themselves to doing an inventory of available units and materiel: about 10,000 to 15,000 troops, airplanes, the aircraft carrier *Charles de Gaulle*, and so on. However, as American preparations intensified in the last weeks of 2002, the French generals became more worried about being caught off guard. They feared that if nothing was done to prepare in advance, it would become increasingly difficult for the French to find a place in the Anglo-American force deployment. Bentégeat "feared that [French political authorities] would ask us to go at the last moment," one French general remembered. By November, the Pentagon was indeed already soliciting possible allied contributions; in this context, Bentégeat felt a need to contact the Americans for two purposes. He wanted to know more about their planning and so be better able to orient the preparations on the French side, and he wanted to ask them to reserve a place—a "slot," in military jargon—in their force deployment should the French decide to participate. Bentégeat argued in this direction with the support of Georgelin, and so in mid-December Chirac authorized him to send General Jean-Patrick Gaviard, his deputy for operations, to Washington. But it was quite clear that Gaviard's mission—about which more will be said later—changed nothing in Chirac's state of mind.[78]

Did the French generals push for an intervention in this period? Many are convinced of this. "Most of the military were burning to participate in the planning" alongside the Americans, Le Maire later wrote.[79] No doubt, at the end of 2002 many of them were indeed ready to take part in a possible war.

Despite France's nonintegration into NATO and the political vicissitudes of relations between the two countries, Franco-American cooperation means a lot to French generals: as a rule, the latter are eager both to show solidarity with their US allies in times of hardship and to maintain a close operational link between French and American forces, out of fear that the French military apparatus otherwise would be demoted in relation to the United States. This desire to keep a strong connection with the Americans had led the French, at the November 2002 NATO Prague summit, to agree to participate in Washington's proposed new NATO rapid reaction force in order to fill the capabilities gap that had appeared—first in Kosovo, and then in Afghanistan—between the American and European armies. (The French also were interested in trying to reestablish the centrality of NATO, which had been marginalized in Operation Enduring Freedom.) In addition, the French military also must have feared seeing the British assert themselves, at French expense, as the Americans' exclusive partners, a problem that already was perceptible in operations in Afghanistan. Overall, and deep down, many in the French military thought, in the words of a former major commander, that "if there was going to be a war, then France had to be there." Yet it would be a mistake to think that the French generals in effect tried to influence the political decision. "There is some truth in the idea that the military wanted to go," this same officer recalled, "[but] this does not mean that they were arguing for French participation. Chirac had said no, and that meant no!"[80] This assertion is confirmed by Bruno Le Maire's testimony: "He told me so with regret," he wrote about Bentégeat's confidential statement concerning Chirac's restrictive instructions on planning, "but with the loyalty of someone who has served the president for years."[81]

"The dope is here"

The adoption of Resolution 1441 had opened a period of calm that would last one month: the time granted to Iraq to transmit the "currently accurate, full, and complete" declaration of its WMD, as required by the resolution. The Iraqis had accepted the return of inspectors in mid-September. The regime had no margin for trickery: the resolution said that the practical measures for resuming the inspections were to be determined by Hans Blix and Mohamed ElBaradei, and implemented without further discussion. A meeting with the Iraqis on this matter had taken place in Vienna on September

30 and October 1. However, the letter of acceptance (required by Resolution 1441) that Baghdad sent to Secretary-General Annan on November 13 did not bode well. In more than nine pages of a text that at times sounded delirious, mixing mystical and historical references, Baghdad mentioned only in passing its intention to "cooperate," while denouncing the resolution and its authors. The United States, the United Kingdom, and their allies were called "a gang of evil." Was this provocation? Or an intuition that the Americans had decided to attack, no matter what happened? In the weeks to come, the Iraqi attitude would oscillate between incoherence and resignation, despite pressure from France and from other "peace camp" countries to bring them to comply without fail. In a telephone conversation with Villepin the same day, Colin Powell nevertheless judged that the letter was tantamount to an agreement, even if it contained "many idiocies" and boded ill for Iraqi cooperation. A second letter from Baghdad, dated November 23, did not go back on its initial acceptance of the resolution—to the comfort of the French, who had tried to dissuade the Iraqis from reneging—though it again denounced Resolution 1441 (albeit in a less virulent manner) and denied that Iraq possessed WMD. On November 27, well before the resolution's forty-five-day deadline, the first UNMOVIC inspection took place, followed by twenty others in the space of a week.[82]

Of course, a derailment was possible at any moment. The hawks would not fail to exploit any misdemeanor by Baghdad, however venial, especially if a more serious incident occurred, for example in the no-fly zones. Yet the succeeding three or four weeks marked an upturn. Received at the Élysée on November 25, Annan told Chirac that war was "no longer inevitable." The French president conceded more guardedly that the tension had somewhat subsided: while many in Washington were pushing for war, he said, the American people seemed less favorable to it, and the risks of an operation were appearing more clearly. Blair, for his part, was encountering growing difficulties in public opinion, he noted. In short, Chirac said that he was now "a little less pessimistic," adding that everything depended on Baghdad's attitude—which meant, he warned, that there still could be "a bad surprise."[83]

As the December 8 deadline for the Iraqi declaration approached, feverishness returned. Although this was hardly their first declaration, the Iraqis told Blix and ElBaradei that they were concerned about the shortness of their deadline for supplying all the information demanded. Meanwhile, in New York, the plans for receiving the declaration gave rise to a psychodrama. Resolution 1441 called for the Iraqis' document to be submitted not only to the inspectors but also to the Security Council; this raised problems, because the document would by nature include information that might be sensitive in terms of proliferation, and therefore it should not be overly disseminated. At the instigation of the Americans, the procedure was refined: UNMOVIC and the IAEA would partially "sanitize" the document with the assistance of the five permanent Security Council members, who would each receive a complete copy. The sanitized report would then be distributed to the whole council. This procedure, of course, irked the nonpermanent members, who saw it as discrimination. The practical method of distributing the text likewise created a stir. The Americans got the Colombian representative, then acting Security Council president, to ensure that the copy destined for the council be handed to the US delegation as soon as the declaration arrived in New York on the evening of the 8th in order for it to be flown by helicopter to Washington. The justification for this sleight of hand was that the US government's photocopying capabilities were superior to the UN's and would enable the copies for the permanent members to be produced more quickly. Left outside of this maneuver—unlike the British—the French representative, Jean-Marc de La Sablière (who had just succeeded Jean-David Levitte at the UN) did not hide his irritation about a procedure that gave Washington access to the document several hours before the other capitals would have it. Meanwhile, the Iraqis were convinced that the Americans simply wanted to manipulate the declaration, and so they proposed that they would give it directly to the French. The interpretation advanced by Jean-David Levitte (who had just replaced François Bujon de l'Estang as France's ambassador to the United States) seems more plausible, given the state of mind that reigned in Washington. In Levitte's opinion, the State Department wanted to demonstrate—even at the cost of disparaging the UN—that the multilateral procedure was not incompatible with a certain kind of efficiency, and that the United States kept the upper hand over the UN process.[84]

Whatever the case, on December 9, the French embassy in Washington—along with the British, Chinese, and Russian embassies—picked up its copy at the State Department and sent it that evening to Paris by the last plane. Philippe Errera, a young diplomat in charge of politico-military issues at the French embassy, was the courier; as soon as he arrived at the Quai d'Orsay the next morning, he handed the Iraqi declaration to Pierre Vimont, Villepin's chief of staff. "The dope is here," Vimont joked to Le Maire, who was in charge of the issue in Villepin's staff. Perceiving the voluminous document, Villepin told his staff, teasingly, "Take courage, my friends!"[85]

Courage would indeed be needed by the UN inspectors in New York and by the experts in the various capitals in order to go through a text of some 12,000 pages with a fine-tooth comb. UNMOVIC launched immediately into the analysis, with Blix planning to present a preliminary evaluation during a Security Council meeting on December 19. It was soon clear that the document— which actually included a main body of "only" 3,000 pages and no less than 5,000 pages of appendices in Arabic—did not meet expectations. Some passages appeared in several places, and there was frequent recycling of declarations addressed to UNSCOM before 1998. Most important, the text contained very few new elements, whether on the issues that had not been resolved prior to 1998 or on later developments, although in this latter respect there were a few pieces of useful information on the ballistic program and on (peaceful) activities in the biological domain. Blix was perplexed. The overwhelming size of the declaration might be explained by the Iraqis' concern to cut short any accusation of ill will by responding with excessive zeal to the exigencies of the Security Council. The formal imperfections could have resulted from the haste with which the document was prepared. But what about the lack of substance? It was difficult for the inspectors not to see this as yet another ploy. "The Iraqi side claimed they had nothing more," wrote Blix. "We doubted this was true, but could not prove it."[86]

On substance, Blix remained quite distrustful about Baghdad, a factor that would prove important as events unfolded. He had hoped, as he told Jean-Marc de La Sablière in mid-December, that US military pressure would lead the Iraqis to "reveal" that they possessed WMD or were pursuing prohibited programs. Blix thought it "quite probable" that the Iraqis had continued to hide certain weapons or capabilities—"probably anthrax and a few Scuds," he said—although he admitted that it was impossible to have a precise idea. He added that "perhaps ultimately it [was] not very significant," nor a matter of an "enormous" volume in relation to the quantities declared by Iraq. (Blix mentioned the 550 artillery shells filled with mustard gas that had not been found, as compared with the 13,000 shells that UNSCOM had counted in 1999.) Blix's confidence shows that he shared the existing suspicions—at least inwardly, though not publicly—about probable Iraqi trickery, although he was also uncertain about the actual importance of the concealments. He later confirmed these sentiments by speaking of his "gut feelings" in that regard.[87] Be that as it may, Blix stuck to his rigorous approach: the Iraqi declaration was not satisfactory, he told La Sablière, since it did not clarify the remaining areas of uncertainty and it contained inconsistencies. Even if UNMOVIC was not in a position to demonstrate that the declaration was deceitful or incomplete, Baghdad's persistent failure to deliver convincing evidence meant that Blix believed that he had "no assurance" of Iraq's effective disarmament. Blix told La Sablière that the tone of his statement to the Security Council would therefore be "rather negative," although he hoped that a "dynamic" favorable to inspections would nevertheless emerge. The bottom line was clear: the Iraqis must furnish the necessary documentation or any other proof of their statements, and it was necessary to carry on with the inspections. This was the approach Blix defended to the Security Council on December 19, and he would not depart from it in the following weeks.[88]

But above all, it was the American reaction that the chancelleries were awaiting in the following days. How would the United States analyze the declaration, and what consequences were they going to draw? The answer to the first question was no surprise: the declaration was "neither accurate nor complete," the State Department told Levitte, stressing both the absence of responses to questions still unresolved in 1998 and the quasi-silence on later developments, at least in regard to the intelligence that the Americans claimed they had (starting with the infamous mobile laboratories). Hence the second line of questions: did the Americans intend to denounce the supposed failures or falsehoods of the Iraqi declaration, and as a result declare that Iraq, having not made "admissions," was again guilty of a "material breach"? And if so, what would the consequences be? These subjects, Levitte was informed, would be debated by the National Security Council on December 18 in the presence of President Bush.[89]

Meanwhile, John Negroponte did not mince words at the Security Council on December 19. Pointing to the declaration's silence on the "areas of uncertainty" that still existed from 1998 (among other things, the 550 shells mentioned by Blix) and calling it "incomplete and fragmentary" on later activities (he cited the Al-Samoud missile, which he said had been modified to augment its range beyond the authorized 150 kilometers), Negroponte stressed that these lacunae were neither oversights nor errors but instead arose from a deliberate decision. Iraq, he declared, had rejected with "contempt" its last opportunity to conform; it thus was guilty of a new material breach. Yet Negroponte did not go on to pronounce a casus belli, as might have been feared. La Sablière remarked that Negroponte's denunciation of an umpteenth "material breach" was not central to the speech, and that instead Negroponte had asked Blix to accelerate the inspections in order to "test" the Iraqi declaration. The French representative concluded that the United States was continuing to play the inspection game. But for how long? Levitte, in Washington, wondered this as well. During a press conference, Powell—citing the aluminum tubes and the mobile laboratories—had pointed to the omissions in the declaration and, like Negroponte, denounced a new material breach. Certainly, Levitte noted, this denunciation was not followed by concrete consequences, but he believed that Powell's intention in his press conference had been to nourish the accusation file for American public opinion and for the international community, in order to be able to conclude Iraqi culpability when the time was right. For the Bush administration, Levitte concluded, this clearly was a new step toward the use of force.[90]

Barely a month after the adoption of Resolution 1441, the veritable start of Franco-American divergences was apparent. The disagreement did not hinge on the evaluation of the declaration in itself, since Paris's own assessment of it was close to the ones made in New York, Washington, and London. The French, too, were perplexed: the Iraqi document—of which some passages were handwritten and others barely legible—had a "comic side," Le Maire remembered. Was this provocation, or else disorganization combined with incompetence or panic?[91] Whatever the case, the SGDN's evaluation pointed to the fact that it contained little that was new, whether on the issues left unresolved by UNSCOM or on the possible pursuit since 1998 of forbidden activities, at least on the basis of available intelligence. The French conclusion resembled that given by the UNMOVIC experts: "The data contained in the declaration does not suffice to remove existing presumptions," although inversely the intelligence services "do not believe they possess sufficient evidence to challenge the information transmitted by the Iraqis . . . ; therefore uncertainty subsists," in particular on the chemical and biological issues.[92] The same tone was heard in London, where at first glance it was thought the declaration was "neither current and accurate nor complete." The British position "is not very different from ours," reported the French ambassador in London, Gérard Errera, after a visit to the Foreign Office—which said that it wanted close cooperation with Paris.[93]

The French, however, did diverge from the British and especially from the Americans about the conclusions that could be drawn from the declaration. Of course, there was no question of hiding its unsatisfactory nature: what was the point of denying the facts? Levitte acknowledged to Paul Wolfowitz that the French and American analyses of the text were "overall convergent."[94] Paris, though, wanted to make a "political" evaluation and not merely a "technical" one. The French evidently intended to defuse in advance the expected

American line of argument that an intervention might be justified solely on the basis of the declaration's inconsistencies. First of all, the French argued, the inspections process was still only in its preliminary phase: only as the inspections built up would it be possible to take stock of the Iraqi programs, and the declaration was only one stage in that process. Next, the reality of the "threat" would have to be evaluated based on the resumed inspections and the fact that a strengthened ongoing monitoring and verification regime would be set up in any case. In other words, the French effectively said, whatever threat existed was now under control. Although the uncertainties concerning the post-1998 developments were potentially serious, they argued further, it should not be forgotten (as the Amorim Report had stated in March 1999) that UNSCOM had dismantled the majority of the programs before December 1998 despite the remaining unresolved issues about a residual part of the arsenal. The French concluded that a mere preliminary analysis of the declaration could not establish a "material breach," and that the remaining uncertainties were precisely the reason why it was appropriate to fully support the inspections.[95] Unsurprisingly, it was the latter point that the French advanced at the Security Council on December 19: the declaration, La Sablière conceded, "brought no clear responses" to issues that UNSCOM had left unresolved, nor did it remove "doubts" about the pursuit of activities after 1998. He pointed to the "areas of uncertainties" that remained, but, he quickly added, "It is precisely because there remain uncertainties that the inspection mechanisms were put in place."[96]

For the time being, Paris and Washington avoided a clash, but the disharmony was now patent. On both sides, in the context of beginning to implement Resolution 1441, the choices that eventually would lead to the Franco-American rupture and then the confrontation were being made in this period. This clearly was the case on the American side. During the NSC meeting devoted to the Iraqi declaration on December 18, Bush had given the impression of having already written off the UN process. Powell had defended the line that Negroponte would follow the next day at the Security Council: to denounce the Iraqi declaration as a material breach, but for the time being without making it a casus belli. But Bush had criticized Powell's approach, revealing his basic thinking. "The question is, is war inevitable after you say 'material breach'?" he had asked Powell; the latter had replied that he did not think so, and in any case they should await the report from Blix planned for January 27. Bush retorted, "I think that it is inevitable," while emphatically repeating that the declaration showed that Iraq was "not cooperating."[97] In short, although the Powell line had seemed to carry the day on December 18, this was because the moment had not yet come, in Bush's eyes, to break *officially* with the logic of "coercive diplomacy." But in private, Bush did not hide his real state of mind; the declaration was "empty," "a joke," he told Spanish prime minister José María Aznar that same day. "We will be measured in response," Bush then said, "[but] at some point, we will conclude enough is enough and take him out." That evening, at a Christmas party for the media at the White House, Bush met veteran *Washington Post* journalist Bob Woodward. As Woodward confided that his new book *Bush at War* (devoted to the response to 9/11 and the campaign in Afghanistan) was a best-seller, Bush hinted that there would be a story to write as a sequel. Woodward joked, "Maybe it will be called 'More Bush at War.'"[98]

Meanwhile, the White House was beginning to focus on how to present to the public whatever intelligence was available to justify the war. Was this somewhat belated concern—more than two months after the NIE had been issued—a new indication that the issue of Iraqi WMD was merely a pretext? Or, as Bush would maintain, was it proof that he believed in good faith that the existing intelligence was sufficiently solid? On December 21, CIA deputy director John McLaughlin reviewed in Bush's presence the pieces of incriminating evidence that could be presented to the public without hindering the work of the CIA, which was careful to protect its sources and methods of investigation. Yet the evidence that McLaughlin showed was hardly compelling: some satellite photos, one of which showed a stand test for rocket engines that was patently oversized in relation to the 150-kilometer limit, and another that showed an alleged chemical weapon facility that had been "cleansed"; a graph showing that a drone might have flown close to 500 kilometers instead of the authorized 150; and an extract from an intercepted conversation between two Iraqi officers concerning nerve agents. Bush was disappointed. "Nice try," he said, adding, "I don't think this is quite—it's not something that Joe Public would understand or would gain a lot of confidence from." Then Bush said to George Tenet, "I've been told all this intelligence about having WMD and this is the best we've got?" Bush stressed that the information that had been presented to him in his briefings over the previous weeks had been much more categorical—which, as mentioned earlier, probably was the case. But Tenet reassured him that it was possible to present the file in a more convincing way; "It's a slam-dunk case," he said, using the basketball expression. Did the confidence portrayed by Tenet comfort Bush about the possibility of justifying the war in public opinion? Quite probably. But did it play a decisive role in his decision to go to war? That is most doubtful. For Tenet, the expression "slam dunk" was subsequently blown out of all proportion by the Bush administration—through Bob Woodward's 2004 book *Plan of Attack*—in order to project onto the CIA the responsibility for a war that the administration had decided upon anyway. (The scene would become one of the most controversial episodes in the whole Iraqi affair.) Whatever the case, the episode does confirm in an indisputable way that at this stage the drive to war had prevailed: the question was no longer about the trustworthiness of the intelligence reports, but about their value in terms of communication.[99]

At the very end of 2002, Bush was indeed heading toward a final decision. The inspections were leading nowhere, he thought—at least, that is how he presented things. (This, of course, was a premature conclusion that retrospectively seems to imply that Bush had never really envisaged a peaceful outcome.) For the first time, he asked at the end of December for Condoleezza Rice's opinion, something he would never do with Powell or Rumsfeld. Should he go to war, he asked? Yes, Rice answered; letting such a threat flourish in this region of the world would "come back to haunt us someday." Bush did not respond, but Rice knew that he was coming to a decision. When Karl Rove came to Crawford, Texas, during the holiday to discuss the need to start preparing for the 2004 reelection campaign, Bush said to him: "We got a war coming, and you're just going to have to wait." It was also at Crawford during the holiday that Bush—again, rare for him—asked his father for advice. "You've got to try everything to avoid a war," the elder Bush replied, "but if [Saddam Hussein] won't comply, you don't have any other choice."[100]

It was also toward the end of 2002 that the French side—in large part as a reaction to the perceived US drive to war—crystallized its decision to hold itself apart from a possible military operation. By this stage, the French generals had obtained confirmation of what they already suspected: the American war machine was well and truly underway. In mid-December, Gaviard had toured the Gulf and met General T. Michael "Buzz" Moseley, the commander of the CENTCOM air component under Franks, at Prince Sultan Air Base, the major US Air Force base in Saudi Arabia. Moseley had confided to Gaviard that an offensive would probably take place before the spring. When Gaviard reported back to Bentégeat upon his return to Paris on December 18, Bentégeat said that Gaviard would be going to Washington in two days' time, armed with personal instructions written in his own hand.[101]

Gaviard's mission, Bentégeat made clear, was "totally confidential and unofficial." Above all, "it did not prejudge the political decision that the French authorities would make when the time came based on the decisions of the Security Council," knowing that there could be nothing "automatic" about a possible French military engagement. (The "non-automaticity" of any French military engagement alongside the United States had been a central tenet of Franco-American military relations since the time of Charles de Gaulle.) The purpose of the mission was to inform the American generals about the forces—land, air, sea, and special forces—that France *might* bring "if it decided to engage." Gaviard was told to stress that France was not asking to be involved in American planning, but because any potential decision to engage would come at a "late" stage, he was instructed to "ask our American friends to study the possibility of reserving for France some slots and platforms that would enable it to be worthily integrated into the plan of attack," especially with regard to its carrier battle group and land forces. Bentégeat concluded his instructions: "We understand the difficulty of this procedure for American planners, but there is a political stake for both our countries; facilitating the possible integration of French forces would be profitable for everybody."[102]

Gaviard's instructions conformed to the line defined by Chirac. It was a matter of establishing contact with the American military in order to preserve the possibility of French participation, but without prejudging a final decision, which implied both strict confidentiality and the absence of any involvement in American planning. When Gaviard was received at the Pentagon on December 21 by General George Casey, the "J5" in the Joint Chiefs of Staff—the chairman's deputy for strategic plans and policy, responsible for relations with allies—and four or five other generals, he did not deviate from that line. Gaviard emphasized that a possible French decision to intervene could be made only by France's highest political authorities and that it would depend on the evolution of the UN process—which in any case would imply a fresh Security Council resolution. He then gave his American colleagues the figures of a hypothetical French contribution, including 10,000 to 12,000 troops and up to a hundred aircraft, plus the aircraft carrier *Charles de Gaulle*. Gaviard insisted on the purpose of his mission: a possible decision could not take place in France for some time, but it would presuppose that a place be reserved now for French forces in American planning.[103]

For the Pentagon generals, Gaviard's approach seemed unusual. A proposition of this kind normally went through government channels, not through contacts between military commanders. But because it was emanating from Bentégeat, whose closeness to Chirac was known in Washington, it was taken seriously. Yet the Pentagon generals did not hide their puzzlement:

the deadlines mentioned for a possible French decision appeared to them to be quite long with respect to the probable acceleration of the calendar on the American side. The remaining uncertainties, notably logistic, about the American plan of attack (especially the roles of Saudi Arabia and Turkey) further complicated the affair. Moreover, it was at CENTCOM that things were being decided from an operational standpoint: the French request therefore would normally have to go through Tampa. But this possibility was seen as premature from the French point of view—and no doubt also from the American—since it would presuppose that a political decision had already been made.

The American generals nevertheless sent the French approach up through their channels. Tommy Franks and General Richard Myers, chairman of the Joint Chiefs of Staff, were duly informed, as were the Pentagon's top civilian leaders and, of course, the White House. But there was no follow-up to the meeting: the Americans were not able to respond to the French military's request as long as France's participation remained hypothetical. The American generals understood full well that their French colleagues wished to be at their side, and they no doubt desired to encourage such a possibility, which is why they welcomed Gaviard. (This was in contrast to the Pentagon's top civilians, who from Rumsfeld down were hardly concerned about being reconciled with an ally that they judged unreliable.) But the Americans also knew that the decision was not up to the French military. "They wanted to go there with us," an American general later remembered, "but we knew that, in France like here, it is the president who decides." The White House, as a matter of fact, was also skeptical about French engagement. "I do not think that at the White House people really believed that France would participate," a former adviser to Bush later testified, adding that "I don't think anybody believed that [the Gaviard mission] represented an opening or that Chirac might change his mind."[104]

Overall, the Gaviard mission merely confirmed the current situation— paradoxically, since the French military wanted to keep the game open. On the American side was a clear intensification of military preparations; on the French side was great circumspection from the political authorities about the prospect of a possible engagement. At the Élysée, it was now evident that the American war machine had been launched and it would be premature at best to insert oneself into it. This indeed is what Chirac would retain from this episode: "Those responsible at the Pentagon implied [to Gaviard] that . . . the more time that passed, the more it would become impossible to reserve slots for French forces," he later wrote, "which presupposed that we commit right now to the preparations for the operation, or else risk being set aside when the time came."[105] And for Chirac, at this juncture there was no question of such a commitment.

Nevertheless, at the end of 2002 the appearance within the international community was one of ongoing cooperation on Iraq. "The inspection path must be and must be seen as an alternative, not a prelude to armed action," Blix noted in his diary on New Year's Eve, adding that "I do not think that the U.S. has made up its mind to go to war even though they are taking all the steps in that direction. It serves to scare the Iraqis." Blix, in other words, still believed on December 31, 2002, in the sincerity of George W. Bush's "coercive diplomacy." Blix's feeling was understandable: after all, the inspections buildup had taken place without incident and had given rise to satisfactory cooperation—at least in procedural terms—on the part of the Iraqis, who had given access without difficulty to all the sites that UNMOVIC wished to inspect. Yet what followed in the early weeks of 2003 would soon disabuse Blix of his initial favorable impressions.[106]

Chapter 5
The Rupture: January 2003

The Franco-American rupture took place in the first weeks of 2003. Until then, appearances were intact: the implementation of Security Council Resolution 1441, against the backdrop of the smooth unfolding of inspections, was still a subject of agreement between Paris and Washington, even if inspections were not producing significant results in the absence of Iraq's active cooperation. In the background, however, the Americans were now clearly oriented toward a military operation. The French were able to confirm this choice in mid-January, and it soon was reflected in Washington's and London's desire to accelerate the timetable at the United Nations. The Americans and the British were now eager to not let the inspection phase be indefinitely prolonged and to prepare the diplomatic ground for an intervention.

Faced with US and British eagerness for action, the French stuck to the line they had adopted since the start of the crisis. In their view, a strict implementation of Resolution 1441 was more than ever in order. In the absence of an incident or the discovery of an incriminating clue, let alone a so-called smoking gun, this implied continuing the inspections. But in the face of the Americans' bellicose determination, a clash arguably was inevitable. The divergences between Paris and Washington, which until then had been masked by the need to appear united over Resolution 1441, appeared in full light in the last days of January, first at the UN and then during the celebrations of the fortieth anniversary of the Franco-German Élysée Treaty—the latter of which marked the emergence of a Paris-Berlin axis against a march to war. Now the terrain was ready for a confrontation that would culminate in the following weeks.

"The train has already left the station"

In early 2003, the situation was still ambivalent. On the one hand, the United States, as suggested by its reaction to the Iraqi declaration on weapons of mass destruction and its ongoing military buildup in the Gulf region, was clearly heading toward the use of force. On the other hand, unknowns remained, if only because of the ongoing inspections and uncertainty about the results. At the start of the year, a muffled debate was taking place within the French diplomatic establishment, with an already perceptible dilemma lurking in the background. Should France stick to its position at the risk of a confrontation with the United States, or should it try to avoid a clash at the cost of resignation, or even alignment with the United States?

Those who advocated continuing the line that had been adopted in the fall stated that France should maintain the same approach of defending the rigorous implementation of Resolution 1441. Faced with the American desire to hurry things along, UN representative Jean-Marc de La Sablière suggested a threefold approach: (1) to encourage the inspectors to conduct "robust" actions in order to obtain results in a reasonable time period; (2) to put pressure on the Iraqis in order to make them switch to "active" cooperation; and (3) to reiterate that France's "judgment" was not "predetermined," while emphasizing that Paris would not be content with "serious doubts" or "presumptions" if it were to envisage resorting to force.[1] This approach was shared by the Quai d'Orsay's UN and Middle East directorates, which both thought that since inspections were taking place without incident and at a steady pace, the date of January 27—when the inspectors were supposed to report to the Security Council—should not be seen as a marker for a possible decision about recourse to force. Paris, they believed, should continue to show its determination to implement the resolution fully and should reject any attempt to legitimize military action through the Security Council as long as the inspectors did not find proofs of Iraqi violations. "We are ready, if necessary, to draw the consequences of such possible violations," the heads of both directorates repeated, "but we won't be able to do this absent these elements of proof."[2]

Yet this approach was not unanimous. At the start of 2003, some French diplomats—those most concerned with Franco-American relations—considered it illusory, if not misguided, to try to oppose Washington's plans: "We seem to be acting as though we believe the train has not left the station," said Gérard Araud, the Quai's director of strategic affairs, adding that "in fact, it has already departed. All we are doing is lying down on the tracks in front of it."[3] Jean-David Levitte went further, advocating an approach that aimed as much as possible to preserve France's entente with the United States—a line close to that of the British. For Levitte, France's ambassador in Washington, it was necessary to avoid a "German-like" posture of opposition that could only lead to "self-marginalization"; the goal of French diplomacy should be less to try to impede American plans than to convince Washington of the risks of launching an operation without UN support. Taking up the arguments he had already advanced at the time of the negotiation over Resolution 1441, Levitte said that this goal would entail remaining credible in American eyes by stating that France was indeed ready to envisage the use of force if necessary. The French position, Levitte believed, should be "clarified" to enable France to be heard in Washington. "Our capacity to influence the Bush administration would be stronger," he continued, "if we could indicate clearly that in the event of a material breach . . . France would vote in favor of a resolution authorizing the use of force and would be disposed to participate in the military operations that would follow." Levitte did also write that France ought to reserve its position in the event that the United States decided to engage in military operations without such a material breach being formally declared by the Security Council. But he did not hide his innermost feelings: if the Americans ultimately decided to resort to force in the absence of a clear report from the inspectors, France, he pleaded, should not try to sabotage the United States at the UN. Such a course of action only risked causing a profound transatlantic split and a lasting marginalization of the UN. Levitte argued for maintaining a "hearty and trusting" dialogue with Washington.[4] Clearly, the debate over a possible French veto was already beginning.

It was up to the president to set the French position. On January 5, having heard the arguments on both sides, Dominique de Villepin submitted to Jacques Chirac the line he was proposing to defend in the coming weeks. Faithful to his energetic image, Villepin advocated all-out diplomatic action: "If we wait passively," he argued, "then the mechanical calendar fixed by the Americans will lead us to war in unacceptable conditions. We must reject this prospect. After the decisive role that we played in the negotiation of Resolution 1441, we must retake the initiative." He then detailed the measures that he proposed to undertake in the following days: to convince the Iraqis to "actively" cooperate with the inspectors, to strengthen the work of the latter by supplying them with "precise" information on the Iraqi programs and by putting fresh means at their disposal, and finally to "widen the scope of the debate" at the UN to the whole issue of the fight against terror, to which France—which held the monthly presidency of the Security Council until the end of January—proposed devoting a ministerial meeting on the 20th. The above initiatives conformed to the line that Paris had defended for months; as a result, Chirac readily agreed to them. Yet Chirac opposed his foreign minister's final suggestion: Villepin, like Levitte, proposed a "clarification" of what France's attitude would be in the event of a "recognized" blockage of inspections, specifying the conditions in which it might envisage military action. The aim was to make French ideas on strengthening inspections more "credible" by making it known to the Americans "at the highest level" that in the event of a Security Council decision to resort to military action on the basis of a "significant and clearly recorded" incident, France would assume its responsibilities by contributing to its implementation. But Chirac reacted negatively to this proposal. It was not the moment to let Washington think that France might he resigned to military action, he said; it was better to "push in the opposite direction."[5]

The French president kept a firm hand on the tiller. He was not ready to depart from the position he had adopted in line with Resolution 1441. The day after his conversation with Villepin, Chirac confirmed his utmost reluctance to envisage French participation in a possible military action. In a note dated January 6, his military chief of staff, General Georgelin, reminded Chirac of the "time constraint" weighing on a possible French decision to engage and asked if it was "still too early" to decide to be involved in American planning—and risk giving the "signal" of possible participation. Chirac answered "yes"—without hesitation, he would later remember. In addition, Chirac was opposed to certain advance preparations, such as requesting visas or rights of passage through the Suez Canal, that would allow French forces to be deployed in the region.[6]

Yet curiously, the next day, Chirac seemed to give a "signal" of possible French participation. In a January 7 speech giving New Year's greetings to the French military, he asked them to be ready for any situation: enumerating all the current theaters of operation, he added that "others, alas, might be opened." This phrase had been inserted into Chirac's speech at the initiative of Georgelin, whose hobbyhorse was the need for the military to be prepared for strategic "surprises." However, in the context of the growing probability of American intervention, many observers in Paris and elsewhere inevitably interpreted the statement as the sign of France's possible change of attitude about the military option—an interpretation which the Élysée tried to deny in the following hours. Yet this apparent change of heart had been merely an optical illusion: it was indeed in the first half of January 2003 that the military option was effectively abandoned. In spite of the acceleration of the American military agenda, Paris was not willing to take the measures that it would need to take to insert itself into the US plan of attack. Chirac evidently believed that such acceleration was not justified, since inspections were going on without a notable hitch.[7] In fact, on January 7, Chirac used another New Year's address, this one to the foreign diplomatic corps, to reaffirm the French position. Chirac's message to the Iraqis was clear: "A last opportunity is given them to disarm in peace, [and] they must understand that there is no other possible outcome than to cooperate actively." But the message he conveyed to the Americans was just as clear: "Let us resolutely reject the temptation to unilateral action," he stressed; "let us continue to give all our trust to the inspectors."[8]

The next day, Villepin wrote to his colleagues on the Security Council. Noting that the inspections were taking place without incident and at a rapid pace, he repeated that it was "imperative" for the Iraqis to cooperate actively in order to dissipate the "areas of uncertainty" contained in the WMD declaration and for the inspectors to be granted all necessary aid, including the communication of all available information. "The members of the Security Council should mobilize to give every chance for peace through the implementation of resolution 1441," he concluded.[9] Villepin then went on an Asian tour, which he wanted to use as an opportunity to ascertain that Russia and China, the two other permanent Security Council members whose positions on the crisis had been close to that of France, would remain on a similar line. As during the negotiation of Resolution 1441, the Russian and Chinese attitudes would be a major factor for French diplomacy if it wanted to influence Washington. Stopping in Moscow on January 8, Villepin noted that this was the case with the Russian position. Foreign Minister Igor Ivanov insisted on the need to respect the calendar of the resolutions and to not "anticipate" the January 27 meeting, which Washington was trying to "dramatize." Russia, Ivanov added, was ready to participate in the ministerial meeting on terrorism. The two foreign ministers then launched a joint appeal to Iraq to cooperate fully in order to clarify the remaining areas of uncertainty, specifying that this cooperation "should not be passive and resigned, but active."[10] The next day, Villepin's stop in Beijing showed him that Chinese diplomacy was on the same wavelength. True, since the start of the crisis Beijing had appeared to take a more wait-and-see attitude than Russia had. Foreign Minister Tang Jiaxuan even asked Villepin about "press rumors"—no doubt the result of Chirac's phrase in his January 7 speech to the military—about possible French participation in an operation, which was a reminder to the French that nothing would displease the Chinese more than to find themselves alone in opposing Washington. Yet after Villepin reaffirmed that the use of force could be only a last resort, Tang concluded that the French and Chinese positions "were essentially identical."[11]

At this stage, contact between Villepin and Powell was still close and cordial. On January 8, Ambassador Jean-David Levitte went to the State Department for one of his regular conversations with the secretary of state, whom he described as "very warm as usual." Powell repeated that Baghdad had wanted "to fool" the international community with its declaration and that nothing in it led anyone to believe that the Iraqis intended to change their behavior. But Powell stated that the January 27 meeting would not necessarily be "decisive": everything would depend on the inspectors' report, he said, implicitly refuting the idea that Washington might have made its decision in advance. Bush, he insisted, continued to put all his hopes in a peaceful solution. Was Powell pretending? Not necessarily: after all, it was only the following week (as shall be seen) that Bush would inform Powell about his choices. The only shadow on the picture, though, was that Powell balked at participating in the ministerial meeting on the fight against terrorism that Villepin wanted to hold at the Security Council on January 20. There was not enough time, Powell objected, and it might be better to wait until Hans Blix had made his report, which was scheduled on January 27. Why not postpone the ministerial meeting to February? Powell's objections poorly concealed both his personal reservations and his political ones. January 20 was Martin Luther King Jr. Day—a federal holiday, and a day on which, as the first African American secretary of state, he had planned to make public appearances at events commemorating the fallen civil rights leader. Moreover, he wanted to avoid anything that might embarrass the United States at the UN at a time that seemed decisive for the Iraqi issue. The next day, however, Villepin called Powell from Beijing and got Powell's consent for the ministerial meeting. Powell said that he was ready to modify his timetable in order to participate in the Security Council session, and he affirmed his "full agreement" with the approach advanced by Villepin in his letter to the Security Council members about the need for increased support for the inspections. Clearly, there still was trust between Powell and Villepin.[12]

Another sign that the time was not ripe for a rupture was that there still were grounds for agreement between Paris and London. Gérard Errera, the French ambassador to London, noted that British leaders had modified their tone on the issue: previously, they had stressed the need to prepare for war to put pressure on Iraq, but now they insisted that war was not inevitable and that inspections should be continued. The explanation was that the military option had far from unanimous support in public opinion, in the political class, and even within the government. In British public opinion polls, for instance, 58 percent considered that the Iraqi threat was not sufficient to justify a war. There was room, Errera wrote, for "better coordination" between France and Great Britain. He therefore recommended organizing a meeting between Tony Blair and Jacques Chirac, during which the latter would advance the "historic" choice that lay before the two countries: either they would have to resign themselves to American military action whatever the result of the inspections, with their only options being to slow it down or to dress it up in UN legitimacy (an approach that France could not accept); or else they would have to combine their efforts to persuade Bush to give every chance to inspections while putting pressure on Saddam Hussein, without excluding the use of force if the "objective" data justified it. Blair seemed to echo Errera's suggested approach during a January 13 press conference, when he stated that war was not inevitable and the inspectors should have enough time to work.[13]

Meanwhile, French diplomacy was eager to proclaim its support for the inspectors. Since Hans Blix and Mohamed ElBaradei were supposed to go to Baghdad on January 19 and 20 and meet with Blair en route, Jean-Marc de La Sablière recommended to Chirac that he receive them as well—an even more desirable gesture in his eyes, since Bush had already received Blix twice. Chirac agreed, and the meeting was set for January 17. In parallel, the French tried to pressure Iraq to supply new elements on its WMD programs during Blix and ElBaradei's visit to Baghdad or, at least, before their January 27 report to the Security Council. Paris proposed that it would transmit to the Iraqis a list of "priority" issues where they might "make a difference" by furnishing clarifications to the inspectors. Paris offered to ask UNMOVIC in advance whether the list, which had been drawn up on the basis of information possessed by French experts, was on target. This initiative was welcomed by Blix, who thought that it might indeed convince the Iraqis to cooperate more. It was all the more desirable, Blix thought, since Baghdad seemed to believe that military action was unlikely as long as the inspectors did not produce a "smoking gun"—that is, irrefutable proof that Iraq possessed prohibited weapons. This was a risky wager, he said, since the Americans might well consider that a mere lack of active cooperation would be sufficient to qualify as a "material breach." For the rest, Blix said that he agreed with the list of priority issues established in Paris and was ready for a meeting with French experts when he visited the French capital.[14]

Blix having given his approval, André Janier (the French chargé d'affaires in Baghdad) received instructions to approach the Iraqi authorities. He was asked to request from them a degree of cooperation that went beyond allowing the unhindered performance of inspections, and to stress that Blix and ElBaradei's visit was a chance that should be taken at all costs to provide answers to the subjects on the list communicated by Paris. Thus, on January 15, Janier went to see Naji Sabri. Sabri's reaction was "measured," Janier noted, but basically raised little hope: although Sabri said that he appreciated the "principled position of France" to reject a war, he did not understand this "unremitting effort" to exhort Baghdad to "more actively" cooperate. The authorities were in no way hindering the inspections, Sabri said; what more could they do? They were ready to clarify areas of uncertainty, he pleaded, but they could not show inspectors what did not exist. (Sabri cited the case of the mobile laboratories—whose presumed existence, he guessed, resulted from a confusion with vehicles from the ministry of health assigned to verify food quality.) In short, he said fatalistically, Baghdad felt that the inspectors were letting themselves be fooled by American "propaganda." He remarked that Iraq had more interest than anyone else in cooperating, so why not believe it when it affirmed that it no longer possessed WMD? History, of course, would confirm Sabri's statements. For the time being, a skeptical Janier noted simply that his position was "predictable."[15]

At the same time, the French learned more about the intelligence that the Americans had started to transmit to UNMOVIC in accordance with the commitments made by Washington and other capitals. This intelligence mainly came from interceptions and satellite images—cross-checked in the best of cases with the testimony of Iraqi defectors—but it was not precise or current enough to reveal a possible "smoking gun," an irrefutably incriminating element. Yet, the French noted, this lack of evidence did not prevent Washington from continuing to make the case for prosecution. The Americans possessed few intelligence elements for the period since 1998—except for those concerning the presumed purchase of uranium and aluminum tubes—but they were determined to use all the means at their disposal concerning the unresolved issues from before 1998. Furthermore, the French observed, Washington had a diehard approach, systematically putting forward these issues (however imprecisely) even when the inspectors already in 1998 no longer considered the corresponding "areas of uncertainty" as a priority. "If the active cooperation of Iraq must be judged by this standard," the French delegation at the UN noted, "it is unlikely that Baghdad will ever be able to fully cooperate."[16]

Given the fatalism of the Iraqis—who were still suspected of ill will in Western capitals—and the extremism of the Americans, things did not seem auspicious. Still, for the time being a cautious approach carried the day, as confirmed at the January 9 session of the Security Council. On that day, the inspectors gave an informal update on their progress. Blix made a mixed statement: on the one hand, inspections were taking place without hindrance and had led to no incriminating discovery; but on the other hand, progress on the substance remained weak because little to no new information had been provided in the December 8 declaration. Blix's update was followed by John Negroponte's fresh denunciation of Iraqi behavior; Negroponte concluded, as he had on December 19, with the phrase "material breach" and cited the "serious consequences" that would ensue if Baghdad remained obstinate. His British colleague Sir Jeremy Greenstock affirmed London's support for inspections and stressed the need to give the inspectors time to work; nevertheless, he added, he was convinced that Iraq was continuing to conceal prohibited activities. For his part, La Sablière took up the arguments contained in Villepin's letter, insisting on the necessary support for inspections as well as the indispensable "active" cooperation of Baghdad. From this roundtable, the French representative took away the impression that even though Washington lacked a now-improbable "smoking gun," it would continue to make a case against Iraq on the notion that Saddam Hussein had had his chance to be given a clean slate but had not grasped it. The British, he noted, affirmed that war might still be avoided, but did not seem to really believe that it could be—or even truly wish that it would be. Blix and ElBaradei's trip to Baghdad, La Sablière concluded, might well be "the last-chance trip"; it was decidedly "important," he wrote, that the inspectors be able to produce a "more positive" report on January 27.[17]

In mid-January, the Iraq issue was in suspense. There was no doubt about the American determination to fight, but the Resolution 1441 process seemed to be proceeding normally, which made many say that the game was still open.

That was the opinion of Kofi Annan, who could hardly be suspected of naiveté regarding American intentions. La Sablière met with Annan on January 14. Bush, Annan said, had a solid political instinct, and American public opinion remained ambivalent about attacking Iraq, especially without the support of the Security Council. In short, Annan thought that even if Bush's entourage spoke a lot, the president himself was keeping his options open and the scenario that the French were trying to privilege—the pursuit of inspections—was not ruled out. "I found the Secretary-General relatively optimistic," La Sablière wrote, adding that "this should be noticed." Colin Powell did not seem to contradict Annan. On January 15, he sent a courteous response to the letter that Villepin had sent to him and the other Council members the previous week; in it, Powell assured his French colleague that Washington continued to support inspections and thanked him for France's contribution to the process.[18]

"The die seems to be cast"

Yet French leaders did not have to wait long before obtaining confirmation that, for Washington, the game was in fact pretty much over. Behind the apparent indecisiveness that reigned over the Security Council, it was during the first two weeks of 2003 that Bush's decision to intervene militarily against Iraq became in effect irrevocable. Bush, as seen above, may have made the decision in his own mind at the end of 2002, but communicating it to his entourage (which until then had been reduced to guesswork) and especially to the representatives of other countries, as he would do in mid-January, made it irreversible. Although he had not revealed his intentions before the holidays, shortly after New Year's Day Bush became more explicit when talking to Condoleezza Rice, who had come to spend a few days in Crawford. Saying that he was convinced that the inspectors were going to be fooled again, he worried that the regime ultimately might be strengthened. Moreover, the American military deployment could not be maintained for very long. Rice again argued for war: "You have to follow through on your threat," she said. Did her advice weigh upon the presidential decision? Bush seemed determined. "We are not winning. Time is not on our side here," he said, adding, "Probably going to have to, we're going to have to go to war." Rice interpreted this as the expression of Bush's definitive decision. Even if the scenario and the deadlines remained vague, she thought that the president had reached the "point of no return" on Iraq.[19]

Of course, the United States was still far from an actual declaration of war, even if Bush played more than ever on the patriotism of a nation at war. Coming to celebrate the New Year at Fort Hood, Texas, on January 3, Bush stuck to his usual statements. Once again denouncing the Iraqi threat and Saddam Hussein's provocative attitude, he insisted that the use of force could only be a last resort if the Iraqi dictator did not yield. Saddam Hussein might still "give up his provocations" and change his "behavior," he assured his audience, adding a martial note to the great pleasure of the military: "Yet, if force becomes necessary to disarm Iraq [and] to secure our country and to keep the peace, America will act deliberately, America will act decisively, and America will prevail because we've got the finest military in the world." "We are ready," Bush concluded to thunderous applause.[20]

In private, Bush proved much more explicit about his opinions. Speaking to journalists on January 6, he did imply that the game was still open. "Thus far it looks like he hasn't complied," he said. "But he's got time, and we continue to call upon Saddam Hussein to listen to what the world is saying." Two days later, however, Bush confided to a group of Republican leaders, "There's a good chance I'll have to address the nation," adding that "it is clear Saddam Hussein is not disarming." Then, on January 9, General Tommy Franks came to the White House to brief the president on how military preparations were progressing. Franks shared the last-minute difficulties created by Iraq's neighbors, starting with Turkey, which was hesitating to authorize the deployment of American forces on its territory to provide northern access to Iraq. Jordan and Saudi Arabia also were worried about the consequences of their engagement alongside Washington. Still, the CENTCOM chief indicated that, if need be, some 400 aircraft were already deployed in the region and some 15,000 troops were present in Kuwait to conduct an operation on a short timescale. For the rest, Franks said that he would be able to go into action in the next three weeks. "I'd be ready in early February, but I'd really like the 1st of March."[21]

On January 10, Bush was very direct with three Iraqi dissidents whom he met in the presence of Dick Cheney: "I believe Saddam Hussein is a threat to America and to the neighborhood. . . . We will remove him from power." One of the visitors stated, "People [in Iraq] will greet troops with flowers and sweets." Bush asked, "How do you know?" All three said that the information came from people on the ground. The conversation then turned to what would happen "afterward." The exchange clearly reveals Bush's underestimation of the difficulties to come: "Your job is to gather the people who want to help and rally their hearts and souls. My job is to rally the world and win the war." He concluded, "Maybe one year from now, we will be toasting victory and talking about the transition to freedom."[22]

It was also in the first half of January that Donald Rumsfeld understood that Bush had made a decision. On January 11, Rumsfeld had ordered the deployment of 35,000 additional troops to the region. Bush asked him when the point of no return would be reached—in other words, when the United States would be too engaged to be able to pull back. Rumsfeld answered that the point would come when Washington asked allies in the region, starting with Saudi Arabia, to commit to supporting the operation and hence taking risks; this moment was approaching rapidly, he stressed. Cheney shared this view: he thought it was now indispensable to involve the principal countries concerned, foremost Saudi Arabia. Given the Saudis' vulnerability—Osama bin Laden had long denounced Saudi Arabia's submission to the United States and other "infidels"—there was a great risk that this crucial ally might be gravely destabilized if Washington, after having enrolled it in a crusade against Saddam Hussein, did not follow through to the end. Thus on January 11, in the presence of Rumsfeld and General Richard Myers, chairman of the Joint Chiefs of Staff, Cheney received the Saudi ambassador to Washington, Prince Bandar bin Sultan. The ambassador was an old acquaintance of Cheney's. The purpose of the meeting was to inform Bandar about the US war plans and to convince Riyadh to grant American forces permission to operate from Saudi territory. In return, Cheney assured him, Saddam Hussein's regime would not survive. Cheney did not mince words: "Once we start, Saddam is toast," he told Bandar. Then Cheney asked Bush to personally receive Bandar to pass a message to Crown Prince Abdullah. The meeting took place on the morning of Monday, January 13. "People are not going to shed tears over Saddam Hussein, but if he's attacked one more time by America and he survives, he will be larger than life," warned Bandar, "and everybody will follow his word." Bush's response was laconic. "You got the briefing from Dick, Rummy [Rumsfeld], and General Myers?" he asked, adding: "That is the message that I want you to carry for me to the crown prince."[23]

On the same day, Bush, in a tête-à-tête in the Oval Office, informed Powell of his decision. "I really think I'm going to have to do this," he declared. "You're sure?" Powell asked, and summarized the arguments he had put forward five months earlier, including his famous "Pottery Barn rule." "You understand the consequences?" he insisted, reiterating the analysis he had been stressing for months, namely that the United States would have to take charge of the country and that the ripple effect in the Middle East and the world could not be predicted. "You know that you're going to be owning this place?" But Bush appeared very determined, making Powell understand that the object of the meeting was to inform him of his resolution, and not to discuss it. For Powell, the possibility of resigning did not arise; for this military soul, such a decision would be a gesture of unimaginable disloyalty. So when Bush asked him, "Are you with me on this?" Powell did not hesitate: "Yes, sir, I will support you. I'm with you, Mr. President."[24]

Yet in Powell's eyes, Bush had not communicated a *formal* decision to enter into war, but rather his conviction that a conflict was inevitable. Powell considered that the diplomatic phase was not at an end: Bush, after all, had not contradicted him when he had indicated during the meeting that he would "continue to see if it were possible to find a diplomatic solution." "The president had come to a conclusion . . . but he didn't say in the same breath, 'And don't try to keep me from doing it,'" he later confided. Powell, in other words, did not leave the Oval Office with the feeling that the affair was definitively settled, and so he did not feel that pursuing the diplomatic avenue would be disloyal. The failure of inspections at this stage was not a foregone conclusion. The situation, Powell thought, had not radically changed since the inspections had resumed, and thus it was still possible to avoid war, at least if Saddam Hussein caved in. As a result, it would be necessary to keep the pressure on him, which required maintaining the unity of the Security Council.[25]

Later events would show Powell's reasoning to be illusory. Yet Bush's conversation with him on January 13 once more illustrated the dysfunctional character of the decision-making process inside the administration as well as the ambivalent nature of Powell's role. At no moment—except when Bush commenced the military action on March 19—was a formal decision taken in favor of war. As for Powell, in the end he never spoke out plainly against a war whose opportunity and timing (though not its very principle) he contested, while at the same time hoping that the UN path—which he was determined to follow for as long as possible—ultimately would enable the United States to avoid it.

That same Monday, January 13, Maurice Gourdault-Montagne—who had replaced Jean-Marc de La Sablière as Chirac's diplomatic adviser the previous month—came to Washington for a series of meetings. His key meeting on that day was with his opposite number, Condoleezza Rice. By a chance of the calendar, the French—even before the United States's closest allies, including the British and the Spanish—would thus be the first to learn of Bush's intentions. Chirac had dispatched Gourdault-Montagne to Washington primarily to remind the Americans of the French position, as he had expounded it during his New Year's greetings to the diplomatic corps a few days earlier. But Gourdault-Montagne's visit also aimed to get a more precise idea of the White House's plans: knowing that the United States was pursuing its military preparations against all odds, Chirac had "scarcely any more doubt about American intentions," he later wrote, but he "wanted to have a clear mind about it."[26]

Gourdault-Montagne, accompanied by Levitte, initially was welcomed to lunch by Rice. The atmosphere was courteous—Rice welcomed her visitors with friendly words about the French president—but cold. Chirac's adviser recalled the French position for her, and defended its constancy. The international community, he said, should continue to stick to the framework of Resolution 1441. France, he added, would participate in a military intervention—if the president of the Republic so decided—only after the Security Council reached an explicit decision on the basis of a reasoned report by the inspectors. This point had not yet been reached, he warned, and one should avoid giving the impression that the failure of the process was a foregone conclusion—an allusion to the intensifying American military buildup. Hence, Gourdault-Montagne stressed, Paris and Washington needed to maintain a "frank" dialogue as the January 27th deadline approached, but also continue it beyond that—a way of reminding Rice that, for Paris, inspections should not be a priori limited in time. France, Gourdault-Montagne reiterated, could not take a decision based on simple "suspicions" or "hypotheses."[27]

Gourdault-Montagne quickly understood that he was up against a brick wall. Although she remained perfectly calm and in control of herself, "Condi" nevertheless forged ahead. She started with a stinging indictment of Iraq in the disarmament issue, following the familiar circular reasoning that prevailed in the US administration. Iraq was not playing the game, Rice said, calling the December 8 declaration a "joke"; "Saddam Hussein is fooling the world" and "hiding his weapons," she declared. Certainly, she argued, utilizing Blix's distinction, Saddam Hussein was cooperating in form, but he was *not* cooperating in substance, as he clearly hoped that the current situation, characterized by "formally correct but unfruitful" inspections, would last "indefinitely." Worse, she stated, "not only was he not cooperating actively, but he had "engaged in a policy of active non-cooperation." As a result, she went on, the January 27 meeting would be important, even though it would not be the "day of decision." If, as was probable, the Blix report were not more substantial than the one presented on January 9, then this would open a "final phase" that would last "a certain time." Certainly, Rice conceded, one should not expect a dramatic casus belli: it was unlikely that a "smoking gun" would be discovered between now and then, since Saddam Hussein had carefully dissimulated his WMD stocks—this, of course, showed Rice's circular reasoning—and he would do anything to avoid a provocation. But for Washington, she concluded, the combination of "lies and omissions" contained in the declaration and of Baghdad's persistent refusal to engage in "active" cooperation would suffice to declare a "material breach." Rice could not have better summarized the prosecution mounted by the Bush administration.

Gourdault-Montagne offered France's evidently very different reading of Resolution 1441 and the need to stick to it—in vain, for Rice did not budge. True, she declared that "President Bush had not yet taken his decision," holding to the line that had been proclaimed for almost one year—a disingenuous statement, in retrospect, since by then she was perfectly aware of the presidential intentions. Yet Rice observed that "time is now short," because US credibility was at stake: "Everybody knows that Saddam Hussein tricks and dissimulates. If the inspectors don't find anything and we do not act," she explained, the countries of the Middle East and the whole world "will recognize our weakness." "We don't want to renew the experience of the eleven years that have passed since the first Gulf War," she emphasized; "the American people will not accept it." It would be difficult to be clearer.

Chirac's emissary then advanced the objections that the French president had raised for months with his American counterpart. Arab leaders, Gourdault-Montagne argued, feared a war that would only destabilize the region and feed not only terrorism but also dissent against their regimes. Rice swept away this objection. "Basically," she said, "the Arab leaders are saying to us: we do not want this war, but they add: 'if you have to go there, then go quickly.'" "No doubt," she went on with a certain cynicism, " there would be demonstrations that these same leaders will tolerate, unless they become too threatening, in which case they will be banned, brutally repressed, and calm will come back as in the past." Rice seemed to confirm the notion that the administration was trying, via a war against Iraq, to provoke a reordering of the Middle East: "After the war, the situation in the region will be more stable. Conversely, things would not go better . . . if we did nothing in the course of the coming years. Recruitment by Al Qaida is already occurring in any case." Washington, she pointed out, "sincerely" wanted the Security Council to be able to "accompany" the United States. A Franco-American entente would be "decisive," she concluded: "Russia and China will follow. Even our British friends need the Security Council to take a position, but it is France that more than any other country can help this decision."

After this tirade, it would have been difficult for Gourdault-Montagne and Levitte not to realize that the die was cast. Nevertheless, the former asked Rice under what conditions a war could still be avoided. Rice could not have been clearer: "The departure of Saddam Hussein and the whole Ba'athist clique, followed by the establishment of a more democratic government. . . . There has to be regime change," she stressed, thereby confirming that this had been Washington's objective from the start. By the end of the conversation, Rice and Gourdault-Montagne could but measure the extent of their divergences while agreeing that contact in the near future between the two presidents was desirable. Meanwhile, Rice offered to call Gourdault-Montagne in the coming days to learn of Chirac's reaction to their conversation.[28]

Gourdault-Montagne's other meetings in Washington—he met Paul Wolfowitz, Richard Armitage, Richard Haass, and Cheney's assistant national security advisor Eric Edelman—merely confirmed what he had heard at the White House. North Korea was the only other topic addressed in these meetings. Three days previously, Pyongyang had announced its withdrawal from the Nuclear Non-Proliferation Treaty, opening up a new crisis. Washington suspected that North Korea had resumed its nuclear military program, and Pyongyang had already broken with the IAEA in December. This was an embarrassing coincidence for Washington, since the Americans had to justify a different approach—in essence, a nonmilitary one—in the North Korean case, where from a nuclear standpoint the danger potentially was more serious than in Iraq. Yet this apparent incongruity did not prevent Wolfowitz from explaining that the Iraqi threat was in fact more serious; unlike Saddam Hussein, Kim Jong-Il was "in his box," he said. The Pentagon's second-in-command stressed that there was no available military solution for North Korea—in other words, that it was inconceivable to invade that country. By contrast, this admission confirmed, at least implicitly, that the Bush administration's choice of Iraq as a target was indeed encouraged by Iraq's military weakness.[29]

While the atmosphere remained courteous, Wolfowitz adopted a particularly harsh tone when it came to Iraq, accusing Paris of giving too much importance to the diplomatic "game" and not enough to the "facts." "This isn't bridge or canasta," he said. Everybody in France, as in the United States, he stressed, knew that Iraq was maintaining WMD programs and that Saddam Hussein continued to dissimulate. "We know that you know," he declared, pointing his finger at Gourdault-Montagne. The inspectors' characterization of the situation was "secondary," he continued, since "what Hans Blix will or won't say has nothing to do with facts." Then Wolfowitz shifted to a contemptuous tone: how could France, he asked, put its foreign policy in the hands of a Swedish diplomat who had at his disposal "fewer men than the chief of police in a French provincial town?" The French, he continued, were reading Resolution 1441 in an unacceptable way when they implied that Saddam Hussein might be exonerated in the absence of incriminating evidence; the resolution foresaw the opposite, namely, that Iraq should declare its WMD and renounce them. It was futile for Gourdault-Montagne to reply that this presentation distorted the French position, for Wolfowitz did not budge: it was not possible to continue wandering around the country in search of the "smoking gun" for another eleven years, he retorted. This line of reasoning was taken up more courteously by Eric Edelman, for whom conducting inspections in an uncooperative country was an "almost impossible" task; he pointed out the contrasting case of countries like South Africa that had chosen to disarm actively. Richard Haass, in turn, remarked that a possible incriminating discovery—which, given the Iraqi attitude, could only happen by chance—could not (as Paris suggested) be interpreted as a sign that inspections could continue. On the contrary, he said, it would confirm that Iraq had lied to the international community. In short, it would be a casus belli.[30]

Returning to Paris, Gourdault-Montagne informed Chirac of the Americans' state of mind. "The die seems to be cast," Chirac would later write. This was not a sudden realization, however. Although French leaders had hoped that adoption of Resolution 1441 would keep the game open, in the weeks following the handover of the Iraqi declaration on December 8 they had started to feel that Washington increasingly was moving toward war. For French leaders—starting with Chirac, who early on had been convinced that the United States wanted to intervene—Gourdault-Montagne's visit to Washington only confirmed their suspicions. Yet Paris remained determined to maintain the line it had adopted at the start of the year, and continue the UN procedure as per Resolution 1441. But was it still a matter of trying to avoid war despite American determination? Or of preventing the United States from making use of the UN in order to provide cover for a unilateral adventure, thereby opposing Washington in the name of principles? Without being formulated in these terms, it was around the middle of January 2003 that a tipping point came between these two objectives, with the latter now clearly prevailing in French policy. Henceforth a clash became inevitable, as illustrated a week after Gourdault-Montagne's visit, during the Security

Council's January 20 meeting on the fight against terror, which had been summoned at Villepin's initiative.[31]

An "ambush"?

In mid-January 2003, the question of the duration of inspections became central. As a consequence of Bush's decision to accelerate the timetable, the Americans and British now let it be known that they would not accept indefinite extensions to the inspections process. A week before, Bush had said that Saddam Hussein still had time to comply, but on January 14 (the day after Gourdault-Montagne's visit) he declared to the press that "time is running out on Saddam Hussein." The same day in New York, Blix was declaring his intention—in line with Resolution 1284, which still governed UNMOVIC activity—to present at the end of March a disarmament work program that included the list of "key tasks" that Iraq should accomplish. But the American and British representatives warned him there was no question of applying the timeline from Resolution 1284, which in their eyes was far too protracted. Washington's and London's change of footing was abrupt; it confirmed that from now on, everything was based on the military timeline being prepared. Resolution 1284 had foreseen that satisfactory Iraqi cooperation and Baghdad's accomplishment of the "key tasks" might lead to the lifting of sanctions, though long-term disarmament monitoring would be maintained. But now the logic of Resolution 1284, especially its calendar, was in contradiction with the possible military timeline, since it would indefinitely postpone the ability to establish Iraq's possible failures; in addition, there was the risk that the inspectors, given time, might actually conclude that the Iraqi WMD were nonexistent—hence Washington's and London's rejection of the procedure and calendar of Resolution 1284.[32]

Faced with this contentious issue, the French (supported by the Russians and Chinese) stressed that Resolution 1441—which did not spell out a final deadline—did not cancel out Resolution 1284. Accepting the American view on this point, they protested, would amount to recognizing that the logic of resorting to force would carry the day, because the inspectors would not have enough time to carry out their work. What was at stake, the French delegation noted, was whether the Security Council would commit after the 27th to a logic of war.[33] The French therefore wanted to encourage Blix to apply the calendar that he had announced on January 14, at least as long as the council did not decide otherwise. Blix's scheduled visit to Paris on January 17, in the company of ElBaradei, provided an occasion to encourage him in this direction. The Élysée wanted to pass along a three-part message of unequivocal support. First, France trusted in the "professionalism and impartiality" of UNMOVIC and the IAEA, and Paris was ready to help both organizations unreservedly by putting at their disposal human and material resources and sharing information with them. Second, the French believed that the presence of inspectors guaranteed that Iraq could no longer develop, produce, or deploy WMD. Third, they saw the Iraqi case as having exemplary value for present and future proliferation crises. As for the timeline, it should be an extended one, since the inspections had just finished their buildup. In short, the French believed, Blix and ElBaradei had to be given sufficient leeway to work without pressure or time constraints.[34]

On January 17, Chirac welcomed Blix and ElBaradei to Paris. From the outset of their meeting, he stressed that he wished to express to them his "total" confidence and to hear their assessment of the situation. Then he listened to their summary of how inspections were proceeding: the form of the inspections process had been satisfactory up to now, they said, though it was more mixed in terms of Iraq's cooperation on substance. Blix said that the situation was "particularly tense," emphasizing that UNMOVIC and the IAEA needed time to work. It was then Chirac's turn to speak. France, he said at the outset, had no "operational element" (i.e., direct intelligence) on any "localization" of WMD production or storage sites in Iraq; as for the United States, he believed that they "very probably" held no precise information. In passing, he remarked that intelligence services had a tendency to "intoxicate" each other—a remark that subsequently would prove accurate. (Blix would later write that during the meeting, Chirac had said that "personally, he did not believe that Iraq had any weapons of mass destruction.") The two visitors noted Chirac's statements with interest, since they seemed to contrast with the dominant tone of the international intelligence services—including the French services, whose representatives had confided in them that it was "conceivable" that "relatively few weapons of mass destruction were retained" in Iraq, though there was "no evidence" of this. Challenging American analyses, Chirac stressed again that the inspections had proved their efficacy from 1991 to 1998 and that only "missteps," which Paris had "deeply regretted" at the time, had led to their interruption. Chirac delivered his deeper thoughts about the American plans. Apart from the "heavy" human consequences, a conflict would have a "disastrous" political fallout by reinforcing anti-Western feelings, in particular in the Arab-Muslim world. Nobody, he went on, could understand why the Israeli-Palestinian conflict was being allowed to "rot"; a war would have an enormous economic impact and financial cost, while the essential needs of the developing world were far from being satisfied and development aid was diminishing. France, he concluded, was not disposed to let itself be dragged without a valid reason into a war that only the Security Council should decide upon on the basis of the inspectors' report. One had to try everything, Chirac said, to persuade Saddam Hussein that unless he quickly gave "clear" signs of his desire to cooperate, war would become inevitable and he would then be "swept out." The problem, he added—a remark that also would prove just as pertinent—was that the Iraqi dictator was "locked up in an intellectual bunker" and his entourage did not dare to tell him the truth.[35]

The meeting concluded with a press conference, during which Chirac issued a warning: if a country wanted to decide unilaterally on war, he said, "it would put itself purely and simply in contravention of international law." Blix and ElBaradei's visit to the Élysée had an impact on both chief inspectors. ElBaradei found Chirac "astonishingly candid" and said that it was "refreshing" to hear a statesman of his stature express himself in total frankness and in sympathy with the IAEA's position. Blix—who later recognized that he had not come to the meeting "with any surplus of admiration" for the French president—left the Élysée with the feeling that Chirac's attitude was less the result of his desire to satisfy a public opinion that was hostile to the war, and more the result of his conviction that Iraq simply did not represent a threat of a nature to justify an intervention.[36]

On January 19, Dominique de Villepin flew to New York to preside over the Security Council session on terrorism he had called for. Villepin, as seen above, had taken this initiative at the start of the month with a view to lowering pressure on the Iraqi issue by going back to "fundamentals." But in the interval, the exercise had become politically risky. The debate, his advisers warned him, might swerve to Iraq and so create ripple effects. Villepin swept this argument aside by stressing that the speech he had prepared would not touch on the subject of Iraq. Events would nevertheless confirm the fears in the French foreign minister's entourage and lead to the first real clash between France and the United States.

As soon as he arrived in New York on the evening of the 19th, Villepin met Colin Powell for a bilateral conversation in the American delegation's suite on the top floor of the Waldorf-Astoria. After an exchange about North Korea, Iraq came up. "Bush has not made a decision," Powell said, adding that he nevertheless remained "very suspicious" about the Iraqis. Less than a week after Maurice Gourdault-Montagne's Washington visit, Villepin and his associates were not duped by this hollow-sounding formula. In response, Villepin launched into a long tirade based on the now well-known French arguments. The inspections should be conducted thoroughly, he stressed, since the danger of Iraqi WMD remained confined as long as the inspections were pursued. Nothing justified resorting to force: the danger of Iraqi proliferation should not be underestimated, but there were other situations—including North Korea, Iran, Pakistan, and Libya—that also raised serious problems, and all these situations should be treated as a whole. A military intervention, Villepin concluded, would be not only illegitimate but also ineffective. It would have "incalculable consequences on the unity of Iraq and the stability of the region," would dig a chasm "between our peoples and our cultures," and would encourage terrorism. After listening to Villepin with some signs of impatience, Powell spoke up. "Don't underestimate our determination, Dominique," he repeated twice, adding that American patience was not "inexhaustible." After the meeting—which had been somewhat tense, despite the good relations that until then had prevailed between the two men—the French delegation went to a neighborhood steakhouse for a "debriefing," and the participants concluded that Powell's statements confirmed those that Condoleezza Rice had made to Gourdault-Montagne the previous week. "I know Condi," said Jean-Marc de La Sablière, "she must have bombarded Maurice [Gourdault-Montagne]: 'You want assurances? The answer is no. More time? No. More inspections? No!'"[37]

The meeting between Villepin and Powell was bound to have an effect on the events of the following day, January 20. The Security Council meeting itself was not affected. During the meeting, German foreign minister Joschka Fischer once again voiced his country's opposition to war, which led to a skirmish with Powell and Jack Straw, but in his own remarks Villepin kept his pledge to Powell and did not depart from the issue of terrorism. At the press conference he gave afterward, though, he raised the Iraqi issue squarely, and thus provoked the "scandal." True, Villepin's introductory statement to the press did not deviate from his previous line: he stressed the necessity of pursuing inspections and of showing an indispensable firmness toward Iraq in order to make Baghdad cooperate "actively" and furnish a "complete and global" picture of its WMD. The statement nevertheless included an explicit condemnation of Washington's plans: "If war is the only way to resolve the problem, we are immediately entering an impasse," he stated, condemning in advance any unilateral intervention as "a victory for the law of the strongest" and an "attack against the primacy of international law and morality." Yet in his response to questions from the American press—which was rather aggressive about the French, who were regarded (as one journalist put it) as "inconsistent"—Villepin crossed a line. When asked, "Is France prepared to use its veto if convinced that Iraq is not manifestly violating its obligations?," he replied, "Nothing justifies envisaging military action." He added that France "will assume all its responsibilities," and declared, "You may believe me that when it comes to respecting principles, we will go to the end."[38]

The effect was immediate. Although the threat of a French veto was merely implicit, the American media summarized Villepin's statement by announcing that Paris was ready to block a possible resolution authorizing the use of force. The *Washington Post* went further by declaring that Villepin had in effect chosen to "ambush" Powell: the former allegedly had taken the initiative of the Security Council meeting on terrorism and convinced the latter to take part in it—despite the hawks' negative opinion and a busy personal agenda on this Martin Luther King Day—with the sole objective of placing himself in the limelight to criticize American policy in a most disloyal manner. Even today, this interpretation remains widespread on the American side, where it is averred that on that day Villepin lost his only "ally" in the administration. (Adding insult to injury, according to this narrative, Villepin had made Powell wait three-quarters of an hour—the time it took to hold his press conference at the UN headquarters—before joining him for the luncheon that La Sablière had offered to the Security Council members.)[39]

Yet the idea of an "ambush" does not stand up to scrutiny. Granted, in scheduling the meeting French diplomacy had aimed to retake the initiative, but Villepin's diatribe was by no means premeditated. In fact, it was quite the opposite, since the initial goal of the meeting was to take the pressure off the Iraqi issue by "banalizing" it in relation to other topics, starting with terrorism. Clearly, though, Villepin's conversation with Powell the previous evening, because it confirmed that the game was over in Washington, had led him to react on the spot during the press conference, thereby departing from his original "script." Villepin was nevertheless eager to call Powell upon his return to Paris the next day to explain himself and try to pick up the pieces. He said that he was "surprised" that the incident seemed to have been blown out of proportion, and defended himself against the charge of having tried to "trap" Powell. He advanced the necessary "frankness" in a period that was going to be "difficult." Powell responded in kind, saying that he was equally astonished by all this noise—which he attributed to the media—and acknowledging that he himself had contributed to it by responding to Fischer during the session in order to shield himself from the hawks' criticism. He later confided that he was convinced that the White House had indeed blown the episode out of proportion in the press, framing it along the lines that "poor Powell went up there and we warned him not to and he got skunked by the French."[40]

Some in Paris, including at the Quai d'Orsay, nevertheless thought this incident was a faux pas on Villepin's part. True, the notion that Villepin might that day have "lost" Powell is not credible in retrospect: the latter already had been marginalized within the administration, and he simply was no longer in a position to prevent the war even if he had wanted to. Yet by implicitly suggesting for the first time in public the possibility of a French veto over a resolution authorizing the use of force, Villepin had played into the hawks' hands. The hawks now found it easy to denounce the impasse in the UN route and to discredit Powell—and, of course, the French, who again became a convenient target. "There always comes a moment when things have to be said," Villepin later said, justifying his response at the press conference. "Powell had laid down America's cards," Le Maire later summarized, and Villepin "had laid down France's cards." Still, in the poker bluffing game that the Iraqi affair had become at the UN, on January 20 Villepin perhaps had revealed his hand a little early: the risk was now that France appeared to be responsible for the rupture. Be that as it may, the confrontation was now inevitable, as subsequent episodes would confirm.[41]

Two days later, there was a further escalation. January 22 saw the long-planned anniversary celebration of the Élysée Treaty, signed in 1963 by Charles de Gaulle and Konrad Adenauer to seal the reconciliation between France and Germany and to make their relationship the cornerstone of European construction. This celebration gave rise to the first joint session of the French Assemblée Nationale and the German Bundestag in Versailles, the symbolic site of a Franco-German enmity that had been transcended in favor of a common destiny in the service of European unification. For Paris and Berlin, this was an ideal occasion to dramatize their entente over the Iraq crisis, and Chirac and Gerhard Schröder did not hesitate to seize the occasion—even if, for the former, this meant amplifying the effect of Villepin's declarations two days previously. The French president now seemed to be aligning with the German chancellor, who had expressed his opposition to a military "adventure" in Iraq ever since the summer of 2002—and consequently had paid a heavy price in German-American relations, which since then had been glacial.

At their joint press conference at Versailles, Chirac and Schröder imme-diately were questioned about Iraq. Were Paris and Berlin ready to defend a common position at the Security Council—where Germany had been sit-ting as a nonpermanent member since January 1—in the face of American bellicosity? "Germany and France have the same judgment about this crisis," Chirac replied. "War is always the worst solution," he said, thus seeming to adopt a pacifist approach which until then he had rejected, and he added that "it is on the basis of this common position" that Paris and Berlin would coordinate with each other at the Security Council. During a joint television interview that evening, Chirac went even further: when Schröder restated that Germany could not approve of or participate in a war against Iraq, Chirac declared, "There you are, that is our joint policy." By approving his partner's statement, Chirac recognized that France would not participate in an intervention, and even opposed its authors' desire to obtain legitimacy for it. Chirac thus broke with the line he had adopted since the summer, namely to not exclude the possibility of French participation in military action if the Security Council decided to sanction it. Previously, this line had dis-tinguished the French position from the German one, since Schröder had excluded such a possibility all along, even if it were based on a new resolu-tion. Chirac's position was confirmed the next day by Villepin, who appeared with Joschka Fischer in Berlin in a joint session of the foreign affairs commit-tees of the Assemblée Nationale and the Bundestag during the celebrations occurring in the German capital. We share a "world view" that is "different" from that of the United States, Villepin said; recourse to force might appear to the Americans as a solution, he added, but for the French and Germans it was "the start of an unstable world."[42]

In retrospect, the Franco-German rapprochement over Iraq, sealed by Chirac and Schröder on January 22, is not a surprise. During their conversa-tion at the beginning of September in Hanover, they had shared the same hostility to American plans. Of course, until January 22, Chirac—unlike Schröder—had not officially excluded a possible French participation in an intervention, but the situation had changed. Whereas at the beginning of the month the French still did not dismiss in principle their possible participation in a military operation, by mid-January they had come round to excluding this hypothesis in light of the American determination to go to war despite the progress on inspections. Coming two days after Villepin's declarations in New York, the Franco-German declarations during the anniversary of the Élysée Treaty highlighted how the French position had evolved in reaction to its confirmation of Washington's plans. In addition, Germany, having started its two-year term as nonpermanent Security Council member, was now in a position that allowed the two nations to coordinate. Thus, the Franco-German rapprochement was not—as some, especially in London and Washington, said at the time—the result of a quid pro quo in which Paris abandoned its "balanced" position on Iraq and rallied to the German point of view in exchange for concessions from Berlin on Europe-specific issues such as the Common Agricultural Policy or the nascent European constitutional treaty. (In fact, at that juncture the Franco-German accord was not yet ironclad. Schröder knew that he had Chirac's commitment to remain shoulder-to-shoulder, but German diplomats—Fischer first and foremost—feared that Germany might find itself isolated if France were ever to cave in; Fischer in particular observed that Chirac, despite Villepin's declarations, had not publicly and explicitly committed to oppose a possible resolution when the time came.)[43]

The Franco-German declarations—coming on top of the alleged "ambush" episode two days before—nevertheless had a resounding impact in Washington. The American press exploded with recrimination. "We are being reproached with aligning ourselves with Germany, with encouraging Saddam Hussein not to play the game, inciting American opinion to worry about the war, and weakening Powell," the French embassy reported. Meanwhile, the hawks in the administration had a whale of a time. On the very day of the Versailles festivities, Donald Rumsfeld pronounced a phrase that would remain in memories: asked by reporters about the Franco-German declarations and the attitude of the Europeans, he replied: "You're thinking of Europe as Germany and France. I don't. I think that's Old Europe." Rumsfeld's declaration unleashed an outcry in Paris and Berlin. Michèle Alliot-Marie, the French minister of defense, did not mince words: "We are no longer in prehistoric times where the one with the biggest club tried to knock out the other to steal his haunch of mammoth," she shot back.[44]

This time, the confrontation was out in the open. "Over the past forty-eight hours, the crisis has taken a familiar turn: France and Germany have become the spearhead of mobilization against American policy," wrote Gilles Andréani, the director of the Quai d'Orsay's policy planning staff. He warned: "The debate risks becoming a predominantly Franco-American one because we are more visible than the Germans on this subject, and also because the American perception is that we have left our position of balance between the United States and Germany to embody an opposition to the war that is even more active than Germany's."[45] In barely a few days, the Iraq crisis had become not merely a Franco-American (and German-American) crisis, but also a transatlantic and intra-European one.

Sixteen Words

French and German opposition, even though it was now in the open, did not hinder American determination. "The United States is moving toward war," Jean-David Levitte summarized the day after the Versailles celebrations. The Bush administration, he reported based on meetings at the White House and the State Department, was more determined than ever to feed the prosecuting case against Iraq, aiming at both American public opinion (which remained hesitant, Levitte noted) and the international community (where the United States found itself more alone than they thought, he stressed).[46] In fact, the White House would use the two important events at end of January—the inspectors' report on the 27th and Bush's State of the Union address on the 28th—for this purpose. Hans Blix, as will be seen, would contribute to this case, no doubt against his will but to the great regret of French diplomats.

Back from Baghdad, Blix had set out to prepare the update that he would give to the Security Council two months after the resumption of inspections, as Mohamed ElBaradei was to do on his side. The session was greatly anticipated: the Americans had hinted that the update might be the opportunity to end the game, especially if they concluded that Baghdad's cooperation was inadequate. The stakes as the meeting approached were clear, Blix would later write: had inspections produced results, or was war inevitable? The meeting was held in an electric atmosphere: the hall of the Security Council was full to bursting and a forest of cameras and microphones covered the horseshoe-shaped table.[47]

The meeting took place at a decisive moment. To be sure, inspections had unfolded without any notable incident in terms of access or discoveries. (In mid-January, the inspectors had found a handful of empty chemical warheads in a depot, and at a scientist's home they had acquired some documentation on uranium enrichment that had no new information.) Yet two months after the resumption of inspections, Blix judged that the situation was not satisfactory. The Iraqis were dragging their heels on agreeing with the inspectors on two particular points. They were delaying agreement on the ways of using the U-2 observation aircraft, as Baghdad was trying to obtain the end of bombing in the no-fly zones as a quid pro quo for such an agreement. They also were stalling on allowing the inspectors to interview Iraqi scientists, as desired by UNSCOM; the inspectors believed that the regime was trying to prevent this by putting pressure on the scientists. In short, Baghdad still seemed tempted to procrastinate. Although the two chief inspectors' visit to Baghdad (their first since the resumption of inspections) had helped resolve some practical questions, such as the limitation of the number of Iraqi "minders" accompanying the inspections, the U-2 and interview issues remained in suspense. In addition, the visit had hardly produced any progress on substance, since Baghdad had not communicated new documents or elements that would provide answers to the inspectors' questions. On his return to New York, Blix judged the overall results "a mixed bag," signaling that the tone of his report on the 27th would be nuanced at the least. The French UN delegation, which had procured a confidential draft version of the text, was concerned. The draft report contained phrasing that could have a devastating effect, such as the notion that Iraq would be "in grave danger of missing the opportunity" granted to it to disarm. The delegation thought that this statement was far from the sort of "factual" tone that was appropriate in such a report: clearly, the French feared that Washington would want to use Blix's statements to justify their decision to invade.[48]

That was exactly what happened. Blix's report notwithstanding, ElBaradei's update on the 27th was clearly positive. The IAEA director-general stressed that in two months of inspections, no prohibited nuclear activity had been found. The IAEA, he noted, had progressed on some specific questions, such as the aluminum tubes. Although the investigation into the tubes was ongoing, the current information tended to show that Baghdad's assertion (that these tubes were designed for missile propulsion) was credible and that they could not be used as part of a nuclear centrifuge unless they were modified. As for Baghdad's alleged efforts to import uranium, ElBaradei indicated that the IAEA did not have enough information to rule on this subject, and so he invited nations to communicate to him whatever information they possessed. ElBaradei asked the Security Council to "continue its unified and unequivocal support for the inspection process." He did warn that Iraq should move from "passive" to "active" cooperation, but he also asserted that if that were the case, then the IAEA might in the coming months be able to "provide credible assurance that Iraq has no nuclear weapons program."[49]

Blix's statement, by contrast, was much less encouraging. Ultimately, the idea that Baghdad was "missing the opportunity" did not figure in his report. Blix recalled the vicissitudes of disarmament since 1991 and recognized that despite the "hide-and-seek" game in which Iraq had indulged for years, the inspections had produced "considerable" results until 1998. But he then issued a sentence that would have a major impact in the coming weeks: "Iraq appears not to have come to a genuine acceptance—not even today—of the disarmament which was demanded of it." Blix acknowledged that Baghdad had played the game in terms of "process" and "access," but he deplored the fact that Iraq basically still did not cooperate actively and reiterated that the Iraqi declaration did not permit the inspectors to resolve issues that had been pending since 1998. In the chemical domain, there were "indications" that Iraq might have produced VX that was purer and in greater quantity than Baghdad had admitted and, contrary to its admissions, it could have militarized the chemical. Moreover, 6,500 chemical bombs were unaccounted for, and recently a few chemical rocket warheads had been discovered. In the biological domain, there were "strong indications" that Iraq might have produced more anthrax than it had recognized and might have kept a certain quantity of it; it also had not declared imports of bacterial growth media. As for ballistic weapons, Blix noted the remaining uncertainties about whether Baghdad had kept some Scud missiles after the 1991 Gulf War and about the possibly illegal nature of activities conducted in this domain since 1998. Supplementary technical investigations would have to be performed before drawing definitive conclusions; for instance, the Al-Samoud missile was said to have been tested at a 183-kilometer range, and its diameter had been augmented beyond the specifications imposed by UNSCOM. Overall, Blix repeated that UNMOVIC did not assume Iraq's guilt or innocence, but the tone of his statement, as the French delegation remarked, tended to suggest a deliberate will to dissimulate. To the disappointment of the French delegation, Blix (unlike ElBaradei) also refrained from asking for more time for inspections, and he did not emphasize (as he had done on January 9) the inherent reassurance that continuing the inspections provided.[50]

Blix's declarations immediately created a stir. A few minutes after the end of the session (which he had chaired), Jean-Marc de La Sablière met Blix and ElBaradei in an adjoining room. The two chief inspectors were manifestly in the middle of a heated exchange that confirmed their divergences in substance as well as in form. La Sablière pointed out to Blix that their statements would have an important impact, since the Americans, who had decided in any case to go to war, would make use of everything the inspectors might say. ElBaradei, who evidently had just reproached Blix along similar lines, upped the stakes by warning him about the "gravity" of the moment; he said that he was convinced that Iraq no longer represented a serious threat and wondered if a war should really be waged over "residual" capacities. Blix responded that one could indeed wonder, while adding that he could not certify that Iraq did not possess significant biological weapon capacities. La Sablière concluded from all this that Blix, despite the warnings that he and others had issued before the session, had not completely understood the impact of his presentation. Blix himself would confirm this later, acknowledging that he had not anticipated that the hawks would be "delighted" at the "rather harsh" tone of the update on inspections as he had presented it.[51]

How can we explain what, for the opponents of military intervention, was undoubtedly a faux pas on Blix's part? The main factor, arguably, was the rigorous approach that Blix had wanted to implement ever since the inspection process had resumed in autumn 2002. This may have led Blix—without his necessarily being aware of it—to effectively endorse the hawks' argument: the burden of proof was incumbent on Baghdad, and if it did not comply, Iraq was exposing itself to intervention. Blix, in fact, would later recognize that by declaring on January 27 that Baghdad had not come to a "genuine acceptance" of disarmament, he had come close to the American point of view that Iraq needed to make a "strategic decision" to disarm. As mentioned earlier, Blix was privately convinced that Iraq had continued to conceal its WMD programs and capacities, and that American military pressure was therefore needed to make Baghdad comply. Although he reaffirmed on January 27 that UNMOVIC did not presume the existence, or absence, of WMD in Iraq, such a frame of mind was likely (if perhaps unintentionally) to bring him to publicly use turns of phrase that could strengthen the hand of those advocating the use of force.[52]

Whatever the case, the Americans and British immediately seized the opportunity. In the debates following the session, John Negroponte again denounced the deceitful character of the December declaration and concluded that it was impossible for the inspectors to verifiably certify the disarmament of Iraq; they were not "detectives," he commented. He also warned that the time when American patience would be exhausted was approaching "at great speed." The same day in Washington, Cheney's assistant national security advisor, Eric Edelman, stressed in front of French and German diplomats that Blix's declarations "clearly indicate" that Iraq "has not taken the path of cooperation." In the weeks and months to come, the Bush administration would effectively, and unashamedly, take advantage of Blix's phrase about Baghdad's "nonacceptance" of disarmament to justify the decision to invade Iraq.[53]

In the days following the presentation of the reports, the French tried to put things right by bringing out the positive elements from both. ElBaradei's report, they pointed out, showed that the nuclear file was almost closed, and Blix's report suggested that the ballistic file was making good progress and that the remaining uncertainties over chemical and biological weapons essentially concerned only old stocks of anthrax and VX, two products of doubtful longevity. Hence, they argued, the existence of an effective threat was all the more debatable, since inspections were preventing Iraq from resuming its programs. In short, the French claimed, the bottom line could not be considered negative, and this finding justified pursuing the inspections for as long as needed, even if Baghdad should be called on to cooperate more actively with them. The French line of argument had an impact on the Security Council—the great majority of whose members did not share London and Washington's viewpoint—and so the council proclaimed a preference for continuing inspections. During informal consultations at the Security Council on January 29, the French representative noted that the Americans and British, despite support from the Spanish, were isolated in their will to assert that "the game is over"—as Jeremy Greenstock had put it that day while denouncing (with Negroponte's support) a new "material breach."[54]

Although Blix's January 27 presentation had contributed to the Bush administration's indictment of Iraq, Washington was aware that it still needed to "consolidate" the file on WMD. Given the improbability of the inspectors' uncovering a "smoking gun," the major objective was now to convince the public of the existence of an Iraqi "threat." The White House had set out to do this; after the December 21 meeting (when Tenet had announced the "slam dunk"), Bush had asked the CIA to compile a document containing the best information it had on the subject. Stephen Hadley and Scooter Libby, two lawyers by training, were tasked with preparing as powerful a presentation as possible on that basis, as would be done for a legal prosecution. One month later, on January 25, Libby and Hadley showed the result of their work to Condoleezza Rice, Richard Armitage, and Paul Wolfowitz. After this presentation, it was decided that it would be Powell's job to reveal their work at a Security Council meeting in a few days' time.[55]

Meanwhile, an opportunity arose to advance the indictment: Bush was to deliver his State of the Union address on the evening of January 28. This time, most of the address was devoted to the administration's economic and social program, but the last third of it was a virulent attack on Saddam Hussein. Recalling that Resolution 1441 had offered Baghdad a last opportunity to disarm peacefully, Bush again accused Iraq of concealing WMD. He advanced the most damning elements in the file, both those going back to 1998 and the suspicions that had emerged since then. Bush was prepared to play with the facts: for instance, when he implied that the inspectors had established in 1999 that Iraq held 25,000 liters of anthrax and 500 tons of VX, which equated capacities that were only unaccounted for with *effectively proven* capacities; or when he again mentioned the aluminum tubes that Iraq allegedly had tried to procure to construct centrifuges, even though ElBaradei had cast serious doubt on this hypothesis the day before; or else when he mentioned that sixteen chemical warheads had been discovered a few days earlier, omitting to say that they were empty. Bush highlighted the most disturbing intelligence, starting with the mobile laboratories whose existence, he said, had been confirmed by three Iraqi defectors.

But if Bush's speech became infamous, it was due to a sixteen-word phrase on the alleged Iraqi attempt to acquire uranium from Niger—allegations that Bush attributed to British intelligence: "The British government has learned that Saddam Hussein recently sought significant quantities of uranium from Africa." Despite the presence of this information in the October 2002 National Intelligence Estimate, the CIA, unlike the British intelligence services, had given it only limited credit; Tenet had even requested that it be removed from Bush's speech in Cincinnati the previous October. Yet less than four months later, Stephen Hadley had let the information remain in the State of the Union address. Even if Hadley later attributed its presence to forgetfulness, the episode confirmed that at the end of January 2003, the Bush administration was ready to use all available means to justify the war, even darkening the picture of the WMD threat. The cherry on the cake was that Bush—who during his address announced that Powell would present Washington's intelligence information to the Security Council on February 5—affirmed again that Saddam Hussein "aids and protects terrorists, including members of al-Qaeda." And, he added: "Secretly, and without fingerprints, he could provide one of his hidden weapons to terrorists, or help them develop their own."[56]

In Paris's eyes, Bush had brought up nothing new that day. The French continued to think that nothing substantiated Baghdad's supposed links with al-Qaeda. French services noted that both the CIA and the FBI had confided to them that they did not believe that there were close relations between Baghdad and the al-Qaeda–affiliated Ansar al-Islam movement or key al-Qaeda figure Abu Musab al-Zarqawi. Furthermore, it was now established that the alleged contact between 9/11 hijacker Mohamed Atta and an official from the Iraqi services in Prague had in fact not taken place.[57] As for Iraqi WMD, the Quai d'Orsay's UN directorate noted, Bush was merely mixing the "key issues" that previously had been raised by UNSCOM (i.e., anthrax, VX) with "uncertain suspicions" (i.e., uranium from Niger, mobile laboratories) or suspicions that were being refuted (i.e., the aluminum tubes). In short, Paris thought. the speech confirmed that Washington did not have a "smoking gun" to show, In light of Iraq's lack of active cooperation with the inspectors, the Quai's UN directorate noted, it was certainly difficult to deny that Baghdad still had not given convincing proof of its will to show that it had disarmed; yet it was just as difficult to deduce that Iraq still possessed WMD. In other words, the situation, as seen from Paris, was characterized by "worrying uncertainties," but "clarifications" nevertheless still seemed possible.[58]

To be sure, at this stage the French intelligence services had not exonerated the Iraqis in the WMD file. On January 27, a new meeting was held at the SGDN to "refine" intelligence assessments. Bruno Le Maire summarized the meeting's conclusions for Villepin: even if (in the absence of definitive proof of existing Iraqi WMD programs) the French had only a "working hypothesis" inspired by the "principle of precaution," he wrote, "an overall picture" of Iraqi programs might be "sketched" drawing on the "presumptions" of the services and the "questions" of inspectors. This picture, according to Le Maire, showed persistent Iraqi capacities in the chemical, biological, and ballistic domains, as well as the maintenance of "know-how" in nuclear matters. However, he added, even if the above capabilities were confirmed, only the chemical and biological domains constituted a "significant" military threat—one, however, that would be limited geographically, since Iraq did not possess long-range ballistic capabilities. Granted, such a threat would not be negligible in case of reprisals against an invasion of Iraq's territory, especially since Baghdad had demonstrated in the past that it was ready to resort to such weapons. But overall, Le Maire concluded, Iraq did not represent a "strategic" threat: at most, it possessed a significant "power of nuisance" that could evolve into a "long-term" threat, but one that would be offset thanks to the pursuit of inspections and the maintenance of monitoring. Le Maire added that Iran—to speak only of the Middle East—was a much more worrying threat.[59]

Thus, the French evaluation, two months after the resumption of inspections, had not changed much in one direction or the other: it still spoke of strong suspicions that Iraq possessed residual WMD capacities, and assessed that the potential "threat" was limited to the local theater. Although this evaluation did not eliminate all danger, it left unchanged the French leaders' conviction that a military intervention was not justified. Villepin, in substance, repeated as much to Jack Straw during a telephone conversation the day after Bush's State of the Union speech. Villepin's statement was aimed as much at London as at Washington: "How can you argue in favor of war," he asked, while the inspectors are offering a "favorable" overview in the nuclear domain and one that admittedly is "nuanced" for the biological and the chemical ones? If the Americans did not offer new evidence, they would have a hard time justifying an intervention, he added. Villepin's assessment arguably was not contradicted by the head of MI6 when he came to Paris three days later— at Straw's insistence—to present to Villepin the British intelligence services' confidential intelligence about Iraqi programs. The visit, in French eyes, was a "flop": after having listened to the British spymaster, the French felt that there was nothing very new or interesting in his presentation.[60]

Meanwhile, the march to war continued to accelerate. "If Saddam Hussein does not fully disarm," Bush had declared in his State of the Union address, to the applause of the whole Congress, "for the safety of our people and for the peace of the world, we will lead a coalition to disarm him." This time war seemed imminent, as he told the armed forces: "Many of you are assembling in or near the Middle East, and some crucial hours may lay [*sic*] ahead," and then adding, "And if war is forced upon us, we will fight with the full force and might of the United States military—and we will prevail." On January 24, Tommy Franks had transmitted to Donald Rumsfeld and Richard Myers his definitive war plan, which called for a total of 140,000 personnel (including 78,000 ground troops) to be deployed by mid-February. Receiving Italian prime minister Silvio Berlusconi on January 30 and ritually repeating that he had not yet made a decision to "disarm" Saddam Hussein, Bush indulged in some bragging: "We have put together a lethal military, and we will kick his ass." The next day, Bush received Tony Blair at the White House. Between the two allies, the subject by then was no longer whether to resort to force, but rather how to situate this decision within the UN process. Blair, for whom UN approval was a vital stake, in light of the rising opposition he was facing in his own country, had come to plead for London and Washington to try to obtain a UN resolution to proceed to action. Bush accepted, but with hesitation, since the Americans did not estimate that such a resolution was necessary from a legal point of view; unlike the British, they considered Resolution 1441 sufficient.[61] Blair's and Bush's decision to seek a fresh resolution would only feed the spiral of confrontation at the UN in the coming weeks.[62]

At this stage, there was no doubt whatever at the Élysée about the White House's intentions; only the precise calendar remained uncertain. "Events are accelerating," Chirac's staff stated on January 29. They noted that Bush, in his speech the day before, had attacked Iraq "virulently" and announced that Powell would come to New York to present "proofs" that Baghdad held WMD; in the meantime, Blair would come to Washington. "All the elements are converging to give the impression that the United States has entered the final phase of preparing a military intervention that might start after mid-February," they wrote, and noted that this date coincided in the Muslim world with the end of the hajj, the pilgrimage to Mecca. Chirac's advisers suggested that he take the initiative of contacting Bush by telephone: "Although there is nothing much to expect from such a conversation given our basic divergences with the United States," they wrote, "it is important that you express your position clearly." "I do not see the utility of this phone call," Chirac replied with his usual red-ink felt-tipped pen. The rupture was well and truly accomplished.[63]

Chapter 6
The Confrontation: February 2003

By the beginning of February 2003, the Franco-American rupture over Iraq was patent. Although Colin Powell's presentation of the "evidence" of the Iraqi threat to the Security Council on February 5 won the previously hesitant American public over to support the war, the presentation had the opposite effect on the international community. The peace camp was growing skeptical about the reality of the threat, especially since Iraq finally was giving signs of more active cooperation with the inspectors. This skepticism was unmistakable on February 14, when Dominique de Villepin, at the Security Council, denounced an unjustified rationale for war in a few sentences that hit the mark, winning him the applause of the audience.

Meanwhile, the Franco-American confrontation was growing into a Euro-American confrontation. In the space of a few days, a double fault line—European and Atlantic—was revealed. The two pillars of the "West," the European Union and the Atlantic alliance, were both on the verge of a major crisis. Beyond that, the United Nations had become the theater of a diplomatic fight that extended to virtually the entire international community. Its stakes now far exceeded the Iraq crisis and bore on the future of the international system as a whole.

Yet French policy—in spite of Villepin's fervent speech—did not deliberately seek confrontation. As will be seen, an all-out clash with the United States was not Chirac's objective. On the contrary, until the end of February, French diplomacy tried to avoid an escalation at the Security Council by dissuading the

Americans and British from seeking UN backing for the war. Their efforts were in vain: the mechanics that would lead in the following month to a Franco-American crisis of an intensity that had not been seen for decades—and then to the unleashing of the war in Iraq—were irrevocably underway.

"And this is an old country . . . ."

Powell's appearance at the Security Council on February 5, announced by President Bush during his State of the Union address, was a major opportunity for the US administration to convince the country and the international community—though the latter, clearly, was a lesser concern—of the justifications for the planned war. Tapping Powell for this task was a clever choice: the "reluctant warrior" enjoyed strong credibility and great popularity in US public opinion. Dominique de Villepin's so-called "ambush" of Powell at the Security Council on January 20 had led Powell to harden his tone on the issue and, in effect, to align himself with the war camp. The hawks were delighted by the role that their favorite whipping boy was getting ready to play. As a good soldier, Powell did not shrink from Bush's demand; he wanted to prepare himself thoroughly for what he knew was a risky exercise, but one that he thought he could control. Powell had placed the bar very high: he took as his model the presentation of proofs of the presence of Soviet missiles in Cuba by UN ambassador Adlai Stevenson at the height of the Cuban Missile Crisis in October 1962. But far from the "Stevenson moment" he had hoped for, Powell was in fact about to face the least shining episode of his career.[1]

Powell and his close advisers would devote an entire week to preparing for the UN presentation. On January 29, Lawrence Wilkerson, Powell's chief of staff, went with a small team to CIA headquarters at Langley, Virginia. They set out to filter the available intelligence in order to select those pieces that appeared to be indisputable proofs—a work that soon proved titanic. Powell himself spent a good part of the weekend at Langley, accompanied by Richard Armitage. George Tenet and John McLaughlin were also present, as were Stephen Hadley and Scooter Libby. Very quickly, Powell and his team realized the fragility of the case, especially since they worked at first on the basis of the document from Hadley and Libby, whose assertions were badly sourced and in which the raw material had been "masticated." This led Powell's team to give up on using Hadley and Libby's materials and to rely mostly on the National Intelligence Estimate from the previous autumn.

At the end of the day, Powell nevertheless deemed—no doubt in good faith—that he had a solid document purged of the most dubious assertions, including the affair of the uranium from Niger, which had figured prominently in the State of the Union address. "I don't know what more he could have done," Armitage would later declare. But if Powell and his team felt that they had separated the wheat from the chaff and had been able to resist those who were ready to dress up the facts, the result—much like the NIE—rested on a foundation that would prove very defective. Powell's prepared briefing contained two elements that soon would become highly controversial. The first element was the aluminum tubes, which Powell mentioned as evidence of Iraq's nuclear intentions, even though he acknowledged that they were the subject of debate among experts. The second was the mobile laboratories, which Powell claimed to exist as a proven fact. He had been encouraged in this by George Tenet, who had assured him that the information was reliable in spite of the fact that it rested on the sole testimony of "Curveball"—and in spite of the fact that Tyler Drumheller, the chief of the European division in the CIA's Directorate of Operations, apparently had once again relayed to Tenet the Germans' skepticism about the intelligence, even as Powell's appearance was being prepared. The dysfunctional working of the intelligence services was again manifest, and Powell would pay a high price for it in terms of personal credibility. For the bulk of Powell's presentation derived from the 2002 NIE—which, the Senate Committee on Intelligence judged three years later, was simply wrong. "The [CIA] let him down big time," Powell's friend Armitage said later.[2]

Yet Powell also helped create his own disaster. He decided to include in his briefing audio excerpts whose interpretation was debatable, like the intercept (which McLaughlin had presented to Bush at the end of December) in which an Iraqi officer, when the inspections were resumed at the end of November 2002, had ordered that the mention of nerve agents be deleted from an instruction manual. This was a potentially incriminating piece of evidence, but one which equally could have indicated that the Iraqis wanted to clean up the manual in order for it to reflect the effective elimination of these weapons. Powell had also decided to include in his presentation a discussion of potential links between Iraq and al-Qaeda by advancing—with some qualifications—the alleged association between Saddam Hussein's regime and Abu Musab al-Zarqawi's network. This satisfied the White House, and especially Dick Cheney; yet the CIA, as seen earlier, from the start thought it impossible to establish any links of dependence between the two. Clearly, Powell wanted to make an impression: he introduced the subject by saying that he wanted to speak about the "sinister nexus" between terrorism and WMD, in effect adopting what since 9/11 had been the motto of the hawks.[3]

At 10:30 a.m. on February 5, Joschka Fischer—Germany held the presidency of the Security Council that month—opened the session and then gave the floor to Powell. Millions throughout the world followed the event live. Powell, who had asked Tenet to sit in the first row of the American delegation as a way of showing that the CIA was behind him, spoke for seventy-six minutes. He addressed successively the Iraqi regime's practices of dissimulation, its WMD properly speaking, and its links with terrorism. Apart from audio extracts, the presentation was punctuated by images (no less than forty-five, including satellite photos) projected on two screens hanging above. Powell was poised and clinical. This did not prevent him from dramatizing as needed: most notably, he exhibited a vial full of a white powder ("an avalanche of camera flashes" froze his gesture, noted Bruno Le Maire, who was sitting with the French delegation), recalling that an envelope containing the same quantity of anthrax had killed two Washington, D.C., post office employees and led to the temporary closure of the US Senate in the autumn of 2001. Predictably, Powell concluded his speech by saying that since the adoption of Resolution 1441, Iraq had constantly aggravated the situation of "material breach" in which it already found itself. In Baghdad, General Amir al-Saadi, the usual interlocutor of the UN inspectors, remarked that Powell's presentation was "a typically American show, complete with stunts and special effects." ABC News, in contrast, commented: "The case for an unpopular war was made by the most popular, the most trustworthy man in the administration."[4]

Powell won full marks in the United States, to the great satisfaction of the White House. Rice saw his presentation as a "tour de force"; Bush judged the performance "exhaustive, eloquent, and persuasive." Powell indeed had "done the job": according to a poll, after Powell's speech, half of Americans questioned were ready to support the war, compared with only a third the month before. Powell's appearance also had the effect of overcoming the skepticism of many opinion-makers. True, Maureen Dowd shrewdly remarked in the *New York Times* that "the case was less convincing than the presenter," wondering why Powell had suddenly placed himself in the war camp. Yet the tone of the rest of the press was clearly favorable. "He persuaded me," wrote Mary McGrory—a figure of Washington journalism who famously had denounced the Vietnam War and the Watergate scandal—in the *Washington Post*, saluting an appearance effected "without histrionics of any kind" and "with no verbal embellishments." The press "gave him a triumph," said the French embassy in Washington.[5]

The same impression was not shared around the Security Council table, however. Even before the session, Igor Ivanov had confided to Villepin that he expected the presentation to be merely "a show designed for public opinion." Le Maire noted: "Nothing seemed to us convincing or new. But we did not count for much. The real jury was sitting in front of TV screens." In the eyes of Jean-Marc de La Sablière, the French UN representative, Powell had "asserted a lot" without furnishing indubitable proof, but his speech was designed "at least as much for American public opinion as for members of the Council." This impression was shared by the Germans, who were surprised by the assertions about the alleged mobile laboratories and the central place they occupied in Powell's statement, since they knew that the "Curveball" testimony was dubious. "It was now clear to us that the Americans had no solid evidence whatsoever," Fischer would later write. As soon as the presentation ended, so did the media attention, Fischer noted. "When I resumed speaking as president to close the session," he wrote, "their attention had declined to zero."[6]

In the following days, the French would confirm the impressions of their UN colleagues. True, the elements Powell had put on the table on February 5 matched the suspicions of the French intelligence services—who, it should be recalled, had not exonerated the Iraqis, particularly in the biological and chemical domains. But the French services also observed that Powell had not brought anything really new to the table; the only exception was Baghdad's dissimulating activities, but the evidence cited by Powell, such as wiretaps and photos, was open to interpretation. The French noted that Powell had not communicated any previously unknown information regarding the weapons themselves. The evidence he had given on the chemical weapons merely presented as facts the questions that had been raised by UNSCOM and taken up by UNMOVIC. As for the biological weapons, Powell's data seemed to match their own, especially on anthrax and on mobile laboratories (whose existence French intelligence, as mentioned earlier, could neither confirm nor deny), but he had no new evidence, either. The same was true in the ballistic and nuclear domains; unlike the Americans, the French did not believe that the Iraqis still possessed missiles from the 1991 Gulf War, and they were not convinced by Powell's evidence concerning the alleged centrifuges. As for the supposed links between Baghdad and terrorist networks, notably that of Abu Musab al-Zarqawi, the French services regarded them as groundless allegations and noted that their American counterparts were far from unanimous in sharing them. Overall, Powell's presentation did not change the French services' analysis. There were strong suspicions of prohibited activities but neither certainty nor proofs of these activities; in any case, any potential remaining threat was merely a limited one. Nor did Powell's presentation remove the critical points that differentiated the French assessment from that of the American services: the latter's constant use of the indicative rather than the conditional tense to describe Iraq's WMD, and their systematic choice of the highest figures in the range of estimates of Iraqi capabilities.[7]

Before the Security Council presentation, the French could not exclude the possibility that Powell might bring up new evidence. But the February 5 session confirmed the fragility of the US case. Until then, the French could surmise that the Americans knew more than they did, and that they had information that other countries did not. Once everything had been put on the table, though, it became clear that this was not the case. As a French decision-maker later recalled, "We had believed the Americans were much more knowledgeable," but Powell's exposition "was simply not credible." Jacques Chirac said much the same thing on the telephone to Vladimir Putin the next day: we have listened attentively to Powell, Chirac said, but he has brought no new evidence that might justify a preventive war, even if the chemical and biological dimensions are still uncertain. Putin, who had just convened his own services, shared Chirac's analysis, and was even more skeptical. There was "nothing sensational" in Powell's statements, he said, adding that there were doubts about the chemical and biological dimensions, but even in these domains Iraq did not seem to have operational capabilities; as for the nuclear, Putin thought, it was a "quasi-certainty" that Iraq had no capability at all.[8]

After Powell's presentation, Villepin had declared that France would examine closely the information communicated by Washington. He had also stressed that inspections were starting to produce results, even if some areas of uncertainty had yet to be dissipated; this clarification, he said, required Iraq's active cooperation. In line with the proposals that Paris had put forward in January, Villepin called for strengthening the inspections by increasing the number of inspectors and means of observation—France offered to put its Mirage IV aircraft at the inspectors' disposal—while appointing a coordinator in Iraq. Villepin's proposals on February 5 had won the support of many delegations: apart from Spain and Bulgaria, which tended to follow London and Washington, the others—with more or less firmness—had declared themselves in favor of pursuing inspections. The French, at this juncture, thus thought there was at least a "blocking minority" in favor of continuing the inspections. It did not seem that the Americans and their allies would be able to obtain nine votes out of the fifteen that would permit—except for a veto—the adoption of a resolution.[9]

Powell, after the February 5 session, had nevertheless confided to Villepin that the "time limit" granted to Iraq would expire on February 14—the date of the next inspectors' report—and that if Baghdad did not change its behavior, there would need to be "talk of a resolution." The next day, Bush himself had announced that "the game [was] over."[10] Paris, in the wake of the proposals sketched out by Villepin, therefore wanted to retake the initiative by further developing Villepin's proposals. Of course, the French, at that point, did not really believe that such an initiative had any serious chance of preventing war unless there was an improbable new development; but they hoped that it might allow them to strengthen the "blocking minority" in the Security Council that had emerged on February 5. As long as such a "blocking minority" persisted, they believed that the Americans and British would hesitate, out of fear of failure, to introduce a draft resolution. To deter Washington and London from doing so, as we shall see, was now Paris's goal in the hope of avoiding an agonizing choice between a veto and abstention.[11]

In the following days, the French launched a major diplomatic initiative that was akin to a three-stage rocket. On February 7, the French UN delegation issued a "non-paper" (in other words, an informal document) specifying the French proposals. Paris wanted to increase the inspections' effectiveness, both from the point of view of disarmament and that of "containment": to do so, they proposed doubling or tripling the number of inspectors (then numbering about 120) in order to increase the visits; diversifying their profiles by including interpreters, accountants, archivists, and other different areas of expertise; and reinforcing the means of aerial detection and interpretation by involving experts in areas such as image analysis. The informal document was then circulated among the inspectors and the Security Council members. Powell, who had so far underestimated the French determination to oppose Anglo-American plans, called Villepin on February 11, somewhat incredulous. Did France really envisage the immediate tripling of the number of inspectors? In a memorandum distributed on the 12th, the Americans swept aside the French proposals. "The problem is not the number of inspectors but the lack of active cooperation from Iraq," the Americans said; as for "containment," that was not their role. It was the same old tune, the French thought.[12]

The second stage of the "rocket" was to obtain the support of Moscow. Paris could count on Berlin: Fischer had unreservedly endorsed Villepin's proposals on February 5. But the French judged it essential to be able to rely on Russia as well: the threat of a veto, first sketched out by Villepin on January 20, would be more credible if Moscow clearly showed the same disposition as Paris, as it had done during the negotiations surrounding Resolution 1441. Yet this concord was by no means a foregone conclusion. Ever since Villepin and Ivanov's declaration at the start of January, the Russians (who basically shared the French point of view) did not conceal their reservations about directly opposing the Americans. They even seemed ready to accept a possible change of regime in Baghdad—their relationship with the current regime was not what it once was—provided that their financial and economic interests in debt repayments, oil contracts, and the like could be preserved. Did the Russians come to side with the French position because they had not been able to obtain the desired guarantees from Washington? Or had Chirac managed to persuade Putin of his determination to go as far as a veto if necessary? Regardless, on February 10, Putin (coming to Paris after a stop in Berlin) put Russia definitively alongside France and Germany by joining a three-way declaration. In it, the three countries, emphasizing their "close cooperation," stated that they were in favor of pursuing inspections and asserted that there was "still an alternative to war," noting that this position was "close to [that of] many countries." By sealing their joint determination, the declaration assuaged the fears in all three capitals that they would find themselves isolated in what increasingly appeared as a challenge to America. Needless to say, as will be seen, the declaration did not go unnoticed in Washington.[13]

The Declaration of the Three on February 10 enabled the launch of the third stage of the "rocket": the search for support of a majority of countries in anticipation of the next Security Council meeting on February 14. Everything indeed seemed to indicate that this next rendezvous, when the inspectors would present a new update, might be the occasion for the Americans and British to blow the whistle for the end of the game by announcing the introduction of a draft resolution authorizing the use of force. In order to dissuade them, it therefore was important to rally as many capitals as possible to the French ideas on inspections and to the tripartite declaration of February 10. Chirac was personally involved in this diplomatic campaign, calling (sometimes twice) the leaders of key nations sitting on the Security Council: apart from Putin, whom he saw shortly after in Paris, he spoke with Vicente Fox (Mexico), Paul Biya (Cameroon), Ricardo Lagos (Chile), Bashar al-Assad (Syria), Jiang Zemin (China), Pervez Musharraf (Pakistan), and Luiz Inácio Lula da Silva (Brazil). (Brazil was not then sitting on the council, but was likely to influence the other two Latin American nations that were.) Villepin, for his part, did the same with his opposite numbers, while the French embassies approached many other capitals, in close cooperation with the Russians and the Germans. The first result of this global canvassing was that China, which until then had remained noncommittal, now publicly gave its support to the Three—thus adding the weight of a possible third veto—as did important countries that were not currently sitting on the Security Council, like Brazil and Indonesia. Other leaders solicited by Chirac said that they were in full agreement with the French approach, even if they (with the exception of Syria) balked at taking part publicly out of fear of a clash with Washington. Thus took shape at the Security Council a group of six "hesitant countries"— Angola, Cameroon, Chile, Guinea, Mexico, and Pakistan—that would be the object of everyone's attention in the weeks to come.[14]

On February 14, the "rocket" was finally sent into orbit. As the new deadline (once more considered "decisive" by the principal capitals) approached, things remained uncertain. On the Iraqi side, authorities still did not seem to have fully understood the need to demonstrate the "active" cooperation demanded of them. Replying to an invitation sent by Baghdad after the January 27 session, Hans Blix and Mohamed ElBaradei again went to Iraq on February 7 and 8. But the result of the visit was again meager: although the Iraqis finally appeared disposed to give credible responses to key questions about anthrax and VX, proposing the use of new techniques to evaluate precisely the quantities of toxic agents that had been destroyed in 1991, they continued to argue that they had not kept the documents that could prove that the weapons stocks had been destroyed. And even though they had been more open on certain points of procedure—such as by facilitating interviews with scientists outside Iraq, as the inspectors had requested—they remained closed on other points, including the U-2 surveillance flights. In short, it appeared that the Iraqis—despite the many messages sent to them, including by the French—did not appreciate the gravity of the situation. On his return, Blix had given Jean-Marc de La Sablière a "mixed" summary of the visit and judged that the situation remained "difficult." As a result, La Sablière expected that ElBaradei would present another report justifying the pursuit of inspections, but that Blix would remain "guarded": "He will point to some positive elements," La Sablière said, "but he is not inclined to showcase these elements" because he considers "that there is no real change of attitude by the Iraqis." "I found Hans Blix still shocked by Baghdad's attitude, which he thought continued to play cat-and-mouse," he added, and worried that Blix might "de facto play the American game" even if he appeared "haunted" by the possibility of an intervention.[15]

The French, therefore, did not have much choice but to stick to their original logic. Faced with the probability that the Americans would rely on a mixed report to announce that they would table a draft resolution, France had to consolidate the "blocking minority" around the Three, now joined by China: hence the speech that Villepin planned to give that day at the UN to defend the French position and refute the Anglo-American arguments. Villepin clearly aimed to make an impression, as shown by the lyrical coda in which he wanted to invoke—in a de Gaulle–like formula that also cocked a snook at Donald Rumsfeld's earlier denigration of both France and Germany—this "old country, France" and this "old continent, Europe." His advisers had prepared the draft, and he had reworked it; it had also been reviewed at the Élysée, where Chirac, who liked the coda, had approved its content. Villepin, no doubt, was aware of the risk of creating a stir: upon his arrival in New York, he called Maurice Gourdault-Montagne to make sure that the Élysée was on board with his text, including the end of the speech—which Chirac's adviser confirmed. La Sablière also encouraged Villepin to keep the ending passage: "This is a strong message," he said. "They will understand."[16]

Villepin would benefit that day from a favorable conjunction. Blix's report—as the latter had hinted during a phone conversation with Villepin the day before—turned out to be more positive than most had expected in the previous days. Stating that UNMOVIC had conducted more than 400 inspections, that all the sites inspected before 1998 had been verified, and that more than 200 chemical samples and 100 biological samples had been analyzed without revealing toxic agents, Blix said again that so far no prohibited weapons had been found, except for the few empty chemical munitions mentioned in his January report. Blix stressed that it still was not possible to determine with certainty whether Iraq still possessed WMD, but he noted progress in the inspection process: inspectors had no problems accessing sites, and Baghdad had just agreed to the inspectors' latest demands, notably on overflights (U-2 and Mirage planes would be able to operate soon) and interviews with scientists (which had begun, as Blix had announced to Villepin). Blix also said that progress also had been made on substance. Without yielding proofs per se, the evidence that Baghdad had supplied during the visit seemed to indicate a more active cooperation from Iraq. Blix, furthermore, was critical of the information communicated to UNMOVIC by intelligence services. He even criticized Powell's presentation, at least regarding one specific element: following a recent visit to the corresponding site by the inspectors, Blix said, Powell's interpretation of certain satellite photos had proved erroneous. "We were not expecting so positive a tone," noted the French delegation, which stressed that the peaceful disarmament of Iraq remained a "realistic" prospect.[17]

Was Blix trying to put things right in relation to his previous report? Be that as it may, his presentation—as well as that of ElBaradei, which was in line with his previous one—was a boon for Villepin. Powell was on the defensive. Leaving aside his prepared remarks, he had to improvise; he denounced yet again the absence of Baghdad's active cooperation, but he refrained from mentioning an ultimatum or speaking of a resolution. Villepin, by contrast, felt that his line of argument had been strengthened. "The inspections are producing results," he declared, and argued for their intensification. Then he launched into a denunciation of American plans: "The option of war might appear at first to be the quickest. But let's not forget that after having won the war, you have to construct the peace. And let's not fool ourselves—it will be long and difficult." "The use of force is not justified today," he went on, stressing that France had never ruled out that force might someday be necessary. And he concluded with the finale that would remain in people's memories: "In this temple of the United Nations, we are the guardians of an ideal, the guardians of a conscience. The onerous responsibility and immense honor we have must lead us to give priority to disarmament in peace. This message comes to you today from an old country, France, from an old continent like mine, Europe, that has known wars, occupation, and barbarism. . . . Faithful to its values, it wants to act resolutely with all members of the international community. It believes in our capacity to construct together a better world." Villepin's voice fell quiet, silence held for a few moments, and then a large part of the hall applauded spontaneously.[18]

After the session, Le Maire remembered, Villepin wore "the grin of a kid who has carried off a prize." The French foreign minister could indeed boast of a fine success. Secretary-General Kofi Annan congratulated him personally on his "brilliant speech"; Annan was impressed by the applause—this "never happens," he stressed. The French, obviously, were pleased. "[It has been] an incontestably favorable day," said La Sablière, who noted that owing to the positive tone of Blix's report, the Americans and British would have a hard time getting the Security Council to declare a material breach.[19] Whatever the justice of the argument and the panache of the speech, Villepin's intervention, however, did not fundamentally change the situation. On the Iraqi side, there was a risk that the regime might misunderstand the sense of the speech, which by no means aimed to exonerate Baghdad. In the following days, French chargé d'affaires André Janier made his umpteenth approach to Iraqi foreign minister Naji Sabri in order to push the Iraqis to confirm and to amplify the signs of cooperation they had begun to give. This time, Sabri considered the message "harsh"—all the more so because Chirac, in an interview given to *Time* magazine two days after the UN session, had declared that "if Saddam Hussein would only vanish, it would without a doubt be the biggest favor he could do for his people and for the world." Meanwhile, on the American and British side, nothing indicated that the February 14 session or the massive demonstrations against the war that took place the next day—which will be discussed later—did any more than simply delay the end of the game by a few days. "Despite the events of recent days," the Quai d'Orsay thought, "the United States has visibly not given up plans for a military intervention in the near future, which might, under British pressure, lead them to introduce a draft resolution."[20] Thus the most tangible result of Villepin's speech, apart from placing him personally in the spotlight, was to accelerate the increasingly clear deterioration in Franco-American relations. On February 12, Jean-David Levitte in Washington had mentioned a "rapid rise in tension" between the two countries that was attributable to the fact that France now figured as the "coordinator of the fight against the American position."[21] This perception was further fed by the fact that the French opposition to the coming war was not limited to the New York scene: for three weeks, the Iraq crisis had been sowing discord well beyond the Security Council, and its shockwaves were increasingly being felt throughout both the EU and the Atlantic alliance.

"They missed a good occasion to keep quiet. . . . "

The Iraq crisis unfolded against the backdrop of major developments in European integration and the transatlantic relationship, which to some extent the crisis revealed. This was foremost the case within the EU. For several months, relations between Paris and Berlin had been assuming a new dynamic. The compromises that the French and Germans had reached in autumn 2002 over the Common Agricultural Policy (CAP) and the constitutional treaty under discussion illustrated Chirac's and Schröder's desire, after the fiasco of the Nice Summit in December 2000, to reaffirm Franco-German leadership and vigorously relaunch European integration. At the same time, this prospect was becoming a concern for Britain. Despite Tony Blair's promising beginnings on European matters, London was afraid of finding itself marginalized by this new dynamic. The Franco-German compromise over the CAP had even given rise to a vivid altercation between Blair and Chirac in October 2002. On top of that tension was the growing resentment of countries like Spain and Italy about a Franco-German couple that was accused of treating other EU member-states as secondary partners.

Furthermore, there were the usual differences among Europeans concerning relations with the United States. Although the French and Germans wished for a Europe capable of counterbalancing Washington's policies in the face of rising American unilateralism, the British wanted to preserve at all costs the primacy of US-Europe relations. They were joined in this sentiment by Italy, a traditionally Atlanticist country, and more surprisingly by Spain, whose prime minister, José María Aznar, wanted to base his foreign policy on Madrid's proximity to Washington—a choice that the events of 9/11 had only confirmed in the name of the war against terror, which strengthened Madrid's hand in the fight against Spain's Basque nationalists. The future EU enlargement to include ten new nations, a decision enacted at the December 2002 Copenhagen summit and planned for the spring of 2004, only accentuated this growing intra-European divide. The future EU members included the three Baltic states and five central and eastern European countries; marked by the experience of Soviet domination, these nations found themselves instinctively in the Atlanticist camp, starting with the most important among them, Poland. In short, when Donald Rumsfeld had spoken of the "old" and "new" Europe, he had merely recognized the existence of an emerging fault line between two conceptions of Europe and of transatlantic relations.

In January 2003, the Iraq crisis began to resonate with this European situation. Although the common position adopted by Chirac and Schröder resulted primarily from their converging opinions on the Iraqi issue, it was also amplified by the ongoing rapprochement between Paris and Berlin. In light of the rising hostility of European public opinion to the war, the Iraq crisis spurred the desire of both countries to speak in the name of Europe in the face of US unilateralism. Yet this outspokenness, in turn, could only alienate those EU member-states (whether present or future) who did not see themselves in this position. "It seems that the celebrations of the 40th anniversary [of the Élysée Treaty] have produced a certain irritation," the Quai d'Orsay noted—in a characteristic understatement—at the height of the European crisis three weeks later.[22]

Meanwhile, the Iraq crisis contributed to a marked degradation in Franco-British relations. At the beginning of January, some in Paris had hoped to avoid a break with London, but Blair's rallying to Bush's policy (manifest even before his visit to Washington on January 31), combined with the French and Germans taking their joint position, only revived the perennial misunderstandings between the two countries: a France seen by Great Britain as viscerally anti-American, and a Great Britain seen by France as systematically following the United States. The January 29 conversation between Tony Blair and Gérard Errera, the French ambassador in London—Errera's visit to 10 Downing Street visit had been planned long before the crisis erupted—illustrated this divide. Errera denied any anti-Americanism in the French attitude and said that it was wrong to approve of a unilateral war in the name of the transatlantic relation. Blair, by contrast, wondered aloud if, in order to influence the United States, one was not bound to go "as far as agreeing with them a priori."[23] There could be no better definition of Atlanticism.

The European crisis exploded at the end of January. On the 27th, the fifteen EU foreign ministers had adopted a consensual text reaffirming the importance of Resolution 1441 and the peaceful disarmament of Iraq, urging the Iraqi regime to cooperate. But everything fell apart on the 30th: the *Wall Street Journal* published on its op-ed page a letter from eight European leaders expressing their support for the United States and their attachment to the transatlantic tie. In addition to Tony Blair, Silvio Berlusconi, and José María Aznar, the signatories were the Portuguese, Dutch, Hungarian, and Polish prime ministers, as well as, emblematically, the Czech president and former dissident Václav Havel, who at the time was only three days from the end of his mandate. Although the letter did not formally advocate a military operation against Iraq, it was no doubt an assault on "old" Europe. The initiative had come from a *Wall Street Journal* editor, Michael Gonzalez, and it had been endorsed by Berlusconi, Aznar, and Blair. The letter, moreover, had been prepared without the knowledge of French and German leaders or of the EU representatives, including European Commission president Romano Prodi, the High Representative for Common Foreign and Security Policy (CFSP) Javier Solana, or the Greek presidency of the EU. Clearly, the initiative aimed to counter France and Germany's stance and to show that these two countries could not claim to speak for Europe as a whole. Even if the Bush administration was not directly involved in the initiative, it evidently was pleased with the operation: "God bless you and Spain," Bush wrote to Aznar.[24]

A few days later, an additional threshold was crossed. On February 5, the same day that Colin Powell presented his evidence to the Security Council, the foreign ministers of the ten countries of the Vilnius Group published a text that echoed the *Wall Street Journal* letter. The Vilnius Group, which included Albania, Bulgaria, Croatia, Estonia, Latvia, Lithuania, Macedonia, Slovakia, Slovenia, and Romania, had been created in 2000 to argue collectively for the enlargement of the Atlantic alliance; during the November 2002 Prague Summit, seven of these countries had been invited to join NATO before 2004. Though the content of both texts was similar, the blast of the declaration of the Vilnius Ten exceeded that of the letter of the Eight. Because the ratification process for their accession to NATO was about to start in the US Senate, the Vilnius Ten declaration evidently was meant as a token of loyalty to the United States. The Vilnius initiative clearly was guided from Washington; Bruce Jackson—a lobbyist with close ties to the Bush administration and to the US weapons industries, who was very active in the issue of enlarging the alliance—had been maneuvering with the blessing of the White House. What made things even more galling in the eyes of "old" Europe was that the Vilnius declaration, which had been drafted *before* Powell's Security Council appearance, said that the United States had provided "compelling evidence" of the existence of WMD in Iraq. This statement clearly confirmed its authors' bias toward Washington's views. An aggravating factor for Paris and Berlin was that three of the signatories of the letter of the Eight (Poland, the Czech Republic, and Hungary) and seven of the signatories of the Vilnius declaration (the three Baltic states, Slovenia, Slovakia, as well as Bulgaria and Romania) were also on the path to EU membership. This confirmed in French and German eyes that these countries had no intention of striking their Atlanticist colors when entering the EU.[25]

This time, the storm really burst. On January 30, the day that the letter of the Eight appeared, Villepin and Fischer had tried to defuse the debate by not overreacting to a text whose substance by and large remained in accordance with the EU declaration of the 27th. But the Vilnius declaration on February 5 lit the tinderbox. Villepin and Fischer became aware of it just before the "proofs" session at the Security Council; it was a "completely ridiculous" text, Fischer whispered to Villepin. Villepin brought up the subject with Powell during their private conversation after the session. Once friendly, the atmosphere was now strained. When Villepin said that he was surprised that the Americans were thus seeking to divide the Europeans, Powell denied any intervention on his part in the declaration of the Ten. "Each now got stuck in incomprehension and animosity," noted Le Maire.[26]

223

The tension between Paris and Berlin on one side, and Washington and London on the other, was now in the open, and the stakes centered on which side could claim to lead Europe. Two days after the Vilnius declaration was published, there was another heated exchange during the Munich security conference, a yearly gathering of experts, journalists, and decision-makers from the United States and Europe. Donald Rumsfeld was combative. Feeling strengthened, in this utmost Atlanticist gathering, by the letter of the Eight and the declaration of the Ten, he lashed out at the French and Germans by flaying them for their opposition to the United States. Rumsfeld's diatribe earned him a rebuke from Fischer: speaking in English to make himself better understood and to capture media attention, he said from the podium: "Excuse me, I'm not convinced!" His French counterpart Michèle Alliot-Marie did not mince words, either: "To be allies does not mean saying that my idea is necessarily right and all those who do not agree with me should be isolated or excluded."[27]

Yet the EU was well and truly divided. Paris and Berlin, although clearly in touch with European public opinion, were not in a position of strength. The French were aware that the project of a political Europe and the future of the CFSP were at stake and had to be protected from the fallout of the crisis; Paris therefore was trying to calm things down. So when the Greek presidency of the EU proposed gathering the European Council on February 17 to seek a compromise on the Iraq issue, the French welcomed Athens' initiative. The Iraq crisis, the Quai d'Orsay noted, exposed the "deep tendencies" of the future enlarged EU, and it revealed the "Atlanticist tropism" of the soon-to-be members as well as the "relative rejection" of the Franco-German couple. France's goal at the meeting, therefore, was to obtain a text that was as close as possible to the French positions on Iraq while avoiding any "blame game" based on the notion that the positions taken by others were incompatible with the imperative of European solidarity. (The risk was indeed that the French and Germans would themselves be criticized for the declarations they had made during the Élysée Treaty celebrations.) For Paris, it was important to abstain from posing the debate in terms of a choice between Europe and the United States. It was a matter of "saving the unity of Europe," Villepin said to his Greek colleague George Papandreou, thanking him for having taken the initiative.[28]

In Brussels on February 17, the fifteen EU leaders—after having met Kofi Annan—adopted a declaration that took up the conclusions adopted by the foreign ministers on January 27 and reaffirmed the goal of the "total and effective" disarmament of Iraq within the UN framework. The declaration stressed that this process should be conducted peacefully, as European public opinion demanded, knowing that such an objective could not be reached without the increased cooperation of Iraq and that the inspections could not be pursued indefinitely without such cooperation. French diplomats were satisfied: the declaration was situated at an "equilibrium point" of all positions. Given the tense climate in which the meeting had begun, this was already an appreciable improvement: before the meeting, Blair and Dutch prime minister Jan Peter Balkenende had sent strong-arm letters expressing their views to Greek prime minister Costas Simitis.[29]

Chirac's impulsiveness, however, soon destroyed this fragile consensus. After the meeting, Chirac talked to the press. Although he expressed his satisfaction with a result that put an end to a European "mini-crisis," the French president opened another such crisis on the spot by lashing out at the declaration of the Ten—which was exactly what his diplomats had wanted to avoid. "Honestly, I find that they have behaved with some thoughtlessness," he said about the candidate nations. "If on the first difficult subject people start to give a viewpoint independently of any consultation with the whole body into which they want to enter, then this is not very responsible behavior. In any case, this is not proper behavior. So I think they missed a good oppportunity to keep quiet." Chirac then suggested that this behavior might complicate the ratification of the EU enlargement by certain member-states, suggesting in barely concealed terms that the all-out pro-Americanism of certain candidates might cost them their entry into the Union. Predictably, Chirac's statement unleashed a wave of protest in the countries concerned, as well as manifestations of well-orchestrated indignation among their American and British protectors, for whom Chirac's statement was obviously a boon: did it not demonstrate that France was itself practicing the same form of intolerance and even intimidation for which it had criticized the United States? Chirac—who later acknowledged his "somewhat excessive language"—had thus helped aggravate the fault line between the "old" and the "new" Europe, paradoxically proving Rumsfeld right. The affair left lasting strains in the relations between France and the future new EU members. At the time, it showed the extent to which the Iraq crisis was dividing Europe and also the extent to which Chirac was now determined to oppose American policy, and not just at the Security Council, at the risk of further exacerbating Euro-Atlantic tensions. The parallel crisis that was being simultaneously played out at NATO only confirmed this.[30]

Just like the crisis within the EU, the NATO one unfolded against profound changes in the institution. The September 11 attacks, coming on top of the Kosovo crisis, had once more exposed the increasing unilateralism of the United States and its growing disinterest in European security. The allies' invocation of Article 5 in the wake of the attacks, combined with the absence of an effective NATO role in the Afghanistan campaign, had confirmed in European eyes the declining importance of the alliance for the United States and its preference for "coalitions of the willing." Washington increasingly saw NATO merely as a framework for legitimizing—rather than conducting—American operations. The November 2002 Prague summit had restored a more harmonious climate, but considering that the summit had taken place a few days after the adoption of Resolution 1441, it was clear that maintaining Atlantic harmony would depend on the evolution of the Iraq crisis, as what followed would amply confirm.[31]

The NATO crisis originated in the Americans' desire to involve the alliance in one way or another, even if just symbolically, in a possible operation in Iraq. Doing so, they felt, would answer European criticisms about the marginalization of NATO and, more important, secure the allies' political endorsement for their intervention. By November 2002, the Americans had begun to consider how to involve NATO in their plans for Iraq, and at the start of December Paul Wolfowitz had gone to Brussels to discuss possible options. In mid-January, he came back with formal proposals, which were endorsed by NATO secretary-general Lord Robertson. By that point, Washington had dismissed the notion of direct NATO participation in operations, which France and Germany seemed unlikely to accept; the Americans, however, wanted to reassign forces from other NATO countries to defend US installations in Europe and to relieve American forces in the Balkans, and above all to deploy AWACS planes and Patriot missiles to ensure the defense of Turkey. This last point was justified, the Americans argued, because Turkey, a NATO member that shared a border with Iraq, was ready to grant the United States the right to use its air bases, which might expose it to Iraqi attacks. Washington pointed out that this scenario fell under the Washington Treaty's article 5, and therefore should allow NATO to establish defensive measures to help Turkey.

Discussions had remained discreet until that point, but everything changed in mid-January, because NATO's hypothetical involvement in Iraq was now mentioned in the press. In the meantime, the subject had become extremely sensitive, for the American decision to go to war had become just as clear as the Franco-German rejection of it. On January 22, the same day as the Élysée Treaty celebrations, France and Germany, followed by Belgium and Luxembourg, blocked the NATO measures. They argued that these measures were not necessary as long as inspections were ongoing, and that taking the Americans' proposed steps would have the effect of making the war seem fully decided. This was the start of a test of strength that would last for three long weeks.[32]

The Americans had no intention of standing still. Not only was the breakaway group of four countries a snub to them, but the alliance of France and the normally docile Germany, plus two other countries of "old Europe," was a dangerous precedent. By ganging up against the United States, the Four embodied an old American fear: the emergence of an autonomous Europe within the Atlantic alliance. Moreover, and even more serious, this NATO setback ran counter to Washington's bellicose projects, because it showed that the United States' closest allies were determined to oppose those projects. The impasse at NATO augured badly for the United States' ability to obtain the Security Council's endorsement for its plans for Iraq.

With Washington ready for a showdown, the situation quickly became inflamed. The debates at the Munich security conference, as mentioned earlier, were dominated by the NATO psychodrama. To get out of the impasse, Paris and Berlin suggested that the measures pertaining to the defense of Turkey be taken bilaterally, without going through NATO. Thus, the US plans would not receive NATO's stamp of legitimacy, but Turkey would be shielded from the potential fallout of the possible implementation of these plans. But the Americans did not want to hear of it: the stakes had become highly political.

Washington knew that, for domestic reasons, Berlin had only limited capacity for resistance. True, Schröder was willing to stand shoulder to shoulder with Paris, Brussels, and Luxembourg in the name of their common rejection of the logic of war. But the German government was under attack from the Christian Democrat opposition, which accused Schröder of stirring up anti-Americanism. Moreover, the German diplomatic apparatus, which wanted to avoid a clash with Washington, was unhappy with the situation. Fischer did not hide this from Villepin, asking him several times in the first days of February to show "flexibility." But while the Quai was ready to find an exit door, Chirac wanted to stand fast, particularly since it would be difficult to yield to the Americans at NATO without being discredited at the UN. "The president has no qualms," warned the Élysée. The Quai d'Orsay could only follow. "A positive decision on our part at NATO would be immediately interpreted as a sign of rallying to a preventive military intervention in Iraq,"

Villepin told Fischer, who was trying to convince him to end the blockage at NATO. "We cannot accept this logic."[33]

The crisis reached its apex the week of February 10. On the 10th, Lord Robertson hoped to force the decision by formally asking NATO's highest body, the North Atlantic Council (NAC), where member countries are represented by their ambassadors, to adopt the defense package. Yet the opponents of the US proposals decided to hold fast: Paris, Berlin, and Brussels maintained their opposition. In response, Ankara—no doubt at Washington's instigation—invoked the very rarely used article 4 of the Washington Treaty, which provides that a member country might demand consultations within the alliance if it believes that its security is threatened. This pushed up the tension even further, since the opponents were implicitly designated as guilty of breaking solidarity with a member country that demanded its allies' protection in the face of a pressing danger. To make matters worse, this episode occurred on the same day that France, Germany, and Russia adopted their tripartite declaration; virulent exchanges took place both at the NAC and in the press. The French ambassador to NATO, Benoît d'Aboville, declared that there was "simply no reason to let NATO implement a policy in contradiction with our objectives"; his American colleague, Nicholas Burns, called the attitude of his opponents "most unfortunate." President Bush lamented that the affair might negatively affect the alliance, while the attitude of opponents was judged "shameful" by Donald Rumsfeld and "inexcusable" by Colin Powell, who warned about the risk of seeing the alliance "breaking itself up." France was accused in Congress and in think tanks of "sabotaging" NATO, Jean-David Levitte reported from Washington.[34]

At this point, it was becoming difficult for Paris not to budge. On the evening of February 10, Fischer, who had been besieging Villepin for several days, called again to ask him to give in. The next day, February 11, Villepin heard from Powell: the solidarity of allies was at stake, Powell pointed out. Lord Robertson did not hesitate to dramatize: "All we are going to do is to kill NATO." The same day, Chirac called his Turkish counterpart, Ahmet Necdet Sezer. The Chirac-Sezer conversation showed that the French position, although coherent with its principles, was not tenable. If Turkey really were threatened, Chirac argued, then France's solidarity was assured, but this was not the case: the American gambit, he said, aimed above all to show that NATO was ready for war. Sezer stated that he shared Chirac's point of view on the need for a peaceful solution to the Iraq crisis. "We are in total solidarity with France," he declared, echoing the majority of Turkish public opinion, which was hostile to the war (while the political class was split), and he confided that he had no acrimony about France's position about NATO, which he said he could even understand. But Sezer's message was clear: it was time to end the blockage and permit the defensive measures to be implemented in Turkey.[35]

The Americans then began a movement that soon would allow them to drive a wedge between Paris and Berlin. On February 12, they offered a reduced "package," one that was more acceptable to Berlin since it no longer called for NATO forces to replace American forces in the Balkans or to ensure the protection of American bases, but included only the measures for the defense of Turkey. At the same time, the United States suggested that the adoption of these measures might be approved not by the NAC but by NATO's Defense Plannning Committee (DPC). This was a shrewd maneuver, since the DPC was composed of the defense ministers of NATO countries *except* for France (which had withdrawn from NATO's integrated military organization in 1966). On the 13th, Fischer was in Paris to find a way out; meeting Chirac at the Élysée, he hinted that Berlin was getting ready to accept the new "package." At that point, the French had no better option than to use the exit door offered by the DPC procedure; since France thus would not be associated with the adoption of the package, Paris would not have to formally reverse its position. The DPC procedure, though, had the disadvantage of singularizing France and its "special" status, just as Paris was trying to downplay its standoffishness from the alliance in order to facilitate France's military rapprochement with NATO. Nevertheless, this arrangement effectively unblocked the situation in Brussels. Although the Belgian government made a gallant last stand for twenty-four hours, it ended up yielding; a compromise was reached at the DPC on February 16, and on the 19th the DPC formally adopted the package of measures in favor of Turkey. (The three "dissidents" nevertheless published a declaration stressing that NATO's decision in no way prejudiced efforts that should continue to be conducted to peacefully disarm Iraq.)[36]

Thus ended a psychodrama that had been a sideshow with respect to the Iraq crisis—one that could have been avoided if Washington had not used the Turkey issue to force the hands of its reluctant allies by making them endorse the United States' bellicose approach. Cautious for this reason, Ankara was not asking for NATO involvement as such, and the issue of defending Turkey could have been solved in another way. The NATO crisis thus revealed a basic tendency, accentuated by 9/11 and the "war on terror," for Washington to see

NATO not as the framework for US involvement in European security—as it had been during the Cold War and in the first post–Cold War decade—but instead as a tool in the service of American global strategy. Yet the crisis also would have assumed lesser proportions if Berlin and Paris had not responded to the American provocation by blocking the defensive measures for Turkey, which in fact were quite limited in scope, at the risk of being accused of undermining the sacrosanct Atlantic solidarity. In other words, Germany and France also had used NATO as a tool to strengthen their position of refusing to sanction a US intervention. In fact, by demonstrating Paris and Berlin's determination to challenge Washington, the NATO episode may well have led Moscow and perhaps Beijing to harden their attitudes in these crucial weeks, thus consolidating the "peace camp" at the Security Council. When Putin telephoned Chirac on February 17 to express concern that the NATO compromise might favor "the march to war," the latter reassured him that this was not the case. The decision that the rest of NATO had made without France, Chirac maintained, had had a "limited" character and was actually a "diplomatic defeat" for the United States.[37]

Yet the NATO episode clearly had a cost for French diplomacy, since it ended with an arrangement that isolated France within the alliance by giving new life to the image of France as only a partial ally—an image that it had been trying to shed. "We are opening a path to our own marginalization within NATO," noted Bruno Le Maire, expressing the dominant skepticism in the diplomatic service with respect to a NATO crisis that many considered counterproductive.[38] In Washington the following months, the hawks would indeed make use of the episode in order to circumvent France within NATO while caricaturing French policy over Iraq as the resurgence of an atavistic "Gaullism," which France's specific status within the alliance exemplified. This incident was a boon for Washington, since such a reading of French policy allowed the United States to clear its name by reducing Paris's opposition over the Iraq crisis to a simple anti-American reflex. French policy was at risk of being interpreted according to this classic schema: receiving Levitte on February 17—a moment that will be discussed in more detail later—Dick Cheney did not fail to mention the NATO episode at the top of a long list of what he saw as manifestations of systematic French opposition to American plans.[39]

If the Iraq crisis had until then been treated on its own merits, Chirac's France was now engaged in an all-out contestation of US policy—a contestation whose primary stakes were no less than the future of the international system. Powell's February 5 UN briefing had been a turning point in that respect, since it was now established that Washington's bellicose plans were not justified simply by the need to defend the United States against a serious threat. It had become patent that American motivations were of a different kind. As a result, the debate shifted inevitably to principles, exposing a line of fracture that touched on the very concept of the international order. "From then on," Chirac would later write, "we entered the second phase of the Iraq crisis, with two opposite visions of the world and of the international community crystallizing." On one side was a "multilateral and legalistic" approach, he wrote, and on the other was a "dominating and Manichean logic that privileged force over law."[40]

This, in any case, was the message that the French president stressed to his interlocutors in the wake of Powell's "proofs" session at the UN, at the cost of increasing tension with Washington by systematizing the Franco-American disagreement. On February 7, Chirac pointed out to Jiang Zemin that the way in which the Iraqi issue was ultimately solved would set a "precedent," and that they risked seeing a "unipolar world" established. The same day, Chirac told Finnish prime minister Paavo Lipponen (who was visiting Paris) that the Iraq crisis carried stakes that went beyond the fate of Iraq itself: it was about "the difficult and demanding construction of a multipolar world." These declarations were echoed in Villepin's UN speech on February 14. By saying that France was "faithful to its values" and desired to "construct together a better world," Villepin clearly placed the debate on the terrain of the defense of principles, thereby stigmatizing American policy and its motivations beyond the Iraqi issue. This positioning, in turn, could but arouse the approval of those— and they were many, as the applause in the Security Council showed—who were hostile to American unilateralism, or quite simply to the United States. Villepin had "expressed himself not only in the name of France but for us all," declared Arab League secretary-general Amr Moussa to the French ambassador in Cairo, Jean-Claude Cousseran. The role of France was "essential," Moussa added, and it "exceeded the strict framework of the Iraqi question"; it was, he said, a matter of "finding the principles of a new international order that was not founded solely on obedience to the United States."[41]

Two weeks later, Chirac's triumphant visit to Algeria on March 2–4 (which had been planned long before the crisis) confirmed widespread adherence to French policy, in particular in the Arab world. It was difficult for the French to resist the temptation to intensify what had become a full-blown diplomatic campaign, in which the objectives relating strictly to the Iraqi issue—to give inspections a chance and to push back against the use of force—now arguably mattered less than the promotion of a "multipolar" world, something that Chirac had been advocating for years. The UN had become a theater whose audience was the international community and whose ambiance was seen as reflecting world opinion. In this arena, French positions were widely supported, as illustrated by the Security Council's public debate on Iraq—a debate widened to all UN members—that took place in New York in the days following Villepin's speech. "The general tone [of the debate] . . . shows that our ideas have support from a wide majority," reported the French delegation, reckoning that out of the sixty delegations that had expressed a view, less than a quarter had rallied to the inevitability of an upcoming war. This survey had the value of a poll for the Quai d'Orsay.[42]

"I am calling you as a friend of the United States"

By mid-February 2003, the Iraq crisis had become a Franco-American confrontation that recalled the clashes between France and America under Charles de Gaulle and Lyndon Johnson over NATO, the dollar, and the Vietnam War almost forty years earlier. Although Paris had often clashed with Washington since then, the shock had never been so head-on: it was difficult for commentators not to hear in Villepin's flight of oratory in the Security Council distant echoes of de Gaulle's speech in Phnom Penh in September 1966, when the General had denounced the derailment of US policy over the conflict in Southeast Asia. In the coming months, the French would pay the price for their opposition to the United States in the form of denigration by American decision-makers and a wave of Francophobia that was fed by some figures in the Bush administration and relayed by the complacency of a large segment of the US media.

Yet it would be a mistake to think that a confrontation of such intensity had been a deliberate decision on the part of the French. Certainly, French decision-makers, not least Chirac, accepted the risk of a severe deterioration in relations with Washington, although initially they likely underestimated the depths to which relations would fall. But they also thought that their policy in this crisis was in a direct line with the attitude adopted by French presidents from Charles de Gaulle to François Mitterrand. They were acting as a France that was the "friend" and "ally" of the United States, but "not aligned" with it, in Hubert Védrine's phrase. But this perception was not at all shared by the Americans, who were still under the effect of the September 11 attacks, prey to a persistant chauvinist fever and preoccupied with their own national security.

For the French, the initial preference was, if possible, to avoid an escalation to extremes: specifically, a French veto to a resolution authorizing the United States to use force. When it became obvious at the end of January that Washington was heading toward a military operation and that the Bush administration, at British insistence, might try to obtain a UN mandate for action against Iraq, French diplomacy wanted to prevent such an escalation, which might have grave consequences for Franco-American relations. The French therefore wanted to dissuade Washington from introducing a draft at the Security Council, which could lead Paris to use its veto. The situation was paradoxical: when the Security Council had adopted Resolution 1441 in the fall of 2002, Washington had affirmed that the resolution would be sufficient to justify a war if it became necessary, whereas Paris considered that a new resolution would be needed as a prerequisite for war. Now, France was trying to avoid having to pronounce on a new resolution. Beyond the apparent contradiction, the French attitude in this new phase of the crisis aimed to manage the divergence with the Americans as best they could. "We should be careful that the inevitable disagreement with Washington does not turn into a confrontation," Jean Félix-Paganon, the head of the Quai d'Orsay's UN directorate, wrote on January 27. This would require avoiding the submission of a new resolution that would force France to choose between a veto, which would open a "major crisis" with Washington, and an abstention, which would be contrary to French convictions. Avoiding a direct confrontation with Washington was all the more important, Félix-Paganon said, because discord over the war should not prevent France and the United States from coming together again on postwar management and, in particular, on the necessary role of the UN in the reconstruction of Iraq. For Paris, this last point was an important consideration. "Nobody," Félix-Paganon concluded, "has an interest in making things worse." The paradox was that the price to pay for dissuading Washington from trying to obtain a resolution and thus for France to avoid casting its veto—namely, a diplomatic campaign that would devastate France's relations with the United States—ultimately would prove just as prohibitive for Paris as the cost of actually casting a veto.[43]

As February began, things were not yet at that stage, despite an already palpable tension between Paris and Washington. The skirmish after the so-called "ambush" in New York on January 20 and the Franco-German celebrations on January 22 had been a warning. When Chirac finally resolved to call Bush on February 7 (two days after the "proofs" session), as his advisers had been suggesting since the end of January, it was in the hope of avoiding a confrontation despite the two nations' obvious disagreement. In his call to Bush, Chirac ostensibly pleaded once more—without "great conviction," he later wrote—for inspections to be pursued. But the real objective of the telephone call was to try to convince Bush that the French opposition to the war should not be understood as a manifestation of hostility, and thereby to prevent an overly severe deterioration in bilateral relations. "I call you as a friend of the United States," Chirac began. "We have two different analyses that raise the issue of war and peace. It is a moral problem. You have one position, we have another. They are two visions of the world, and we have to deal with that. But this should not prevent us from talking to each other. . . . We are not anti-American. Our relationship is an old one and it has always survived all difficulties. I am attached to a transatlantic relationship that contributes to the equilibrium of the world and to the security of Europe. But in this affair, what is at stake is not transatlantic relations but rather the relations we have with the Middle East, where a war will have catastrophic consequences, including in terms of terrorism." He pleaded that even if a war took place, France and the United States would work together to reconstruct Iraq, "an immense task to which everybody should contribute."[44]

Bush responded in a similar tone, but with a note of disdainful irony. Thanking Chirac for his statements, he assured him that he, too, valued their "personal relationship" as well as the relationship between France and the United States. Saying that he appreciated Chirac's "consistency" and "compassion," he insisted that he did not like war, either, and that like any head of state he felt the "responsibility" of someone who decides to send troops into combat. "I'm responsible for hugging the families of those who've lost their lives in war," he said. But then, using an argument that left no room for debate, Bush stressed what separated him from Chirac. "I view an armed Saddam Hussein as a direct threat to the American people," he said, which might explain their difference of views on the inspections calendar—an understated reference to their complete disagreement over the war. The conversation ended with Bush thanking Chirac once more for the good cooperation between the two countries with respect to intelligence, and noting his wish for a solution to the ongoing NATO crisis.[45]

Behind the ostensibly polite nature of the conversation, both men had strong opinions. Chirac, according to witnesses, rolled his eyes when he listened once again to Bush justifying the war by the "threat" that Iraq represented to America. Meanwhile, Bush, as he wrote later, pulled a face when hearing Chirac speak of the "moral" problem about a war against a brutal dictator. In short, the disagreement was total: two world visions, in effect, opposed each other. "Our dialogue was no longer anything but that of two men who had run out of arguments," Chirac would later note, though he emphasized that "the tone, on both sides, was courteous, calm, and measured" and that "it always remained so." Chirac was right: if the relationship between him and Bush cooled off for several months, there was no personal affront. (This was a marked contrast to the bad blood between Bush and Schröder. Bush judged that Schröder had first promised not to oppose the war and then had denounced it for reasons of domestic policy, a reading of events that Schröder later would contest.) The American president credited his French counterpart with saying to him in private what he said in public.[46]

Yet both leaders clearly overestimated their capacity to preserve Franco-American relations from the negative fallout of the disagreement over Iraq. Chirac, as his February 7 conversation with Bush suggests, reasoned according to the conception of his predecessors since de Gaulle—who believed that disagreement over "peripheral" issues did not contradict the fundamentals of Franco-American relations—without seeing that America had changed after 9/11. As for Bush, he did not seem to have fully realized Chirac's determination to oppose the American desire to obtain UN approval to legitimize the war. (At this stage, Colin Powell still thought that France would probably abstain on an Anglo-American draft resolution in the Security Council.) It would not be long before events disabused both of them of these notions.[47]

The deterioration in bilateral relations, perceptible since the first half of February, was now abrupt. Both the State Department and Bush's associates had until then underestimated French resolve. (The hawks in the Pentagon and on Cheney's staff, by contrast, had been hell-bent for months against French policy.) Everything changed in a few days. The trigger was the France-Germany-Russia declaration of February 10. "It was galling to see the United States' NATO allies hug Russia in opposition to the United States on a matter of national security,"[48] Condoleezza Rice later remembered. The coalition of "old" Europe and Russia infuriated Washington: not only were Paris and Berlin failing to support the Americans in a crisis that they believed—whether in good faith or not—involved US vital interests, but they had not hesitated to make common cause with Washington's former Cold War nemesis. Combined with the NATO crisis that culminated at the same time, the tripartite declaration lent credit to the image of a disloyal France—Germany showed itself as less extreme in the NATO context—that was ready to do anything to hinder Washington's plans. The rebuff that Chirac inflicted a few days later on Washington's "new" eastern European allies obviously confirmed this image in the eyes of the Americans.

Two days after the tripartite declaration was issued, Jean-David Levitte was worrying about a "rapid rise" in tension: veteran observers like Henry Kissinger and Zbigniew Brzezinski, he reported from Washington, had had to go back to France's exit from NATO's integrated military organization in 1966 to find a period of similar hostility. At the White House, he wrote, the tone was becoming not only "unpleasant" but even "menacing." Daniel Fried, Bush's adviser on European affairs and a habitually urbane diplomat, had accused France of being the "coordinator" of the fight against the American position and warned that it would pay "dearly" and "for a long time" for pursuing such an attitude, particularly in NATO. The same tone prevailed in Congress, where French bashing was rapidly growing. Levitte found the outrageous language of someone like Representative Peter King—a Republican from New York State who attributed France's attitude to the fact that it had supposedly lost the two world wars—less disturbing than the hostile declarations of prominent senators from both sides of the aisle, like Arizona Republican John McCain and Florida Democrat Bob Graham. Levitte was all the more worried because there was now talk of a boycott of French products, although in his view it was an unlikely possibility because it was a minority position. It was especially the press, he noted, that was "raging" against France; whereas some moderate newspapers like the *New York Times* maintained a balanced approach, the television networks—led by Rupert Murdoch's Fox News— were unanimous in their vituperation. Undoubtedly, the most worrying sign was the "spectacular" drop in the popularity of France in American opinion. According to a recent poll, while Great Britain remained stable at 89 percent in favorable opinions, Germany had lost 12 points and France 20 points compared to the previous poll: France now had a 59 percent favorable opinion rating. Another more anecdotal illustration of the situation in Washington in mid-February 2003 was that on February 13, about a hundred students from Georgetown University had demonstrated in front of the French embassy on Reservoir Road (across the street from the university) with slogans like "Stop Saddam," "Save Turkey, not Iraq"—or, even more explicitly, "First Iraq, then France." Opposite them, some antiwar students had wanted to proclaim their support of the French position with the slogan "We are with you"—but there had been only a dozen of them.[49]

On February 17, three days after Villepin's Security Council speech, Levitte went to see Dick Cheney. The meeting left no doubt about the rapid deterioration in Franco-American relations. Levitte started the discussion. He wanted to reduce the drama of the Franco-American differences: Paris and Washington, he stressed, were in agreement on what was essential about Iraq, both about the nature of the regime and the necessity of its disarmament, including by force if needed. The only real difference, he argued, related to the need (or not) to pursue inspections at this stage. But Cheney did not want to put up with diplomatic language. He warned that he would be "frank" and that he would express himself without the "forms" that Bush would use. (This was Cheney's way of saying, Levitte inferred, that Bush thought as Cheney did.) Cheney went straight to the point: the state of Franco-American relations had never been so "abominable" for thirty-five years, with many in Washington harboring "serious doubts" about whether France was still the ally of the United States, for Paris was opposing Washington on a matter that went "to the heart" of American security and had thus made the "tragic" choice of causing "serious damage" to bilateral relations. And Iraq was only one element, Cheney said. Pointing to the long blockage that had just ended at NATO and congratulating himself that the United States had been able to circumvent France, he wondered if French policy now consisted of "defining" itself by a systematic opposition to the United States.

Then, Cheney launched into a justification of the coming war. Of course, it would have consequences, he conceded, but were not governments obliged to ensure the security of their citizens? A merely defensive strategy was inadequate: "The threat has to be destroyed at the source," he stressed, saying how "decisive" the American response to the September 11 attacks had been. Cheney then took up the arguments about the supposed links between Baghdad and Ansar al-Islam; Levitte noted that Cheney even went beyond Powell's February 5 declaration by asserting that Baghdad was effectively financing the al-Zarqawi group. The coming war against Iraq, Cheney was arguing in essence, was an integral part of the "war on terror." This, Cheney said, was what fundamentally separated Europeans from Americans: the September 11 attacks had occurred on US soil, and so Europe's solidarity had been merely fleeting and its perception of the threat had quickly diminished. To this remark, Levitte responded that he would never forget watching, from his UN office, the Twin Towers being "transformed into dust." He recalled that it was under the French presidency that the Security Council had adopted Resolution 1368 the next day, identifying the events of 9/11 as a threat to international peace and security, and he pointed to the European governments' determination to fight terrorism as well as their total solidarity with the United States. But Cheney was dismissive: another attack that this time would cause 7,000 deaths, or a bioattack on an American city, would no doubt trigger a new surge of European solidarity, he conceded with icy irony, but the United States simply could not wait passively for this to happen.

The conversation illustrated the chasm that now separated America from "old" Europe, and particularly from France. "Cheney does not like France," Levitte cabled after the meeting. "This is not new, but the violence contained in his statements speaks volumes about the level of exasperation toward us that prevails in the conservative camp." Levitte was struck by the fact that Cheney had used "a Franco-American disagreement over Iraq (a major one, to be sure) to describe France as behaving as a systematic adversary of the United States on the international scene." Levitte concluded, "We have become the leaders of the resistance to an impending war. For the conservatives who dominate the Bush administration, this is an unpardonable crime, since in doing so we are endangering the security of America at the very moment when it is realizing its vulnerability and is determined to undertake any action necessary to eradicate 'evil.'"[50] Levitte's assessment was an excellent description of how the Manichaeism and polarization that dominated American policy, both foreign and domestic, was leading to a confrontation with a France that refused to fall into line.

Paris feared such a clash. The majority of officials at the Quai d'Orsay did not hide their anxieties about a major Franco-American confrontation. "I've been talking with the directors of the ministry and our ambassadors in major capitals, and most of them are worried to say the least," Le Maire noted, adding: "Our diplomacy is convinced that since great maneuvers have been launched by Washington, the wisest thing, if rallying is not possible, is to run for shelter. . . . The course is steered by two or three directors, just as many ambassadors, the advisers [of the minister] who are in charge of dealing with this crisis, [and] the [minister's] chief of staff and assistant chief of staff." A meeting that had been called on February 7 by the Quai d'Orsay's secretary-general, the top civil servant in the French Foreign Ministry, confirmed Le Maire's description. At this meeting, which had been held two days after Powell's Security Council briefing, participants had discussed the attitude to adopt in case the Americans and British introduced a new draft Security Council resolution. The prospect of a French veto was still unanimously rejected; although it was considered "coherent" with the line defended for months, this option appeared the most "costly" since it was likely to provoke a grave crisis with the United States and to cause France's "lasting isolation"—without preventing the war.[51]

Defense circles were just as troubled. Although the French military had accepted the fact that the political authorities had decided not to participate in a military operation, they disliked the pacifist phraseology that Chirac had employed at the end of January, which echoed German discourse. They had made their displeasure known at the Élysée; they were especially worried about the consequences of a crisis with Washington for military cooperation with the United States, which they considered essential. The civilian leaders at the Ministry of Defense dreaded a confrontation for the same reasons, and also because French security policy in the wider sense—starting with nonproliferation policy, a major priority for Paris—implied close cooperation with the United States. In short, as one person close to Chirac later recalled, "a great many French officials [wondered] if there could be a Franco-American crisis" over Iraq without France paying dearly for its consequences.[52]

The rejection of a confrontation with the United States was just as clear outside the state apparatus. This was the case in the "Atlanticist" fringe of the French political spectrum. Only a handful of prominent politicians, like the former center-right minister Alain Madelin, declared squarely for the war. But some, like Pierre Lellouche—a member of parliament from Chirac's own political party, RPR (Rassemblement pour la République, Rally for the Republic)—fretted publicly about the turn that Franco-American relations had taken after January and February. Other politicians were content to air their concerns in private, like former RPR prime minister Edouard Balladur, as well as Interior Minister Nicolas Sarkozy and even Prime Minister Jean-Pierre Raffarin (both of whom kept their concerns quiet to preserve government solidarity). The same was true of some intellectuals and journalists, including the philosopher André Glucksmann; the editor-in-chief of the weekly *Le Point*, Claude Imbert; and the director of the journal *Commentaire*, Jean-Claude Casanova—the last of whom had expressed alarm during a luncheon to which Villepin had invited them at the end of January. Casanova, a disciple of noted French political scientist Raymond Aron, was the most forthright in his criticism of the turn taken by French policy, no doubt expressing the sentiments of a significant part of the small community of French strategists. "You have defended a certain vision of international affairs," he stated, "and that is fine. But you have been drawn along too far by the Germans, and in a register that is not our own: that of pacifism. Now that the game is over, be reasonable and return to the ranks. Nothing would be more damaging to our security, and for our economic interests, than a lasting confrontation, head to head, with the United States."[53]

Another group that was sensitive to the risk of confrontation with Washington was of course the business community, which was worried about a US boycott of French products. Ernest-Antoine Seillière, the chairman of Medef (France's national business association), sent messages about this to the Quai d'Orsay and to the Élysée in early 2003. Overall, influential circles mostly advocated moderation in contesting the United States. Yet all these were milieux, in a political system dominated by the presidency, that had only a limited weight when it came to foreign policy decision-making: "It was from the élites or those presumed to be such" that discordant voices were heard, Chirac later remarked. In this comment, he was taking up a classic Gaullist theme: the defense of the national interest when elites were inclined to abandon it.[54]

The Gaullist paradigm was indeed a determining factor in France's stance in the Iraq dossier. The "genetic code" inherited from the founder of the Fifth Republic explained the propensity of French decision-makers, Chirac foremost, to assume—rather than to actively seek—a frontal clash with the United States. Chirac, after all, had always claimed the heritage of de Gaulle (however distant in time), and so he was ready to follow in de Gaulle's footsteps. "There was evidently no question for me of challenging, not even remotely, the friendship that unites us with the American people," he later wrote, "but our political and diplomatic relation with the United States in my view had to remain more than ever faithful to the principle that had been ours since 1958: solidarity within independence."[55] French diplomacy, therefore, was ready to defend its views toward the United States, but it did not pursue a confrontation. This was in essence what Bernard Emié, the head of the Middle East directorate at the Quai d'Orsay and a former Chirac aid at the Élysée, told Sharon Wiener, the minister-counselor for political affairs at the US embassy in Paris, on February 10. When Wiener told Emié that she hoped that "serenity" would continue to prevail in Franco-American relations but was worried that the hawks in Washington might try to "punish" France by excluding its businesses from the reconstruction of Iraq if Paris continued to oppose the United States, Emié's answer was quintessentially Gaullist: France wanted to preserve its friendship with the United States, he said, but its policy was not driven by commercial interests. "Our ambition is not to ensure at all costs our place in Iraq after the fall of the regime," Emié added, emphasizing that French policy is "founded on principles."[56]

The Gaullist reflexes of French leaders were of course stimulated by another determining factor: the weight of a public opinion that now was massively opposed to the war. At the end of the summer of 2002, 58 percent of the French were hostile to an intervention in Iraq; by the start of January, the figure had risen to 76 percent, and was at 87 percent in mid-February. During this same month and a half, those who were "totally opposed" to a military intervention went from 42 percent to 57 percent. This opposition derived primarily from a rejection of American policy: three-quarters of those polled justified their attitude by the fact that they disapproved of the way the United States was handling the Iraq crisis, while only 13 percent and 9 percent mentioned, respectively, the fact that French interests were not involved or the fact that Iraq and Saddam Hussein did not represent a threat. Eighty-seven percent thought that US foreign policy—beyond the Iraq crisis—was motivated by the defense of US interests, while only 10 percent thought that it was determined by the defense of freedom and democracy in the world. In short, the French followed their leaders in seeing larger stakes in the Iraq crisis, as well as finding it the result of a preexisting American tendency toward unilateralism. Clearly, the latter was responsible for the steady deterioration in the image of the United States that had been going on for several years in France and in Europe against the backdrop of a growing transatlantic divorce over "values," including such issues as the death penalty or religion. So were Chirac and Villepin deliberately surfing on the wave of a resurgent anti-Americanism, as they later would be reproached for doing? As seen earlier, it would be simplistic to assert this. Whatever the case, in February 2003, 62 percent of the French said that they had a favorable opinion of Chirac, a rise of four points compared to January, and for the first time since the September 11 attacks, Chirac's popularity rating was positive even among a majority of left-wing sympathizers.[57]

European public opinion as a whole—including in Great Britain, Spain, and Italy, whose leaders said that they stood by the United States—seemed to prove French leaders right. Public opinion polls were corroborated by the huge demonstrations that succeeded one another in the major European cities. On February 15, the day after Villepin's UN speech, almost a million people took part in a major antiwar demonstration in London, one to two million gathered in Rome, and almost a million marched against the war in Madrid and Barcelona. (The demonstrators were less numerous in Berlin or Paris, no doubt due to their governments' positions.) Did French leaders, in this context, risk getting carried away? Some thought it was clear that Chirac was riding the antiwar wave for his own benefit in domestic politics; they observed that he had recovered a popularity rating close to the 82 percent of votes he had won in the second round of the 2002 presidential election, allowing him to revive a respectable left-right unanimity and make people forget that his reelection had owed much to the unexpected success of far-right nationalist Jean-Marie Le Pen in the election's first round. Some critics thought that Villepin, after his UN speech, was now skillfully playing the card of opposition to America to secure his own popularity and to forge a national political destiny. Others accused both men of working each other up to an anti-American frenzy. By managing the crisis with only the close circle of their respective entourages and feeling the massive support of French, European, and even world opinion behind them, critics said, Chirac and Villepin had become impervious to counsels of moderation and were losing the sense of proportion over what had become a Franco-American confrontation of an unprecedented intensity.[58]

Yet the fact remains that until the end of February, Chirac's diplomatic efforts went into trying to avoid an escalation at the UN. The French, as mentioned earlier, wanted to convince the Americans to give up on the idea of asking for a new resolution; this scenario appeared to be possible because the Americans thought that they could intervene in Iraq on the basis of existing resolutions, starting with Resolution 1441. "This option [no new resolution] presents advantages," Villepin's entourage stressed. It would disengage France from any responsibility in a conflict that it considered illegitimate; place the British face-to-face with their own contradictions; and, finally, allow Paris to position itself more easily in the postwar situation by advancing the necessary role of the UN, which might permit French involvement alongside the United States in Iraq's reconstruction. This option, Villepin's diplomats continued, presupposed presenting the Americans with a statement along the following lines: "We know that we will not be able to prevent you from conducting this war, and our intention is not to hamper you; but do not take the risk of a rejection [of a draft resolution] at the United Nations because we would be obliged, to our regret, to go right to the end."[59] Unsurprisingly, Levitte made himself the most active defender of this approach; it was he who took the initiative toward the Americans. Underlining that a "major confrontation" would be in nobody's interest, he had suggested to Cheney during their meeting on February 17 that if the United States decided to go to war, it might do so "without going back to the Security Council" since it originally had thought that Resolution 1441 would allow it to do so. Yet Cheney, carried away by his virulent denunciation of the French attitude, had not even acknowledged Levitte's suggestion. The next day, Levitte sent the same message to Daniel Fried and to Marc Grossman, the third-ranking official at the State Department, who simply took note of it.[60]

To push forward with his proposal, on February 21 Levitte seized on an opportunity to talk with Stephen Hadley, who was filling in for Rice. (Rice had left for Crawford, where Bush was welcoming his faithful ally José María Aznar.) The conversation, in contrast with the one with Cheney, was courteous: the two men did not even bother to linger over the fundamentals of the Iraqi issue, as the disagreement was obvious. But Levitte quickly understood that his suggestion, which he had reiterated to Hadley, was going nowhere. Although Hadley saluted it as "constructive," he objected to it as "impracticable": the Bush administration had been accused of practicing unilateralism and had chosen to "prove the contrary" by going through the UN, he explained, so it would be "very difficult" to make a U-turn at the Security Council. Moreover, Hadley said, a certain number of countries allied with Washington absolutely needed this second resolution for political reasons— clearly, he had Britain in mind. Hadley then advanced a proposal of his own, one that he no doubt knew had almost no chance of being accepted by Levitte: why not try to refine a resolution whose text would be limited to noting that Saddam Hussein had not fulfilled his obligations, he asked, since this would allow Paris to not use its veto? After all, Hadley argued, France had said that it shared this view. But Levitte could only reiterate the French position: Paris did not see the need for a fresh resolution, and would be led to oppose it.[61]

Levitte's attempted overture amounted to offering a gentlemen's agreement to Washington: the Americans would do without a resolution—on the model of the operation in Kosovo in 1999—and the French would promise not to be virulent in their denunciation of a unilateral decision, even if it ran counter to their interpretation of Resolution 1441. Levitte, of course, was not acting without the approval of his superiors: if the idea came from him, the initiative had been agreed on in Paris, where it was conceived as a gesture of appeasement. It was "legally questionable," a former Élysée official recognized, "but it would have allowed for 'damage limitation.'" Chirac, the official added, was scarcely convinced of its chances of success, but he was at least inclined to let his former diplomatic adviser go through the motions. It was a "last-ditch effort," a person close to Villepin later remarked, adding that "we knew we were going into a clash and that we would eventually have to take a position." This expectation was confirmed by the Levitte-Hadley meeting: although the

Americans wanted above all to help their British ally and secondarily to appear to play the UN game that they had themselves initiated, by that point they had indeed resolved to introduce a draft resolution, thinking (or claiming to think) that they had the necessary Security Council majority to secure its adoption. In doing so, they were ready to take the risk of a French veto that Washington and London would denounce as illegitimate while carrying on regardless.[62]

This resolve became apparent the very next day. On February 22, Bush and Aznar held a conference call from the Crawford ranch with Blair and Berlusconi. During the call, they decided that the moment had come to file a draft resolution declaring that Iraq had not conformed to Resolution 1441. On February 23, Powell called Villepin to warn him: the next day, Washington and London would present a text to the Security Council; there would be "neither ultimatum nor deadline," he said, but a "simple and direct" resolution noting the "material breach" of which Iraq was guilty, as Hadley had told Levitte. Villepin could only answer that Paris would not accept the new resolution "in the absence of new elements leading to acknowledging the failure of inspections." Furthermore, he deplored that the United States did not "seem any longer to take into account possible positive gestures from Iraq."[63]

Three days later, in a speech to the American Enterprise Institute, a premier neoconservative Washington think tank, Bush, echoing his UN speech, issued a warning. "Another resolution is now before the Security Council. If the council responds to Iraq's defiance with more excuses and delays . . . , the United Nations will be severely weakened. . . . If the members rise to this moment, then the [c]ouncil will fulfill its founding purpose." But the essence of Bush's statement lay elsewhere. Even though he declared that he hoped that Iraq "would disarm fully and peacefully," listeners could not doubt that he had decided to disarm it by force. Bush delivered a summary of the motives for an impending war, reviewing one more time the arguments that he had been putting forward for a year: it was a matter of confronting a dictator who was "hiding weapons" that could allow him to "dominate the Middle East and to intimidate the civilized world," and who "had close ties to terrorist organizations" to which he might supply "the terrible means to strike this country"; "the safety of the American people depends on ending this direct and growing threat," Bush declared. But for the first time, the American president explicitly took up the neoconservative argument in favor of the war: namely, to reorder the entire Middle East by means of regime change imposed by force. Invoking the German and Japanese precedents of 1945, Bush made the postconflict democratization of Iraq an objective in itself and for the whole of the Middle

East. "A new regime in Iraq would serve as a dramatic and inspiring example of freedom for other nations in the region," he asserted, stating that "success in Iraq could also begin a new stage for Middle Eastern peace," including between Israel and a democratic Palestinian state that might definitively break with terrorism. In short, Bush was justifying the theory that the road to Jerusalem went through Baghdad. He ended his speech by reaffirming the exceptionalism, even the messianism, that was at the heart of America's "mission": "We trust in the power of human freedom to change lives and nations. By the resolve and purpose of America . . . , we will make this an age of progress and liberty."[64] This time, the die was cast.

Chapter 7
The War: Spring–Summer 2003

At the end of February 2003, the last phase of the crisis opened. The United States had now resolved to intervene soon, and so the final diplomatic battle opened at the United Nations. London and Washington formally proposed another resolution. This proposal aimed to obtain the UN sanction that the British in particular needed; the stakes were no longer war or peace, as the United States and Great Britain claimed, but the legitimacy of the coming war. The crisis reached its apogee in the first two weeks of March. Faced with the "Anglo-Saxons," France appeared more than ever as the leader of the "peace camp" in a now-global confrontation, as illustrated by the race for Security Council votes that took place in those crucial weeks. In early March, this race would lead Dominique de Villepin to embark on a spectacular African tour, and would bring Jacques Chirac to brandish the threat of a French veto in New York.

When the British and Americans gave up on obtaining the coveted resolution in the face of opposition from France and many other countries, London and Washington put the blame on a "failure of diplomacy." Now nothing could prevent the war, which began on the night of March 19–20. It would last for three weeks; on April 9, Saddam Hussein's regime fell, symbolically, in front of cameras from around the world when the dictator's statue was toppled with the help of American soldiers. The stunning Anglo-American victory opened a period of euphoria, whose climax was reached on May 1 when George W. Bush stood under a "Mission Accomplished" sign on a US aircraft carrier. This phase of triumphalism would be brief, however. From the summer on, the evidence was clear; the war in Iraq was only beginning. In retrospect, the French had been right—and in this context, France tried to turn the page quickly on the confrontation in order to reestablish normal relations with the United States as soon as possible.

"Whatever the circumstances, France will vote No"

On February 24, the British put "in blue" (that is, made official) a draft resolution of which the Americans were only "co-sponsors" with the Spanish. That London was playing first fiddle is not surprising in light of the important stakes for Tony Blair in getting UN validation for the war. The actual content of the proposed resolution was very short: invoking Chapter VII of the UN Charter, which in itself signaled the possibility of the use of force, the Security Council decided that Iraq had failed "to take the final opportunity [to disarm] afforded to it by resolution 1441." But the essence lay in the eleven-paragraph preamble, which accused Iraq of being in "material breach" and under the threat of the "serious consequences" of which the council had warned it. That day, Sir Jeremy Greenstock delivered a lengthy presentation that covered Iraq's failings: the obstacles to inspections, foot-dragging cooperation, and the absence of answers to unresolved issues (starting with the anthrax and VX). Iraq, Greenstock concluded, was not disarming and had no intention of doing so. Yet he declared that the council was not being asked to act on these findings immediately, and that Baghdad still had time to make the "good choice": in short, recourse to force supposedly had not yet been decided upon, and it was simply a matter of putting more pressure on Iraq.

The French were not misled. The deliberately vague nature of the text, they believed, aimed to make it acceptable to the "hesitant" countries, when it was in fact an authorization to resort to force, albeit through language of paraphrase and allusion. Jean-Marc de La Sablière stressed this belief in his answer to Greenstock: such a resolution would be tantamount to a "rubber stamp" to a planned war, he said. The Russians and Germans were on the same wavelength. That day, Paris, Berlin, and Moscow issued a memorandum that expanded on the "non-paper" of February 7: the three countries, supported by Beijing, wanted to show that there still was an alternative to war. This alternative involved a further intensification and acceleration of the inspectors' work. It called for a presentation by the UN inspectors on March 1—namely, three weeks in advance—of the work program mentioned in Resolution 1284, and in particular of the "key remaining disarmament tasks," which should be put in a hierarchy to incite Iraq to cooperate more actively. Furthermore, every three weeks the inspectors would present reports to the Security Council, and progress would be evaluated after the 120 days stipulated in Resolution 1284.[1]

Previously, Paris's objective had been to dissuade London and Washington from demanding a new resolution; now it was to prevent its adoption. It was no longer a matter of preventing the war since, as Bruno Le Maire noted, it was now clear that it would take place. The goal, rather, was to prevent the Americans and their allies from obtaining UN legitimacy. "We risk making the United Nations endorse a disaster," Le Maire wrote. Chirac told his Mexican and Brazilian counterparts the same thing after the British draft resolution was made official. The United States, he explained to Mexico's Vicente Fox, wanted to enter the war for motives other than the claimed Iraqi threat—which did not justify an immediate war—and first and foremost in order to change the Iraqi regime and reshape the political landscape of the Middle East. This, he said, was a "dangerous strategy" that would only "play the game of Islamist extremism." And Chirac told Brazil's Luiz Inácio Lula da Silva that if the United States wanted to lead an intervention that would constitute a "serious precedent" and would have "disastrous consequences," it was "a responsibility that it should assume alone" and without trying to obtain the "complicity" of the international community.[2]

This final phase of the crisis at the UN was thus characterized by a double bluff. The "Anglo-Saxons," in trying to obtain a resolution authorizing the use of force (which they said gave Saddam Hussein a last chance to comply), were claiming that they wanted to avoid a conflict, whereas in fact they wished to legitimize a war they had already decided upon. Meanwhile, the French-led "peace camp," in refusing to adopt such a resolution, also were claiming that they wanted to avoid a conflict, whereas they really were trying to avoid granting UN legitimacy for a war that they now knew was inevitable.

A resolution that would reconcile the two points of view appeared quite illusory. Conceivably, a possible compromise could consist of extending the time period granted to Iraq to perform its obligations, at the end of which it would be declared disarmed or, failing that, would be subject to a military intervention. But an agreement on this basis was highly improbable: the Americans and the British wanted to be able to proceed quickly to action, whereas the French and their allies, concerned with giving inspections a chance, wished for a "realistic" timetable (counted in months, not weeks) and rejected anything automatic about the use of force—on which, in any case, the Security Council would have to pronounce. In effect, the two sides were going back to the debate over Resolution 1441, but this time without any real prospect of agreement since the deadlines were now imminent. The Canadians, for instance, proposed a one-month deadline that the French judged unacceptable because it amounted to a "disguised ultimatum." Of course, Paris said that it was open to discussing the issue, not wanting to appear divisive or alienate the "hesitant" countries that might support it. But in fact, things were quite clear. "Any formula for real compromise has no chance of being accepted by the Americans," said the Quai d'Orsay's UN directorate—an analysis shared by the French delegation in New York.[3]

Although the French had not succeeded in preventing the Americans and the British from tabling a draft resolution, they could still hope to bring them to withdraw their proposal if it was not certain that the resolution would obtain the nine indispensable positive votes. Paris would thereby be spared casting a veto, and if the text nevertheless was put to the vote without obtaining the needed nine votes, a negative vote from France or another permanent member would not formally count as a veto, since the resolution had not received the necessary support. With the "war camp" having four assured votes (the United States, Great Britain, Spain, and Bulgaria) and the "peace camp" having five (France, Germany, Russia, China, and Syria), to block the resolution at least two of the "hesitant" countries (the three African countries of Angola, Cameroon, and Guinea; the two Latin American countries of Chile and Mexico; and Pakistan) would have to abstain. (As will be seen below, a plain negative vote by any of these countries would be unlikely, given the consequences of such a vote on their relations with Washington.) This outcome did not appear out of reach, even if the French knew that the pressure—financial and other—that Washington and London were able to exert on the hesitant nations was such that the result might be close. Therefore, it was necessary to "cultivate" them by targeting particularly the two Francophone African countries, Cameroon and Guinea, without neglecting the two Latin American ones.

Quickly, however, it appeared that persuasion might not suffice, whatever the merits of the French arguments. The "hesitants," starting with the Chileans and Mexicans, pointed out that a mere abstention on their part would have a high cost on their relations with the United States. To "share the burden," they said, the permanent members, starting with France, would have to make it clearly known that they would vote against the text even if there were a majority of nine votes; this, they said, would permit them to better resist the pressure from Washington. The point was made: if France (and Russia and China, for that matter) were to content itself with proclaiming its intention to abstain and counting on the same attitude from the "hesitants" in order to prevent the text from being adopted—as many in Paris had wished from the start to avoid the "clash" with Washington—it ran the risk that the Americans would use pressure to rally some of the hesitants, and thus the resolution might pass. Washington and London, in fact, were busy spreading the rumor that Paris eventually would abstain, precisely to weigh on the hesitant capitals. This scenario, as we shall see, would lead the French in the first days of March to brandish the threat of a veto in the hope of not having to use it. Such a scenario was detectable between the lines of the new declaration that France, Germany, and Russia adopted on March 5. Reiterating the goal of the "peaceful and complete" disarmament of Iraq, the Three declared that they "will not let a proposed resolution pass that would authorize the use of force" and specified that "Russia and France, as permanent members of the Security Council, will assume all their responsibilities." Although it was only implicit, the threat of a double Franco-Russian veto—and a German "no"—was now clear.[4]

On March 7, the Security Council was again scheduled to listen to inspectors present the UNMOVIC trimester report under Resolution 1284, covering the period from December 1 to February 28. Things did not look good. The document, which first had been presented to the UNMOVIC commissioners at the end of February, made a rather negative assessment of Iraqi cooperation since the resumption of inspections. Although Hans Blix denied any bias in the report, the French judged the draft report overall as very critical on both substance and procedure. The key message was that Iraq could have made more efforts over the past three months, a position that the French delegation noted might "play the Anglo-Saxon game." Furthermore, Blix, in order not to appear to choose sides, was not willing to advance the presentation of his work program to March 1, as the French, Russians, and Germans had suggested in their memorandum of February 24 in order to give credibility to the pursuit of the inspections process.[5]

At the approach of the March 7 meeting (which might well be the last of its kind) the Baghdad regime seemed once more on the point of shooting itself in the foot. At stake was the fate of the hundred-some Al-Samoud missiles held by Iraq. UNMOVIC had established that, despite Iraqi denials, the missiles were able to exceed by several tens of kilometers the authorized 150 kilometers. In a letter addressed to Baghdad on February 21, Blix had required their destruction before March 1. These missiles were not fully operational, and their military value was not very significant, but it was a test: an Iraqi refusal to destroy them would no doubt represent a new "material breach." On February 24, in an interview with Dan Rather of CBS, Saddam Hussein seemed determined to resist the injunction. Immediately, the peace camp led by the French and Russians mobilized to pass a firm message to the Iraqis. The day before, French chargé d'affaires André Janier had warned Tariq Aziz that not complying would give a "present" to the Americans and would be indefensible. In the following days, Chirac was personally involved in trying to make the Iraqis budge: during telephone conversations with Syria's Bashar al-Assad and Pakistan's Pervez Musharraf, he asked his counterparts to convey to the Iraqis that a refusal would amount to "giving an enormous advantage to those who want a war." In the end, on February 28 Baghdad announced that shortly it would start destroying the missiles, which somewhat compensated for the negative effect of the trimestral report that was published the same day. But this new episode of Iraqi equivocation came at the worst possible time. The day before, Colin Powell had warned Villepin that the Iraqis likely would end up complying, but that would change nothing; there was simply no hope, Powell said bluntly, that Baghdad would adopt a "change of heart" leading to "a truly sincere and effective cooperation."[6]

In this tense context, the March 7 session turned out to be a pleasant surprise for the French delegation. Two days earlier, Blix had declared to the press that Iraqi capabilities were "much weaker" than they had been in 1991, all the more so because the country was now under surveillance. His presentation was cautious as usual, but its bottom line was positive. Blix stressed the recent efforts at cooperation by Baghdad: the beginning of destruction of the Al-Samoud missiles, a desire to clarify the quantities of biological and chemical weapons that the Iraqis claimed they had destroyed in 1991, and the submission of documents concerning anthrax and VX. Baghdad, Blix said, was now "active," even "proactive." Arriving after three months, this cooperation could not be called "immediate," he acknowledged, but it was nevertheless "welcome." Blix said that he soon would be ready to present his work program, knowing that the cooperation might be evaluated as a function of the "key disarmament task" that remained to be elucidated. This task, he specified, would take time that could not be counted in days or years, but in months. Blix's proposal was close to the timeline suggested by the French, and it contradicted the idea that Iraq could give immediate proofs of its disarmament, as the Americans and British maintained.[7]

But it was the report from Mohamed ElBaradei that made a sensation that day. Mentioning the "important progress" made by the IAEA in three months and underlining that it had detected no sign of a resumption of nuclear activities in Iraq, he said that he would be able to present an "objective and thorough" assessment in the "near future." ElBaradei, noted the French after his presentation, was not far from considering that the nuclear file might be closed soon. Better still, in his presentation he had given elements that invalidated two of the principal items of evidence in the American accusation. First, on the aluminum tubes, he was now able to confirm (as he had implied in his previous report) that there was no evidence that they were meant for anything other than rocket production; the thesis of centrifuge production, as a result, was practically disproved. Second, on the uranium from Niger, he announced that the corresponding allegations rested on documents that "[were] in fact not authentic."[8] This was the conclusion that Jacques Baute, the head of the IAEA Iraq Action Team, had reached a few days earlier after examining the evidence sent in February by the CIA to the IAEA at its request. These documents had turned out to be gross forgeries, and it would later be found that they had been transmitted to the Americans in the autumn of 2002 by an Italian intelligence crook.[9]

Overall, the positive impression given that day by the inspectors' reports was once again in favor of the peace camp, but with the deadlines approaching fast it did not fundamentally change the situation. Bush stamped his foot: he was under attack from the hawks in the media for being indecisive, since the war had still not started, and for having wrongly chosen the UN road, as shown by the Declaration of the Three. On March 5, Donald Rumsfeld and Tommy Franks had briefed him on the state of the military arrangements: 208,000 personnel (137,000 from the army) were present in the region, and 50,000 were ready to reinforce them in two weeks, on top of 44,000 men in the coalition, mostly British. Franks declared that the war could be launched at any moment. So on the evening of March 6—the day before the inspectors' presentation—Bush held a press conference that preempted the next day's debates, while in effect responding to the trio that had met the day before in Paris. Although he continued to maintain that a military operation had not been decreed ("I've not made up our mind," he said in his unmistakable syntax), he insinuated the exact opposite: arguing that the Iraqis were hiding biological and chemical agents, he said that "the final stages of diplomacy" had arrived. "We're calling for the vote," he warned, using poker-style language. "It's time for people to show their cards." Ironically, at this same moment,

Powell and Villepin were meeting in New York, and their aides were passing the time together by watching the president on television.[10]

Under these conditions, the debates that followed the inspectors' presentations at the Security Council the following day held no surprises. The meeting was held again at the foreign-minister level: Villepin, Igor Ivanov, and Joschka Fischer had announced that they would be present, forcing Powell and Jack Straw to be there as well. The peace camp, in this final phase, wanted to get a maximum impact from the debates. Villepin reiterated France's rejection of a resolution authorizing automatic recourse to force, but he then made an overture: the 120-day disarmament evaluation period called for by Resolution 1284 and mentioned in the February 24 Franco-German-Russian memorandum might be shortened if the inspectors judged that it would be useful to do so, he suggested. Villepin nevertheless denounced a planned war whose real motives were not those proclaimed, and he called for the UN to be placed back at the heart of international affairs. He concluded with a breathtaking proposal—considered unrealistic even by his own diplomats—that the upcoming Security Council vote should be conducted at the level of heads of states and of governments, because it was a matter of war or peace. Powell, for his part, repeated that the issue was not about whether or not to prolong inspections, but rather about the choice that Baghdad had to make to disarm; the inspectors' report, he stressed, was a catalogue of noncooperation. Straw, whom the French judged "rather aggressive," continued to claim (against all the evidence) that the draft resolution on the table did not imply automatic recourse to force, and that it aimed merely to increase the pressure on Baghdad. In short, the foreign ministers were at an impasse.[11]

The British, however, began on that day a movement that could undermine the position of the peace camp by introducing, in agreement with the Americans, a change to their planned resolution. In substance, Iraq would be offered a "*last* last chance" until March 17, after which there would be war unless the Security Council concluded that Baghdad had met its obligations. The French delegation analyzed that the six "hesitants" might be tempted by this formula, since it would throw back onto the Iraqis the responsibility for war in case of their (probable) failure to meet the deadline. The hesitants then in good conscience could rally to the Anglo-American resolution and avoid a clash with Washington. The Six were indeed interested in the British amendment and were ready to negotiate: on March 8, they undertook a joint approach to ask Blix what he believed should be the "criteria" or "benchmarks" for evaluating the reality of Iraq's disarmament on March 17. This approach worried the French delegation, which knew that Blix was favorable to issuing an ultimatum combined with "benchmarks." The proposed British amendment was indeed worrisome: if a sufficient number of hesitants supported the resolution, it would ensure a majority of nine for the Anglo-Americans—especially since London and Washington, La Sablière warned, were ready to make "purely cosmetic" concessions to achieve their ends. He pleaded for an offensive strategy: Paris should maintain contact with the Six, including at the highest level, and send them the following message: "Make no mistake: the Anglo-American resolution, even if amended, means war, and war in unacceptable conditions" given the positive results of inspections.[12]

The call was heard in Paris, and in the following days it would prompt French leaders to intensify their activity in the hope of making the Anglo-Americans fail, even if this meant upping the ante. On March 9, Chirac went again to his telephone. He talked first with Gerhard Schröder and Vladimir Putin. Schröder was entirely in agreement with refusing a formula that contained either an ultimatum or automatic recourse to force, and he said that he was ready to come to New York for the vote. Putin was more evasive on his own possible attendance, but he confirmed his opposition to any resolution authorizing war. Then the French president called his Pakistani, Mexican, and Chilean counterparts. Pervez Musharraf agreed on the line to take but did not say that he would come to New York, on the pretext of the short deadline. Vincente Fox and his Chilean counterpart, Ricardo Lagos, were also reserved; invoking the need not to add to the division in the Security Council, the two Latin American presidents—who were clearly working in tandem—declared that they had not ruled out Paris's approach entirely, but they wanted to find a compromise on the basis of a delay that would be granted to Iraq. Their response confirmed their interest in finding a formula that would allow them to avoid a clash with the United States; Washington was manifestly redoubling pressure on them, raising the risk of their rallying to the resolution.[13]

For Paris, the main concern was the three African countries. For several days, the French noted how much pressure the Americans and British were putting on them to obtain their votes. In New York, the French delegation observed that the representatives from Angola, Guinea, and Cameroon were shaky; even the two Francophone nations, in which Paris placed its hopes, seemed like "weak links." At the end of February, Tony Blair had sent Baroness Valerie Amos—a member of the House of Lords of Guyanese origin—to the three countries, where she apparently had been persuasive. The Americans were not lagging behind: the assistant secretary of state for African affairs had even taken advantage of a Franco-African summit held in Paris at the end of February to canvass the entourages of the three African presidents. (The summit had nevertheless adopted a declaration that conformed to the French position.) The "Anglo-Saxons" promised the African countries a lot, the French believed: debt relief, tolerance for their failures in human rights, investments—plus other tangible incentives. In short, the French realized that Africa, even the Francophone parts, was no longer their preserve.[14]

For the French, it was difficult to fight on the same ground, if only because they wanted ostensibly to give priority to "principles" when discussing the Iraq issue. True, they were ready to consider gestures like granting supplemental aid to Guinea ("we offered them a new road," an Élysée adviser recalled) or else implying that the "Angola-gate" affair (an arms trafficking case that had been poisoning relations between Paris and Luanda for several years) might have a favorable judicial result. But should they send a high-level emissary to the leaders of the three countries? Cameroon president Paul Biya asked for this: such a gesture would encourage him to face up to the United States, he implied. But Paris hesitated, as such an initiative would only raise the tension level with the Americans. "Chirac was not very much in favor," a person close to Villepin remembered. In the end, though, the risk of seeing the three African countries go over to support the resolution convinced French leaders to act. Returning from New York the morning of March 9, Villepin departed for Angola the same evening.[15]

On March 10, French worries were confirmed in Luanda. Villepin held out debt relief and a possible resumption of military cooperation—all as part of postconflict assistance to Angola, which was getting over a long civil war—but in vain; he obtained nothing on the subject that interested him. Deploring that the Iraqi issue had become a combat of "giants" at the UN, President Eduardo Dos Santos pointed out that small countries had to "protect themselves," implying that he might support the Anglo-American position. When Villepin traveled to Yaoundé on the same day, the result there was hardly more encouraging. Biya, whose country proclaimed neutrality, seemed to waver. "We would have liked . . . more public engagement on our side" from the African country closest to us, the French said with regret, though they hoped that it was only a matter of "tactics" and that Yaoundé would ultimately show solidarity. Yet the final leg of the tour, in Conakry, was no more conclusive. (President Lansana Conté was ill and unavailable, and so Villepin was received by the prime minister.) Although the French had hoped to play on the atavistic anti-imperialism of their former colony, Guinea seemed not to have made up its mind and would not commit to either side. On the whole, Villepin's tour was not the anticipated success. Moreover, Baroness Amos was on his heels: on the evening of the 10th, London announced that she was undertaking a new trip to Africa.[16]

This disappointing result from Villepin's diplomatic visits no doubt explained Chirac's statement during a live television interview on the evening of March 10. The drama was high: a vote was expected two days later, and Chirac and Schröder's proposed trip to New York had made headlines minutes before. From the start, Chirac put himself on principled ground, attacking the aims of the Bush administration beyond the immediate crisis. "We have to know in what world we want to live," he declared, invoking as usual a "multipolar" world. He stressed that the "inspectors say that cooperation has improved" and that they are able to "pursue their work." Above all, he confirmed that France would oppose the resolution, which he thought would not get the required majority of nine votes; as a result, he said, "there will be no problem of a veto." Pushed by journalists who demanded to know if he would do the same even if a majority emerged, Chirac declared, "My position is that, whatever the circumstances, France will vote 'no' because it considers this evening that there is no reason to go to war."[17] This time, it was said aloud: France, if necessary, would use its veto.

"The French laid down their cards"

Chirac's statement was the high point of a strategy that brandished the "atomic weapon" of the veto in order not to have to use it. He was giving the six hesitant countries—especially the two Latin American ones—the signal of the French determination that they had said they needed to resist American pressure and abstain in a possible vote. A few days later, this strategy would have the hoped-for result, but at the price of aggravating the Franco-American confrontation and a Franco-British psychodrama.

Although the Americans were furious about the public clarification made that evening by Chirac, it was the British who led the counteroffensive. The situation in London was critical: faced with a public opinion that was massively hostile to the war—especially if there was no UN mandate—and a rebellion by some of his own troops in the House of Commons and within the Cabinet, the survival of Tony Blair's government was at stake. "Without a UN resolution specifically agreeing to military action," Blair summed up, the political situation could become "possibly terminal." Chirac's television appearance on March 10 was a hard blow, since it ended any hope of obtaining the resolution. Yet Blair still hoped to be able to gather in New York a majority of nine that would enable him to denounce an "unreasonable" French veto, or failing that, to point out that he had tried everything to obtain a resolution, which might help him save the situation at home by making the French take the rap for its failure. Of course, Blair continued to claim that he was pursuing a resolution that would avoid war by putting a final pressure on Baghdad, in the hopes that Saddam Hussein would "capitulate."[18] But he was clearly doing so against all evidence, for who could still believe that the Iraqi dictator was ready to "capitulate"—or, for that matter, that Bush would give up on the war?

The American president was indeed extremely reluctant to go along with this final British maneuver at the UN. Once he heard about Chirac's declaration, Bush wanted to end the diplomatic game as soon as possible, as he thought it was dragging on and uselessly delaying the start of operations. Only Blair's likely fate dissuaded Bush from blowing the whistle on the game in New York. The fall of Blair's government, which the Americans did not rule out, would be a reversal for Washington; Bush even confided to Blair on March 9 that he would rather have the British not participate in operations, at least initially, if that might save Blair's government. Blair, unsurprisingly, rejected this scenario: he did not intend to give up, whatever the political cost. Yet Bush's proposal confirmed that in American eyes, the political stake of Britain's support vastly exceeded the military interest of its actual participation. Rumsfeld, with his customary roughness, also confirmed this perspective when he declared publicly on March 11 that British nonparticipation was not to be ruled out in light of Blair's difficulties, and that Bush would consider options in the days to come. Was this misspeaking, or sabotage? In either case, Rumsfeld's remarks infuriated the British: it seemed to put them in the position of backup troops, without which the Americans could do just as well.[19]

The British margin of maneuver at the UN—even if they claimed that they were now only one vote short of a majority—was extremely limited because of the Americans' fixed military calendar. Washington had no wish whatsoever to prolong negotiations in New York. In the days following Chirac's declaration, the definition of the "benchmarks" that Iraq would have to respect in the remaining lapse of time became the critical issue. The French were not dupes: for the British, it was a matter of reaching a "mix" of realistic and unattainable criteria that would be derived from the UNMOVIC reports in order to make them credible to the undecided. But apart from the fact that this final attempt clearly was aimed not to prevent a war but instead to legitimate it, it soon appeared that it was hampered by the huge gap between the Americans, who merely gave lip service to the idea of benchmarks out of fear that the outcome would be revealed as not clearly negative, and the six "hesitants," who wished to define objective and realistic criteria. On March 12, Sir Jeremy Greenstock—visibly tense, noted the French—presented six "tests" that Iraq would have to fulfill, starting with a televised speech by Saddam Hussein in Arabic, in which he would recognize that Iraq had in the past hidden its WMD but that it had made a "strategic decision" to give them up. Greenstock also implied that the March 17 deadline would be negotiable and that the British would do everything possible to push back the ultimatum by several days, hinting that they were ready to put pressure on the Americans to that effect. But the proposal was a flop: the Americans did not really support it and the Six, starting with the Mexicans and the Chileans, were not convinced. That same evening, Blair asked Bush to try one last time to convince Fox and Lagos to vote for the resolution. The result was categorical: despite Bush's insistence, Fox remained elusive and Lagos said no. Also on the same day, Powell and Villepin had a telephone conversation in which they acknowledged the impasse. The former noted Chirac's "radical" opposition to any resolution authorizing the use of force, whereas the latter argued, once again, that a peaceful solution remained possible, and rejected the use of force except as a last resort. Recognizing that an intervention carried "risks," Powell appealed to history, which he said showed that the United States had been able to conduct wars that led to "improving things."[20]

The end of the game was now close. On March 13, the six undecided nations—who, the week before, had said that they were ready to examine the British proposals—rejected them, and the British, Americans, and Spanish announced yet again that the vote on the draft resolution would be postponed. The British went to-and-fro by suggesting that the first criterion, the declaration by Saddam Hussein, might be abandoned. (Everybody knew that there would be no chance of his accepting it, since it would be a major humiliation.) Yet the Americans were now unwilling to make any concessions, leading the Six to put a stop to the current compromise attempt. This dénouement demonstrated that the Anglo-Americans, despite their maneuvers, did not in fact possess a Security Council majority to validate their decision to enter a war. "The general feeling," La Sablière wrote on March 14, "was that the Security Council process had reached its end." As a matter of fact, two days later, Bush, Blair, and Aznar were meant to meet in the Azores—and nobody seriously imagined that the intent of this meeting was to prolong the diplomatic route.[21]

Since the end of January, Franco-British relations had been in a difficult period. During the Franco-British summit in Le Touquet at the start of February, Blair and Chirac had agreed to "confine" their disagreement over Iraq by advancing their cooperation in other domains, starting with defense. But as the final showdown approached, this pact of nonaggression was harder to observe. The political difficulties of the British government over the coming war were a major factor in the growing Franco-British frictions; by opposing the adoption of a resolution, Paris considerably complicated Blair's task, on which his political survival depended. The French were aware of this, but they believed that Blair had only himself to blame, since his difficulties stemmed from his own choices and mistakes, notably about French policy. "Because they have wanted to believe that our attitude derives from a systematically anti-American posture," Gérard Errera wrote the day after Chirac's March 10 television appearance, "[the British] have not taken the full measure of our determination." Nor, Errera added, had they understood that the French position rested on fundamental questions of principle that were shared by British opponents of the war. Errera—who had not missed Rumsfeld's statement the same day, and drew the conclusion that Blair's support was not returned—concluded that after the Iraqi "adventure," Blair "will not be able to escape asking himself questions about the nature of the U.K.'s interest: either to continue to stick to the United States to exercise some kind of illusory control, or else to redefine, with us and the Germans, the bases of a new relation, healthier and less unequal, with the United States."[22] In the meantime, he said, the Blair government might well be tempted to launch a press campaign against France to better disown its difficulties.

Errera's prediction was correct. Blair did not hesitate—at the cost of a fallacious argument—to stigmatize France's alleged responsibility for the expected failure of the resolution and even for the unleashing of the war, in the hope of closing ranks around the government as the hostilities approached. Chirac, it is true, had inadvertently offered Blair and his "spin doctors" a golden opportunity by declaring on March 10 that he would oppose a resolution "whatever the circumstances." Of course, Chirac had referred to the votes of the other members of the Security Council—whether or not a majority existed—and he had not meant to signal a refusal a priori to negotiate over a text that did not include the "automatic" use of force. But extracted from its context, Chirac's phrase served Blair's purposes: was this not the "unreasonable" veto that Blair had denounced in advance, and would not the French attitude make the war inevitable by preventing the international community from putting a final pressure on Baghdad? There was, of course, a flagrant lack of honesty in this line of reasoning, since Blair clearly was trying to obtain validation for the war, not to prevent it. Be that as it may, on March 11 he denounced the fact that a country (which he did not name) "talk[ed] about using a veto in all sets of circumstances." The next day, Errera set the record straight for the press and for his British governmental interlocutors, denouncing the "deliberate misrepresentation" of Chirac's statement. On March 13, Maurice Gourdault-Montagne did the same to the British ambassador in Paris. But when Villepin telephoned Straw, contesting the British interpretation, the latter responded that he had a "different reading" of Chirac's statements and threw the fault back on Paris. Straw used the same specious reasoning; blocking the resolution, he argued, would mean missing the opportunity to apply final pressure on Baghdad and thus play the game of those in Washington who wanted to ignore the UN.[23]

The British deliberately ignored the French effort to set the record straight. "The French can hardly be surprised [by our position]," wrote John Holmes, the British ambassador in Paris, "[or by] the fact that we are using Chirac's words against him." He added, somewhat perfidiously, "He did say them, even if he may not have meant to express quite what we have chosen to interpret."[24] Even more cynically, Blair and his communication advisers—led by Alastair Campbell—decided to conduct a full-fledged press campaign against France, using newspapers like the *Sun*, Rupert Murdoch's tabloid. "There is no doubt that Tony Blair and Jack Straw knew what they were doing," Stephen Wall, then Blair's adviser on European affairs, later testified, commenting that "in British politics, playing the anti-French card is a pretty sure-fire successful card to play." The British were looking for a scapegoat by attacking France, Villepin noted on March 14 during a conversation with his Spanish counterpart, Ana Palacio. Palacio recognized that Blair was stuck in a "very complicated" situation. "I am like a man walking across a precipice on a tightrope with only a straw to balance with," Blair confided to Wall. Clearly, he was ready to try all means to save his government.[25]

Once the impasse in New York came to a head on March 14, matters swiftly accelerated. The day before, Bush had indicated to his aides that he wished to organize a summit with Blair to dissipate the nebulous impression that had resulted from the interminable palavers in New York. But Blair feared being absent from London even for a short period, given the political situation: in November 1990, had not Margaret Thatcher lost her post when she went to a summit in Paris while the Tories were in full rebellion? The idea of a meeting in Bermuda was dismissed as being too near the United States and too far from the United Kingdom, as was a visit by Bush to London, which was considered too risky, given the hostile public opinion. Thus it was in the Azores, a symbolic site of the transatlantic relationship, that Bush, Blair, and Aznar met at the invitation of Portuguese prime minister José Manuel Barroso, who also sided with the Anglo-Americans.

The meeting took place Sunday, March 16, on Lajes Air Base on Terceira Island. Although it was not presented as such, the summit—which Aznar unashamedly called the "last chance for peace"—looked like a war council. The participants agreed to put an end to the diplomatic process the next morning if no compromise was reached; in other words, if the peace camp did not rally to the Anglo-American resolution, which was still formally on the table. Earlier the same day, Chirac had given CNN and CBS an interview in which he said that he was open to a compromise that would give the inspectors from one to three months—their choice—to finish their work, but this proposal was promptly swept aside by Bush, who chose to see Chirac's overture only as a delaying tactic. Meanwhile, Cheney and Powell, on the US weekend talk shows, adopted the same tactic that Blair had used in throwing the responsibility onto France. At the end of the Azores meeting, Bush—who had a hard time concealing that war was imminent—followed suit in front of the cameras: "I was the guy that said they ought to vote," he declared in his macho, poker-playing tone. "France showed their cards. . . . They said they were going to veto anything that held Saddam to account. So cards have been played, and we'll just have to take an assessment after tomorrow to determine what that card meant."[26]

Returning to Washington, Bush warned Franks on the morning of the 17th to be ready to launch operations within seventy-two hours. He had his spokesman announce that the "diplomatic window is closed" and that he would address the nation that evening. In New York, the American, British, and Spanish representatives announced that morning that they were giving up asking for a vote on their proposed resolution, justifying this decision by the "intransigence of a permanent member" and the probability of the resolution being vetoed. La Sablière retorted—and repeated to the press—that a veto would have signified the existence of a majority that in reality did not exist. In the Security Council session, La Sablière asked Hans Blix about the timescale that he would need to conduct his work program, and Blix repeated that several months would be necessary but that the timescale could be shortened if certain "key tasks" were chosen to "test" Iraq's disarmament. Some of these tests, like the destruction of remaining missiles or the holding of interviews with Iraqi scientists, could be accomplished quickly. Others, like tasks concerning anthrax or the mobile laboratories, if Iraq did have them, would take longer. (Blix was now ready to recognize that it was much more difficult to prove their absence than their presence.) He even stated that Baghdad had made a good deal of effort to prove its good faith over VX and anthrax, and that seventy Al-Samoud missiles had been destroyed up to that date. Blix's statements clearly vindicated France's approach, but it was too late. "Nobody seems to doubt that the die is cast and that the diplomatic avenue is finished," wrote La Sablière.[27]

At 8:01 p.m. on March 17, President Bush addressed his fellow citizens for fifteen minutes to announce that the decisive moment had come. Bush's speech summarized the usual arguments, starting with the well-known assertions about WMD and Iraq's ties to al-Qaeda, and placed the responsibility for the "failure of diplomacy" on "some permanent members of the Council" that had announced that they would veto "any resolution that compels the disarmament of Iraq." This was not a formal declaration of war, but an ultimatum: "Saddam Hussein and his sons must leave Iraq within 48 hours," Bush declared, adding that "their refusal to do so will result in military conflict, commenced at a time of our choosing." Of course, it amounted to the same thing: everybody understood that the war would start in two days' time. Unsurprisingly, the patriotic reflex prevailed. The next day, it was clear that public opinion and Congress unfailingly supported Bush.[28]

On March 18, Blair fought for his political survival in the House of Commons. The previous evening, he had lost a heavyweight: former foreign secretary Robin Cook had resigned his post as Leader of the House of Commons, a key government portfolio, to protest Blair's position. Bush had done everything he could to facilitate his ally's task. He had removed overly bellicose aspects from his address of the previous day, and had addressed the Israeli-Palestinian conflict by announcing the forthcoming publication of the "roadmap" for peace in the Middle East. Both lent credit to the idea that Blair was paid back for supporting the United States. That evening, over the course of more than an hour, Blair gave one of his most brilliant speeches. It was profoundly argued—even if his arguments were debatable—and eloquent in form. He managed to save the day: the government carried the confidence vote by 412 to 149. France once again had served as scapegoat for supposedly being opposed to any new resolution of any kind, thus bearing the responsibility for the failure of diplomacy and ultimately for the war. This was the climax of the Franco-British breach. Chirac was beside himself. The next day he asked Villepin to call Straw to convey his thinking to Blair. The French president, said Villepin, was "shocked and pained" by statements he judged "unacceptable" and "not worthy of a friendly country and a European partner," statements that did "not conform to reality" and that "will fool nobody." Yet Blair had scored a hit at home: the polls showed less hostility in public opinion and a predictable reflex of national unity in light of a likely entry into war.[29]

At this stage, only the departure of Saddam Hussein could change the situation, but nobody could reasonably believe that this would happen. In the hope of avoiding war, in the first weeks of 2003 some countries in the region had studied this scenario. In January, Saudi Arabia, Syria, and Turkey had envisaged a negotiated solution that involved Saddam Hussein's voluntary exile in exchange for personal guarantees given by the Americans, but such an option appeared unrealistic from the start. In January and February, Washington had publicly mentioned the possibility that promises of amnesty might be given to those close to power; much as in 1991, it was hoped that this offer would encourage Iraqi elites to overthrow the dictator. But Bush was not ready to grant such guarantees to Saddam Hussein himself. In February, Saddam Hussein's close entourage apparently sounded out Egypt's Hosni Mubarak on whether Saddam Hussein and his family might settle in Egypt—with two billion dollars in cash and ingots. Mubarak had ruled out the possibility of allowing such a sum of money to enter his country, but he had responded positively about the Iraqi leader's family. However, he had warned the requesting parties that he would have to have American agreement to extend the offer to Saddam Hussein and senior regime officials. When Mubarak's son Gamal raised the question with Bush in mid-February, Bush had refused any idea of granting protection to Saddam Hussein. "If you are looking for assurances from me that we will or won't do something," he replied to Gamal Mubarak, "you don't have those assurances."[30]

The French were informed of these various attempts to prevent the coming war, but they could hardly believe in their chances of success. "We did not take that seriously," one person close to Villepin remembered. In fact, with the war approaching, this kind of scenario seemed increasingly improbable. Saddam Hussein himself was opposed to leaving Iraq. The Russians tried their luck, but with no more success: on February 23, Igor Ivanov reported to Villepin that former prime minister Yevgeny Primakov—a connoisseur of Iraq and the Middle East—had just come back from Baghdad convinced that Saddam Hussein would never leave. Two weeks later, the president of the Duma, Gennadiy Seleznyov, confirmed this impression; received on March 10 for three hours by a "serene" and apparently well-informed Saddam Hussein, Seleznyov had heard a diatribe that left no doubt about the dictator's state of mind, full of both bluster and resistance. The Americans would experience their own "Stalingrad," Saddam Hussein had prophesied; there was no question of his leaving power and being dragged in front of the courts like Serbia's Slobodan Milošević. Faithful to the image of a modern Saladin, which he liked to cultivate, he emphasized that "[he would] follow the fate of [his] people to the end." Three days later, Egyptian foreign minister Ahmed Maher had confirmed to the French ambassador in Cairo, Jean-Claude Cousseran, that Saddam Hussein would never accept exile and that his entourage affirmed that Iraq would resist the American army. The Arab League also had just renounced sending a last-chance mission to Baghdad. Saddam Hussein's departure, in any case, would have changed nothing. "Even if Saddam Hussein leaves, we'll go in anyway," Bush had declared to congressional leaders two hours before launching his ultimatum on March 17. Was this the ultimate bravado, or a denial of reality? On March 18, Iraqi foreign minister Naji Sabri responded to Bush's ultimatum: "The only way to avoid armed conflict is to provoke the departure of the prime warmonger in the world. This crazy man must go, as well as his acolyte Blair."[31]

"Mission Accomplished"

The war began in an unexpected way on the evening of March 19, or the early hours of March 20, in Baghdad. A volley of Cruise missiles and two F-117 bombers equipped with "bunker busters" reached Dora Farms, a compound located in a palm grove on the southern periphery of the capital, and known to be visited occasionally by Saddam Hussein. That morning, George Tenet had informed the White House that the CIA had reliable intelligence that the dictator and his sons would be present there that night. Hitting this target was tempting: success in eliminating Saddam Hussein even before the start of the operations could only facilitate or shorten them, and so Bush had given the green light to the operation. At 10:16 p.m. in Washington, when the raid was just starting and the sirens were sounding in Baghdad, the American president went on television to announce the start of operations aiming "to disarm Iraq, to free its people and to defend the world from grave danger."[32]

For a time, Tenet thought that the raid had hit its target. In fact, this was not the case: Saddam Hussein probably was not there that evening. (The same scenario would occur three weeks later, when the Americans targeted a Baghdad restaurant.) While US Special Forces had been in Iraqi territory for almost forty-eight hours to control part of the western desert in order to prevent any hypothetical launch of Scud missiles at Israel, it was on March 21 at dawn (Iraqi time) that Operation Iraqi Freedom truly began. Surprisingly, the US Army units based in Kuwait, less than 150,000 troops in total, crossed the border even before the start of the air campaign—Franks had decided on this action at the last moment. Nicknamed "Shock and Awe," the air campaign started a few hours later and turned out to be brief. This was a reversal of the first Gulf War a dozen years before, and it marked a clear break with the Powell Doctrine: instead of a long and intensive air campaign followed by an overwhelming land assault, the new strategy relied on a "targeted" use of the air force and on the use of land forces involving speed and surprise. This strategy was the result of more than sixteen months of planning, spurred by Rumsfeld along the lines of his desired "transformation" of the US military—at the price of constant pressure on reluctant generals. In the eyes of Pentagon strategists, Operation Iraqi Freedom aimed to erase the image of an "American Way of War" that until that point had been relying on the massive use of the air force at the cost of considerable collateral damage. In short, the war was meant to showcase the extraordinary military power and know-how of the United States.[33]

The start of the operation appeared to validate these choices. On March 21, the American and British forces penetrated at least a hundred kilometers into Iraqi territory and encountered only weak resistance, losing only a dozen men in a helicopter accident. The Americans reached Nasiriya and then advanced to the north along the Euphrates River, while the British turned off toward the sector of Basra, for which they were responsible. The next day, Franks announced to Bush from his headquarters in Doha that the most advanced American units had already traveled more than 200 kilometers. Blair and Bush, who spoke by telephone on the evening of March 22, were optimistic: Iraqi forces seemed literally to disintegrate at the arrival of coalition troops. Of course, things were already becoming more complicated. Certain Iraqi units were more combative, and very few chose to surrender, contrary to American expectations. Starting on the second day, American forces faced the first attacks by snipers embedded in the Iraqi population; a few days later, in Najaf, they would be the target of the first suicide attack, which would cost the lives of four US soldiers. Still, the operations as they unfolded in the first days of the invasion seemed to turn to the advantage of the allies.

The French followed operations closely. The Secretary General for National Defense, under Jean-Claude Mallet, prepared a daily synthesis of events for French government authorities on the basis of the available information. Although it was clear that the fate of the conflict would be favorable to the Americans and their allies—the result was "known in advance," Chirac told Bashar al-Assad—there were two different readings of events as seen from Paris. The military believed in a rapid US victory, given the massive advantage of the coalition. By contrast, the intelligence services were expecting resistance that would make victory costly. In the end, both would prove right, yet for the time being the first scenario appeared more probable. On March 25, the Quai d'Orsay's Middle East directorate noted that even if the "blitz" announced by the Pentagon was off to a slow start and even if there was no Iraqi military collapse as such, the coalition forces were progressing rapidly toward Baghdad, with relatively limited losses.[34]

The start of the war placed the peace camp in a novel situation. Should they stick to opposition at the risk of aggravating tensions with the belligerents, or else demonstrate flexibility at the price of renouncing their own principles? The French, like the Germans, chose the second attitude without qualms. Officially denouncing the war as illicit in the absence of a UN mandate, they reckoned, would only feed tensions with the Americans and raise issues with respect to the airspace authorizations granted to the belligerents, which might be legally contested. In these conditions, it was deemed best not to declare a position on the subject.[35] Because it had been against the use of force, France logically should have denied its airspace to the coalition, but the political price would have been prohibitive: in 1986, France's refusal to grant the Americans access to its airspace to conduct a raid in Libya against Colonel Muammar Gaddafi had led to a severe episode of "French-bashing" in the United States. (At the time, Jacques Chirac had been prime minister, and François Mitterrand was president.) This precedent no doubt explains the attitude adopted by Chirac even before the start of the conflict: "If the Americans need to overfly our territory, it goes without saying that among allies these things are done," he had declared during his March 10 television interview. The same logic led Villepin to say on March 17 that if Iraq should use chemical or biological weapons—which could not be ruled out—then

France would indeed "show its solidarity." Villepin's declaration echoed statements made by General Bentégeat two days before; such a scenario might lead France to "reconsider" its attitude, Bentégeat had said. Officials remained elusive in public as to the precise measures that France might take, but in all likelihood France, in such a situation, would have put at the disposal of the coalition a medical assistance unit specialized in nuclear, biological, and chemical warfare. Meanwhile, the unleashing of operations in no way challenged a fundamental given of the Franco-American relation since 9/11: the maintenance of close cooperation in intelligence.[36]

For the rest, French leaders were keen to avoid throwing oil on the fire in their public expressions. Chirac's early declarations after Bush's ultimatum were harsh. Condemning a decision "contrary to the will of the Security Council," he stressed that the Security Council alone was authorized to legitimize the use of force, and he called for "respect of international legality," implicitly denouncing an illegal war conducted for motives different from those stated. But two days later, he adjusted his aim. Wishing that operations "might be the quickest and least deadly possible," Chirac noted that "tomorrow, we will have to find ourselves with our allies and with the whole international community in order to meet together the challenges that await us." In private, French leaders also tried to smooth things over: on March 29, Chirac sent Blair his condolences for the fallen British soldiers and repeated that he wished that the war would have a "rapid culmination with the least destruction possible." He would do the same with Bush when contact was renewed in mid-April. In short, the start of military operations changed the situation; whatever their reservations about the conflict, the French did not want to appear to be extremists.[37]

On March 25, the horizon grew darker, inaugurating a difficult week for the coalition. A sandstorm accompanied by strong rain beat down on Iraq for three days, grounding helicopters and preventing the coalition forces from advancing. Moreover, the American and British forces were now facing increased resistance from irregular units coming from paramilitary groups—the Saddam Fedayeen, commanded by Uday Hussein, one of the dictator's sons. "The enemy we're fighting is different from the one we'd war-gamed against," the commander of the US Fifth Corps confided to journalists. Such statements were bound to feed the criticism that by then was being raised over troop strength: was there not a contradiction between the war's objectives—to put an end to the regime—and the limitation of means imposed by Rumsfeld? Had not the operation been planned on a mistaken hypothesis—namely, the rapid collapse of the Iraqi regime? Later, this polemic would only intensify; for the time being, Bush feigned impassiveness. "I'm not paying attention to the press," he told a group of veterans on March 28.[38]

The Americans and the British tried to be reassuring. The situation was "confused" but there was nothing "abnormal" about it, Straw had told Villepin on March 25. Powell sounded the same note: the American forces had arrived at the gates of Baghdad in six days, which was "a real performance," he stressed. The peace camp, unsurprisingly, was split between concern and, already, the feeling of having been right. Joschka Fischer was alarmist: the Americans had been "completely mistaken" in their calculations, he told Villepin on March 29; they would surely win the war, but victory would be hard, he added, evoking a "nightmare scenario" in which Saddam Hussein, having become the "hero of the Arab world," would fight "until the end." Two days later, Fischer and Villepin met again in Paris, and this time it was Villepin who painted a somber picture of what might happen. Underlining the error of the Americans in believing that they would be welcomed as liberators in Iraq, he was worried about the risks of an American military escalation, to which the Iraqis might respond by using chemical weapons in a symbolic site like the holy city of Karbala in the hope of extending the conflict to the whole region, starting with Iran. (Villepin's remark points again to the fact that the French had not excluded the possibility that Iraq had kept some WMDs.) Fischer, however, considered this scenario implausible: US public opinion and Congress would not accept such an escalation, he said, and the Iraqis, according to the Russians (who were far and away the best informed in this domain), did not have sufficient chemical capabilities.[39]

The situation on the ground changed completely in barely a few days. On March 29, returning from Camp David where he had met with Bush, Blair confided to Chirac that some Iraqi elements continued to fight "fiercely" and that what happened in the coming days would be decisive. Four days later, on April 3—the conflict was then entering its third week—the 3rd US Infantry Division occupied Baghdad International Airport, west of the capital. On April 5, the Americans, giving up the previously planned tactic of gradually encircling the city, attempted an entry in force into the capital with a column of armored tanks at full speed. They met with strong resistance. At this stage, the affair still seemed uncertain: that very day, Putin and Chirac agreed that their previous fears had been corroborated and they were worried to see the conflict drag on. The French president labeled the war unleashed by the Americans and British "a triple error: moral, political, and strategic."[40]

On April 7, an armored column again made an assault on the capital and reached the presidential complex situated in the center of Baghdad, on the left bank of the Tigris. This time, American forces occupied the heart of the metropolis. The fall of the regime assumed an almost comic turn: the Iraqi minister of information, Muhammad Saeed al-Sahhaf, stated during a press conference at the Hotel Palestine that there was no enemy military presence in Baghdad, and that any American units that were approaching ought to surrender or else risk destruction. Was this the final bravado of a regime that knew it was finished? Maybe not: the Americans would later determine that al-Sahhaf, who soon was captured by the occupiers, probably believed what he was saying, since the Iraqi military in those critical days preferred to hide the disastrous reality from their hierarchy out of fear of reprisals. In any case, on April 9, Saddam Hussein's regime was truly finished, both as a symbol and in reality. At the center of Baghdad, American soldiers helped a small group of Iraqis to topple a statue of the dictator in front of the television cameras. The same day, Franks briefed Bush by video-conference. We had "a good week," he said, presenting an assessment of the situation: in the south of Iraq, all the enemy units had been destroyed; in the center, 90 percent of the equipment of Iraqi forces had been annihilated; in the north, the regular army was much weakened. Throughout this third week of the conflict, euphoria grew in the United States. Commentators who had been doubtful the previous week were now ecstatic about the operation's speed and efficiency. Bush's popularity was at its zenith: his approval rating, which had reached 92 percent after 9/11 and then had fallen below 60 percent, rebounded to 77 percent.[41]

The weeks that followed soon showed how much this euphoria was misplaced. As the most clear-sighted among American generals already suspected—far from the complacent optimism of Pentagon civilians—difficulties had only begun over an occupation about which nobody could predict the duration. Their intuition soon would be verified when the Americans and their allies failed to consolidate their victory in the wake of the fall of the regime. Even as soon as the day following the fall of the regime, acts of vandalism occurred throughout the country, in particular in Baghdad; the national museum was looted without the Americans intervening. "Stuff happens," Rumsfeld famously (and cynically) commented on April 11, illustrating the Americans' glaring unpreparedness, starting with how to maintain order, in the face of the coming difficulties. Rumsfeld's offhand remark was a stunning admission that would come to summarize the monumental error of the American military adventure in Iraq. The Americans "do not seem to have understood the complexity of events," Villepin commented that day during a telephone conversation with Fischer, stressing the "confusion" that reigned in Iraq. In retrospect, this was an understatement.[42]

In mid-April, the mood among the victors was optimistic, even triumphalist. After the fall of Baghdad, the French embassy in Washington judged it probable that this "three-week war" would remain a "model" of efficiency and speed, even if the operations were not yet over and the occupation had only begun. Those who were less bellicose, like Colin Powell, remained guarded. "The military campaign is practically over," he said to Villepin on April 16. "What is at stake now is security." Powell used the same tone during a fresh exchange ten days later: although he acknowledged that there were "concerns" regarding the situation in Baghdad and in the center of the country—the "Sunni triangle," which would be the heart of the insurrection in the months to come—he claimed that overall the evolution was "positive," and that despite "sporadic" confrontation, the coalition forces were witnessing a "slow return to normal."[43] But the hawks did not hide their jubilation. On April 13, Cheney gave a dinner for a few friends—including Paul Wolfowitz and Scooter Libby, two of the principal architects of the war—to celebrate victory. One of the guests was Kenneth Adelman, a veteran of Republican administrations who was close to Cheney and Rumsfeld and had supported the Bush administration with his public positions. That evening, Adelman set the tone. Declaring that the war had been "awesome," he raised a toast to Bush, whose determination had "blown him away." Cheney fully agreed. "After 9/11," he said, "the president understood what had to be done. He had to do Afghanistan first . . . but after Afghanistan . . . , the president knew he had to do Iraq." Libby added that all this was "wonderful." The only false note was that Adelman was surprised that the WMD had not been found. "We'll find them," Wolfowitz replied; Cheney stressed that "it's only been four days" since the regime fell. In short, the atmosphere that evening was one of self-congratulation, a sentiment widely shared in Washington's power circles—to the point of ignoring the warning signs that had already started to flash yellow, not least the apparent absence of WMD and the deterioration of the security situation. On April 28, Wolfowitz declared to the press, "We're not going to need as many people to do peacekeeping as we needed to fight the war." Wolfowitz's statement was made at the very moment when serious incidents were occurring in Tikrit, Saddam Hussein's native city, and in Fallujah, the heart of the Sunni triangle.[44]

On May 1, American triumphalism reached an almost Hollywood-like apogee. That day, Bush landed on the aircraft carrier *Abraham Lincoln* off San

Diego. He had arrived on board a military aircraft, from which he emerged dressed in a "Top Gun"-style flight suit. Then, to the strains of "Hail to the Chief," applauded by the crew assembled on the deck, he advanced to pronounce a speech to the nation. The setting sun was at his back. "Major combat operations in Iraq have ended. In the battle of Iraq, the United States and our allies have prevailed," he declared. True, he wanted to avoid giving the impression that the conflict was over: "We're bringing order to parts of that country that remain dangerous" he said, recognizing that "we have difficult work to do in Iraq." "The transition from dictatorship to democracy will take time," he said. Yet the speech could only be interpreted as a premature proclamation of victory: "The battle of Iraq is one victory in a war on terror that began on September 11th, 2001," Bush said. Meanwhile, in the background the crew displayed a banner that read "Mission Accomplished."[45]

"Punish France"

France and its allies had not been able to prevent the war; that, in itself, marked a failure that the American triumph in Iraq further highlighted, inaugurating a difficult period for the peace camp. The coalition's swiftly won victory appeared to validate their enterprise and refute their opponents' warnings. Early signs of the difficulties to come, which had multiplied after the fall of Baghdad, would soon change the situation in the summer and confirm the accuracy of those warnings. Yet for now, in the spring, the French, Germans, and Russians seemed marginalized, even isolated in the postwar phase. The Americans, with British help, had a clear path to take charge of the reconstruction and democratization of "liberated" Iraq and to make it the showcase of a Middle East transformed by the unequaled military power and "benevolent" hegemony of the United States.

At the end of the operations, the Americans confirmed their intentions: the victors would manage Iraq for as long as necessary. There would be no Iraqi provisional government, at least at first, and the UN would have merely a limited place in reconstruction—quite the opposite of the "Afghan model" that had been used in 2001. This approach had the merit of consistency; Washington judged that the UN had "failed" and so there was no question of giving it more than an auxiliary role. Condoleezza Rice confirmed this plan on April 4, even before the fall of Baghdad. Ruling in favor of the Pentagon, the White House decided that Iraq would indeed be administered by the coalition. (Unsurprisingly, the Department of State had tried to take a more flexible line.) "For those who still had doubts," the French embassy commented, "this confirms that Iraq will be governed by the US Army, meaning in reality by the ideologues at the Pentagon."[46] To be sure, the British pushed for an increased UN role, but without success. Blair and Bush, who met in Belfast the day Baghdad fell, announced a "vital" role for the UN, but their aim was clearly to obtain its technical help—especially for humanitarian issues—while the coalition kept full power.

By the end of April, the Americans had begun to approach some forty countries—France, Germany, and Belgium were deliberately excluded—to ask them to contribute to the security force that was to ensure order after the fighting. Of course, this force would be placed under American command, without any explicit UN mandate. NATO might be called upon for help in a form that was yet to be determined, such as by offering logistical support to contributing countries that might need it, like Poland. Apart from the fait accompli of the occupation of Iraq outside any UN framework, the US approach validated the principle that the mission defined the coalition. On top of this, the Americans (with tacit British consent) confirmed their intention to get around France within NATO by systematically resorting to the Defense Planning Committee, based on the precedent of providing assistance to Turkey. Clearly, the danger of France's marginalization after the war in Iraq was very serious.[47]

The Franco-American relationship, which had been deteriorating for several weeks, now sank to its lowest point. French-bashing, which had steadily intensified in the United States during the UN confrontation in March, culminated during the war with the blessing of the White House. "Chirac has pushed it to the point where there's a huge anti-French backlash in America," Bush told Irish prime minister Bertie Ahern on March 13; "he's taken it too far."[48] The derisory gesture that remains in memories occurred when the congressional cafeteria, at the instigation of a handful of legislators, replaced "French fries" on its menu with "Freedom fries." This sneer soon was imitated by the staff on board Air Force One, where on March 26, in the middle of the war, "French toast" became "Freedom toast." More seriously, threats of boycott of French products became more explicit, even if they seemed difficult to put into effect, since American enterprises would also be hurt as a result. The manifestations of Francophobia intensified, especially in the conservative media, as illustrated by the success of the expression "cheese-eating surrender monkeys" to characterize the French—a joke going back to an old episode of the animated television series *The Simpsons* that was adopted by conservative activists.

Whether these jokes were seen as funny or disgraceful, they denoted an anti-French climate that became frankly alarming after the war began. A state of alert was reached at the end of March with a series of attacks on persons, including the murder by a drunken ex-Marine of a Florida bartender who had had the bad idea of expressing himself against the war and speaking French to his girlfriend on the telephone—a murder that was recognized as racist by the court. This time, the French embassy decided to react by transmitting to the American authorities a list of incidents of which it had knowledge, and on March 28 the Quai d'Orsay's spokesman expressed the French government's concern about the turn of events. The protest was not well received by American authorities, who tended to minimize the situation. But the situation was serious enough for Chirac to take advantage of the resumption of contact with Blair on March 29 to ask him to pass a message to Bush: expressing his "vivid concern" about a campaign with "racist connotations" and "totally injurious" declarations emanating from certain milieus in the United States, Chirac asked Blair to make Bush understand that "certain limits" could not be crossed.[49]

Another manifestation of the Franco-America deterioration, fed by some within the Bush administration, was a number of deliberately orchestrated press leaks intended to discredit France on the basis of incriminating—and erroneous—information. The phenomenon was not new: such "revelations" had surfaced periodically for years during Franco-American frictions over Iraq, and they had reappeared in the autumn during the negotiations over Resolution 1441. These alleged leaks, which claimed that French businesses were delivering sensitive materials and even weapons to Iraq, reached a peak between March and May 2003. Carried by right-wing papers like the *Washington Times*, they also appeared in more moderate ones like the *Washington Post*, the *New York Times*, and *Newsweek*. Given the flawed coverage of the issue of Iraqi WMD, even in the mainstream media, it is not surprising that false information concerning so-called French collusion with Baghdad came up, despite the systematic denials by the French authorities. The French attributed these leaks to the Pentagon's civilians—in particular to Douglas Feith and his "Office of Special Plans"—and to the "communicators" at the White House around Karl Rove and Scott McClellan. Their goal, as seen from Paris, was obvious: to discredit the position of France by tarnishing its motivations in opposing the US war in Iraq.[50]

In the aftermath of the conflict, this situation led Jean-David Levitte to take an unusual initiative. The French ambassador wrote an open letter—which made the front page of the *Washington Post* on May 15—in which he denounced an "organized campaign of disinformation" aiming to "destroy the image of France," and to which was attached a list of various press articles along with the corresponding denials. Levitte said that it was a matter of reestablishing a relationship of trust between the two countries as friends and allies, in which denigration and lies should have no place. The initiative was risky, but the goal was reached: "The campaign of disinformation stopped from one day to the next," he later wrote.[51]

Still, in the immediate aftermath of the conflict the bilateral relationship was deeply affected. Hostility to France was not confined to zealots among Pentagon civilians, Cheney's entourage, or Washington conservative "think tanks"; the rift also appeared among reputedly moderate administration officials. When Levitte, during a conversation with Steven Hadley after the fall of Baghdad, stressed the French desire to "turn the page" and demonstrate "pragmatism," Hadley—referring to Chirac's March declaration expressing the wish for a quick American victory—observed that many in Washington thought it "incredibly telling" that the French "felt the need to say out loud what went without saying." Hadley's comment showed that the acrimony reigning in Washington was such that even a gesture of goodwill could be interpreted as evidence of France's disloyalty. Levitte chose to take a positive view: Hadley's attitude, he wrote, still distinguished him from the "vengeful and vindictive" posture of someone like Paul Wolfowitz, who had declared publicly three days earlier that the French ought to "pay" for their opposition to the United States.[52]

"Turning the page" and quickly reestablishing contact at the highest level: this was indeed the goal set by French leaders after the fall of the Iraqi regime. This was soon done with the British who, the French understood, had an interest in smoothing things over. Not only were Britain's ideas about the postwar situation—specifically, the role of the UN and efforts to relaunch the Israeli-Palestinian peace process—closer to those of the French than to those of the Americans, but Blair wanted to get out of his isolation from France and Germany. Even if they should not wait for any "gifts" from the British, the French reckoned that relations with them would be less durably difficult than with the Americans. After their telephone call on March 29, Blair met Chirac in mid-April during a European Council meeting in Athens. Blair was satisfied with their conversation, thinking that the French president had made an effort toward him. The months that followed would confirm that despite continuing disagreements, starting with the perennial one over transatlantic relations, a proper Franco-British relationship had been reestablished.[53]

The affair was clearly more delicate with the Americans. As combat ended, Chirac thought that the moment had come to revive contact with Bush, with whom he had not spoken since February 7. First, he asked his diplomatic adviser to sound out the American president's entourage, so Maurice Gourdault-Montagne called Condoleezza Rice. When he shared with her the French wish to cooperate in the postwar, Rice proved harsh. "There are those who were in and those who were out," she told him. "We have paid for this victory with our blood and treasure," she continued, adding, "We don't need you." This reaction was scarcely surprising to the Élysée in the context of the prevailing triumphalism in Washington. It was around this time that Rice famously quipped in front of Bush and a few staff members that the administration's motto should be "Punish France, forgive Russia, and ignore Germany"—a comment that quickly made its way into the press. But Chirac nevertheless decided to go ahead and reach out to Bush, persuaded that the more reasonable among administration officials, especially those at the State Department, would wish for a quick overture to the peace camp.[54]

The telephone conversation that took place on Chirac's initiative on April 15 confirmed that it would take time for things to return to normal. Observing that he and Bush had not spoken "for some time," Chirac pointed out that, with the Iraq issue entering a "new phase," it had seemed to him "useful" to renew contact. Stressing that his analysis of the war had not changed, he congratulated Bush that the conflict had been brief and, while repeating his condolences for the losses suffered by the United States, he stressed that France, like all democracies, was "pleased" by the fall of the dictatorship. He wanted to "turn toward the future" with an "open and constructive" spirit. The tone was set: no French contrition for the opposition to the war, but a desire to turn the page by demonstrating cooperation in the postwar situation.

Chirac also wanted to give a token of his goodwill. To stress that France was attached to the Atlantic alliance—as shown by its decision to participate in the NATO Response Force—he indicated that Paris would be ready to consider a NATO role in Iraq, on condition that this role was "reasonable." Bush welcomed Chirac's overture: some in his entourage, he said bittersweetly, were convinced that the French goal was to "destroy NATO." Chirac retorted that such assertions arose from the "anti-French campaign" led by some sectors of the administration, to which Bush responded that he was not aware of the existence of such a campaign, and concluded on a sardonic note that in any case he would have "good news to announce" to those who doubted France's desire to see NATO play a role in Iraq. Bush spoke as if he had not heard that the French president had mentioned a *reasonable* role for NATO, so at this stage of the conversation Chirac explained the French postconflict position more plainly: "The sooner the United Nations is associated with reconstruction, the better," he indicated to Bush. Although Chirac affirmed his wish for a "pragmatic" approach to the UN role, between the lines he was saying that a significant NATO involvement could be envisaged only if a Security Council mandate placed the postconflict transition in a formal UN framework—which, of course, was a scenario that the Americans did not want to hear. The rest of the conversation made it clear to Chirac that the United States, predictably, was determined to exploit its victory to change the situation elsewhere in the Middle East. In particular, Washington wanted to increase pressure on Yasser Arafat as a precondition of the application of the roadmap for solving the Israeli-Palestinian conflict. The Americans also wanted to put pressure on Syria, suspecting that Damascus had allowed fleeing Iraqi leaders onto their territory, perhaps even with chemical weapons. Chirac was skeptical about these suspicions, given the old contentions between the two Baathist regimes, but said he would pass a message of prudence to Bashar al-Assad. (The Syrian issue, as will be seen, would become a central element in the Franco-American reconciliation in the coming months—but the two countries were not quite there yet.)[55]

Although the April 15 conversation confirmed that Franco-American dialogue had resumed at the highest level, it also showed that it would take time to rebuild the bilateral relationship. The following week, the press reported that a meeting had been held at the White House, presided over by Stephen Hadley, to study what might be done to "punish" France, in particular by bypassing it in international bodies, starting with NATO. An embarrassed Colin Powell defended himself in a telephone call to Dominique de Villepin. Powell sought to dissipate the "misunderstandings" fed by the media, but he was obliged to recognize that the "major disagreement" between the two countries over Iraq would have lasting consequences for the bilateral relationship, if only because of "strong pressure" from congressional and public opinion. The French, as April ended, saw how hard it would be to push up the slope.[56]

Not surprisingly, the first real test of the improvement in Franco-American relations in the spring of 2003 was about the role of the UN after the conflict. Once major military operations ended in mid-April, the Americans logically wanted the Security Council to lift the sanctions on Iraq. Not only did it no longer make sense to maintain them, because the "disarmament" of Iraq had now been imposed by force, but lifting them also was a precondition for Iraq's reconstruction. For Washington, it was also a matter of obtaining from the Security Council at least an indirect form of ex post facto legitimation of the war and of the administration of Iraq by the United States and its allies without subjecting the coalition to any UN tutelage. This created a dilemma for the French and their allies. For them, a central role for the UN in Iraq was indispensable to Iraq's stabilization and reconstruction, which they believed were doomed to failure in the event of an occupation without UN legitimacy. So they wondered: should they use their acceptance of the lifting of sanctions as a lever in order to obtain an increased role for the UN, but at the risk of again appearing to obstruct Washington? (One option would be to make the lifting of sanctions conditional on establishing a sovereign Iraqi government or on UN inspectors certifying disarmament, neither of which the Americans wanted for obvious reasons.) Or, on the contrary, should they show flexibility on this matter, but at the expense of any substantial role for the UN in postwar Iraq?[57]

In May 2003, Paris chose the second option, preferring pragmatism once the war was over. Faced with an Anglo-American resolution proposed on May 8, which simply called for sanctions to be lifted and gave the UN no substantial role or oversight in Iraq, the French quickly saw their limited margin of maneuver. The Russians and Germans shared the French point of view, but they privileged reconciliation with Washington. In line with Rice's earlier quip, the American tactic consisted of differentiating the three countries and driving wedges between them—and it paid off. To this position was added the very strong pressure that Washington was putting directly on Paris. The message was clear: a positive vote in New York—and not a simple abstention— would be, said Bush's European adviser Daniel Fried, "the best thing" that could happen for Franco-American relations, especially with the approach of the G8 summit at Évian, which was crucial for Paris. So in return for a few concessions, including an agreement to allow the UN secretary-general to designate a "special representative" in Iraq and not a simple "coordinator," the French decided to vote for the Anglo-American plan. On May 22, Resolution 1483 was adopted with fourteen votes in favor, with Syria not taking part in the vote. After Resolution 1483, a former Élysée staff member recalled, Chirac gave instructions to "recreate a consensus on the Iraqi issue." (Chirac's instructions, as will be seen, were soon complicated by the worsening of the on-the-ground situation in Iraq in the following months.)[58]

The Bush-Chirac meeting at the G8 summit in Évian on June 1–3, 2003, marked the first result of this approach. For the Élysée, it was an occasion to demonstrate that contact at the highest level was indeed reestablished. "This meeting has extreme importance and could give the signal for a gradual reestablishment of good cooperation between our two countries, or on the contrary confirm a durable break," Levitte had written ahead of the summit, while stressing that the personal relationship between the two presidents—unlike the Bush-Schröder relationship—was "preserved." Yet the Évian success was hard-won. During the April 15 telephone conversation, Bush had not positively committed to coming, ostensibly because of worries about the risk of antiglobalization demonstrations during the summit, as had happened at the G8 summit in Genoa two years earlier. Then, as the summit approached— preparations were made in a frosty, unpleasant climate, French "sherpas" (personal diplomatic advisers) would later remember—there were press leaks to the effect that the American president would not stay in Évian, but across the border in neighboring Switzerland. In the end, Bush did come to Évian, but he flew off before the summit's closure and headed for the Middle East, a way of showing what his real priorities were.[59]

The Bush-Chirac meeting on June 2 nevertheless took place in a positive climate. Thanking Chirac for his hospitality, Bush "hoped that over Iraq we will not let ourselves be stopped by the disagreements of the past;" Chirac responded that these disagreements should not undermine bilateral relations, but that "friendship and solidarity" called for "frankness." Then, he launched into an uncompromising exposition of the situation in Iraq. Warning Bush about the difficulties of establishing democracy there—free elections, he said, would bring to power the Shiites, who have no democratic tradition— he presaged that the process would be "long and perilous" and that the United States had every interest in not "assuming it alone," but rather in using the framework of the UN. Then the conversation turned to other problems in the region. On Iran, which was on its way to becoming the new proliferation crisis since the Western powers had discovered in 2002 that it was conducting a clandestine nuclear program, the Franco-American positions were far apart. Bush was alarmist about a nuclear Iran, but Chirac was skeptical about the existence of such a threat, though he assured Bush that he was ready to work with the United States. On Syria, however, their positions were getting closer. Chirac, who had his own grievances against Damascus over its meddling in Lebanon, was harsh toward the regime of Bashar al-Assad; he concurred with the American demands, starting with the closing of Syria's border with Iraq

279

and the cessation of all aid to its former leaders. Chirac was clearly changing his footing: the Syrian question, about which more will be said later, would be at the heart of the Franco-American reconciliation in the coming months. "Here is an opportunity for cooperation" between the two countries, Bush said with enthusiasm.

But Chirac's most concrete gesture bore on Afghanistan. At the Évian summit, Chirac announced to Bush that France had decided to place a hundred members of its special forces under American command as part of Operation Enduring Freedom. (One may recall that a plan to send these forces had been envisaged after 9/11, but it had fallen through.) General Bentégeat, who wanted to avoid the deterioration in Franco-American military relations after the Iraqi conflict, had strongly advocated this gesture, and Chirac had agreed to it despite his initial reservations. The French and Germans also agreed that NATO would take over the ISAF command in Kabul. With these gestures, the French president wanted to show—despite his basic skepticism about operations in Afghanistan—that Franco-American cooperation in the struggle against terrorism had not been undermined by the rupture over Iraq. He also wanted to stress in passing the contrast between the Iraqi adventure and the legitimate fight against the Taliban and Osama bin Laden—the "good" and the "bad" war, as it were.

The conversation in Évian was a first step toward the reestablishment of a suitable relationship between Chirac and Bush. When the former announced his intention to go to the UN General Assembly in September and his wish to meet with Bush in New York, the latter declared that he would be "welcome." Bush, indirectly responding to Levitte's open letter of two weeks before, came back to the irritating subjects: the press was "blowing up out of all proportion" the disagreements between the two countries, he said, assuring Chirac that he did not wish to "personalize debates." Adding that there might be "uncontrolled individuals," Bush "wanted naturally to deny that his administration was organizing any anti-French campaigns." Chirac assured him that the French authorities were not themselves involved "either closely or distantly" in any anti-American campaign.[60]

"It was predictable"

Until early summer 2003, the postwar period remained under the insignia of "mission accomplished." Yet the ingredients for disaster already had been assembled. To the unpreparedness of the American military—who were convinced that they would be welcomed as "liberators" and would go home soon—was added the mistakes committed by the occupiers. At the start of May, after the first troubles in Baghdad, the White House fired General Jay Garner from his position as director of the Coalition Provisional Authority that the Pentagon had set up in Iraq. In May, Garner's replacement, Paul Bremer, made two early decisions that would prove disastrous: the complete "de-Baathification" of Iraqi society, and the dissolution of its army and security forces. These decisions were inspired by a flawed historic parallel with the US occupation of Germany and Japan after World War II, reflecting both a deep misunderstanding of Iraq and the hubris of the American plans to "transform" Iraq and the region. Whether or not Saddam Hussein— as is plausible—had planned the insurrection in advance is secondary; the fact is that these two decisions powerfully contributed to the insurrection by bringing tens of thousands of Iraqis into the struggle against the occupier and alienating a major part of Iraqi society. The effect of these two decisions would soon be amplified by a third one. Bremer decided that it would be too difficult to quickly assemble an Iraqi government, and therefore the United States would prolong the occupation indefinitely.[61]

The result was not long in coming. From July, acts of violent opposition to the American military presence multiplied. At this stage, there were no major events, but rather a succession of targeted attacks involving snipers or roadside bombs, each provoking a small number of victims in the ranks of American soldiers. The deterioration was nevertheless clear. Soon, the denials by American political authorities, starting with Donald Rumsfeld, were no longer tenable; by mid-July, General John Abizaid, who had just replaced Franks at the head of CENTCOM, was speaking of "guerrillas." The lucidity of those in charge about the real situation was a function of their positioning in the earlier debate about unleashing the war: although Richard Armitage did not hesitate to speak to Maurice Gourdault-Montagne, who was visiting Washington in mid-July, of a "terrible situation" in the Sunni triangle, Scooter Libby for his part proclaimed relative optimism in the face of what he described as organized but small and isolated groups.[62]

For the French and their allies, this deterioration was not astonishing. "It was predictable," said Chirac to Vladimir Putin during a telephone conversation at the start of July. A few days later, Villepin gave Igor Ivanov a French reading of events: the acts were perhaps deeds by some Baathist elements, but this was more likely the start of a "resistance" to the occupation. Yet for the

French there was no question of showing any schadenfreude about the difficulties encountered by the Americans, or about the fact that no WMD had yet been found—an outcome that already fed polemics in the United States and in Great Britain. French authorities refrained from boasting that they had been right. "The problem should not be posed in these terms," Villepin declared on July 10, adding that "the war did take place. . . . We see from day to day how difficult the situation is. The instability that prevails in Iraq is a source of worry for us all." The White House appreciated the "elegance" of Villepin's statement, Hadley told Gourdault-Montagne a few days later."[63]

Still, the messy situation in Iraq changed things. Finished were the declarations by US officials disdainfully rejecting the offers of service from the peace camp, as Rice had done with Gourdault-Montagne in April: now was the time for more or less discreet appeals for these countries to help stabilize and reconstruct Iraq. From mid-July, "authorized" Republican legislators publicly called for reconciliation with Germany and France—as if that would suffice, noted an amused Levitte, to obtain the sending of French contingents to Iraq. Members of Congress were increasingly worrying about the US capacity to face up financially and militarily to the deterioration of the situation, the French embassy noted; it was now clear that the necessary means would vastly exceed the optimistic prewar estimates. This worry was even sharper because the prospect of reinforcements from other countries suddenly collapsed. In mid-July, India refused to send a contingent of 17,000 troops that the Americans had hoped would reinforce coalition forces in Kurdistan. This was a hard blow for Washington.[64]

The deterioration of the situation posed a dilemma for the French and the peace camp. They said that they were in favor of the Americans' success, so to what extent should they actively contribute to it? Could they envisage actual involvement in the stabilization of Iraq, whether directly or in the framework of a NATO force or an operation under the aegis of the EU? These options were discussed in various capitals as the summer began. Despite their wish to repair the Franco-American relationship, the French were more than hesitant, especially in the absence of a central role for the UN. Speaking to Putin on July 4, Chirac said that he was "very reserved" about the prospect of French involvement in Iraq, which in any case would presuppose a real transfer of responsibilities to the UN. Schröder agreed with him, Chirac confided to his Russian colleague. It was a matter of "coherence," the Quai d'Orsay stressed: how could the French participate in a stabilization force that the Americans (except for an improbable devolution of the operation to the UN) wanted to keep under their control, when France had been opposed to a war that appeared more and more unjustified? There was no question of getting onto the slippery slope in the name of reconciliation, Villepin confirmed to Ivanov on July 8. "Participating in the operation without a United Nations mandate would be both unacceptable and ineffective," he repeated, adding that there had to be a UN mandate authorizing a peacekeeping force at the same time as an acceleration of the calendar for reestablishing Iraqi sovereignty: "It is only under these conditions that we could reflect on the possibility of participation," Villepin said, but it was "out of the question" in the absence of these preconditions for France "to rally" to the Americans despite their veiled appeals.[65]

Levitte, once again, suggested another approach. For him, the improvement in the bilateral relationship—and it was going better, he thought—should be translated into an effective French involvement in Iraq and not solely rest on words. Of course, Levitte recognized, this would necessitate a change of American strategy and acceptance of the return of the UN to center stage, but he thought that this prospect was not out of bounds, since the deteriorating situation on the ground might lead the administration to rethink its approach under pressure from public opinion and Congress. Bush was a pragmatist, Levitte believed, and his reelection the following year would depend on the situation in Iraq. Levitte concluded: "What is in play in the Iraq game is fundamental. The neoconservatives wanted to demonstrate that the United States in the twenty-first century has the capacity to transform the world alone, by the sole force of their incomparable military strength. . . . If we play our cards well, we might well be in a position to bring the Bush administration to accept tomorrow for Iraq what they arrogantly refused yesterday—and doing so, to lead America, through the management of this emblematic issue, to agree that the time of empires is over and that the security of all comes through the collective management of threats."[66]

But this plea for involvement in Iraq in the name of Franco-American reconciliation and the return of the United States to multilateralism—whose arguments echoed those that Levitte had employed in the lead-up to the war in the hope of avoiding a rupture with Washington—would soon run up against the facts. During August, it became clear that the collapse of the security situation in Iraq, far from leading the Bush administration to accept multilateralism in the country's management or an accelerated return to Iraqi sovereignty, was on the contrary being translated into a reassertion of US unilateral action. The Americans wanted even more to keep complete control of the military situation. The adoption in mid-August of a new Security Council resolution

(Resolution 1500), which remained in line with 1483, confirmed this assessment: Washington and London wanted the international community to be involved in Iraq—whether in terms of military or financial means—without sharing the responsibilities.[67]

Yet the situation on the ground was only getting worse. In the middle of the summer, the insurrection truly began, in the form of a series of spectacular attacks. On August 7, a car bomb in front of the Jordanian embassy in Baghdad caused the deaths of eleven people. The situation really tipped on August 19, when a truck full of explosives crashed into the wall of the UN headquarters in Baghdad, destroying a whole side of the building and killing twenty-two people. Among the casualties was the Brazilian diplomat Sérgio Vieira de Mello, the special representative designated by Kofi Annan after the adoption of Resolution 1483. A universally respected international civil servant, Vieira de Mello died of his injuries shortly after the attack. The episode was a dramatic illustration of the gravity of the deterioration, despite the optimistic discourse of American leaders. The attack's obvious purpose was to deliver a fatal blow to the hope of significant UN involvement in Iraq, and it worked: over the following weeks, the UN reduced its personnel in Iraq from 800 to 15 persons.[68]

At the start of the summer, things might have pointed to convergences between the coalition and the peace camp, but by the end of August this was no longer the case: each side stuck to its own logic. On August 23, Villepin spoke on the telephone with Kofi Annan, who was attending a memorial service for Vieira de Mello in Rio de Janeiro. As long as there was no shift from a "logic of occupation" to a "logic of sovereignty" supported by "strong gestures" like rapid elections, Villepin thought, then the situation could not get better. Annan agreed with him: "the hearts and minds of the Iraqis" had to be won, which presupposed a "clear mandate" for the UN. Two days later, Villepin realized that this prospect was illusory. Colin Powell told him that a rapid return to Iraqi sovereignty would be difficult, even as he repeated Washington's wish to see other contingents join the coalition while nevertheless insisting on the necessary "unity of command"—clearly, a code word for *US* command. When Villepin and Joschka Fischer pleaded with Jack Straw at the start of September for a "radical change" by stressing that the strategy conducted by the Americans, combined with their lack of knowledge of the region, risked leading to the disintegration of Iraq, the Briton pleaded for short-term priorities. They had to make the country secure and proceed "step by step," Straw answered. "The Americans aim solely to obtain more troops and money," Chirac said with regret on September 5, during a telephone conversation with Putin. "We are not far from chaos," Putin agreed.[69]

At the end of the summer of 2003, a dialogue of the deaf once again prevailed between Paris and Washington. The Americans and British wanted a new Security Council resolution, giving way to fresh dissensions. Powell and Villepin discussed the matter on September 8; although the former believed that a return to "immediate" Iraqi sovereignty was impossible, the latter thought it indispensable to organize a "devolution" of power with UN support. A few days later, the French delegation confirmed that the Americans were not willing to budge. It seemed to be a return to the worst hours of the confrontation in the spring: on September 18, the *New York Times* published an op-ed piece by Tom Friedman, titled "Our War With France," in which France was described as "becoming an enemy" of the United States. On September 21, Chirac, who was in New York with Villepin for the General Assembly, invited Annan to dinner. The French noticed once again that they saw eye-to-eye with the UN secretary-general about Iraq. Both Chirac and Annan argued for a transfer of sovereignty as rapid as possible, along the Afghan model, and Annan insisted on the necessity of an inclusive process. But everybody had to bow to the evidence: the United States would not rapidly change its policy in Iraq.[70]

On September 23, Bush and Chirac met in New York, as they had agreed at Évian. Powell, Rice, and Negroponte on the American side, and Villepin, Gourdault-Montagne, La Sablière, and Levitte on the French side, witnessed the conversation. The tone was proper, despite a strained atmosphere. The press was watching for the least signs of a new disagreement. When Chirac arrived for the meeting at the US mission, the rumor ran that Bush had refused to shake his hand, which was not the case. The conversation bore first of all on regional matters. On Iran's nuclear program, Chirac stressed that proliferation was a "major" subject on which the two countries were in agreement; he explained to Bush the initiative that Paris, London, and Berlin had just taken to persuade Tehran to suspend its enrichment program. As for Syria, Chirac said that he was "concerned" by the Assad regime's support for terrorist organizations like Hezbollah and its negative attitude toward the Israeli-Palestinian peace process. Bush suggested that Paris and Washington jointly put pressure on Damascus, and Chirac replied that the French were "available." A dialogue over Syria was now underway, the results of which would be seen a few months later.

But when the two presidents tackled Iraq, the tone on the American side hardened considerably. "I hope that you want a free Iraq and success for the

United States," the American president told his French colleague. "To go to sovereignty too quickly is a nonstarter." And, Bush warned, "Even if we have a disagreement on the policy to follow in Iraq, it is important, to preserve the image of France in the United States, that you appear favorable to our success." Chirac defended himself: France had the "same objectives" as the United States, but there was a "real divergence in analysis." The French analysis, he declared, was that American policy was "erroneous" since it generated among the Iraqi population "a hatred" that would be "very difficult to master," hence the necessity of "changing footing" and going as quickly as possible toward Iraqi sovereignty. "That said," Chirac added, moving to the topic of the resolution under discussion, "we have no intention of embarrassing you in New York; if you integrate into your plan an allusion to the transfer of sovereignty, even without a date, we will vote in favor." Bush did not mince words: "I am in total disagreement with your analysis," he responded. "It is true that some people hate us in Iraq. But the majority likes us. Those who hate us are those who supported Saddam Hussein." And, he concluded, "We want France to participate in the reconstruction of Iraq," adding, "You are rich." Chirac wanted to be conciliatory. France would study what might be done from a financial point of view, as well as the possibility of contributing to the training of the Iraqi army and police—bearing on the final content of the resolution. Paris was approaching the negotiation "in a positive spirit," he repeated. But he did not want to prolong the debate on the validity of the American approach in Iraq. "History will judge," Chirac said.

Their last subject was about the state of the bilateral relationship. Chirac, in turn, did not mince words, saying that he was "shocked" by some of the comments in the American press, which he judged "unworthy" of two countries whose friendship went back more than 226 years. Bush replied that he did not read the press much, and Rice intervened to say that the French president was no doubt alluding to Friedman's *New York Times* op-ed. Newspaper columnists sometimes use "uncontrolled" language, Bush recognized, explaining the phenomenon by noting the "difference in perception" between the French and the Americans. For the majority of the latter, Iraq was a "threat"; hence the "negative reaction" of public opinion to the French attitude, which Bush assured Chirac once more was not "encouraged" by the administration. Bush added that the moment had come to turn the page: "You are right, Jacques, let's revive this friendship. We need it." But he could not refrain from a final piece of "friendly" advice, which at the same time was an admission about the Manichaeism that prevailed in the United States: "Be attentive, in everything you say, to the permanent question of American journalists: 'Is this a friend or a foe? Is he against America?'" And Bush completed this remark with bravado: "As for me, I know that they treat me like a cowboy, and I take that as a compliment."

The conversation had been direct but courteous, which showed that the personal relationship was "preserved," wrote Levitte, who had been the note taker. But Levitte did not hide that he had been struck by Bush's implicit threat that France would pay a high price—its degraded image among Americans—if it persisted in not falling into line. "This unusual language between allies," he wrote, reflected the decisive importance of the Iraqi issue for the US image in the world and for the political future of Bush one year away from the 2004 presidential election. It also expressed, Levitte thought, the current weakness of the Bush administration, whether on the domestic level, at the UN, or of course in Iraq.[71]

At the end of summer 2003, two pages were turned. First, six months after the start of what was supposed to have been a lightning war, the illusions of the victors were shattered. Although the war apparently had been won in three weeks, the peace was on its way to being lost. The occupation, which was supposed to have ended quickly and yielded to a transformed country and region, was turning into a nightmare. If the Americans had once hoped that the international community would acknowledge their success and share with them the burden of stabilization and reconstruction, they now had to face the facts: Iraq had become their "thing," making Powell right when he said: "*You break it, you own it.*"

The second page was turned in the relationship between France and the United States. The severe crisis that had erupted in the spring was being overcome gradually; at the highest level, contact had been reestablished. Of course, it would leave some aftereffects in terms of public opinion as well as in diplomatic relations: not until George W. Bush's second term, as shall be seen, would Franco-American relations and, more generally, transatlantic relations resume a normal course. Yet from now on, the will to put the pieces back together was present on both sides. The deterioration in Iraq, nevertheless, changed the situation: whereas before the summer the Americans, blinded by their premature triumphalism, were under the illusion that the French and the whole peace camp would go to Canossa and ask to be forgiven for their opposition to the war by becoming involved in Iraq according to the United States' wishes, this was not the case. In the summer of 2003, the French chose to avoid making the situation worse, in particular at the UN, but it was clear that even if Franco-American reconciliation led to increased cooperation on other issues, it would not imply that France—or the international community—would be significantly involved in Iraq. For the rest, as Chirac had told Bush, "history [would] judge."

Epilogue
Reconciliation: 2003–2007

By the autumn of 2003, it had become clear that the United States was facing a widespread insurrection in Iraq. The country was sinking into violence and disorganization, belying the optimistic scenarios of a rapid return to stability and a serene transition to democracy. Faced with this situation, the Bush administration responded with a denial of reality that would last at least three years: only gradually did the evidence of a badly prepared fiasco of a war with contestable motivations impress itself on Americans. This did not prevent George W. Bush from being reelected in November 2004, but while the Bush administration remained obstinate (at least until the end of 2006) in not wanting to change its approach in Iraq, starting in 2005 the larger framework of American foreign policy began to change significantly. This change made the transatlantic reconciliation possible.

France had sought this reconciliation since the immediate aftermath of the Anglo-American intervention. Jacques Chirac wanted to turn the page of confrontation by showing France's readiness to cooperate with the United States, though without renouncing his Iraq stance and within the boundaries of firm "red lines." But while the Iraqi question ceased to be a major apple of discord between Paris and Washington after 2004, the deterioration of the situation in Iraq precluded any significant French involvement in what had become a quagmire. This did not prevent the bilateral relation, meanwhile, from returning to normal, or Franco-American cooperation from becoming more satisfying, and even decisive on some other issues. By the end of Chirac's second term in the spring of 2007, another era had begun.

"Some assholes have just lost the war for us"

In autumn 2003, the scenario of Iraq's rapid stabilization and reconstruction had collapsed, leading the White House to ask Congress for an additional envelope of $87 billion—an effort without precedent since the Marshall Plan. Yet the security situation continued to decline. Whereas American soldiers had been the targets of ten to fifteen daily attacks during the summer, in mid-October the figures were between twenty and thirty-five. The country sank into chaos. In September, Paul Bremer had declared that the occupation would end only when Iraq had a constitution and a government—implying that American forces would be there for a while—but in mid-November, the White House announced that the United States would restore Iraqi sovereignty at the end of June 2004, less than eight months later. Although the Americans did not trumpet this change, the most ambitious goals of "nation-building" were scaled back. Nevertheless, for three long years the approach of the Bush administration remained characterized by an evident denial about the situation in Iraq.[1]

The capture of a bearded and haggard Saddam Hussein on a farm near Tikrit in mid-December 2003 seemed at first to bring an improvement. The occupiers hoped that with Saddam Hussein in US custody, the insurrection would now run out of steam. Yet nothing of the sort happened: the revolt was not motivated solely by loyalty to the former dictator, but rather was fed by deep resentment about the war and the occupation, and it sealed a formerly improbable alliance between Baathist nationalism and jihadi terrorism. The spring of 2004 confirmed this, with the start of the battle of Fallujah at the heart of the Sunni triangle (triggered by the lynching of four employees of the private security contractor Blackwater), and then with the battle for Najaf, which pitted the Americans against the militia of the radical Shi'a leader Muqtada al-Sadr. Combined with an increase in attacks across the country, these events showed that the Americans were faced with a large-scale conflict in Iraq. "I have seen the movie," declared General Anthony Zinni, a committed opponent to the war who did not hesitate to speak the V-word: "It was called Vietnam."[2]

The United States, in that spring of 2004, was losing the battle on moral grounds. The revelation at the end of April of the serious abuses at Abu Ghraib prison near Baghdad, carried out by American military personnel, exacerbated things enormously, and was compounded by the nonchalance that Donald Rumsfeld once again demonstrated toward such illegal actions. The scandal could not help but taint the motivations of a war that had been conducted in the name of freedom and human rights. (The moral outrage over these abuses would be aggravated the following year by press revelations of the scope of the CIA's human rights violations in the war on terror, whether involving secret detention centers, extraordinary renditions, or the use of interrogation techniques that in some cases amounted to torture.) By feeding the resentment of Iraqis and the Arab and Muslim world as a whole, Abu Ghraib further compromised an already difficult political and military situation. "Some assholes have just lost the war for us," said a young Marine when he saw television coverage of Abu Ghraib.[3]

Moreover, another justification for the war—the Iraqi "threat"— crumbled at about the same time. In January 2004, David Kay, the leader of the Iraq Survey Group (ISG) whose mission was to search for Iraq's supposed weapons of mass destruction, resigned. Kay was a former UN inspector who had supported the war and who had been appointed to the ISG by George Tenet after the fall of the Saddam Hussein regime. Kay's resignation confirmed what had become obvious over the past six months: these weapons did not exist any longer, probably because they had been destroyed by orders from Saddam Hussein in 1991, as Baghdad had always maintained. "We were all wrong," Kay declared. This was confirmed in the final report submitted in autumn 2004 by his successor as ISG head, Charles Duelfer—despite a perceptible "spin" based on the "intentions" of the Iraqi regime, which the report portrayed as having intended to resume its WMD programs in time. The Duelfer Report had two hefty victims: Colin Powell, who discovered how much he had been led astray in the preparation of his Security Council appearance on February 5, 2003; and George Tenet, who resigned in the summer of 2004. Meanwhile, another argument—one that even the CIA doubted, as we have seen—that had lent credit to the Iraq "threat," namely the supposed links between Iraq and al-Qaeda, was definitively invalidated in the summer of 2004. The final report of the 9/11 Commission, released on July 26, concluded that this assertion was erroneous.[4]

For all these reasons, the spring of 2004 was a turning point, first and foremost in the United States. The war, which in one year had cost the lives of 800 military personnel, was now judged negatively by the Americans. At the end of May, for the first time a majority of them thought that it was not worth the pain. The press, until then rather uncritical, began a turnaround. Prominent columnists who had declared themselves in favor of the war now lambasted how it was being conducted. Tom Friedman in the *New York Times* called for "a total overhaul," pointing to the risk of "a total disaster." At the same time, the *Times* began to wonder about the quality of Judith Miller's articles on Iraqi WMD; it was now established that Miller had relied on toxic sources like Iraqi National Congress leader Ahmed Chalabi. Meanwhile, the "coalition" was crumbling. In May 2004, Spain announced that it would withdraw its contingent, following the electoral defeat of José María Aznar by the socialist José Luis Zapatero in the wake of an al-Qaeda–sponsored terrorist bombing of the Madrid train system on March 11.[5] Hungary withdrew its forces at the end of the year, followed in early 2005 by the Netherlands and Ukraine. Poland, Bulgaria, and Italy also announced their coming withdrawals. Only the British seemed to remain alongside the United States. One year after the fall of the regime, the balance sheet was damning.[6]

In this context, from autumn 2003 to summer 2004 Paris tried to get beyond the Iraq crisis. This effort meant avoiding useless tensions on the subject with the United States and abstaining from any self-satisfaction, despite the temptation to do so. Some in Washington who had shared French reservations about the war were now saying that "the French were right."[7] Thus, for Paris, there was a delicate balance to be struck between the desire to be "constructive" and "pragmatic" in the face of American demands and the need to remind them of French "red lines," in particular on France's potential contribution to the stabilization and reconstruction of Iraq. France wanted to keep its contribution in Iraq within strict limits, albeit without appearing to refuse a priori to help.

In autumn 2003, the turning point in Franco-American relations was still a long way off. After the Bush-Chirac conversation at the UN General Assembly meeting in New York in September, negotiations over the resolution desired by the Americans had been difficult and tense. In mid-October, the French, Germans, and Russians had finally decided to vote for it despite the lack of progress on the role of the UN and on a return to sovereignty, and Resolution 1511 was finally adopted. The White House was resigned to "definitive disagreement" with France, US diplomat Robert Blackwill told French member of parliament Pierre Lellouche a few weeks later. (A hawk who was known for his blunt positions, Blackwill was now in charge of coordinating Iraq policy at the National Security Council.) Washington's decision in mid-November to advance the transfer of sovereignty to the end of June 2004 changed the situation somewhat: the Élysée thought that things were moving "in the right direction."[8]

Unsurprisingly, the Americans put back on the table the question of the involvement of the international community. When Maurice Gourdault-

Montagne met Condoleezza Rice at the end of November 2003, Rice asked what the French were "ready to do," again advancing the idea—which had been on the back burner for a few months—of NATO involvement in Iraq. A few days later, Senator Joe Biden, a Democrat who had supported the war but now was critical of how it was being conducted, defended this same idea to Chirac, whom he went to see at the Élysée. Was Biden trying to test the angle of attack the Democrats would use in the coming presidential election, namely the denunciation of the Bush administration's failure to rely on allies in the war in Iraq? Biden, in any case, did not hesitate to flatter his host to convey his point: events, he said, had proved Chirac right, but now he should be "magnanimous." Chirac was the only person who might still "save the situation," so he should "extend his hand" to Bush to get him to accept an internationalization of postconflict management, including NATO's involvement. Chirac did not budge: "The past [is] past," he said, and if France could do something "useful" to help the Americans to "get out of the Iraqi wasps' nest," it would do so "willingly." But, he added, the French were not ready "to do whatever," judging a possible NATO involvement "dangerous." Without totally ruling out this possibility, Chirac (in characteristically vague terms) said that he was ready to think about ways in which France might help.[9]

In parallel, the Americans opened another front: that of a financial contribution to Iraq's recovery by erasing its debt, since the three countries of the "peace camp," along with the United States and Japan, were its principal creditors. But from the French standpoint, this affair was just as sensitive. Not only was the Iraqi debt consequential—on the order of $3 billion for France, $3.6 billion for Russia, and $2.2 billion for Germany—but such a gesture raised a problem. Iraq was a country with "strong potential," and so erasing its debt would constitute a precedent; moreover, the rules of the group of creditor countries known as the Paris Club required negotiations with a sovereign government on the basis of an agreement with the International Monetary Fund. And how could the French agree to take part in Iraqi debt relief when the Americans continued to proclaim their wish to exclude France and other opponents of the war from contracts for Iraqi reconstruction, as the Bush administration had announced after the end of major operations? Yet for Paris to refuse any gesture seemed difficult. When he was received by Chirac on December 16, former secretary of state James A. Baker III, whom Bush had appointed to manage this issue, took advantage of Saddam Hussein's arrest two days earlier to ask for the French position. Chirac told Baker that he would accept a 50 percent reduction of the debt, but he would not go any further.[10]

Gourdault-Montagne's visit to Washington at the end of January 2004 was an opportunity to sketch out France's "red lines." In conversation with Rice, he summarized France's effort. In addition to the partial forgiveness of the Iraqi debt, France was considering (in concert with Germany and Japan) a possible contribution in humanitarian terms, such as education and health, and was studying a plan for a police training school that might be implemented when Iraq was sovereign. But when questioned by Rice about a possible French military involvement in Iraq, Gourdault-Montagne was clear that such a possibility was not now on the agenda. (Gourdault-Montagne's response to Rice confirmed implicitly that although, for a few months, there had been a window for France's involvement on the ground, it had closed owing to the worsening security situation.) As for a possible role for NATO—which, said Rice, might take over the sector that Poland would occupy until 2005—he reminded her that Paris could only accept such a role on two conditions: first, if a sovereign Iraqi government existed (therefore, after June 30), and second, if NATO had been provided with a UN mandate to intervene (something that Washington did not want, as the French well knew).[11]

The aggravation of the situation starting in the spring of 2004 obviously did not change French opinion. After the events in Fallujah and Najaf, Lakhdar Brahimi, UN secretary-general Kofi Annan's special envoy for Iraq, was received at the Élysée. Brahimi was not reassuring; there might be a slide toward a civil war, he told Chirac, stressing that the shift to sovereignty at the end of June might be somewhat illusory. The Americans wanted to maintain an embassy of more than 3,000 personnel, Brahimi said, adding that the Iraqi ministers would be paraded around by American advisers. The French were becoming resigned to the situation, as they understood that it would be futile to try to moderate American policy in the direction of both internationalization and "Iraqization." The deteriorating situation no longer permitted it, anyway. At the end of May, when the United States put forward a draft Security Council resolution to accompany the transfer of sovereignty, the Élysée noted that this was a fig leaf. The future multinational force would merely prolong the occupation force, particularly since the resolution did not fix its duration. But Washington stuck to its guns. "It would be a mistake to want to limit the duration [of the multinational force]," Bush stressed to Chirac during a telephone conversation on May 25, saying in the same breath that there was "no doubt" that the transfer of sovereignty ought to be "complete," and thanking his colleague for sharing his vision of a "free and democratic" Iraq that would be a "model" for the region. The French believed that the US administration was more than ever in "denial" mode, but Paris was no longer willing to resist and run the risk of uselessly quarreling with the Americans. Resolution 1546, adopted on June 8, approved the formation of an Iraqi interim government that would succeed the Coalition Provisional Authority and rely on a multi-national force, with elections scheduled for January 2005.[12]

As the transfer of sovereignty at the start of the summer of 2004 approached, the French refrained from throwing wrenches in the wheels of the Americans at the UN. Yet they were increasingly wary about a possible NATO role in Iraq, let alone a French military involvement, which simply was no longer in the cards. The administration was again trying to share the burden in Iraq in order to answer criticism from the Democrats in an electoral year, but Paris once more marked its "red lines." It was all right to extend the supporting role that NATO was already playing for Poland to allies who wanted to participate in the multinational force, and for NATO to contribute to training officers in the new Iraqi army by allowing them access to its training centers, but there was no question of going beyond that. The Élysée considered it "very danger-ous" to envisage an effective NATO presence on the ground in Iraq, for fear that it might be seen as "an alliance of Western armies against the Arab-Muslim world." In short, Paris did not want to see the NATO flag flying over Baghdad. At the approach of the NATO summit in Istanbul on June 28 and 29, 2004, new transatlantic frictions were perceptible. Paris and Berlin opposed the train-ing of Iraqi officers taking place in Iraq itself, as Washington wished to do in order to better showcase NATO's active involvement in Iraq. Although the French did not entirely rule out such a scenario in the future if the government to be elected in 2005 asked for it and if the UN gave a green light to it, one year after the invasion of Iraq it was clear that anything more than a marginal NATO engagement was not acceptable. The Americans knew that they had to live with this: in mid-June 2004, Bush declared to Chirac that Washington had no intention "either of requiring France to send troops to Iraq, or giving the impression that NATO was engaged" there, and stressed that he would not make this a subject of confrontation. On the eve of the transfer of sovereignty, the Americans realized that there was not much to expect from their oldest European allies to help them save their wager on Iraq.[13]

Limiting tensions over Iraq was key to improving the bilateral relation-ship, as Paris desired. From the summer of 2003 to the summer of 2004, this improvement was gradual, despite French efforts at all levels. Chirac was per-sonally involved, never losing an opportunity to show his American visitors his most affable and thoughtful side, at which he excelled, whether by receiving

Laura Bush at the Élysée at the end of September 2003 or wishing George H. W. Bush a happy eightieth birthday in June 2004.[14] Meanwhile, Jean-David Levitte conducted a charm offensive in Washington. In June 2003, he hosted at his residence the annual Opera Ball, and got Hermès to give each woman attending a scarf decorated with the French and American flags. At the same time, Levitte tried to reach the deep country. On the occasion of the sixtieth anniversary of D-Day in June 2004, he took the initiative to invite a hundred US veterans to the Normandy celebrations, accompanied by their families. The invited veterans were awarded the Legion of Honor, and a hundred other veterans would receive this highest of French distinctions in each of the following years, with abundant press coverage. The message that Levitte wanted to send to US public opinion was simple: "We can disagree, [but] that does not mean that the French have forgotten what we owe to the Americans."[15]

Meanwhile, Levitte modified his embassy's ways of operating. Until then, French diplomats in Washington had focused almost exclusively on traditional contacts with the executive branch. The 2003 crisis had revealed the image problem from which France permanently suffered in the United States, particularly the appearance of being a disloyal ally. To correct this, the embassy and consulates multiplied their press appearances to reach a wider audience. Washington's venues of influence were another target of Levitte's offensive. Levitte wanted to increase the French presence in key think tanks, whose impact on the foreign policy agenda had been made clear by the crisis, and to establish direct links between the embassy and Congress, which until then had been almost nonexistent. To do this, he recruited a former congressional staffer to work in the embassy; in the autumn of 2003, the first tangible result of this outreach was the creation in Congress of a French Caucus with forty-five members, among which were influential representatives and senators. This figure would double in the years to come. Here, too, Chirac made an effort: receiving in February 2004 a delegation from the French Caucus and its president, Amory Houghton—a Republican congressman whose father had been ambassador in Paris in the 1950s—he declared that anything that might damage the ties between France and America was "dangerous and useless." The two countries might diverge occasionally, as had been the case over Iraq, but they had to avoid "dramatization," Chirac said, adding that he had been neither "impressed" nor "disturbed" by the "excessive words" that had been used the previous year, since their quarrels did not touch what was "essential."[16]

All this time, the French had been trying to restart effective diplomatic cooperation. A regular dialogue should be restored, Gourdault-Montagne told

Rice at the end of January 2004. Relations between Dominique de Villepin and Colin Powell became satisfactory once again, but they were less central to the bilateral relationship; Villepin left the Quai d'Orsay in the spring of 2004 after a ministerial reshuffle, and was replaced by Michel Barnier, whom the Americans judged to be less abrasive but also less influential. Thus the king-pin of rapprochement was Gourdault-Montagne, who as Chirac's diplomatic adviser from then on came periodically to Washington to talk with Rice.[17]

Rapprochement between Paris and Washington crystallized, first of all, on the issues over which cooperation had remained effective even during the 2003 crisis, starting with the fight against terrorism. Paris wanted to further intensify cooperation between US and French intelligence services, which had remained close despite the breach over Iraq.[18] Meanwhile, the sending of French special forces to Afghanistan in the summer of 2003 (about which the public was not informed until the spring of 2004) had a positive impact on American perceptions. It also enabled the French to point out that their rejection of the war in Iraq issued neither from a systematic anti-American attitude nor from a pacifist posture. The same was true of other hot spots, starting with the Iranian nuclear issue, which the French wanted to utilize to demonstrate to the Americans the seriousness with which they considered the danger of nuclear proliferation. It extended to other regional crises, such as in Côte d'Ivoire, Haiti, or the Balkans, over which cooperation was satisfactory. In all these dossiers, the French wanted to show that relations with the United States were "globally good," and that despite Iraq the two countries worked well together on many subjects: "We should not let the tree hide the forest and we should give our many convergences [with Washington] still more consistency and visibility," Chirac's diplomats at the Élysée advised at the start of 2004.[19]

Paris also wanted to clear mines on the usual touchy subjects in Franco-American relations. The Iraq crisis had reanimated the old NATO issue between the two countries, and the Tervuren summit outside Brussels at the end of April 2003—in which the French, Germans, Belgians, and Luxembourgers had wanted to restart the European defense project by giving it a headquarters autonomous from NATO—had not helped. So the French wanted to seize all opportunities to highlight their commitment to the alliance, whether in the Balkans, in Afghanistan, or within the NATO Response Force, to which France wanted to be the prime contributor. "Never has France been so close to NATO," the Élysée believed. Paris had reached a compromise with London in the autumn of 2003 over the question of the European military headquarters, at the cost of watering down the ambitions of Tervuren. The Élysée argued that the April 2003 Franco-German-Belgian proposals had been misunderstood and tried to convince the White House that there was nothing in the Franco-British compromise solution that might weaken NATO. Relying on the military operations that the EU was undertaking in the Balkans and in Africa, Paris wanted to demonstrate that the buildup of the European Security and Defense Policy was not in contradiction with the transatlantic tie and to better explain the meaning of the "multipolar" world advocated by Chirac. Far from any idea of a "counterweight," the French explained, this approach was a matter of strengthening the ties between the two "poles," Europe and America. All the same, it did not prevent the need for an international organization that was "sufficiently strong to set the law," Chirac told Congressman Amory Houghton, implicitly reminding him of the primacy of the UN.[20]

Paris also tried to reestablish bilateral cooperation with respect to defense, where the vindictiveness of Pentagon civilians (by contrast to the generals, who wanted to turn the page on Iraq) was felt for a long time after the 2003 crisis. Bad feelings had blocked the joint exercises and exchanges of all kinds to which the military in both countries were attached. Cooperation over weapons was also affected, with the Pentagon suspending the delivery of sensitive equipment to the French armed forces; particularly concerned were catapults for the *Charles de Gaulle* aircraft carrier. When Maurice Gourdault-Montagne complained to Rice about such "petty and incomprehensible vexations" in November 2003, she pointed to the "zeal" of some "intermediary" echelons, but Rice's assertion was scarcely credible, inasmuch as the obstructive role of Donald Rumsfeld was patent. "He simply loathed us," a French general recalled. For months, the Pentagon opposed the appointment (desired by Paris) of two French generals to NATO's integrated military structure for the first time since 1966, a move that reflected the French desire to remain in close contact with the US armed forces despite France's nonintegration in NATO, and to prevent a military gap from emerging between France and the United States. In a sign that French efforts were starting to bear fruit, in early 2004 Rice announced to Gourdault-Montagne that the White House had made a favorable decision on this case, which effectively unblocked the situation in NATO. By mid-2004, the Élysée once more considered that cooperation over defense was satisfactory on essential matters, such as cooperation in theaters of operations where the two countries were engaged side by side, starting with Afghanistan. The Pentagon civilians nevertheless continued to block military exchanges; the situation did not return to normal until Rumsfeld resigned as secretary of defense at the end of 2006.[21]

Overall, in the first months of 2004, French efforts began to pay off. During Gourdault-Montagne's Washington visit at the end of January, Rice had been kind to him. "We always have time for our great French friends and allies," she even said, and he reported that the atmosphere had been "excellent" and characterized by Rice's "attentive listening." The following weeks confirmed the change of atmosphere. One year after the beginning of the war, the crisis over Iraq "had not exhausted its effects," the Élysée observed in March 2004, but the climate definitely had improved. The announcement of Bush's participation in the ceremonies to mark the sixtieth anniversary of D-Day confirmed this lightened mood. Chirac had invited him back in December, hoping that the event would mark a return to normal relations, but at first the White House had dragged its feet: "Our decision has not yet been made," Rice had told Gourdault-Montagne in January. Finally, on March 19, Bush telephoned to tell Chirac that he would be coming to Normandy in June. (He took advantage of the occasion to ask Chirac to make an additional effort on the Iraqi debt.) Bush's acceptance symbolically marked a high point in the reestablishment of the transatlantic relationship, especially since the French had also invited Gerhard Schröder to the Normandy ceremonies.[22]

Beyond its symbolism, Bush's trip to Normandy effectively illustrated the return to normal relations, as shown by his conversations with Chirac in Paris the day before the D-Day anniversary. The atmosphere was positive. Bush, facing a reelection campaign, was anxious to answer criticism from the Democrats about his failure to obtain the support of the allies. Of course, Bush and Chirac still held diverging opinions, notably over the critical situation in the Israeli-Palestinian conflict and the future of the Middle East region more generally. On the one hand, the Americans were eager to promote their "Greater Middle East" initiative; in the wake of regime change in Baghdad, this approach aimed to make manifest the neoconservative vision of how promoting democracy would profoundly transform the whole region. The French, on the other hand, were profoundly skeptical about the possibility for the West to impose changes on the region from the outside after the Iraqi fiasco, and they tried to moderate the scheme's most debatable aspects while carefully avoiding a clash with Washington over the matter. But compared with the stormy UN encounter in September 2003, Iraq in itself was no longer really a point of discord, despite the basic disagreement that remained on the issue. Chirac again expressed to Bush his concerns about the situation on the eve of the transfer of sovereignty, saying that he feared a scenario that combined the Shi'a assumption of power, a violent reaction from the Sunnis, and independence moves from the Kurds. Bush did not seem offended by Chirac's remarks, calling such a hypothetical chain of events a "catastrophic scenario" that the United States would "do everything to avoid." Given the growing instability on the ground that prevailed by the summer of 2004, it was obvious that the management of Iraq had become solely the problem of the Americans (and, to a lesser extent, of the British). Franco-American relations therefore ceased to be directly affected by the Iraqi situation, which permitted the two countries to come back to effective cooperation, if not yet to real convergence, on other subjects: "It was around that time that we found ourselves again on speaking terms," a former Chirac aide would later remember.[23]

"This is a great moment"

Starting in 2005 with the second term of George W. Bush, a full Franco-American reconciliation began to take place. In the November 2004 election, Bush had defeated his Democratic challenger, Senator John Kerry. During the campaign, Bush and his team, advised by Karl Rove, had once again exploited the "9/11 effect" and the patriotism that still prevailed among the Americans, and at the same time succeeded in pushing the Iraqi fiasco into the background. The election result caused consternation in Europe, where a wide majority had hoped for a Kerry victory. Still, from the outset Bush's second term seemed set to take a different turn from the first. The Democrats' willingness to make difficulties for the president over the way in which the war had been conducted and over his inability to obtain the support of the allies during or after the conflict had led Bush, in the last months of his first term, to demonstrate that America was not isolated—hence his trip to Normandy in June 2004.

Bush's second term soon confirmed this revised orientation. Of course, Bush did not lower his colors, nor did he renounce the missionary inspiration or the "transformational" ambition of his foreign policy—which aimed, as he declared during his inauguration on January 20, 2005, at no less than "ending tyranny in our world."[24] American foreign policy remained marked by the proclaimed desire to propagate democracy as a response to the challenge of terrorism, first of all in the Middle East. Yet behind this rhetorical continuity, a basic moderation in the direction of realism could be seen. Condoleezza Rice, who had succeeded Powell as secretary of state shortly after Bush's inauguration, now spoke of "practical idealism." She benefited from a more advantageous situation than her predecessor, as Dick Cheney and Donald Rumsfeld had been discredited by their respective roles in the Iraqi fiasco—the former for having been the principal advocate of the war, the latter for having been responsible for the calamitous management of the postwar phase. Rice was thus truly in charge of foreign policy during the second term. The president himself was weakened by unpopularity, partly resulting from a growing awareness among Americans that the war had indeed been a fiasco. (Bush's disastrous management of the consequences of Hurricane Katrina, which had devastated Louisiana and much of the Gulf Coast at the end of the summer of 2005, compounded this sense of failure.) The fundamentals of American power were also weakened, starting with finances and the armed forces, both of which had been compromised by the two wars. Congress and the press, long passive in the name of national unity in the face of an omnipotent presidency, gradually rediscovered their roles in the "checks and balances" process. In sum, the Bush administration's international margin of maneuver had been considerably reduced. All of the above explains the administration's marked return to pragmatism and even a shift toward multilateralism: America, during Bush's second term, rediscovered that it needed allies.[25]

Bush opened his second term with a gesture toward Europe. In going to Brussels at the end of February 2005 for a NATO summit and a summit with the EU, during which he reaffirmed US support for the European project, the American president—who also stopped in Germany—in essence signaled that the policy of playing the "new" Europe against the "old" had ended. Of course, transatlantic relations were far from tranquil, but the search for cooperation once again had become the rule: both sides had an interest in it. The erstwhile war camp was weakened. Spain's José María Aznar had left power in 2004; Tony Blair had carried his party to victory in the British elections in May 2005, but had been weakened by the Iraq fiasco; and Silvio Berlusconi had lost in the April 2006 Italian elections. But the same was true of the former peace camp: in the spring of 2005, almost 55 percent of the French, followed by the Dutch, had rejected the plan for a European constitutional treaty. This negative vote dealt a blow to the ambitions of "old" Europe and to the French vision of a "Europe-power" that would be able to assert itself as a decision-making pole to rival the United States. Meanwhile, in Germany, the September 2005 elections led to the defeat of Gerhard Schröder by Angela Merkel. Merkel, a Christian Democrat who headed a so-called "grand coalition" government with the Social Democrats as junior partners, had clearly demarcated herself from Schröder over the Iraq crisis, and Schröder's loss deprived the French president of his closest partner and placed German policy again on a more classically Atlanticist path. All these factors would contribute to transatlantic reconciliation in general and to Franco-American rapprochement in particular.

In November 2004, Chirac (who had not made the mistake of underestimating the incumbent US president's chances of being reelected) congratulated Bush shortly after the election. Bush declared his wish to work closely with Chirac. "We are not in agreement on everything, but when we work together the results are always positive," he said.[26] The upturn in the bilateral relationship was already quite clear in the first weeks of Bush's new term. In early February 2005, Rice came to Paris in advance of Bush's trip to Europe. After giving a speech on transatlantic relations at Sciences Po—Paris's prestigious institute for political studies as a venue for the speech was a clever choice, in that regard—she was welcomed by Chirac, who was not short of praise for her talk. The French president was solicitous as usual: accompanying his guest after an hour's discussion, he assured her of the "pleasure" he would have in meeting Bush in Brussels and of the "fundamental importance" he attached to the transatlantic tie.[27]

The Bush-Chirac meeting in Brussels on February 21, 2005, indeed marked a turning point in Franco-American relations: it was an "excellent conversation" that "enabled tackling" the principal issues of the day in a "relaxed and cordial atmosphere," the French side summarized. Whether this shift was the result of the regular trips taken by Gourdault-Montagne to Washington to meet Stephen Hadley (who succeeded Rice at the White House), or Rice's visits to the Élysée, or the direct contacts between the two presidents, starting in 2005 the French and Americans rediscovered a closeness that had been forgotten for almost four years. Even Paul Wolfowitz would declare to Jean-David Levitte in February 2005, "We really want to work with you," which said a lot about the change in climate.[28] It is true that Wolfowitz, at this juncture, was interested in not antagonizing the French, as he coveted the presidency of the World Bank. He achieved his purpose: although Wolfowitz had been "very aggressive," Chirac said to Bush, France did not want to create difficulties over his nomination to succeed James Wolfensohn as World Bank president; Chirac added that "this was the past." In the name of Franco-American reconciliation, the French agreed to this gesture—as they had done with the near total erasure of the Iraqi debt, which Paris had ended up accepting at the end of 2004.[29]

The Syria issue had provided a strong impetus for Franco-American reconciliation at the end of the summer of 2004. In September, at the joint initiative of Paris and Washington—something that had not been seen for years—the Security Council had adopted Resolution 1559, which required respect for the independence of Lebanon and the withdrawal of foreign (meaning Syrian) forces as well as the disarmament of militias. This joint initiative was the fruit of a French idea that had been welcomed at the White House, because it would show, a few weeks before the presidential elections, Bush's capacity to work again with "old" allies. Resolution 1559 resulted from a convergence between the priorities of Paris (to defend the integrity of Lebanon) and Washington (to put pressure on Damascus to stop it from helping the Iraqi insurrection and supporting terrorist movements such as Hezbollah and Hamas), and it also demonstrated the desire of both countries to seize this opportunity to put their reconciliation on track. But it was Bush and Chirac's February 21 meeting in Brussels that sealed their alliance over this issue. The meeting took place a week after the assassination of Rafik Hariri, the former Lebanese prime minister and a close friend of Chirac's. The Americans and the French had no doubt that Damascus was behind the Hariri assassination. Chirac wanted to persuade Bush that regime change in Syria, which the Americans did not hide was their goal, could be effected not by direct confrontation with Damascus but by the effective implementation of Resolution 1559, which had remained until then a dead letter. Forcing Syria out of Lebanon, the French president explained to his American colleague, would bring the ruin of Syria's Alawi power system, which drew its force from the exploitation of Lebanon. Bush was enthusiastic. "This is a very important plan," he exclaimed, adding that this was "a great moment." Against the backdrop of an effective Syrian retreat from Lebanon, the following months would illustrate the close cooperation between Paris and Washington on this issue, confirming a rapprochement that was marked by pragmatism on both sides. In essence, the French recognized the new realities in the Middle East after the Iraqi conflict, even as they tried to push US policy toward moderation. In the case of Syria, this meant accepting the need to put pressure on Damascus and even the possibility of regime change, while at the same time trying to avoid a possible American intervention.[30]

The Franco-American and transatlantic rapprochement over the Iranian nuclear issue starting in 2005–6 occurred along similar lines. The French, Germans, and British wanted to work to resolve this problem within a multilateral framework and to try to involve the United States, both to make their approach more credible in the eyes of the Iranians and to reduce the risk of a unilateral American action. "We need the cooperation of the United States to obtain results," the French pleaded to the Americans. The goal did not appear out of reach. After having dragged its feet in the name of refusing to "legitimize" the Iranian regime, Washington brought its support to the "EU3" in March 2005, and in June 2006 the Americans decided to participate in the negotiations with Iran. To be sure, the persistence of American doubts on the possibility of obtaining results through negotiation, combined with Iranian ill will, meant that the problem would not be easily solved; still, the Iranian nuclear dossier was characteristic of the Euro-Atlantic reconciliation post-Iraq.[31]

It would be a mistake, though, to think that France and the United States, starting in 2005, systematically understood each other. On the American side, the adoption of a more conciliatory style did not imply a renunciation of the fundamentals of the Bush policy; on the French side, recognition of the situation resulting from the war in Iraq and the desire to reconcile with the United States did not signify that they had rallied to the American vision of the Middle East or of the international system. Divergences persisted on many issues, first of all on the Middle East, where the Americans and French continued to have clearly different points of view on the Israeli-Palestinian conflict and over the question of "democratizing" the Arab world and the means of doing so. Similar divergences arose over the "color" revolutions in eastern Europe: the Rose Revolution in Georgia in 2003 and the Orange Revolution in Ukraine in 2004. The French feared that a marked American interference in these revolutions, in the name of propagating democracy or the desire to "roll back" Russia, might lead to a backlash from Moscow, especially if these countries were invited to join NATO. Chirac's France, in other words, feared the possibility of Washington's beginning a new Cold War with Vladimir Putin's Russia at the urging of the "neo-cons." There were also divergences over relations with China, particularly on the issue of lifting the European embargo on arms sales to Beijing: the Americans wanted to dissuade the Europeans from lifting sanctions in the name of their strategic interests, while the latter (led by the French) saw it as a necessary gesture toward China almost twenty years after the Tiananmen Square repressions that had prompted the imposition of sanctions. Finally, the Franco-American reconciliation did not erase disagreement over world governance, as shown by the issue of climate change, where the United States did not budge, or the UNESCO convention on cultural diversity (an idea that Chirac had generated) that was adopted in the autumn of 2005 despite Washington's opposition. But these disagreements were now managed pragmatically and without drama. In November 2005, Rice took up her pen to thank Chirac for his welcome at the Élysée during her most recent trip. "The President and I attach great importance to the dialogue our two countries have established. We value our commitment to democratic ideals, multilateral diplomacy, and eliminating terrorism, and I look forward to working with you to achieve our common goals," she wrote. This declaration would have been unimaginable two years previously.[32]

Meanwhile, the situation in Iraq continued to deteriorate, which pushed Washington to compromise on other issues. Although the year 2005 was marked by a series of events that could be seen as raising hopes for stabilization, a prospect that the White House advanced at every opportunity, in truth the situation was not getting better at all. The Iraqi elections of January 30 took place without incident and were considered at the time to be a success, arousing hope of improvement, but in fact that was not the case. The Sunnis had largely boycotted the vote, confirming their marginalization in the political process, which in return fed the insurrection. This political dysfunction was repeated during the October 15 constitutional referendum—which was held even though the Sunnis had rejected the plan for a constitution—and again on December 15, when fresh elections were held. Despite a semblance of institutional order, the reality was in fact political instability—indeed, it would take months for the Iraqis to form a government—and an aggravated insurrection. During October 2005, there were more than 3,000 insurgent attacks, the highest figure since the fall of Saddam Hussein. At the end of 2005, it seemed that Iraq was sinking into a civil war and that the situation was getting out of anyone's control.[33]

Paris was aware of the continuous deterioration. After the January 2005 Iraqi elections, the Élysée had soberly judged that the situation remained "delicate," but four months later the degradation was considered "worrying," and on the eve of the October referendum the Élysée believed that there was now a serious threat that Iraq would break up. But whereas the French were still convinced that the only way of getting out of the vicious cycle was to set a date for the US withdrawal, to push the Iraqis to include the Sunnis in the political process, and to involve other countries in the region (including Iran) in stabilizing Iraq, Paris could only regret that Washington was far from such an approach. Instead of announcing a prospective US withdrawal, the Americans, the French observed, were linking it to the reconstitution of Iraqi forces that would be capable of ensuring the country's security on their own, which appeared quite elusive. French leaders considered it even more necessary for a "complete change of logic" to occur, including an American disengagement and Iraq's return to full sovereignty, but by the end of 2005 they had given up trying to persuade the Americans of this. "Might you not consider starting a withdrawal from Iraq after the end of this year," if necessary with a "modulation"? Chirac had asked Rice during her visit to Paris on February 8, 2005. But when he received her again on October 14, they barely mentioned Iraq, and they did so only in connection with Syria.[34]

In these conditions, the French more than ever ruled out any direct involvement in Iraq, especially a military one. Unsurprisingly, the question had come back to the table after the January 2005 Iraqi elections: might France help train the security forces and strengthen Iraqi institutions? Rice had asked Chirac in February. Chirac had replied that Paris had offered to train 1,500 police and would be ready to help with institutional strengthening, while also supporting the EU's efforts in Iraq. But France, Chirac had made it clear once more to Rice, was not ready to send military personnel on the ground, in particular in a NATO framework. "It was clear from the start," the Élysée stressed before the NATO summit at the end of February 2005, when the Americans again pressured for NATO involvement, "that our preference was for training [Iraqi troops] outside Iraq and that no [French] soldier would go there."[35] In short, the more the situation in Iraq was aggravated, the less realistic a French presence was.

The Americans did not want to turn this disagreement into a drama, however: the fallout from the 2002–3 crisis, in this sense, was over, even if the French attitude remained a nagging source of irritation for leaders in Washington. At the end of 2005, Jean-David Levitte asserted that the Americans thought that they had "pardoned" the French for their opposition to the war—which, he noted, bespoke the absence of any repentance on their part—but since they were aware of the excellent bilateral cooperation that was taking place on an issue like Syria, they did not understand why Paris would not make an effort on Iraq, not because a French engagement there would change things on the ground but because it would represent a recognition of the legitimacy of US Iraq policy. Levitte argued that the French needed to better showcase what they had already done for Iraq, such as voting on resolutions at the Security Council and reestablishing diplomatic relations with Iraq in July 2004.[36]

Despite the improvement in Franco-American relations starting in 2004–5, the relationship was caught up in the delayed effect of various affairs linked to the Iraqi conflict, whose fallout now interfered with the ongoing reconciliation. Foremost among them was the "Oil-for-Food" scandal that broke in the fall of 2004, in the aftermath of the publication of the Duelfer Report. Based on documents discovered in Iraq and leaked to the press over the previous months, the Duelfer Report pointed fingers at France (and Russia) with the revelation that Baghdad had tried to influence French policy toward Iraq—in particular over sanctions—by systematically privileging French businesses in distributing contracts and by associating French individuals reputably close to power with embezzlements set up by the Iraqis. But, as seen earlier, while the French at the time were fully aware that the Iraqis were trying to make use of the Oil-for-Food program for these ends, nothing supported the allegation that these considerations had significantly influenced French policy. That French personalities were individually involved—including two former ambassadors and a former minister—was confirmed the following year in a report by Paul Volcker, who had been charged by the Security Council with investigating corruption in the Oil-for-Food program. (Paris, in fact, had cooperated fully with the Volcker inquiry.) But while the "Oil-for-Food" scandal testified to the persistence of the role in France (as in other countries) of an Iraq "lobby" and its abuses, it did not incriminate French policy or leaders as such. The alleged French leg of the scandal was nevertheless highlighted in Washington, where the old accusations against France resurfaced, leading Paris to react vigorously. ("It was bullshit," a former CIA official said about the rumors circulated by some in Washington to try to personally discredit French leaders, including Chirac.)[37] The same delayed effect took place over intelligence: while various inquiries in the United States had concluded as early as 2005 that the intelligence about WMD that US authorities had possessed before the conflict had been false, the Bush administration, to justify itself, now tried to argue that the "peace camp" had had the same data, a claim that the French forcefully denied.[38]

In light of all of these difficulties, it was not until 2006 that the Franco-American reconciliation became a durable reality. At the start of the year, the *Washington Post* published an article by its diplomatic correspondent, David Ignatius, whose title—"Bush's New Ally"—made a sensation. France, Ignatius wrote, had become "the best ally" of the Bush administration. Ignatius's article revealed the close ties between Maurice Gourdault-Montagne and Stephen Hadley: the former's regular Washington visits, on top of their weekly telephone calls, constituted a veritable "French Connection," Ignatius quipped. Although France continued to be a target in the US media and in public debate, Ignatius continued, it had become, if discreetly, one of America's most effective allies as the Iraqi fiasco now pushed the two countries to operate "in tandem." Paris was even playing the role of facilitator to rally other countries, such as Russia and China, in policy areas where Washington wanted to involve the UN. Ignatius recounted the intense Franco-American cooperation over Syria and Iran: by sharing roles in the classic "good cop–bad cop routine," the French and the Americans had achieved results that they could not have achieved separately. "Paris and Washington still disagree sharply on the substance of many issues," Ignatius concluded, "but they seem to have concluded that they'll get more of what they want if they collaborate rather than bicker."[39]

Despite its somewhat provocative headline, the *Washington Post* article accurately described Franco-American relations at the approach of the third anniversary of the war in Iraq. Bush, during a phone conversation with Chirac three weeks later, said that he was "very satisfied" with the coordination established between Gourdault-Montagne and Hadley and that he wanted them to stay in close contact. Events in 2006 demonstrated cooperation between the French and the Americans in areas where convergences existed. Regarding Iran, Paris and Washington had agreed to transfer the nuclear issue to the Security Council, and they maintained strong pressure on Syria. That summer, the war in south Lebanon between Israel and Hezbollah gave rise to the adoption of Resolution 1701, on the initiative of both Paris and Washington, on August 12. This concord did not prevent the two countries from differing over many issues; it was, classically, the case with regard to various issues involving the Atlantic alliance, whether concerning its possible enlargement to Ukraine and Georgia (about which France was extremely reluctant), the expansion of the International Security Assistance Force's role in Afghanistan (which Paris accepted only grudgingly), or the assertion of a "political" role for NATO (which the French feared the Americans wanted to promote in order to transform NATO into an "alliance of democracies" that would compete with the UN). But on all these issues, which were tackled at the NATO summit in Riga in November 2006, Paris and Washington were able to find compromises. Franco-American relations were again "normal," said the US ambassador in Paris, Craig Stapleton.[40]

Yesterday's adversaries were both on the decline, which could only push them to want to move beyond their quarrel. On the French side, widespread riots in housing projects in the Paris area in 2005, along with the failure of the European referendum and the vascular cerebral incident (a minor stroke) that Chirac had suffered in early September 2005, made for a difficult last part of Chirac's presidency; it seemed like the end of a reign. On the American side, the second half of Bush's second term was almost like a descent into hell. When he left his post as White House chief of staff in the spring of 2006,

Andrew Card—as faithful and loyal to Bush as one could be—recognized that incompetence and arrogance, two traits now associated with the president's public image, had come to characterize the presidency in the perception of many Americans. The stinging defeat of the Republicans and their loss of the Senate and the House in the November 2006 midterm elections underscored the failure of the Bush presidency and announced a probable Democratic victory in the 2008 presidential election. Two issues in particular stood out in this failure: Hurricane Katrina and the Iraq war.[41]

The year 2006 was the *annus horribilis* of the Bush presidency; it was also when the denial over Iraq finally ended. In March, Bush still believed he could reassure his fellow citizens with fine words: "Our strategy is getting results," he declared, saying there was "evidence of real progress." Two months later, in May, the insurgent attacks had reached a peak of 113 per day on average. Meanwhile, critics lashed out at the administration in the wake of a series of revelations about the dubious conditions under which the choice for war had been made in 2002–3. By autumn 2006, the administration was in complete disarray. At the end of October, Jean-David Levitte talked with John Warner, a loyal though independent-minded Republican who was chairman of the Senate's Armed Services Committee. Warner, on his way back from a trip to Iraq, had been received by Bush: "I told the president that we were faced with a disaster and that it was impossible to maintain the current policy," he told Levitte, and added, "For the first time, I found him receptive." Bush would be ready to adopt another line after the election on November 7, Warner went on, though he acknowledged that "nobody had a clear idea" on the matter. And, he concluded, "I wish that we had a dialogue with France over Iraq; you know the Arab world, do you have suggestions?" The French ambassador noted that these remarks said a lot about the confusion that prevailed in Washington.[42]

Two months later, James Baker and the former Democratic congressman Lee Hamilton made public the conclusions of the Iraq Study Group, an independent commission appointed by Congress to analyze the Iraqi situation and make proposals, over which they had presided jointly. The Baker-Hamilton report's conclusions were irrevocable. "The situation in Iraq is grave and deteriorating," the authors began, and pointed to the administration's mistakes, starting with its refusal to set a timetable for the American withdrawal. Baker and Hamilton called for a radical change in approach: an inclusive reconciliation process in Iraq, the involvement of regional actors, and a new military strategy whose goal would be to result in "responsible" US disengagement. For the French, it was difficult not to see here the justification of their own warnings before the war and their admonitions afterward.[43] Yet in the wake of the report, Bush decided to increase the US military effort in Iraq, while adopting a new "counter-insurgency" strategy. The "surge" led to the deployment, in the first months of 2007, of 20,000 additional troops. But four years after the war began, in March 2007, the surge was still far from bearing fruit; it was "a somber anniversary," wrote the French embassy in Washington, noting the morose mood dominating the American capital. Two months later, Nicolas Sarkozy was elected president of France at the end of a campaign in which he had asserted his wish to reestablish definitively Franco-American friendship. "Washington would appreciate France reflecting on what it might do to help America in Iraq," Rice said to Levitte in July, when he came to say farewell after having been named diplomatic adviser to the new French president.[44]

Afterword

More than twelve years after the events, what assessment can we make of the war in Iraq and its consequences? By all the evidence, the verdict is dismal. Iraq, after almost a decade of occupation that ended with the departure of US troops in 2011, can barely escape its lingering violence and its ethnic and religious fractiousness. Despite a semblance of political order, the country is far from representing the model that it was called upon to become when Operation Iraqi Freedom was launched. Looking beyond Iraq, it is an understatement to say that the whole region has not experienced the positive transformation that had been predicted by the architects of the war. While the defenders of George W. Bush's policy at first wanted to view the "Arab Spring" of 2010–11 as a retrospective validation of US policy, changes over the past few years far from confirm that. Instead of a transition to democracy, the Arab Spring countries—with the exception of Tunisia—have now sunk into repression and an authoritarian backlash, essentially marking a return to the status quo, not least in Egypt. Instability and rejection of the West now characterize the situation throughout most of the Middle East. In Syria, the bloody civil war that has been dragging on since 2011 has devastated the country and nurtured the emergence of the Islamic State on both sides of the Iraq-Syria border. In barely two years, the Islamic State—originally an offspring of the post-2003 anti-American Sunni insurgency in Iraq—has grown into a major threat for the region and beyond. From Tunis to Paris to California, the various attacks perpetrated throughout 2015 by the Islamic State, or in its name, have been felt across the world. Today, the Israeli-Palestinian conflict is at more of an impasse than ever, even though the neoconservatives had promised

311

that Saddam Hussein's fall and the predicted transformation of the region would contribute to its solution. Overall, even if all the troubles that agitate the Middle East are not attributable to the 2003 war, the US adventure in Iraq nonetheless can be characterized as a fiasco of historic proportions.

Beyond that, the grandiose Bush vision of a post–Cold War world order resting on the expansion of democracy and Western values, with the unequaled power of America (military above all) and the exceptionalism of its mission as its keystone, has floundered. The transformation of the international system over the past decade or so has been characterized by the rise of emerging powers—starting with China, now a peer and a strategic competitor of the United States—whose values and interests are most often in opposition to those of the West. Two wars have led to a decade-long quagmire whose human, moral, political, and economic costs have proved enormous for American leadership and capabilities, and have diverted it from addressing other important challenges. In spite of the election in 2008 of a president who promised to turn the page on this dark period in his country's history, America has not yet surmounted the Iraq disaster. Future historians will likely rule that May 1, 2003—the day Bush stood beneath the "Mission Accomplished" banner on the deck of the *Abraham Lincoln*—was the date on which the United States reached the zenith of its power. To be sure, the exceptional situation experienced by America over the decade that followed its "victory" in the Cold War, that of an unparalleled hyperpower, arguably was destined to be fleeting. But it seems hard to dispute in hindsight that the choices made after 9/11, largely imputable to the hubris of power combined with a new feeling of vulnerability, accelerated the relative decline of the United States. A dozen years after the Iraq war, one thing seems clear: the twenty-first century will not be another American century.

Of course, in retrospect, the American fiasco can be seen as proving the French right, along with the other members of the 2003 "peace camp" who had warned the United States about the risks of the Iraqi adventure. By opposing the US-led war, French diplomacy enjoyed its hour of glory, for a time reviving the Gaullist grandeur. In denying the United States the legitimacy of its war and preventing the Iraq invasion from receiving the international community's seal of approval, France proved that a medium power could, in the name of principles, oppose the United States. Yet even though it certainly complicated the American task—and paid the price for it—France ultimately was not successful in preventing the war. Moreover, it was not able to build on its resounding "no" to the United States.

On the regional level, while the war in Iraq, as the French had warned, illustrated the impasse of any democratic transformation imposed from outside, in the years that followed France itself proved unable to change its long-time attachment to a policy of preserving the political status quo in the Middle East and in the Arab world. Its awkward reaction to the Arab Spring, marked by an initial wait-and-see attitude to the popular protests (not least in Tunisia and Egypt), illustrated this initial reluctance to consider new policy options. The desire to overcome Paris's failure to anticipate the Arab Springs and to regain influence in that part of the world then led French diplomacy to a sudden U-turn in the spring of 2011, with Paris now encouraging the revolutions in these pivotal countries as well as in Syria. In an astonishing turn of events, France (together with Britain) in effect became the spearhead of a regime change by force of arms in Libya, leading a war that resulted in the fall of Colonel Gaddafi in the fall of 2011. Meanwhile, on the global scale, the international system that Jacques Chirac had called for even before the Iraq crisis did not see the light of day. Over the past decade or so, the world has indeed become more "multipolar" due to the relative decline of the United States and the emergence of new powers, but this multipolar system is not the one that French leaders imagined, remote as it is from the ideals of multilateralism and collective security built around the United Nations.

If France failed to build constructively on its "no" to America, this failure was first and foremost clear in the European dimension. French leaders had hoped—even if this was not their prime motivation, as we have seen—that the 2003 confrontation over Iraq would hasten the advent of a *"Europe-puissance"* that France had been trying to promote for decades, and so the subsequent disillusion was strong. Yet two years later, the French people rejected a European constitution that they ultimately judged to be inadequate and incapable of producing a coherent governing ensemble, protecting its citizens from the excesses of globalization, or bringing influence to bear on America. The French "no" to the European constitutional treaty in the spring of 2005 was a confirmation of the limits of France's European ambitions and highlighted the delusions of a *Europe-puissance*. Since then, the various European crises—from the Greek debt crisis that has been lingering since 2009 to the refugee crisis that erupted in 2015—have also confirmed that the European Union has proved to be a fragile and dysfunctional construct, not a coherent actor able to assert itself on the global stage. Meanwhile, over the past few years, Franco-German relations have been tested by growing imbalances between Germany and France and their increasing divergences over the direction of the European project.

313

The two countries' decision to stand shoulder to shoulder in the face-off with America during the 2003 Iraq crisis seems, in retrospect, to have fueled the illusion of an ever-closer Franco-German, and European, union.

Another of France's long-held goals, the reshaping and equilibration of the transatlantic relationship, which French leaders had hoped would take place after the events detailed in this book, also appear to have stemmed from wishful thinking. While Charles de Gaulle and his successors had long dreamed of a rebalanced but still close relationship between the United States and Europe, today the transatlantic relation is marked by America's growing disinterest in Europe and by the EU's inability to organize itself to remain the United States' privileged partner. This change has taken place against the background of the declining weight of the "West" in world affairs and, as a corollary, the rise of the "Rest," as shown by the United States' pivot toward the Asia-Pacific region under the Obama administration. Compared with de Gaulle's "no" to US dominance in the 1960s, a legacy to which the French leaders of 2003 laid claim, the French "no" to the war in Iraq—however well founded it might have been—has proved to be an incantatory refusal rather than a constructive move. This assessment illustrates that only the further construction of Europe can allow a medium power like France to count in a multipolar world, particularly with regard to America—even a declining one.

And yet, the enduring paradox of Franco-American relations has never been as apparent as it is today. For barely a dozen years after their worst crisis in decades, it is no overstatement to say that these relations have never been so close. France arguably may even have become America's foremost ally, as illustrated by the various crises and conflicts in which the two countries, in recent years, have closely cooperated—with France at times even leading the way. Although Washington famously described the US role in Libya in 2011 as one of "leadership from behind," France, together with Britain, was clearly the engine behind the intervention that brought down the Gaddafi regime, whatever the vital supporting role played by the United States. In late summer 2013, France once again was in the forefront when Paris called for Western strikes in Syria after Bashar al-Assad's regime had been found guilty of using chemical weapons against its own population. In this instance, however, Paris found itself left hanging out to dry when London and then Washington decided not to intervene. A few months earlier, in January 2013, France had launched Operation Serval in Mali with some 5,000 French troops to prevent northern jihadist rebels from taking over the capital, Bamako, to the satisfaction and admiration of Washington. From the US perspective, France's intervention in Mali was a major contribution to the global war on terror in the Sahel region. (Operation Serval would later be replaced by Operation Barkhane, an antiterrorist intervention involving 3,000 French troops covering a large swath of the Sahel region and headquartered in Chad's capital, N'Djamena.) In summer 2014—barely a decade after the US-led invasion that it had staunchly denounced—France joined the US-led aerial coalition against the Islamic State in Iraq. Then, after major terrorist attacks in Paris in January and especially in November 2015 (for which latter the Islamic State claimed responsibility), France stepped up its participation and took the lead in forging a global coalition against the Islamic State, not least by reaching out to Russia, with American acquiescence.[1]

It is thus no exaggeration to say that France is now at the forefront of the very "global war on terror" that Chirac had once cautioned the Americans against launching when he visited Bush in Washington barely a week after the September 11 attacks. Future historians will have to explain this dramatic reversal in French policy. All this aside, the United States now sees France as a major contributor to the fight against global jihadism, particularly in Africa and the Middle East. As for France, it sees the continuing US involvement in the security of Europe and its periphery as vital. One thing seems evident today: both countries, in a period of rising danger, see themselves as essential to each other and to the future of the transatlantic relationship.

Paris
March 11, 2016

Abbreviations in Notes

AD	Archives Diplomatiques
AFEW	Archives of the French Embassy in Washington
AN	Archives Nationales, Paris
ANMO	Afrique du Nord–Moyen Orient [Middle East and North Africa Directorate, Quai d'Orsay]
ASD	Affaires Stratégiques et Désarmement [Strategic Affairs and Disarmament Directorate, Quai d'Orsay]
CAP	Centre d'Analyse et de Prévision [Center for Analysis and Planning, Quai d'Orsay]
CIA	Central Intelligence Agency (US)
DFRA	Délégation française
DGSE	Direction Générale de la Sécurité Extérieure
DST	Direction de la Surveillance du Territoire
FCO	Foreign and Commonwealth Office (UK)
FOIA	Freedom of Information Act (US)
MAE	Ministère des Affaires Étrangères

NUOI	Direction des Nations Unies et des Organisations Internationales [UN Directorate, Quai d'Orsay]
TD	Télégramme diplomatique
UN	United Nations
UNMOVIC	United Nations Monitoring, Verification, and Inspection Commission
UNSCOM	United Nations Special Commission
WMD	weapons of mass destruction

Notes

Introduction

1. See, e.g., Bob Woodward, *Plan of Attack* (New York: Simon & Schuster, 2004); or Thomas E. Ricks, *Fiasco: The American Military Adventure in Iraq* (New York: Penguin Books, 2006).

2. See Melvyn P. Leffler, "The Foreign Policies of the George W. Bush Administration: Memoirs, History, Legacy," *Diplomatic History* 37, no. 2 (2013): 190–216.

3. This is the case for the British role in the Iraq war, which was investigated by the Chilcot Inquiry (the Iraq Inquiry) from 2009 to 2016. The inquiry's report was published on July 6, 2016, as this book was going to press. Although its final findings could not be incorporated into the text, this book includes material that the inquiry has made available over the years; see www.iraqinquiry.org.uk.

4. Although the US public archives on these events remain essentially closed, I must nevertheless cite the efforts of institutions such as the National Security Archive at George Washington University in Washington, D.C., to obtain and make available certain documents through Freedom of Information Act (FOIA) declassification requests: see http://nsarchive.gwu.edu/.

5. See Leffler, "Foreign Policies."

6. On the issue of manipulation of intelligence, see, e.g., John Prados, *Hoodwinked: The Documents That Reveal How Bush Sold Us a War* (New York: The New Press, 2004). See also the testimony of former White House spokesman Scott McClellan: *What Happened: Inside the Bush White House and Washington's Culture of Deception* (New York: Public Affairs, 2008).

7. See, e.g., Dominique de Villepin's account, *Le Requin et la mouette* [The shark and the seagull] (Paris: Plon/Albin Michel, 2004), 79–130.

8. This is particularly the reading that Blair had of French politics: see Tony Blair, *A Journey: My Political Life* (New York: Alfred A. Knopf, 2010), 421; and George W. Bush, *Decision Points* (New York: Crown Publishers, 2010), 245.

9. For a critical reading of French policy issued shortly after the events, see, e.g., Pascal

Cuche, "Irak: et si la France s'était trompée?" [Iraq: What if France was mistaken?], *Politique étrangère* 68, no. 2 (2003): 409–22. There are to date few books on French policy and the Franco-American conflict in the Iraq crisis; Stanley Hoffmann and I devoted a book of interviews to these events shortly after they occurred: Stanley Hoffmann and Frédéric Bozo, *Gulliver Unbound: America's Imperial Temptation and the War in Iraq* (Lanham, MD: Rowman and Littlefield, 2004). See also Henri Vernet and Thomas Cantaloube, *Chirac contre Bush: L'autre guerre* [Chirac versus Bush: The other war] (Paris: JC Lattès, 2004), and Leah Pisar, *Orage sur l'Atlantique: la France et les États-Unis face à l'Irak* [Storm over the Atlantic: France and the United States faced with Iraq] (Paris: Fayard, 2010).

10. On Iraq's WMD, see the US Central Intelligence Agency's 2004 Duelfer Report: Central Intelligence Agency (CIA), *Comprehensive Report of the Special Advisor to the DCI on Iraq's WMD* (Washington, DC: US Government Printing Office, 2005), http://www .gpo.gov/fdsys/pkg/GPO-DUELFERREPORT/content-detail.html. For an analysis of the WMD/disarmament issue based on Iraqi sources and in particular the recordings of Saddam Hussein's conversations, see Kevin M. Woods, David D. Palkki, and Mark E. Stout, *The Saddam Tapes: The Inner Workings of a Tyrant's Regime, 1978–1991* (Cambridge, UK: Cambridge University Press, 2011), esp. 254 ff. For recent academic studies of Saddam Hussein's regime, see Joseph Sassoon, *Saddam Hussein's Ba'th Party: Inside an Authoritarian Regime* (Cambridge, UK: Cambridge University Press, 2011); and Amatzia Baram, *Saddam Husayn and Islam, 1968–2003: Ba'thi Iraq from Secularism to Faith* (Washington, DC: Woodrow Wilson Center Press, Baltimore: Johns Hopkins University Press, 2014).

11. At the request of most of these individuals (the list of which is to be found at the end of the book), their testimonies are not attributed by name in the endnotes.

12. On this relationship, see David Styan, *France and Iraq: Oil, Arms and French Policy in the Middle East* (London: I. B. Tauris, 2006).

13. For developments in American foreign policy in the 1990s as a prelude to the events of 2001–3, see Derek Chollet and James Goldgeier, *America Between the Wars: From 11/9 to 9/11* (New York: Public Affairs, 2008); on Franco-American relations in the 1990s and French positioning in the face of the rise of the "hyperpower," see Richard F. Kuisel, *The French Way: How France Embraced and Rejected American Values and Power* (Princeton, NJ: Princeton University Press, 2011).

14. Condoleezza Rice, *No Higher Honor: A Memoir of My Years in Washington* (New York: Simon & Schuster, 2011), 212–13.

15. See Andrew Cockburn and Patrick Cockburn, *Saddam Hussein: An American Obsession* (London: Verso, 2002).

16. See on this point Leffler, "Foreign Policies." On the neoconservatives, see Justin Vaïsse, *Neoconservatism: Biography of a Movement*, trans. Arthur Goldhammer (Cambridge, MA: Belknap Press, 2010).

17. Many questions also remain regarding the role of Great Britain and the politics of Tony Blair, above all about his motives: did they derive from a conviction about the Iraq problem, or an obsession with the "special relationship"? Here, too, the French angle does not provide a definitive answer, if only because a trusting Franco-British dialogue was lacking at the height of the crisis in 2002–3; yet an analysis of the available information leans heavily toward the second interpretation. The recently published Iraq Inquiry report and, in particular, its Executive Summary, seem amply to confirm this.

18. For an anthology of these charges (the vast majority of them fanciful) and, more generally, for an illustration of the kind of "French bashing" that prevailed in Washington in the aftermath of the Iraq war, see Kenneth R. Timmerman, *The French Betrayal of America* (New York: Three Rivers Press, 2004).

19. For an attempt to reconstruct the attitude of the regime in the run-up to the 2003 war, see Kevin M. Woods, Michael R. Pease, Mark E. Stout, Williamson Murray, and James G. Lacey, *Iraqi Perspectives Project: A View of Operation Iraqi Freedom from Saddam's Senior Leadership* (Washington, DC: Joint Center for Operational Analyses, 2006). See also Woods, Palkki, and Stout, *The Saddam Tapes*; CIA, *Comprehensive Report*; and Sassoon, *Saddam Hussein's Ba'th Party*.

20. Chirac, as one of his closest advisers testified, was "not anti-American" and did not determine his foreign policy "against or as a function of the United States": see Jean-Marc de La Sablière, *Dans les coulisses du monde. Du Rwanda à la guerre d'Irak, un grand négociateur révèle le dessous des cartes* [In the world's backstage: From Rwanda to the Iraq war, a great negotiator reveals the untold stories of international politics] (Paris: Robert Laffont, 2013), 169. In my opinion, this remark applies equally to Chirac's predecessors, from de Gaulle to Mitterrand; for an introduction to French foreign policy after World War II, see Frédéric Bozo, *French Foreign Policy since 1945: An Introduction*, trans. Jonathan Hensher (Oxford: Berghahn Books, forthcoming 2016).

21. Retrospectively, the option of a French abstention in the Security Council was hardly practicable given the circumstances, as will be seen in chapters 6 and 7. For the sake of full disclosure, at the time I personally defended this option in an op-ed piece, and I now believe I was wrong: see Frédéric Bozo, "Conseil de Sécurité: dans le doute d'abstenir" [Security Council: When in doubt, abstain], *Le Figaro*, February 28, 2003.

22. The clash between France and the United States probably was aggravated by mistaken analysis in Washington and London. At the end of 2002 and early 2003, many were largely convinced (in light of what had happened in 1990–91) that even if Paris was being a "difficult" ally as usual, it eventually would fall into line—if not by participating in the operation, then at least by causing no obstacle, particularly at the UN. Colin Powell, in particular, held this opinion: see, e.g., Philip H. Gordon and Jeremy Shapiro, *Allies at War: America, Europe, and the Crisis over Iraq* (New York: McGraw-Hill, 2004), 105.

23. After the events, the Élysée sought to influence the narrative of the crisis by reaffirming Chirac's preeminent role in French decision-making—including in relation to Villepin, who former Chirac aides described as having in fact oscillated or even vacillated when faced with the US determination to go to war; see, e.g., Pierre Péan, *L'Inconnu de l'Élysée* [The unknown man in the Élysée] (Paris: Fayard, 2006). In truth, ever since the Iraq crisis, the personal relationship between Chirac and Villepin has fed the chronicles. Some believe that the president and his foreign minister got each other worked up and that the latter exercised a hold over the former, encouraging him to adopt a confrontational attitude with the United States. The reality is more prosaic: if a close relationship did exist between them, the fact remains that, in accordance with the functioning of French institutions under the Fifth Republic, it is the president who sets the line in foreign policy and the foreign minister who executes it. But personal "style" also counts, and Villepin's notoriously flamboyant personality no doubt helped to create the impression of him swerving around and shifting almost without transition, from

seeking an understanding with Powell in the fall of 2002 to denouncing the American war at the UN in the spring of 2003.

24. This is the thesis of Gordon and Shapiro, *Allies at War*.

25. Geir Lundestand, ed., *Just Another Major Crisis? The United States and Europe since 2000* (Oxford: Oxford University Press, 2008).

26. See Chollet and Goldgeier, *America Between the Wars*, ix–xvi.

Prologue

1. All citations in the prologue are from Meeting Chirac-Bush, November 26, 1997, 5AG5 BE/11, Archives Nationales, Paris (hereafter, AN).

Chapter 1

1. See Bruce W. Jentleson, *With Friends Like These: Reagan, Bush, and Saddam, 1982–1990* (New York: Norton & Company), 31–33.

2. See Styan, *France and Iraq*.

3. Jacques Chirac, *Chaque pas doit être un but. Mémoires 1* [Each step should be a goal: Memoirs, vol. 1] (Paris: NiL, 2009), 194 (hereafter, *Mémoires 1*).

4. Jentleson, *With Friends Like These*, 68–93.

5. Although France had an important role in supplying conventional arms to Iraq, its contribution in terms of WMD was more limited. Despite the original sin of "Osirak," Paris had refrained from reestablishing nuclear cooperation with Baghdad after the June 1981 Israeli raid; in the other WMD areas, other countries were far more involved than France was, starting with Germany's chemical sales. See Kenneth R. Timmerman, *The Death Lobby: How the West Armed Iraq* (London: Bantam Books, 1992); and Jentleson, *With Friends Like These*, 48–51 and 105–23.

6. See Jentleson, *With Friends Like These*, 94–138; and Styan, *France and Iraq*, 171–75.

7. Quoted in Hal Brands, *From Berlin to Baghdad: America's Search for Purpose in the Post–Cold War World* (Lexington: University Press of Kentucky, 2008), 48.

8. Final report by Maurice Courage, ambassador to Baghdad, January 31, 1985–July 19, 1990, Série Directeur politique 1988–1991, box 291, Ministère des Affaires Étrangères (hereafter, MAE), Archives Diplomatiques (hereafter, AD).

9. Quoted in Brands, *From Berlin to Baghdad*, 49–50.

10. George Bush and Brent Scowcroft, *A World Transformed* (New York: Alfred A. Knopf, 1998), 326 and 333.

11. See notably Brands, *From Berlin to Baghdad*, 54 *ff.*; and Richard N. Haass, *War of Necessity, War of Choice: A Memoir of Two Iraq Wars* (New York: Simon & Schuster, 2009), 66 *ff.*

12. Kohl-Mitterrand breakfast meeting, July 6, 1990, 5AG4 CDM33/1, AN.

13. Kohl-Mitterrand dinner meeting, December 6, 1990, 5AG4 CDM33/1, AN.

14. See Pierre Favier and Michel Martin-Roland, *La Décennie Mitterrand*, Vol. 3, *Les*

défis, 1988–1991 [The Mitterrand decade, vol. 3, Challenges, 1988–1991] (Paris: Le Seuil, 1996), 439 *ff.*

15. Kohl-Mitterrand dinner meeting, December 6, 1990.

16. Kohl-Mitterrand meeting, February 15, 1991, 5AG4 CDM33/1, AN.

17. Brands, *From Berlin to Baghdad*, 62–64. Among many other consequences, the persistence after 1991 of a threatening Saddam Hussein had the effect of maintaining American forces in Saudi Arabia, even though they were supposed to have left the country after the conflict. Throughout the following decade, the American presence would feed Osama bin Laden's anti-American and anti-Western rhetoric. See, e.g., Richard A. Clarke, *Against All Enemies: Inside America's War on Terror* (New York: The Free Press, 2004), 66 and 148.

18. Cited in Andrew Cockburn and Patrick Cockburn, *Saddam Hussein: An American Obsession* (London: Verso, 2002), 32 and 38. See also Haass, *War of Necessity*, 139; and Christian Alfonsi, *Circle in the Sand: The Bush Dynasty in Iraq* (New York: Vintage Books, 2007), 194.

19. Brands, *From Berlin to Baghdad*, 63–64; Cockburn and Cockburn, *Saddam Hussein*, 22 and 32; and David M. Malone, *The International Struggle over Iraq: Politics in the UN Security Council 1980–2005* (Oxford: Oxford University Press, 2007), 75.

20. See Alfonsi, *Circle in the Sand*, 194 *ff.* and 233–34; and Cockburn and Cockburn, *Saddam Hussein*, 14 *ff.* and 38.

21. Personal interviews. On the Security Council's role in the Iraq question, see Malone, *The International Struggle over Iraq*; and also La Sablière, *Dans les coulisses du monde*, 56–57.

22. See Malone, *The International Struggle over Iraq*, 114 and 153.

23. On these aspects, see Pascal Teixeira da Silva, "Weapons of Mass Destruction: The Iraqi Case," in *The UN Security Council: From the Cold War to the 21st Century*, ed. David M. Malone (Boulder, CO: Lynne Rienner, 2004), 205–18; and Malone, *The International Struggle over Iraq*, 152–54.

24. Resolution 688 was not placed under chapter VII (the Soviet Union and China were opposed) and did not mention them explicitly, so the no-fly zones zones were in effect imposed by the three major Western nations with the tacit consent—at least at the beginning—of the other two permanent members. More generally, after the Gulf War, these three countries were in agreement in their belief that the various resolutions adopted allowed them to resort to force against Iraq in the event of a "sufficiently serious" violation. See Malone, *The International Struggle over Iraq*, 84 *ff.*; and MAE, Direction des Nations unies et des organisations internationales (NUOI), note pour le Ministre, a/s Le Conseil de sécurité et le recours à la force contre l'Irak depuis 1991, April 17, 2002, série NUOI, Z/Irak/P box 430, AD. See also La Sablière, *Dans les coulisses du monde*, 57–67.

25. Quoted in Alfonsi, *Circle in the Sand*, 235.

26. Haass, *War of Necessity*, 148 *ff.* See also Kenneth M. Pollack, *The Threatening Storm: The Case for Invading Iraq* (New York: Random House, 2002), 58 *ff.*

27. On these issues, see Malone, *The International Struggle over Iraq*, 152 *ff*; and Teixeira, "Weapons of Mass Destruction." For a detailed account of the activities of UNSCOM, see Jean E. Krasno and James S. Sutterlin, *The United Nations and Iraq: Defanging the Viper* (Westport, CT: Praeger, 2003); and Graham S. Pearson, *The Search for Iraq's Weapons of Mass Destruction* (New York: Palgrave, 2005). See also the Duelfer Report; and Charles Duelfer, *Hide and Seek: The Search for Truth in Iraq* (New York: Public Affairs, 2009).

28. Krasno and Sutterlin, *The United Nations and Iraq*, 41 *ff.*; and Mohamed ElBaradei, *The Age of Deception: Nuclear Diplomacy in Treacherous Times* (New York: Metropolitan Books, 2011), 25.

29. See, e.g., Teixeira, "Weapons of Mass Destruction"; Pearson, *Search*; and Krasno and Sutterlin, *The United Nations and Iraq*. See also United Nations Special Commission, "Chronology of Main Events," United Nations, December 1999, http://www.un.org /Depts/unscom/Chronology/chronologyframe.htm.

30. Note a/s Le Conseil de sécurité et le recours à la force contre l'Irak depuis 1991, April 17, 2002.

31. Quoted in Pearson, *Search*, 37

32. The accounts of Saddam Hussein's interrogations by George L. Piro, an Arab-speaking FBI agent who established an open dialogue with him after his arrest in December 2003, are a remarkable source. See "Interview Session No. 4, February 13, 2004," in *Saddam Hussein Talks to the FBI: Twenty Interviews and Five Conversations with "High Value Detainee #1" in 2004*, National Security Archive Electronic Briefing Book No. 279, ed. Joyce Battle (Washington, DC: National Security Archive, July 1, 2009), http://nsarchive .gwu.edu/NSAEBB/NSAEBB279/index.htm.

33. Quoted in Alfonsi, *Circle in the Sand*, 313.

34. Bush-Mitterrand meetings, La Martinique, March 14, 1991, private papers.

35. Alfonsi, *Circle in the Sand*, 267–68 and 316–17.

36. Quoted in Martin Indyk, *Innocent Abroad: An Intimate Account of American Peace Diplomacy in the Middle East* (New York: Simon & Schuster, 2009), 38.

37. Shortly after the event, CIA had advanced the hypothesis that Kuwait might have tried to falsely incriminate Iraq; see "U.S. Defers Response to Iraqis' Plot Against Bush," *New York Times*, June 8, 1993. Indeed, no evidence of preparations for such an attack seems to have been found in the Iraqi archives seized by the Americans in 2003; see Michael Isikoff, "Saddam's Files," *Newsweek*, March 22, 2008, http://www.thedailybeast .com/newsweek/2008/03/22/saddam-s-files.html. Whatever the truth of the matter, US intelligence—at least until 9/11 changed the situation—believed that Baghdad had not tried subsequently to attack American interests by using terrorism: see Clarke, *Against All Enemies*, 80–84 and 231.

38. On all this, see Indyk, *Innocent Abroad*, 30 *ff.*; and Pollack, *Threatening Storm*, 65 *ff.* See also Chollet and Goldgeier, *America Between the Wars*, 179 *ff.*

39. Report of the Secretary-General on the Status of the Implementation of the Special Commission's Plan for the Ongoing Monitoring and Verification of Iraq's Compliance with Relevant Parts of Section C of Security Council Resolution 687 (1991), S/1994/1138 (October 7, 1994), http://www.un.org/Depts/unscom/sres94 -1138.htm.

40. Quoted in Pollack, *Threatening Storm*, 69.

41. Duelfer Report, 9 *ff.*; Duelfer, *Hide and Seek*, 91 *ff.*; and Pollack, *Threatening Storm*, 68 *ff.* See also Teixeira, "Weapons of Mass Destruction"; and UNSCOM, "Chronology."

42. See Malone, *International Struggle*, 117 *ff.*; especially Peter van Walsum, "The Iraq Sanctions Committee," 181–93. See also Chirac–Boutros-Ghali meeting, January 12, 1996, private papers

43. Duelfer, *Hide and Seek*, 96–106; and Indyk, *Innocent Abroad*, 165.

44. Note by the Secretary-General, S/1995/1038 (December 17, 1995), http://www .un.org/Depts/unscom/sres95-1038.htm. See Duelfer, *Hide and Seek*, 107–15; Pearson, *Search*, 44–47; and also Robert Jervis, *Why Intelligence Fails: Lessons from the Iranian Revolution and the Iraq War* (Ithaca, NY: Cornell University Press, 2010), 136.

45. Duelfer, *Hide and Seek*, 117–35; and Duelfer Report, 49. Hans Blix would later remark that "neither UNSCOM nor UNMOVIC ever found weapons [of mass destruction] on sites that had not been declared"; in other words, the inspectors never discovered WMD (in the strict sense) that had been hidden. Hans Blix, *Disarming Iraq* (New York: Pantheon Books, 2004), 257, as well as 28 and 71.

46. Pollack, *Threatening Storm*, 82; and Indyk, *Innocent Abroad*, 182–83. See also Alfred B. Prados, *Iraq: Post-War Challenges and U.S. Responses, 1991–1998*, Report for Congress 98-386 F (Washington, DC: Congressional Research Service, 1999), 17.

47. Wolfowitz's name is also associated with the 1992 Defense Planning Guidance, a document prepared at the end of the George H. W. Bush presidency by his Pentagon team (some of whom, like Lewis "Scooter" Libby, Stephen Hadley, and Eric Edelman, would also play an important role in 2002–3). Its central theme was the need for the United States to keep the upper hand in the military domain after the Cold War in order to prevent the emergence of any new strategic "competitor." Although the final version was toned down, an early draft of the document was more explicit and it had unleashed a controversy after being leaked to the press. Retrospectively, the guidance may be seen as having laid the groundwork for the hegemonic policy of the George W. Bush administration, heralding the "preventive strategy" that it would adopt ten years later. See Chollet and Goldgeier, *America Between the Wars*, 43–48.

48. Quoted in Chollet and Goldgeier, *America Between the Wars*, 189.

49. Chirac–Boutros-Ghali meeting, January 12, 1996.

50. Jacques Chirac, speech at the University of Cairo, April 8, 1996, available through the French Ministry of Foreign and European Affairs Documentary Database, http:// basedoc.diplomatie.gouv.fr/exl-doc/e024926.pdf.

51. Personal interviews. See also Edouard Balladur, *Le Pouvoir ne se partage pas. Conversations avec François Mitterrand* [Power cannot be shared: Conversations with François Mitterrand] (Paris: Fayard, 2009), 334.

52. MAE, Centre d'analyse et de prévision (CAP), note a/s: La France et les EU face à l'avenir de l'Irak, June 24, 1997, ANMO 5 Irak, Archives of the French Embassy in Washington (hereafter, AFEW).

53. Speech by Jacques Chirac at University of Cairo, April 8, 1996.

54. Duelfer, *Hide and Seek*, 104–5; Krasno and Sutterlin, *The United Nations and Iraq*, 17; and personal interviews.

55. See note a/s: Le Conseil de sécurité et le recours à la force contre l'Irak depuis 1991, April 17, 2002; and Balladur, *Le Pouvoir*, 311. See also Gilles Delafon and Thomas Sancton, *Dear Jacques, Cher Bill. Au cœur de l'Élysée et de la Maison Blanche 1995–1999* [Dear Jacques, Dear Bill: Inside the Élysée and the White House, 1995–1999] (Paris: Plon, 1999), 259; and Indyk, *Innocent Abroad*, 183.

56. Personal interviews; see also Eric Aeschimann and Christophe Boltanski, *Chirac d'Arabie. Les mirages d'une politique française* [Chirac of Arabia: Mirages of French policy] (Paris: Grasset, 2006), 255 *ff.*, and David Styan, "Jacques Chirac's 'non': France, Iraq, and the United Nations, 1991–2003," *Modern and Contemporary France* 12, no. 3 (2004): 371–85.

57. Note de Bernard Emié à l'attention du Secrétaire Général. Objet: Irak. Entretien du Ministre avec les présidents d'Elf et Total, December 6, 1995, 5AG5 BE/11, AN; and personal interviews.

58. Chirac-Albright meeting, February 17, 1997, private papers.

59. Quoted in Cockburn and Cockburn, *Saddam Hussein*, 263; see also Pollack, *Threatening Storm*, 86–87.

60. Letter to President William J. Clinton, Project for the New American Century, January 26, 1998, archived at the Library of Congress Web Archives Collection, http://webarchive.loc.gov/all/20030527201806/http://www.newamericancentury.org /iraqclintonletter.htm. See also Chollet and Goldgeier, *America Between the Wars*, 192–93.

61. Note by the Secretary-General, S/1995/301 (April 11, 1997), http://www.un.org /Depts/unscom/sres97-301.htm.

62. La Sablière, *Dans les coulisses du monde*, 48 and Duelfer, *Hide and Seek*, 138; see also TD Stockholm 383, July 29, 2002, NUOI, Z/Irak/P box 430, AD; and personal interviews.

63. Duelfer, *Hide and Seek*, 137 ff.; UNSCOM, "Chronology"; and personal interviews.

64. Letter from Clinton to Chirac, November 24, 1997, 5AG5 JFG/11, AN; see also letter from Chirac to Clinton, TD Diplomatie 39266, November 21, 1997, ibid.

65. See Chirac-Bush meeting, November 26, 1997, 5AG5 BE/11, AN. See also Madeleine Albright (with Bill Woodward), *Madam Secretary: A Memoir* (New York: Miramax Books, 2003), 276–80; Indyk, *Innocent Abroad*, 187–89; and Delafon and Sancton, *Dear Jacques, Cher Bill*, 311 ff.

66. Chirac-Clinton telephone conversation, December 19, 1997, 5AG5 BE/11. See also Delafon and Sancton, *Dear Jacques, Cher Bill*, 311 ff.

67. Chirac–Hassan II telephone conversation, December 23, 1997, detailed account by Bernard Emié, 5AG5 BE/11, AN.

68. Chirac-Clinton telephone conversation, January 30, 1998, 5AG5 BE/11, AN.

69. Chirac-Annan meeting, February 19, 1998, 5AG5 BE/11, AN; see also Chirac-Prodi meeting, February 10, 1998, ibid.

70. Chirac-Annan meeting, February 23, 1998, 5AG5 BE/11, AN.

71. Chirac–Abdullah of Saudi Arabia telephone conversation, February 26, 1998, 5AG5 BE/11, AN.

72. Chirac–La Messuzière telephone conversation, March 6, 1998, 5AG5 BE/11, AN.

73. Chirac-Aziz meeting, May 14, 1998, 5AG5 BE/11, AN.

74. Chirac-Annan meeting, May 12, 1998, private papers; and Chirac-Blair telephone conversation, February 23, 1998, 5AG5 BE/11, AN.

75. De Gliniasty–Indyk meeting, TD Washington 1961, May 22, 1998, and de Gliniasty–Pickering meeting, TD Washington 2711, July 21, 1998, ANMO 5 Irak, AFEW; see also Duelfer, *Hide and Seek*, 150–51.

76. Duelfer, *Hide and Seek*, 150–51.

77. Quoted in Chollet and Goldgeier, *America Between the Wars*, 195–96.

78. See Clarke, *Against All Enemies*, 162–63.

79. Chollet and Goldgeier, *America Between the Wars*, 199.

80. MAE, NUOI, Note pour le cabinet du Ministre, January 6, 1999, a/s Griefs français à l'encontre de M. Butler, confidential, ANMO, Irak III IR III C3 A1 1999–2002, AD.

81. Duelfer, *Hide and Seek*, 152–53; Pollack, *Threatening Storm*, 90; Krasno and Sutterlin, *The United Nations and Iraq*, 68–69; and Teixeira, "Weapons of Mass Destruction." Duelfer and the Iraq Study Group would never manage to reach a definitive conclusion about the VX issue; see personal interviews. See also ElBaradei, *The Age of Deception*, 31–32.

82. Duelfer, *Hide and Seek*, 154–55.

83. Chirac-Annan telephone conversation, September 17, 1998, private papers.

84. Duelfer, *Hide and Seek*, 156; Indyk, *Innocent Abroad*, 194; Pollack, *Threatening Storm*, 91; and Albright, *Madam Secretary*, 284–85.

85. Chirac-Annan meeting, November 28, 1998, private archives; and Delafon and Sancton, *Dear Jacques, Cher Bill*, 344 *ff*.

86. MAE, NUOI, Note pour le cabinet du Ministre, a/s Griefs français à l'encontre de M. Butler, January 6, 1999; see also Duelfer, *Hide and Seek*, 157–61; Pollack, *Threatening Storm*, 92; Indyk, *Innocent Abroad*, 198–200; and personal interviews.

87. SGDN, Comité interministériel du renseignement, Secrétariat permanent, compte-rendu de la réunion Moyen-Orient du 28 janvier 1999, February 8, 1999, ANMO, Irak III IR III C3 A1 1999–2002, AD. See Pollack, *Threatening Storm*, 92–94.

88. Pollack, *Threatening Storm*, 94–100; Chollet and Goldgeier, *America Between the Wars*, 202–4.

89. TD Washington 2082, June 9, 1999, 5AG5 JFG/11, AN. See also MAE, ANMO, note de synthèse, a/s Irak: situation et perspectives, February 25, 1999, ANMO, Irak III IR III C3 A1 1999–2002, AD.

90. Note a/s Entretien avec le président Bill Clinton, Washington, February 19, 1999, 5AG5 JFG/32, AN.

91. Note a/s Irak – Contribution à la recherche d'une solution, January 12, 1999; TD Washington 166, 15 January 1999; and Directions NUOI et ANMO, note pour le cabinet du Ministre, a/s Iraq – Mémorandum français, ANMO, Irak III IR III C3 A1 1999–2002, AD. See also Teixeira, "Weapons of Mass Destruction."

92. See Malone, *The International Struggle over Iraq*, 165 *ff*.; and Teixeira, "Weapons of Mass Destruction."

93. MAE, ANMO, note a/s Compte rendu de mission en Irak (7–17 octobre 1999), October 10, 1999, ANMO, Irak III B, Questions politiques, relations politiques avec la France 1999–2002, AD.

94. MAE, ANMO, note pour le directeur de cabinet, a/s l'Irak après 10 ans d'embargo, July 25, 2000, Irak III B, Questions politiques, relations politiques avec la France 1999–2002, AD.

95. See Pollack, *Threatening Storm*, 100 *ff*.

96. Amorim Report, S/1999/356 (March 30, 1999), http://www.un.org/Depts/unmovic/documents/AMORIM.PDF.

97. Chirac-Kok (Dutch prime minister) telephone conversation, February 11, 1998, 5AG5 BE/11, AN.

98. Annan-Chirac meeting, January 27, 1998, TD Diplomatie 3593, February 2, 1998, private papers.

99. Personal interview; see also Pollack, *Threatening Storm*, 93.

100. Védrine-Cook breakfast meeting, January 8, 1999, MAE, ANMO, Irak III IR III C3 A1 1999–2002.

101. Chirac-Clinton meeting, June 17, 1999, 5AG5 JFG/11, AN.

102. Albright, *Madam Secretary*, 286–87.

103. See Pollack, *Threatening Storm*, 102–3

104. MAE, ANMO, note pour le ministre, a/s Cadrage de ma prochaine mission à Bagdad, February 4, 2000, and TD Baghdad 85, January 31, 2000, ANMO, Irak Irk III B Questions politiques, relations politiques avec la France 1999–2002, AD.

105. TD Diplomatie 63733, August 30, 2000, AFEW, ANMO 5 Irak, AD.

106. In 2001, Serge Boidevaix, a former secretary-general of the Quai d'Orsay who was active in commerce with Iraq in the 1990s, ended up receiving a warning letter on this subject from his former administration: see Aeschimann and Boltanski, *Chirac d'Arabie*, 308 *ff.*; see also MAE, ANMO, note, a/s L'Irak après dix ans d'embargo/Point de situation et propositions d'actions bilatérales, July 25, 1990, ANMO, Irak Irk III B, Questions politiques, relations politiques avec la France 1999–2002, AD; and personal interviews. Boidevaix would later be involved in the "Oil for Food" scandal; see note 37 in the Epilogue.

107. TD Washington 3372, November 7, 2000, AFEW, ANMO 5 Irak, AD.

108. TD Baghdad 1882, 17 October 1999, and 124, January 29, 2001, ANMO, Irak III IR III B Questions politiques, relations politiques avec la France 1999–2002, AD; and MAE, Direction des affaires économiques et fianancières, note: "Où en sont réellement les échanges commerciaux franco-irakiens?," October 3, 2002, ANMO, Irak III IR III C3 A1 01-02/2003, AD.

Chapter 2

1. See Ivo H. Daalder and James Lindsay, *America Unbound: The Bush Revolution in Foreign Policy* (Washington, DC: Brookings Institution Press, 2005), 35.

2. TD Washington 3756, December 14, 2000, 5AG5 JFG/34, AN.

3. Bush-Chirac meeting, December 18, 2000, 5AG5 JFG/34, AN; see also Vernet and Cantaloube, *Chirac contre Bush*, 23 *ff.*; Jacques Chirac, *Le temps présidentiel. Mémoires 2* [The presidential years: Memoirs vol. 2] (Paris: NiL, 2011), 320–22 (hereafter, *Mémoires 2*); and personal interviews.

4. Bush-Chirac telephone conversation. February 1, 2001, TD Diplomatie 8682, February 2, 2001, Digital archives (DA), AD.

5. Personal interviews.

6. TD Washington 993 and 996, March 28, 2001, DA, AD.

7. Chirac-Powell meeting, April 11, 2001, TD Diplomatie 27971, April 12, 2001, DA, AD; and Bush-Chirac telephone conversation, February 1, 2001. See also Vernet and Cantaloube, *Chirac contre Bush*, 49 *ff.*

8. Bush-Chirac telephone conversation, April 23, 2001, TD Diplomatie 30345, April 24, 2001, DA, AD.

9. Annan-Chirac telephone conversation, June 18, 2001, private papers.

10. Vernet and Cantaloube, *Chirac contre Bush*, 54–55; and personal interviews.

11. Bush-Chirac meeting, December 18, 2000; see also Daalder and Lindsay, *America Unbound*, 39–40; Donald Rumsfeld, *Known and Unknown: A Memoir* (New York: Sentinel,

2011), 418; Bob Woodward, *Plan of Attack* (New York, Simon & Schuster, 2004), 12; and George Tenet, *At the Center of the Storm: The CIA during America's Time of Crisis* (New York: HarperCollins, 2007), 136.

12. Thomas E. Ricks, *Fiasco: The American Military Adventure in Iraq* (New York: Penguin Books, 2006), 26–27; and Haass, *War of Necessity*, 173.

13. MAE, ANMO, Note a/s Irak – Entretien avec M. Nizar Hamdoun – Point de situation/Éléments de langage, February 19, 2001, Irak III B, Questions politiques, relations politiques avec la France 1999–2002, AD.

14. Pollack, *The Threatening Storm*, 105. See also Ricks, *Fiasco*, 27–28; Douglas J. Feith, *War and Decision: Inside the Pentagon at the Dawn of the War on Terrorism* (New York: HarperCollins, 2008), 203; and Clarke, *Against All Enemies*, 231–32.

15. Woodward, *Plan of Attack*, 15; and Haass, *War of Necessity*, 174–75; see also Karen DeYoung, *Soldier: The Life of Colin Powell* (New York: Alfred A. Knopf, 2006), 310 *ff.*

16. See, e.g., Woodward, *Plan of Attack*, 15–16; Rumsfeld, *Known and Unknown*, 419 *ff.*; and Feith, *War and Decision*, 210–11.

17. Woodward, *Plan of Attack*, 21–22.

18. Ibid.

19. MAE, ANMO, note pour le ministre, Yves Aubin de La Messuzière, a/s Irak: bilan politique du projet de "sanctions intelligentes," June 18, 2001, ANMO, Irak III IR III C3 A1 1999–2002, AD; and personal interviews.

20. TD Bagdad 122, January 29, 2001; and ANMO, note a/s Irak: entretien avec M. Nizar Hamdoun. Point de situation et éléments de langage, February 10, 2001, ANMO, Irak III B, Questions politiques, relations politiques avec la France, 1999–2002, AD.

21. See Clarke, *Against All Enemies*, 26 and 227 *ff.*; and *The 9/11 Commission Report: Final Report of the National Commission on Terrorist Attacks Upon the United States* (New York: W. W. Norton & Company, 2004), 174 *ff.* and 254 *ff.* In December 2000, during the transition, Clinton had declared to Bush, "I think you will find that by far your biggest threat is Bin Ladin and the al Qaeda." He added, "One of the great regrets of my presidency is that I didn't get him [Bin Laden] for you, because I tried to." *The 9/11 Commission Report*, 199.

22. George W. Bush, *Decision Points* (New York: Crown Publishing, 2010), 126–28 and 138–39; and Bob Woodward, *Bush at War* (New York: Simon & Schuster, 2002), 37.

23. Chirac, *Mémoires 2*, 326–27; and Mikaël Guedj and Yoanna Sultan-R'bibo, *11 Septembre. Paris, 14h46* [September 11: Paris, 2:46 p.m.] (Paris: Stock, 2011), 85–88 and 92–93.

24. Tony Blair, *A Journey: My Political Life* (New York: Alfred A. Knopf, 2010), 351.

25. UN Security Council Resolution 1368, Threats to International Peace and Security Caused by Terrorist Acts, S/RES/1368 (September 12, 2001), http://undocs.org/S/RES/1368(2001).

26. Guedj and Sultan-R'bibo, *11 Septembre*, 63–65; Vernet and Cantaloube, *Chirac contre Bush*, 62; and personal interviews.

27. Guedj and Sultan-R'bibo, *11 Septembre*, 76–78; Daalder and Lindsay, *America*, 79–80; and personal interviews.

28. Présidence de la République, note de Jean-Marc de La Sablière, rencontre avec le président Bush (18–19 septembre), September 14, 2001, 5AG5 JFG/34, AN.

29. DGSE, "Acteurs, finalités et conséquences des attentats anti-américains," September 13, 2001, in Alain Chouet (with Jean Guisnel), *Au cœur des services spéciaux: La menace*

islamiste, fausses pistes et vrais dangers [At the heart of the special services: The Islamist threat, false leads, and real dangers] (Paris: La Découverte, 2011), 308–10; see also 106 *ff.* and 146 *ff.*; and personal interviews.

30. Guedj and Sultan-R'bibo, *11 Septembre*, 78–79; Vernet and Cantaloube, *Chirac contre Bush*, 61– 62; Chirac, *Mémoires 2*, 327–28; and personal interviews.

31. La Sablière memo, September 14, 2001; and note a/s Entretien avec M. George Bush, président des États-Unis d'Amérique (mardi 18 septembre 2011), September 18, 2011, 5AG5 JFG/34, AN.

32. La Sablière memo, September 14, 2001; see also Guedj and Sultan-R'bibo, *11 Septembre*.

33. Bush-Chirac meeting, September 18, 2001, TD Washington 2667–68, September 20, 2001, 5AG5 JFG/34, AN; and Chirac, *Mémoires 2*, 328.

34. Bush-Chirac meeting, September 18, 2001; and personal interviews; see also Guedj and Sultan-R'bibo, *11 Septembre*, 107.

35. Chirac, *Mémoires 2*, 328; Guedj and Sultan-R'bibo, *11 Septembre*, 104–7; and personal interviews.

36. TD DFRA New York 3247–48, September 19, 2001, 5AG5 JFG/34, AN.

37. Daalder and Lindsay, *America*, 77–78.

38. George W. Bush, "Address to a Joint Session of Congress and the American People," George W. Bush White House, September 20, 2001, http://georgewbush-whitehouse.archives.gov/news/releases/2001/09/20010920-8.html.

39. Daalder and Lindsay, *America*, 90.

40. Donald H. Rumsfeld, "A New Kind of War," *New York Times*, September 27, 2001.

41. Philip H. Gordon and Jeremy Shapiro, *Allies at War: America, Europe, and the Crisis over Iraq* (New York: McGraw, Hill, 2004), 63.

42. Personal interviews; see also Feith, *War and Decision*, 89–91; and Rumsfeld, *Known and Unknown*.

43. Quoted by Guedj and Sultan-R'bibo, *11 Septembre*, 158.

44. Personal interview; see also Guedj and Sultan-R'bibo, *11 Septembre*, 139 *ff.*; and Vernet and Cantaloube, *Chirac contre Bush*, 67 ff.

45. Bush-Chirac telephone conversation, October 26, 2001, TD Diplomatie 80089, October 26, 2001, AE, AD. See also Guedj and R'bibo, *11 Septembre*, 158 and 190–6; and Vernet and Cantaloube, *Chirac contre Bush*, 67 *ff.*

46. Daalder and Lindsay, *America*, 104–7.

47. Note a/s Entretien et déjeuner avec M. George Bush, mardi 6 novembre 2001 à 10h45, November 6, 2001, 5AG5 JFG/34, AN.

48. Bush-Chirac meeting, November 6, 2001, TD Washington 3225-27, November 8, 2001, AE, AD.

49. Bush-Chirac meeting, November 6, 2001; personal interview; and Guedj and Sultan-R'bibo, *11 Septembre*, 198–200.

50. Personal interviews; and Guedj and Sultan-R'bibo, *11 Septembre*, 207–24.

51. See Tenet, *At the Center of the Storm*, 200 *ff.*; Chouet, *Au cœur des services spéciaux*, 116–17; and *9/11 Commission Report*, 273–77.

52. Tyler Drumheller, *On the Brink: An Insider's Account of How the White House Compromised American Intelligence* (New York: Carrol & Graf, 2006), 93–94; see also

Chouet, *Au cœur des services spéciaux*, 113–15; and Direction de la Surveillance du Territoire (DST), note, "État de la menace terroriste en France et de la coopération avec les services américains," 5AG5 JFG/34, AN.

53. Tenet, *At the Center of the Storm*, 229; Chouet, *Au cœur des services spéciaux*, 156; and personal interviews.

54. Bush, *Decision Points*, 159.

55. Chirac, *Mémoires 2*, 334.

56. "War Without Illusions," *New York Times*, September 15, 2001; Wolfowitz quotes in *New York Times*, September 13, 2001.

57. Quoted in Woodward, *Bush at War*, 26; see also Ricks, *Fiasco*, 30–31; Rumsfeld, *Known and Unknown*, 359; Feith, *War and Decision*, 12–17 and 47 *ff.*; Tenet, *At the Center of the Storm*, 306; Clarke, *Against All Enemies*, 32; and *9/11 Commission Report*, 334–36.

58. *9/11 Commission Report*, 336.

59. Bush-Chirac meeting, November 6, 2001; and personal interviews. See also "Bush Advisers Split on Scope of Retaliation," *New York Times*, September 20, 2001; and Guedj and Sultan-R'bibo, *11 Septembre*, 139–41.

60. Bush, *Decision Points*, 151.

61. Ibid., 158.

62. The foregoing analysis owes a great deal to my frequent conversations with Melvyn Leffler when we were both invited scholars at the Wilson Center in 2010–11; see also Leffler, "Foreign Policies."

63. Haass, *War of Necessity*, 237.

64. On this, see Feith, *War and Decision*, 1–21 and 47–88; Rumsfeld, *Known and Unknown*, 342 *ff.*; and Bush, *Decision Points*, 190–91.

65. See DeYoung, *Soldier*, 349.

66. Letter to President George W. Bush, Project for the New American Century, September 20, 2001, archived at the Library of Congress Web Archives Collection, http://webarchive.loc.gov/all/20030526233959/http://www.newamericancentury.org/Bushletter.htm.

67. See, e.g., Rumsfeld, *Known and Unknown*, 418.

68. Woodward, *Plan of Attack*, 162; see also Clarke, *Against All Enemies*, 265.

69. See Murray Waas, "Key Bush Intelligence Briefing Kept From Hill Panel," *National Journal*, November 22, 2005. As early as September 18, Richard Clarke had sent a memo to Bush along these same lines: see Clarke, *Against All Enemies*, 33; and *9/11 Commission Report*, 334.

70. On intelligence and WMD, see chapter 4, 143 *ff.*

71. See Tenet, *At the Center of the Storm*, 305–6. For years, Wolfowitz had peddled the theory (which, however, had been clearly disproved by intelligence agencies) that Iraq had been behind the 1993 truck bomb attack against the World Trade Center, arguing that such an operation could not have been mounted without a "state sponsor," which could only be Iraq. To Clarke's surprise, Wolfowitz had once again shared this conviction in the early months of the Bush administration as he was making the case for an active policy of regime change in Iraq, and he would naturally come back to this line of argument in the aftermath of 9/11: see Clarke, *Against All Enemies*, 30–31, 94–95, and 231–32.

72. Rumsfeld, *Known and Unknown*, 355–56.

73. Tenet, *At the Center of the Storm*, 258 *ff.*, in particular 264; and Ron Suskind, *The One Percent Doctrine: Deep Inside America's Pursuit of Its Enemies Since 9/11* (New York: Simon & Schuster, 2007), 61–62.

74. Clarke, *Against All Enemies*, 265.

75. See Feith, *War and Decision*, esp. 17–21 and 214–16.

76. Bush, *Decision Points*, 229.

77. Tenet, *At the Center of the Storm*, 305.

78. Woodward, *Bush at War*, 2.

79. Woodward, *Bush at War*, 1–8 and 31–44; see also Bush, *Decision Points*, 234–35.

80. Bush, *Decision Points*, 191, 230, and 234; see also Leffler, "Foreign Policies."

81. Quoted in Woodward, *Bush at War*, 36.

82. See, e.g., "Key Bush Intelligence Briefing;" and *9/11 Commission Report*, 228–29.

83. See Ricks, *Fiasco*, 35.

84. MAE, Direction NUOI, note pour le Ministre, Irak–Perspectives aux Nations unies, October 29, 2001, NUOI, Z/Irak/430, AD.

85. TD DFRA New York 4476, November 16, 2001, NUOI, Z/Irak/430, AD.

86. TD DFRA New York 4664, November 27, 2001; and 4715-6, November 29, 2001, NUOI, Z/Irak/430, AD.

87. TD DFRA New York 4664, November 27, 2001.

88. TD DFRA New York 4715–16, November 29, 2001.

89. TD Bagdad 1155, December 15, 2001, Irak III B, Questions politiques, relations politiques avec la France 1999–2002, AD.

90. TD Bagdad 1189, December 23, 2001, Irak III B, Questions politiques, relations politiques avec la France 1999–2002, AD.

91. TD DFRA New York 5009, December 20, 2001, NUOI, Z/Irak/430, AD.

92. TD Washington 3484, December 3, 2001, ANMO 5 Irak, AFEW.

93. Woodward, *Bush at War*, 52–66.

Chapter 3

1. George W. Bush, "President Delivers State of the Union Address," George W. Bush White House, January 29, 2002, http://georgewbush-whitehouse.archives.gov/news/releases/2002/01/20020129-11.html.

2. On this, see Woodward, *Plan of Attack*, 85–95.

3. Quoted in Woodward, *Plan of Attack*, 115. On all this, see also Woodward, *Plan of Attack*, 75–84 and 96–106; and Ricks, *Fiasco*, 37–38.

4. See Woodward, *Plan of Attack*, 130 (quotations from 103, 120, and 130).

5. Ibid., 111–112.

6. On all this, see Haass, *War of Necessity*, 206–10.

7. Blair memorandum for Jonathan Powell, March 17, 2002, The Iraq Inquiry (hereafter, the Chilcot Inquiry), http://www.iraqinquiry.org.uk/media/50751/Blair-to-Powell-17March2002-minute.pdf. See also Blair's own evidence given to the Chilcot Inquiry, January 21, 2011, http://www.iraqinquiry.org.uk/media/50865/20110121-Blair

.pdf, 7 *ff.*, 36 *ff.*, and 42 *ff.*; and Blair, *Journey*, 395 *ff.*

8. Blair, *Journey*, 399; Blair memorandum for Powell, March 17, 2002; and Blair evidence, 42 *ff.*

9. Blair, *Journey*, 400.

10. Blair evidence, 48.

11. Ibid., 8–9. See also Extracts from FCO Diptel 73 of 101727Z, April 10, 2002, Chilcot Inquiry, http://www.iraqinquiry.org.uk/media/42691/fco-diptel-73of101727Z.pdf.

12. Bush, *Decision Points*, 232

13. Blair, *Journey*, 401.

14. Feith, *War and Decision*, 237–38; see also Haass, *War of Necessity*, 212–13.

15. Haass, *War of Necessity*, 212–13; and DeYoung, *Soldier*, 399.

16. Feith, *War of Necessity*, 245–47; DeYoung, *Soldier*, 398–99; and personal interviews.

17. TD Washington 445, February 17, 2002, and TD DFRA New York 545, February 13, 2002, MAE, ANMO, Irak III C3 A/B [2002], AD; and TD Diplomatie 13938, February 20, 2002, AD, ANMO, Irak III C3 A1 [1999–2002], AD.

18. MAE, ANMO, note a/s Réunion sur l'Irak présidée par le Ministre, April 11, 2002, MAE, ANMO, Irak III C3 A/B [2002], AD.

19. TD Washington 978–79, April 15, 2002, ANMO 5 Irak, AFEW.

20. Hubert Védrine, interview with France-Inter radio, Paris, February 6, 2002, available through the French Ministry of Foreign and European Affairs Documentary Database, http://basedoc.diplomatie.gouv.fr/exl-doc/e013582.pdf.

21. Hubert Védrine, press conference, Brussels, February 18, 2002, available through the French Ministry of Foreign and European Affairs Documentary Database, http:// basedoc.diplomatie.gouv.fr/exl-doc/e013519.pdf; see also Gordon and Shapiro, *Allies at War*, 67–68; and Vernet and Cantaloube, *Chirac contre Bush*, 83–84.

22. Haass, *War of Necessity*, 238–39; and Vernet and Cantaloube, *Chirac contre Bush*, 92–98.

23. TD Washington 1418, June 3, 2002, AD, DA; see also Vernet and Cantaloube, *Chirac contre Bush*, 87–89.

24. TD Diplomatie 41808, May 28, 2002; and TD Washington 1413–15, June 3, 2002, AD, DA.

25. MAE, Note NUOI/P n°152, a/s Irak – entretiens des directeurs politiques français et britanniques, January 23, 2002, NUOI, Z/Irak, 430, AD.

26. MAE, note a/s Iraq – Éléments de réflexion, February 12, 2002, MAE, ANMO, Irak III C3 A/B [2002], AD.

27. TD Diplomatie 13233, February 19, 2002; and TD Diplomatie 16350, February 19, 2002, AD, NUOI, Z/Irak, 430; TD Diplomatie 13938, February 20, 2002, ANMO, Irak III C3A1 [1999–2002], AD.

28. TD Washington 445, February 17, 2002.

29. TD DFRA New York 545, February 13, 2002.

30. TD Washington 445, February 17, 2002.

31. TD Bagdad 122, 136, and 144, February 4, 7, and 11, 2002, AD, NUOI, Z/Irak, 430, AD.

32. Hans Blix, *Disarming Iraq* (New York: Pantheon Books, 2004), 60; TD DFRA New York 883, March 7, 2002; and TD Diplomatie 22947, March 2, 2002, NUOI, Z/ Irak, 430, AD.

33. Haass, *War of Necessity*, 211–12; and Blix, *Disarming Iraq*, 60–61.

34. TD DFRA New York 1640, May 3, 2002, NUOI, Z/Irak, 430, AD.

35. TD DFRA Vienne 164, May 17, 2002; and TD Bagdad 377, May 8, 2002, NUOI, série Z/Irak, carton 430, AD; and Blix, *Disarming Iraq*, 62–63.

36. "President Bush Delivers Graduation Speech at West Point," George W. Bush White House, June 1, 2002, http://georgewbush-whitehouse.archives.gov/news/releases/2002/06/20020601-3.html. See also Ricks, *Fiasco*, 38–39; and Woodward, *Plan of Attack*, 130–33.

37. Woodward, *Plan of Attack*, 133–38, 145–48, and 321–22; Ricks, *Fiasco*, 40–43 and 48–49; and personal interviews.

38. Ricks, *Fiasco*, 46 *ff.*; Tenet, *At the Center of the Storm*, 310; and personal interviews. See also Robert Jervis, *Why Intelligence Fails: Lessons from the Iranian Revolution and the Iraq War* (Ithaca, NY: Cornell University Press, 2010), 132.

39. Ricks, *Fiasco*, 38–39.

40. Haass, *War of Necessity*, 4–6 and 213–16.

41. Blair, *Journey*, 403–4.

42. Blix, *Disarming Iraq*, 66; and TD DFRA New York 2508–9, July 15, 2002, NUOI, Z/Irak, carton 430, AD.

43. Woodward, *Plan of Attack*, 148–53 and 162; and DeYoung, *Soldier*, 401–3. (Covers following three paragraphs.)

44. Woodward, *Plan of Attack*, 155–57 and 161; and Rice, *No Higher Honor*, 179–80.

45. Woodward, *Plan of Attack*, 159–60; Rice, *No Higher Honor*, 178–79; and Bush, *Decision Points*, 238.

46. Woodward, *Plan of Attack*, 161–62; see also Memorandum by the Rt Hon Jack Straw MP, Chilcot Inquiry, [n.d.], http://www.iraqinquiry.org.uk/media/43119/jackstraw-memorandum.pdf, 7.

47. Woodward, *Plan of Attack*, 164; and Ricks, *Fiasco*, 49.

48. Haass, *War of Necessity*, 220; and Ricks, *Fiasco*, 51.

49. Haass, *War of Necessity*, 218.

50. Tenet, *At the Center of the Storm*, 315–16; see also Ricks, *Fiasco*, 50–51.

51. Ricks, *Fiasco*, 51.

52. MAE/ANMO, note pour le directeur de cabinet, August 28, 2002, a/s Irak – Compte rendu de la réunion présidée par le ministre en marge de la conférence des ambassadeurs, 27.08.02, ANMO, Irak III C3 A1 [1999–2002], AD.

53. See Dominique de Villepin, speech at the opening of the ambassadors' conference, Paris, August 27, 2002, available through the French Ministry of Foreign and European Affairs Documentary Database, http://basedoc.diplomatie.gouv.fr/exl-doc/e012721.pdf; and TD Bagdad 713, September 1, 2002, ANMO, Irak III C3 A1 [1999–2002], AD; see also TD Diplomatie 63613 and 64661, August 22 and 28, 2002, NUOI, Z/Irak/P 430, AD.

54. Chirac, *Mémoires 2*, 368–69; Jacques Chirac, speech at the ambassadors' conference, Paris, August 29, 2002, available through the French Ministry of Foreign and European Affairs Documentary Database, http://basedoc.diplomatie.gouv.fr/exl-doc/e012710.pdf; and TD Bagdad 713, September 1, 2002.

55. TD Washington 2057–58, September 3, 2002 (with a note from La Sablière), 5AG5 AP/6, AN.

56. TD Washington 2056, September 3, 2002, 5AG5 AP/6, AN.

57. Annan-Chirac meeting, September 6, 2002, TD Diplomatie 66632, September 6, 2002, ANMO, Irak III C3 A1 [1999–2002], AD; and personal interview.

58. Blair-Chirac telephone conversation, September 6, 2002, TD Diplomatie 66449, September 6, 2002, ANMO, Irak III C3 A1 [1999–2002], AD.

59. Bush-Chirac telephone conversation, September 6, 2002, TD Diplomatie 66630, September 6, 2002, 5AG5 AP/6, AN.

60. See La Sablière, *Dans les coulisses du monde*, 195–96; see also Chirac, *Mémoires 2*, 370; Vernet and Cantaloube, *Chirac contre Bush*, 100–103; and personal interviews.

61. See Chirac, interview with the *New York Times*, September 9, 2002, available through the French Ministry of Foreign and European Affairs Documentary Database, http://basedoc.diplomatie.gouv.fr/exl-doc/e012654.pdf; and "Jacques Chirac; French Leader Offers America Both Friendship and Criticism," *New York Times*, September 9, 2002.

62. Rice, *No Higher Honor*, 179–80; and Woodward, *Plan of Attack*, 167–79.

63. Blair, *Journey*, 406; and Bush, *Decision Points*, 239. See also Sir David Manning's evidence given to the Chilcot Inquiry, November 30, 2009, 23–35, http://www.iraqinquiry.org.uk/media/40459/20091130pm-final.pdf; as well as Alastair Campbell's evidence, Chilcot Inquiry, January 12, 2010, http://www.iraqinquiry.org.uk/media/42384/20100112am-campbell-final.pdf.

64. Rice, *No Higher Honor*, 183; and Woodward, *Plan of Attack*, 180–85.

Chapter 4

1. See Woodward, *Plan of Attack*, 220–23; and DeYoung, *Soldier*, 411 *ff.*

2. TD DFRA New York 3156–58 and 3342, September 12 and 18, 2002, MAE, NUOI, Z/Irak/P 431, AD; on the negotiation of Resolution 1441, see also La Sablière, *Dans les coulisses du monde*, 197–206.

3. TD New York 4523–34, September 25, 2002, NUOI, Z/Irak/P 431, AD.

4. Note pour le Ministre, a/s Irak – Clause automatique de recours à la force. Analyse stratégique d'un véto de la France, September 26, 2002, NUOI, Z/Irak/P 431, AD.

5. TD DFRA New York 2523–24, September 25, 2002.

6. MAE, NUOI, Note pour le Ministre, a/s Irak – Projet de résolution américano-britannique, September 26, 2002; and TD Diplomatie 71497, September 26, 2002, NUOI, Z/Irak/P 431, AD. See also DeYoung, *Soldier*, 414 *ff.* and Kofi Annan (with Nader Mousavizadeh), *Interventions: A Life in War and Peace* (New York: Penguin, 2012), 247.

7. Chirac-Bush telephone conversation, September 27, 2002, TD Diplomatie 71942, September 28, 2002, NUOI, Z/Irak/P 431, AD.

8. TD Diplomatie 71924 and 71926–27, September 27, 2002, NUOI, Z/Irak/P 431, AD.

9. TD Diplomatie 72292, September 30, 2002, NUOI, Z/Irak/P 431, AD.

10. TD Washington 2454, October 15, 2002, and 2536, October 23, 2002, NUOI, Z/Irak/P 431, AD.

11. Chirac-Bush telephone conversation, October 9, 2002, TD Diplomatie 75624, October 10, 2002, NUOI, Z/Irak/P 431, AD; and La Sablière, *Dans les coulisses du monde*, 201.

12. Villepin-Straw telephone conversation, October 4, 2002, TD Diplomatie 74486, October 4, 2002, NUOI, Z/Irak/P 431, AD.

13. Villepin-Powell telephone conversation, October 7, 2002, TD Diplomatie 74791, October 9, 2002, and TD DFRA 3748, October 8, 2002, NUOI, Z/Irak/P 431, AD; Chirac-Bush telephone conversation, October 9, 2002; and Chirac, *Mémoires 2*, 380.

14. Villepin-Straw telephone conversation, TD Diplomatie 76267, October 11, 2002, NUOI, Z/Irak/P 431, AD.

15. Juppé-Powell meeting, October 23, 2002.

16. "President Bush Outlines Iraqi Threat," October 7, 2002, George W. Bush White House, http://georgewbush-whitehouse.archives.gov/news/releases/2002/10/20021007-8.html.

17. Rice, *No Higher Honor*, 184; Woodward, *Plan of Attack*, 194–204; TD Washington 2416 and 2418–19, October 10, 2002; 2426, October 11, 2002; and 2605–6, October 31, 2002, NUOI, Z/Irak/P 431, AD.

18. TD DFRA New York 3843, October 12, 2002; TD Diplomatie 76813, October 14, 2002, NUOI, Z/Irak/P 431, AD. See also Gordon and Shapiro, *Allies at War*, 110.

19. MAE, NUOI, note pour le Ministre, October 25, 2002, a/s Irak – Projet de résolution américaine: quelles perspectives pour les négociations en cours?, NUOI, Z/Irak/P 431, AD. For detailed coverage of the whole negotiation, see the aforementioned box.

20. Powell telefax for Villepin, October 31, 2002, NUOI, Z/Irak/P 431, AD.

21. Villepin telephone conversations with Straw, Ivanov, and Powell, TD Diplomatie 83429, November 7, 2002, NUOI, Z/Irak/P 431, AD. On this point, Woodward's account is approximate (see *Plan of Attack*, 224–25); the same is true in Vernet and Cantaloube, *Chirac contre Bush*, 118. Both accounts erroneously relate the "and/or" issue to the beginning of paragraph 4—which calls "false statements or omissions" *and* "failure to comply" a "further material breach"—whereas in fact it relates to the articulation between paragraph 4 and paragraphs 11 and 12.

22. Chirac-Putin telephone conversation, November 6, 2002, TD Diplomatie 82988, November 6, 2002; and TD Damas 1090, November 12, 2002, NUOI, Z/Irak/P 431, AD.

23. TD Diplomatie 838896–97 and 83789, November 8, 2002, NUOI, Z/Irak/P 431, AD; Chirac, *Mémoires 2*, 382; and personal interviews.

24. MAE, NUOI, note pour le directeur de cabinet, a/s Irak – Résolution 1441: les progrès enregistrés, November 8, 2002, NUOI, Z/Irak/P 431, AD.

25. Rice, *No Higher Honor*, 184–85; Woodward, *Plan of Attack*, 226–27; Gordon and Shapiro, *Allies at War*, 113–14; and Bush quote in DeYoung, *Soldier*, 420.

26. TD Washington 2734, November 12, 2002, NUOI, Z/Irak/P 432, AD.

27. Quoted in Ricks, *Fiasco*, 51.

28. Tenet, *At the Center of the Storm*, 321; see also Woodward, *Plan of Attack*, 194–95.

29. The 2002 NIE was partially declassified in 2004, but only the "Key Judgments" that summarize its findings have escaped important redactions. The document was made accessible on the website of the George Washington University's National Security Archive: see "Iraq's Continuing Programs for Weapons of Mass Destruction," NIE 2002-

16HC, National Intelligence Council, October 2002, http://nsarchive.gwu.edu/NSAEBB
/NSAEBB129/nie.pdf.

30. Quoted in DeYoung, *Soldier*, 422; see also Woodward, *Plan of Attack*, 194–95.

31. Commission on the Intelligence Capabilities of the United States Regarding Weapons of Mass Destruction [Silbermann-Robb Commission], *Unclassified Version of the Report of the Commission on the Intelligence Capabilities of the United States Regarding Weapons of Mass Destruction* (Washington, DC: US Government Printing Office, March 31, 2005), 45–46, https://www.gpo.gov/fdsys/pkg/GPO-WMD/pdf/GPO-WMD.pdf.

32. See Jervis, *Why Intelligence Fails*, 123.

33. "Iraq's Continuing Programs," 25; *Report of the Commission on the Intelligence Capabilities of the United States Regarding Weapons of Mass Destruction*, 58 *ff.* and 75 *ff.*; and Tenet, *At the Center of the Storm*, 325–26, 333–34, and 450 *ff.* On this convoluted issue, see Peter Eisner and Knut Royce, *The Italian Letter: How the Bush Administration used a Fake Letter to Build the Case for War in Iraq* (New York: Rodale, 2007). See also John Prados, *Hoodwinked: The Documents That Reveal How Bush Sold Us a War* (New York: The New Press, 2004), 186 *ff.*; and, for the French side, Roger Faligot, Jean Guisnel, and Rémi Kauffer, *Histoire politique des services secrets français* [Political history of the French secret services] (Paris: La Découverte, 2012), 541 *ff.*

34. *Report of the Commission on the Intelligence Capabilities of the United States Regarding Weapons of Mass Destruction*, 80 *ff.*; and Tenet, *At the Center of the Storm*, 328 *ff.* and 375 *ff.*

35. *Report of the Commission on the Intelligence Capabilities of the United States Regarding Weapons of Mass Destruction*, 49–50; and "Iraq's Continuing Programs."

36. Quoted in Ricks, *Fiasco*, 50–51.

37. Jervis, *Why Intelligence Fails*, 126.

38. Tenet, *At the Center of the Storm*, 338. See also Woodward, *Plan of Attack*.

39. Woodward, *Plan of Attack*, 197–99; and Tenet, *At the Center of the Storm*, 333–35 and 370. See also James Risen, *State of War: The Secret History of the CIA and the Bush Administration* (New York: Free Press, 2006), 121; and John Prados and Christopher Ames, ed., *The Iraq War – Part III: Shaping the Debate*, National Security Archive Electronic Briefing Book No. 330 (Washington, DC: National Security Archive, October 4, 2010), http://nsarchive.gwu.edu/NSAEBB/NSAEBB330/index.htm.

40. See *Report of the Commission on the Intelligence Capabilities of the United States Regarding Weapons of Mass Destruction*; and Jervis, *Why Intelligence Fails*.

41. See Risen, *State of War*, 4 *ff.*; and personal interviews.

42. Tenet, *At the Center of the Storm*, 337; see also *Report of the Commission on the Intelligence Capabilities of the United States Regarding Weapons of Mass Destruction*.

43. Drumheller, *On the Brink*; and personal interviews.

44. Quoted in Michael Gordon and Bernard Trainor, *Cobra II: The Inside Story of the Invasion and Occupation of Iraq* (London: Atlantic Books, 2006), 154.

45. Quotations in Ricks, *Fiasco*, 50–57, and Woodward, *Plan of Attack*, 197; see also Risen, *State of War*, 109 *ff.*; and personal interviews.

46. Drumheller, *On the Brink*, 121. See also Risen, *State of War*, 11 *ff.*

47. Tenet, *At the Center of the Storm*, 317 and 449–50; see also Risen, *State of War*, 109 *ff.*

48. Tenet, *At the Center of the Storm*, 329–30; and Drumheller, *On the Brink*, 87–88; see also Sydney Blumenthal, "Turning Truths into Lies," *Guardian*, September 7, 2007, http://www.guardian.co.uk/commentisfree/2007/sep/07/turningtruthintolies/; and personal interview.

49. Paul Wolfowitz, interview with Sam Tanenhaus, *Vanity Fair*, May 9, 2003; see also Tenet, *At the Center of the Storm*, 321.

50. "President Bush Outlines Iraqi Threat"; Haass, quoted in Haass, *War of Necessity*, 230.

51. Drumheller, *On the Brink*, 77; and Haass, *War of Necessity*, 231.

52. Richard Clarke—who in the meantime had left his position as national coordinator for counterterrorism—later wrote: "Both the White House and the CIA must have known there was no 'imminent threat' to the U.S., but one claimed the opposite, and the other allowed them to do so uncorrected." Clarke, *Against All Enemies*, 268.

53. See Woodward, *Plan of Attack*, 203–4; see also McClellan, *What Happened*, 112.

54. Bush, *Decisions Points*, 242; see also Jervis, *Why Intelligence Fails*, 134.

55. MAE, ANMO, Note pour le cabinet du Ministre, a/s Réunion de crise sur l'Irak: guide de réunion (mercredi 11 septembre 2002), September 11, 2002, ANMO, Irak III C3 A1 [1999–2002].

56. Personal interviews.

57. Personal interviews; see also MAE, ANMO, Note pour le cabinet du Ministre, a/s Réunion de crise sur l'Irak: guide de réunion (mercredi 11 septembre 2002), September 11, 2002; and Bruno Le Maire, *Le Ministre. Récit* [The minister: A tale] (Paris: Grasset, 2004), 148–49 and 168–69.

58. Personal interviews; see also Faligot, Guisnel, and Kauffer, *Histoire politique*, 541 *ff.* See also chap. 7, 338 and note 9, and epilogue, note 38.

59. Personal interviews.

60. Personal interviews.

61. Personal interviews.

62. Personal interviews.

63. Personal interviews.

64. Personal interviews; and Le Maire, *Le Ministre*,161–62.

65. Personal interviews; see also Le Maire, *Le Ministre*, 125–26.

66. Le Maire, *Le Ministre*, 167–68; and personal interviews. See also La Sablière, *Dans les coulisses du monde*, 217, and below, chap. 7, note 9.

67. "Irak: ne pas brûler les étapes" [Iraq: We need to proceed step by step], *Le Monde*, October 1, 2002.

68. Personal interviews.

69. MAE, ASD/QA, François Richier, Note, a/s Irak et prolifération: problème du langage public, September 9, 2002, ANMO, Irak III C3 A1 [1999–2002].

70. Jacques Chirac, *Mémoires 2*, 383.

71. Chirac, *Mémoires 2*, 370.

72. Chirac-Bush telephone conversations, September 27 and October 9, 2002.

73. Chirac-Mubarak meeting, Alexandria, October 16, 2002, TD Alexandrie 112, October 17, 2002, NUOI, Z/Irak/P 431, AD.

74. Vernet and Cantaloube, *Chirac contre Bush*, 123–26; and personal interviews.

75. Personal interviews.

76. Vernet and Cantaloube, *Chirac contre Bush*, 131 *ff.*; and personal interviews.

77. Le Maire, *Le Ministre*, 23–24; and personal interviews.

78. Chirac, *Mémoires* 2, 383; Vernet and Cantaloube, *Chirac contre Bush*, 131 *ff.*; and personal interviews.

79. Le Maire, *Le Ministre*, 27–28.
80. Personal interviews.
81. Le Maire, *Le Ministre*, 24.
82. MAE, NUOI, Note a/s Résolution 1441: lettre de l'Irak sur son intention de se conformer à la résolution, November 13, 2002; TD Diplomatie 84668 and 86428, November 13 and 20, 2002; and TD DFRA New York 4574–75, November 25, 2002, NUOI, Z/Irak/P 432, AD; and Blix, *Disarming Iraq*, 89–90 and 95–97.
83. TD DFRA New York 4436–37 and TD Diplomatie 87862, November 15 and 26, 2002, NUOI, Z/Irak/P 432, AD.
84. TD Diplomatie 90676, December 6, 2002; DFRA New York 4705, 4717, 4735, 4750–51, December 5–9, 2002; TD Washington 3006, December 11, 2002; and TD Bagdad 1118, December 12, 2002, NUOI, Z/Irak/P 432, AD. See also Blix, *Disarming Iraq*, 102–7. In his memoir of the Iraq crisis, Le Maire echoes the suspicion that Washington might have tried to use these circumstances in order to redact embarrassing information, in particular for US firms (Le Maire, *Le Ministre*, 29–30); this appears unlikely, if only because the IAEA and UNMOVIC each detained a copy of the original Iraqi document.
85. TD Washington 2983, December 9, 2002, NUOI, Z/Irak/P 432, AD; and Le Maire, *Le Ministre*, 28–29.
86. TD DRFA New York 4784–85, 4863, and 4935, December 10, 16, and 18, 2002, NUOI, Z/Irak/P 432, AD; Blix, *Disarming Iraq*, 106–7.
87. TD DFRA New York 4863 and 4935, December 16 and 18, 2002; and Blix, *Disarming Iraq*, 112.
88. TD DFRA New York 4863 and 4935, December 16 and 18, 2002; and Blix, *Disarming Iraq*, 107–8.
89. TD Washington 3089–90, December 16, 1990, NUOI, Z/Irak/P 432, AD.
90. TD DFRA New York, 4954–55 and TD Washington 3138, December 19, 2002, NUOI, Z/Irak/P 432, AD.
91. Le Maire, *Le Ministre*, 29.
92. TD Diplomatie 93468–69, December 16, 2002, Objet: Déclaration irakienne du 8 décembre: éléments d'évaluation politique; and TD Diplomatie 93597, December 18, 2002, NUOI, Z/Irak/P 432, AD.
93. JIC/Iraq-Initial DIS Assessment of the currently accurate, full and complete declaration, n.d., "Secret UK/French Eyes Only"; and TD Londres 1703, December 19, 2002, NUOI, Z/Irak/P 432, AD; and personal interviews.
94. TD Washington 3089–90; and TD Washington 3115, December 18, 2002, NUOI, Z/Irak/P 432, AD.
95 TD Diplomatie 93468–69, December 16, 2002.
96. Mission Permanente de la France auprès des Nations Unies, "Déclarations au Conseil de Sécurité," December 19, 2002, available through the Internet Archive (saved January 15, 2003), https://web.archive.org/web/20030115064519/http://www.un.int/france/frame_francais/declarations_a_l_onu/cs_chronologique.htm.
97. Feith, *War and Decision*, 339–43.
98. Woodward, *Plan of Attack*, 240–41 and 244–45.
99. Woodward, *Plan of Attack*, 245–50; Bush, *Decision Points*, 242; and Tenet, *At the Center of the Storm*, 359–67.

100. Bush, *Decision Points*, 243; and Woodward, *Plan of Attack*, 254–56.
101. Personal interviews.
102. Bentégeat's handwritten instructions for Gaviard, December 18, [2002], private papers.
103. Personal interview. See also Vernet and Cantaloube, *Chirac contre Bush*, 131 *ff.* The date given by Vernet and Cantaloube for Gaviard's Washington visit—December 16—is inaccurate.
104. Personal interview.
105. Chirac, *Mémoires 2*, 383.
106. Blix, *Disarming Iraq*, 109–10; see also Gordon and Shapiro, *Allies at War*, 117.

Chapter 5

1. TD DFRA New York 4994-96, 24-27 December 2002 MAE, ANMO, Irak III C3 A1 [2002], AD.
2. Note NUOI/ANMO pour le directeur de cabinet du ministre, a/s Irak, January 4, 2003, ANMO, Irak III C3 A1 [01-02/2003], AD.
3. Quoted in "The Divided West: How the Western Alliance Was Torn Apart," *Financial Times* special issue, June 2003, 4; and personal interview.
4. TD Washington 11–12, January 3, 2003, NUOI, Z/Irak/P 432, AD.
5. Bruno Le Maire email to Jean Félix-Paganon, Stanislas de Laboulaye, Gérard Araud, and Bernard Emié, January 6, 2003 (with an attached note drafted by Le Maire and Christophe Farnaud and handed by Villepin to Chirac the previous evening), NUOI, Z/Irak/P 432, AD; and Le Maire, *Le Ministre*, 51–52.
6. Georgelin memorandum for Chirac, "Contraintes 'temps' sur éventuelle participation militaire française à une intervention militaire internationale en Irak," January 6, 2003, 5AG5 DB/63, AN [access to this document was denied]; and Jacques Chirac, *Mémoires 2*, 383; see also Péan, *L'Inconnu de l'Élysée*, 427–28; and personal interviews.
7. Chirac's New Year's greetings to the French military, January 7, 2003, available through the French Ministry of Foreign and European Affairs Documentary Database, http://basedoc.diplomatie.gouv.fr/exl-doc/e011997.pdf. See also Le Maire, *Le Ministre*, 92–93; Vernet and Cantaloube, *Chirac contre Bush*, 139–40; and personal interviews.
8. Chirac's New Year's greetings to the diplomatic corps, January 7, 2003, available through the French Ministry of Foreign and European Affairs Documentary Database, http://basedoc.diplomatie.gouv.fr/exl-doc/e011998.pdf.
9. Villepin letter to Powell, 9 January; and TD Diplomatie 1348, 8 January 2003, NUOI, Z/Irak/P 432, AD.
10. Note a/s Irak—Entretien du ministre avec son homologue russe, Moscou, January 8, 2003; TD Moscow 30, January 8, 2003; and Villepin-Ivanov joint declaration, Moscou, January 8, 2003, NUOI, Z/Irak/P 432, AD.
11. TD Beijing 55, January 10, 2003, 2003, NUOI, Z/Irak/P 432, AD.
12. TD Washington 72–73, January 8, 2003 and TD Diplomatie 1458, January 9, 2003, NUOI, Z/Irak/P 432, AD. On Powell's reservations regarding the January 20 date, see DeYoung, *Soldier*, 431–32; and Gordon and Shapiro, *Allies at War*, 121.

13. TD London 14, 47, and 60, January 6, 10, and 13, 2003, NUOI, Z/Irak/P 432, AD.

14. Memorandum by André Parant, Irak – éventuelle à Paris de M. Blix (vendredi 17 janvier 2003), January 7, 2003; Parant memorandum, January 15, 2003, 5AG5 AP/15, AN; TD Diplomatie 2181–82, January 6, 2003; and DFRA New York 110, January 13, 2003, NUOI, Z/Irak/P 432, AD.

15. TD Diplomatie 2928, January 14, 2003; and TD Baghdad 67, January 15, 2003, NUOI, Z/Irak/P 432, AD.

16. TD DFRA New York 77, January 9, 2003; see also TD Washington 67, January 7, 2003, NUOI, Z/Irak/P 432, AD.

17. TD DFRA New York 57, 78–80, and 109, January 8, 9, and 13, 2003, and TD Diplomatie 1513, January 8, 2003, NUOI, Z/Irak/P 432, AD.

18. TD DFRA New York 129, January 14, 2003; Powell letter to Villepin, January 15, 2003, NUOI, Z/Irak/P 432, AD.

19. Woodward, *Plan of Attack*, 253–54.

20. "President Rallies Troops at Fort Hood," George W. Bush White House, January 3, 2003, http://georgewbush-whitehouse.archives.gov/news/releases/2003/01/20030103.html.

21. Woodward, *Plan of Attack*, 257–58.

22. Ibid., 258–60.

23. Ibid., 260–7; see also Rumsfeld, *Known and Unknown*, 443.

24. Woodward, *Plan of Attack*, 269–73.

25. DeYoung, *Soldier*, 429–30; and Woodward, *Plan of Attack*, 269–73.

26. Chirac, *Mémoires 2*, 384–85; see also Vernet and Cantaloube, *Chirac contre Bush*, 141–42.

27. TD Washington 157–58, January 13, 2003, AD, DA; and personal interviews.

28. TD Washington 151–52, January 13, 2003, AD, DA. The circulation of this telegram, which was drafted by Levitte after the meeting, was extremely limited: the only recipients were Chirac via Gourdault-Montagne, and Villepin via his chief of staff Pierre Vimont.

29. TD Washington 155, January 13, 2003, AD, DA.

30. TD Washington 157–58; and personal interview; see also Vernet and Cantaloube, *Chirac contre Bush*, 141–45; and Haass, *War of Necessity*, 239.

31. Chirac, *Mémoires 2*, 386; and personal interviews.

32. TD DFRA New York 129, January 14, 2003; see also Blix, *Disarming Iraq*, 113 *ff.*; and Woodward, *Plan of Attack*, 275.

33. TD DFRA 152 and 170–71, January 15 and 16, 2003, NUOI, Z/Irak/P 432, AD.

34. Note, Entretien avec MM. Blix et ElBaradei, January 17, 2003, 5AG5 AP/15, AN.

35. TD Diplomatie 4119–20, January 17, 2003, 5AG5 AP/15, AN; see also Blix, *Disarming Iraq*, 127–29, and ElBaradei, *Age of Deception*, 65–66.

36. Blix, *Disarming Iraq*, 127–29; and ElBaradei, *Age of Deception*, 65–66; see also the transcript of the Chirac-Blix-ElBaradei press conference, Paris, January 17, 2003, available through the French Ministry of Foreign and European Affairs Documentary Database, http://basedoc.diplomatie.gouv.fr/exl-doc/e011950.pdf.

37. Le Maire, *Le Ministre*, 121–31; and TD DFRA New York 193, January 20, 2003, NUOI, Z/Irak/P 432, AD. See also La Sablière, *Dans les coulisses du monde*, 207–10.

38. Villepin Security Council statement and press conference, New York, January 20, 2003, available through the French Ministry of Foreign and European Affairs Documentary

Database, http://basedoc.diplomatie.gouv.fr/exl-doc/e011936.pdf (Security Council statement) and http://basedoc.diplomatie.gouv.fr/exl-doc/e011937.pdf (press conference). See also Le Maire, *Le Ministre*, 133 *ff.*; and Joschka Fischer, *"I am not convinced": Der Irak-Krieg und die rot-grünen Jahre* (Cologne: Kiepenheuer & Witsch, 2011), 199–201.

39. TD Washington 247, January 21, 2003, NUOI, Z/Irak/P 432, AD; see also Woodward, *Plan of Attack*, 284–85; and "The Divided West." La Sablière denies this account, explaining that Powell and Jack Straw themselves created this alleged incident by insisting on holding their own press conference before Villepin, which had the effect of delaying Villepin's arrival at La Sablière's uptown residence: see La Sablière, *Dans les coulisses du monde*, 208–9.

40. TD Diplomatie 4851, January 21, 2003; and DeYoung, *Soldier*, 434–35.

41. Le Maire, *Le Ministre*, 136–39.

42. Chirac/Schröder joint press conference with France 2 and ARD, Paris, January 22, 2003, available through the French Ministry of Foreign and European Affairs Documentary Database, http://basedoc.diplomatie.gouv.fr/exl-doc/e011923.pdf; Vernet and Cantaloube, *Bush contre Chirac*, 165; and TD Berlin 163, January 24, 2003, NUOI, Z/Irak/P 432, AD.

43. Chirac, *Mémoires 2*, 372–73; Fischer, *"I am not convinced,"* 201–4; and Gordon and Shapiro, *Allies at War*, 125–28; see also Dieter Dettke, *Germany Says No: The Iraq War and the Future of German Foreign and Security Policy* (Washington, DC: Woodrow Wilson Center Press; Baltimore, Johns Hopkins University Press, 2009), 193–94; and Stephen F. Szabo, *Parting Ways: The Crisis in German-American Relations* (Washington, DC: Brookings Institution Press, 2004), 38–39.

44. TD Washington 283, January 23, 2003, NUOI, Z/Irak/P 432, AD; see also Gordon and Shapiro, *Allies at War*, 128; and Vernet and Cantaloube, *Bush contre Chirac*, 166.

45. Andréani email to Félix-Paganon, January 24, 2003, with attached draft Note a/s: Crise irakienne, January 24, 2003, NUOI, Z/Irak/P 432, AD.

46. TD Washington 270, January 23, 2003, NUOI, Z/Irak/P 432, AD; see also TD Washington 250–51, January 22, ibid.

47. Blix, *Disarming Iraq*, 138.

48. TD DFRA New York 269, January 24, 2003, NUOI, Z/Irak/P 432, AD; and Blix, *Disarming Iraq*, 117–18 and 132–34.

49. Mohamed ElBaradei, "The Status of Nuclear Inspections in Iraq," IAEA, January 27, 2003, http://www.iaea.org/newscenter/statements/2003/ebsp2003n003.shtml#; see also TD DFRA New York 286–88, January 27, 2003, NUOI, Z/Irak/P 432, AD.

50. Hans Blix, "Briefing of the Security Council, 27 January 2003: An Update on Inspections," UNMOVIC, January 27, 2003, http://www.un.org/Depts/unmovic/new /pages/security_council_briefings.asp#5; and TD DFRA New York 286–88 and 295, January 27, 2003, NUOI, Z/Irak/P 432, AD.

51. TD DFRA New York 289–90 and 296, January 27, 2003, NUOI, Z/Irak/P 432, AD; and Blix, *Disarming Iraq*, 141–42.

52. Blix, *Disarming Iraq*, 139–42.

53. TD Washington 318-9, January 27, 2003, NUOI, Z/Irak/P 432, AD; Rice, *No Higher Honor*, 184; and Bush, *Decision Points*, 244.

54. TD DFRA New York 302–3 and 321–23, January 28 and 29, 2003; TD Diplomatie 7065, January 28, 2003; and NUOI note pour le cabinet du ministre, a/s Irak – Rapports

de la COCOVINU et de l'AIEA du 27 janvier: éléments pour une position française, January 28, 2003, NUOI, Z/Irak/P 432, AD.

55. Woodward, *Plan of Attack*, 288–92; see also Tenet, *At the Center of the Storm*, 369 *ff.*

56. "President Delivers 'State of the Union,'" George W. Bush White House, January 28, 2003, http://georgewbush-whitehouse.archives.gov/news/releases/2003/01/20030128-19 .html; see also Woodward, *Plan of Attack*, 294–95; and Tenet, *At the Center of the Storm*, 369 *ff.* and 449 *ff.*

57. MAE, ASD, Note a/s Irak et terrorisme international, confidentiel, February 4, 2003, NUOI, Z/Irak/P 432, AD.

58. TD Washington 348, January 29, 2003; and NUOI note a/s Réunion du Conseil de sécurité du 5 février: quelles preuves sur quels éléments?, January 31, 2003, NUOI, Z/Irak/P 432, AD.

59. MAE, Cabinet du Ministre, Note pour le Ministre, January 28, 2003, a/s: Menace irakienne, NUOI, Z/Irak/P 432, AD; see also MAE, ASD, Note a/s Irak—Armes chimiques et biologiques, January 31, 2003, ibid., and Le Maire, *Le Ministre*, 147–48.

60. TD Diplomatie 6330 and 7334, January 27 and 29, 2003, NUOI, Z/Irak/P 432, AD; and Le Maire, *Le Ministre*, 158–60.

61. See, e.g., P. F. Ricketts to Private Secretary, "Iraq: Resolutions: The Kosovo Option," Chilcot Inquiry, October 3, 2002, http://www.iraqinquiry.org.uk/media/50778/Ricketts -to-PS-Iraq-Resolutions-Kosovo-Option-3October2002.pdf. In substance, the Foreign Office considered that the 1999 Kosovo precedent—during which NATO had intervened against Serbia without an explicit UN Security Council mandate—could not be used in the case of Iraq, and that a British failure to obtain a second resolution authorizing the use of force would in effect translate into the absence of any legal base for an intervention. This finding matched the French position.

62. Woodward, *Plan of Attack*, 287–88 and 296–97; and Bush, *Decision Points*, 244–45. See also Blair's evidence to the Chilcot Inquiry, January 29, 2011, http://www.iraqinquiry .org.uk/media/45139/20100129-blair-final.pdf, 95 *ff.*; and TD Washington 416, February 7, 2003 NUOI, Z/Irak/P 432, AD.

63. Note from André Parant and Maurice Gourdault-Montagne, January 29, 2003, a/s Irak, 5AG5 AP/6, AN.

Chapter 6

1. TD Washington 318–19 and TD DFRA New York, January 27 and 30, 2003, NUOI, Z/Irak/P 432, AD; on this episode, see Ricks, *Fiasco*, 90 *ff.*; Gordon and Trainor, *Cobra II*, 150 *ff.*; DeYoung, *Soldier*, 439 *ff.*; Woodward, *Plan of Attack*, 297 *ff.*; Tenet, *At the Center of the Storm*, 371 *ff.*; and Haass, *War of Necessity*, 240 *ff.*

2. See Ricks, *Fiasco*, 90 and 92; see also John Prados, ed., *The Record on Curveball*, National Security Archive Electronic Briefing Book No. 234 (Washington, DC: National Security Archive, November 5, 2007), http://nsarchive.gwu.edu/NSAEBB/NSAEBB234 /index.htm; and Drumheller, *On the Brink*, 100 *ff.*

3. DeYoung, *Soldier*, 444–45; and Woodward, *Plan of Attack*, 300–1.

4. "Feb. 5, 2003: Colin Powell on WMD," *ABC News* video, 4:05, February 5, 2003, http://abcnews.go.com/Archives/video/feb-2003-colin-powell-wmd-12802420; see also Le Maire, *Le Ministre*, 177.

5. Rice, *No Higher Honor*, 200; Bush, *Decision Points*, 245; Ricks, *Fiasco*, 93; DeYoung, *Soldier*, 451; and TD Washington 466, February 6, 2003, NUOI, Z/Irak/P 432, AD.

6. Le Maire, *Le Ministre*, 176–77; TD DFRA New York 416-9, February 6, 2003, NUOI, Z/Irak/P 432, AD; and Fischer, *"I am not convinced,"* 208–9.

7. MAE, ASD, note by G. Araud, Analyse des déclarations de M. Powell au Conseil de sécurité (5 février), confidential, February 11, 2003, NUOI, Z/Irak/P 432, AD.

8. TD Diplomatie 9407-8, February 6, 2003, NUOI, Z/Irak/P433, AD.

9. TD DFRA New York 359–61, January 30, 2003; MAE, note NUOI, 31 January 2003, a/s Irak – Réunion du Conseil de sécurité du 5 février: quelle position française? Intervention du Ministre, version non définitive; TD DFRA New York 420–22 and 424, February 5, 2003, NUOI, Z/Irak/P 432, AD; and personal interviews.

10. TD Diplomatie 9221, February 6, 2003, NUOI, Z/Irak/P 432, AD; and TD DFRA New York 457, February 7, 2003, NUOI, Z/Irak/P 433, AD.

11. TD DFRA New York 457, February 7, 2003; and MAE, ANMO note, a/s Irak – Réunion du Conseil de sécurité du 14 février: quelle position française?, February 8, 2003, NUOI, Z/Irak/P 433, AD.

12. TD DFRA New York 439, February 6, 2003; Projet de non-papier, February 7, 2003; TD Diplomatie 10040 and 10632, February 10 and 12, 2003; Aide-mémoire américain remis à l'Auswärtiges Amt par l'ambassade des États-Unis à Berlin; and TD Diplomatie 10958, February 12, 2003, NUOI, Z/Irak/P 433, AD.

13. TD Moscou 208 and 293-294, January 25 and February 3, 2003, NUOI, Z/Irak/P 432, AD; déclaration commune Russie Allemagne France sur l'Irak, February 10, 2003; TD Berlin 295, February 10, 2010; and TD Moscou 4410, February 13, 2003, NUOI, Z/Irak/P 433, AD; personal interviews; see also Fischer, *"I am not convinced,"* 214.

14. TD Diplomatie 9407–8, 9884, 10626–27, 10962, 11100, and 11338, February 6, 8, 11, 12, and 13, 2003; TD Pékin 233, February 12, 2003; TD Berlin 310, February 13, 2003; and email from R. Salins to M. Lafont-Rapnouil, February 14, 2003, NUOI, Z/Irak/P 433, AD.

15. TD DFRA New York 495–96 and 498–99, February 12 and 14, 2003, NUOI, Z/Irak/P 433, AD; and Blix, *Disarming Iraq*, 161–66.

16. Personal interviews; and Le Maire, *Le Ministre*. 196–97. See also La Sablière, *Dans les coulisses du monde*, 9–11.

17. TD Diplomatie 11337, February 13, 2003, and TD DFRA New York 518–19, February 14, 2003, NUOI, Z/Irak/P 433, AD. For Blix's Security Council briefing, see Hans Blix, "Briefing of the Security Council, 14 February 2003: An Update on Inspections," UNMOVIC, February 14, 2003, http://www.un.org/Depts/unmovic/new/pages/security_council_briefings.asp#6.

18. TD DFRA New York 520, 521–23, and 527–28, February 14, 2003, NUOI, Z/Irak/P 433, AD; see Villepin's Security Council speech, New York, February 14, 2003, available through the French Ministry of Foreign and European Affairs Documentary Database, http://basedoc.diplomatie.gouv.fr/exl-doc/e011766.pdf.

19. Le Maire, *Le Ministre*, 198–200; TD DFRA New York 526 and 527–28, February 15, 2003, NUOI, Z/Irak/P 433, AD.

20. MAE, NUOI, note pour le directeur de cabinet, a/s Irak: perspectives au Conseil de sécurité et propositions, February 17, 2003; see also TD Bagdad 231 and 243, February 15 and 18, 2003, and TD Diplomatie 11938, February 17, 2003, NUOI, Z/Irak/P 433, AD.

21. TD Washington 562, February 12, 2003; and TD Diplomatie 10626, February 11, 2003, NUOI, Z/Irak/P 433, AD.

22. MAE, Service de la PESC, note a/s Conseil européen informel extraordinaire (Bruxelles, le 17 février 2003), Eléments de cadrage, February 17, 2003, NUOI, Z/Irak/P 433, AD.

23. TD Londres 179, January 30, 2003, AD, NUOI, Z/Irak/P 433, AD.

24. See "United We Stand," *Wall Street Journal*, January 30, 2003; and Gordon and Shapiro, *Allies at War*, 128–32; see also "The Divided West," 6–7 (the Bush quote is on page 7).

25. Gordon and Shapiro, *Allies at War*, 132–33; and "The Divided West," 6–7.

26. TD Diplomatie 7687 and 9221, January 30 and February 6, 2003, NUOI, Z/Irak/P 432, AD; and Le Maire, *Le Ministre*, 149, 155, and 179.

27. Vernet and Cantaloube, *Chirac contre Bush*, 170. See also Gordon and Shapiro, *Allies at War*, 136–37; Fischer, *"I am not convinced,"* 211–12; and TD Berlin 285, February 9, 2003, NUOI, Z/Irak/P 433, AD.

28. TD Diplomatie 9899 and 11543–44, February 9 and 14, 2003, NUOI, Z/Irak/P 433, AD; and MAE, Service de la PESC, note a/s Conseil européen informel extraordinaire (Bruxelles, le 17 février 2003).

29. TD Diplomatie 12264, February 12, 2003, NUOI, Z/Irak/P 433, AD.

30. Chirac's European Council press conference, Brussels, February 17, 2003, available through the French Ministry of Foreign and European Affairs Documentary Database, http://basedoc.diplomatie.gouv.fr/exl-doc/e011754.pdf; see also MAE, Direction de la coopération européenne, note a/s Réaction des pays candidats d'Europe centrale aux propos du président de la République à l'issue du Conseil européen extraordinaire de Bruxelles (17 février), February 27, 2003, NUOI, Z/Irak/P 433, AD; Vernet and Cantaloube, *Chirac contre Bush*, 182–84; Gordon and Shapiro, *Allies at War*, 133–34; and Jacques Chirac, *Mémoires 2*, 389.

31. On this, see, e.g., Frédéric Bozo, "La relation transatlantique et la 'longue' guerre contre le terrorisme" [The transatlantic relationship and the "long" war on terrorism], *Politique étrangère* 67, no. 2 (2002): 337–51.

32. MAE, ASP, note a/s OTAN/Irak, February 25, 2003, ANMO, Irak III C3 01-02/2003, AD; see also Gordon and Shapiro, *Allies at War*, 136–37; Brian Knowlton, "Allies Delay Decision on U.S. Requests: NATO Wavering on War with Iraq," *New York Times*, January 23, 2003; and Craig S. Smith, "Debate Over Iraq Raises Fears of a Shrinking Role for NATO," *New York Times*, January 26, 2003.

33. Le Maire, *Le Ministre*, 174–75, 181–82, and 186; TD DFRA New York 441, February 6, 2003, and TD Diplomatie 9900, February 9, 2003, NUOI, Z/Irak/P 433, AD; see also Gordon and Shapiro, *Allies at War*, 137; and personal interviews.

34. Gordon and Shapiro, *Allies at War*, 138; and Craig S. Smith with Richard Bernstein, "3 Members of NATO and Russia Resist U.S. on Iraq Plans," *New York Times*, February 11, 2003.

35. TD Diplomatie 10632 and 11058, February 11 and 12, 2003, NUOI, Z/Irak/P 433, AD; and Le Maire, *Le Ministre*, 188.
36. MAE, ASP, note a/s OTAN/Irak, February 25, 2003; Gordon and Shapiro, *Allies at War*, 139–40; and Le Maire, *Le Ministre*, 192.
37. TD Diplomatie 11985, February 17, 2003; see also TD Pékin, February 12, 2003, NUOI, Z/Irak/P 433, AD. The NATO episode complicated Turkish-American relations, hence Chirac's comment to Putin: indeed, on March 1, the Turkish parliament rejected Washington's request to use Turkish territory in case of an Iraq invasion, thus depriving the US military of the possibility of opening a second front in northern Iraq.
38. Le Maire, *Le Ministre*, 192–93.
39. TD Washington 208, February 17, 2003, NUOI, Z/Irak/P 433, AD.
40. Chirac, *Mémoires 2*, 388.
41. TD Diplomatie 9884 and 10349, February 8 and 11, 2003, and TD Le Caire 195–96, February 14, 2003, NUOI, Z/Irak/P 433, AD.
42. TD DFRA New York 546, February 19, 2003, NUOI, Z/Irak/P 433, AD.
43. MAE, NUOI, Note pour le conseiller diplomatique de la présidence de la République, January 27, 2003, NUOI, Z/Irak/P 432, AD; see also Note pour le Ministre, a/s Entretien avec le PR—Eléments de langage [attachment to an email of 30 January from Bruno Le Maire to Pierre Vimont and other addressees], ibid.; and MAE, ANMO, Note pour le cabinet du Ministre, a/s Irak – Réunion du conseil de sécurité du 14 février, February 8, 2003.
44. Note, Entretien avec le président Bush, 7 février 2003, éléments de langage; and TD Diplomatie [no number], February 7, 2003, 5AG5 AP/6, AN; see also Chirac, *Mémoires 2*, 391.
45. TD Diplomatie [no number], February 7, 2003; see also Chirac, *Mémoires 2*, 391; and Woodward, *Plan of Attack*, 313.
46. TD Washington 609, February 18, 2003, NUOI, Z/Irak/P 432, AD; Vernet and Cantaloube, *Chirac contre Bush*, 199; and Bush, *Decision Points*, 233–34 and 245.
47. Woodward, *Plan of Attack*, 314.
48. Rice, *No Higher Honor*, 202.
49. TD Washington 560 and 562, February 12, 2003, and TD Washington 574 and 575, February 13, 2003, NUOI, Z/Irak/P 433, AD.
50. TD Washington 605-6, February 17, 2003, NUOI, Z/Irak/P 433, AD.
51. Le Maire, *Le Ministre*, 99 and 144; MAE, note ANMO, a/s Irak – Réunion du Conseil de sécurité du 14 février: quelle position française?, February 8, 2003; see also Chirac, *Mémoires 2*, 389; and personal interviews.
52. Personal interviews.
53. Le Maire, *Le Ministre*, 151–52; Vernet and Cantaloube, *Chirac contre Bush*, 151 and 232–35; and personal interviews.
54. Chirac, *Mémoires 2*, 389.
55. Ibid., 390.
56. TD Diplomatie 10301, February 10, 2003, NUOI, Z/Irak/P 433, AD.
57. Figures from the CSA polling institute (Paris), quoted in Vernet and Cantaloube, *Chirac contre Bush*, 149; and figures from the IPSOS polling institute (Paris), www.ipsos .fr. On the issue of French anti-Americanism, see Kuisel, *The French Way*, in particular 329 *ff.*; and Sophie Meunier, "The Distinctiveness of French Anti-Americanism," in *Anti-*

Americanisms in World Politics, ed. Peter J. Katzenstein and Robert Keohane (Ithaca, NY: Cornell University Press, 2007), 129–56.

58. Gordon and Shapiro, *Allies at War*, 144; and Vernet and Cantaloube, *Chirac contre Bush*, 149–51.

59. Note pour le Ministre, a/s Entretien avec le PR—Eléments de langage, January 30, 2003; MAE, ANMO, Note pour le cabinet du Ministre, a/s Irak – Réunion du Conseil de sécurité du 14 février, February 8, 2003.

60. TD Washington 605–6 and 609, February 17 and 18, 2003.

61. TD Washington 650, February 21, 2003, NUOI, Z/Irak/P 433, AD.

62. Personal interviews; and TD Washington 650, February 21, 2003.

63. TD Diplomatie 13318, February 23, 2003, NUOI, Z/Irak/P 434, AD; and Woodward, *Plan of Attack*, 319–20.

64. "President Discusses the Future of Iraq," George W. Bush White House, February 26, 2003, http://georgewbush-whitehouse.archives.gov/news/releases/2003/02/20030226-11 .html.

Chapter 7

1. TD DFRA New York 245, 605, 606, and 607, and TD Diplomatie 13640, February 24, 2003; TD Diplomatie 14388, February 26, 2003; and NUOI, note pour le directeur de cabinet, a/s Irak – Deuxième résolution: éléments sur la procédure au Conseil de sécurité, March 3, 2003, NUOI, Z/Irak/P 434, AD. On the UN endgame, see also La Sablière, *Dans les coulisses du monde*, 212 *ff.*

2. Le Maire, *Le Ministre*, 203 and 208; and TD Diplomatie 14313 and 14429, February 26, 2003, NUOI, Z/Irak/P 434, AD.

3. TD DFRA New York 570, February 20, 2003, AD, NUOI, Z/Irak/P 433; TD DFRA New York 622, February 25, 2003; NUOI, note pour le directeur de cabinet, a/s Irak – Conseil de sécurité: quelle attitude tenir face à la proposition canadienne?, February 27, 2003, NUOI, Z/Irak/P 434, AD; and personal interview.

4. Russia-Germany-France declaration, Paris, March 5, 2003, available through the French Ministry of Foreign and European Affairs Documentary Database, http://basedoc .diplomatie.gouv.fr/exl-doc/e011669.pdf; see also MAE, NUOI, note pour le directeur de cabinet, a/s Irak – Perspectives au Conseil de sécurité et propositions, February 21, 2003, and note a/s Irak – Renforcement de notre langage public sur notre opposition au projet anglo-américain, March 5, 2003; TD Diplomatie 16563, March 5, 2003, NUOI, Z/Irak/P 434, AD; and personal interviews.

5. TD DFRA New York 633–34 and 720–22, February 26 and March 5, 2003, NUOI, Z/Irak/P 434, AD; and Hans Blix, *Disarming Iraq*, 198–202.

6. MAE, le directeur politique, note pour le ministre, a/s G8—Directeurs politiques- point Irak, February 25, 2003; TD Bagdad 280, February 26; TD DFRA New York, 633–34 and 658–59, February 26 and 28, 2003; TD Diplomatie 14319, February 26, and 14716, 15000, and 15002, February 27, 2003, NUOI, Z/Irak/P 434, AD; and Blix, *Disarming Iraq*, 188 *ff.*

7. Hans Blix, "Oral Introduction of the 12th Quarterly Report of UNMOVIC," UNMOVIC, March 7, 2003, www.un.org/depts/unmovic/SC7asdelivered.htm.

8. Mohamed ElBaradei, "The Status of Nuclear Inspections in Iraq: An Update," IAEA, March 7, 2003, https://www.iaea.org/newscenter/statements/status-nuclear-inspections -iraq-update.

9. Incredulous from the start on the Niger affair, the DGSE had reached the same conclusion several months before, based on the same documents. Yet the DGSE seems not to have conveyed its assessment in categorical terms to the Quai d'Orsay, unless the Quai officials—perhaps influenced by other sources, like Thérèse Delpech—ignored or dismissed its assessment. Quai officials only discovered the fraud when Baute informed them a few days before ElBaradei's UN appearance; see TD DFRA New York 260–61, January 24, 2003; note N°224 QA a/s Irak: programme nucléaire; tentative d'acquisition d'uranium au Niger, January 30, 2003, NUOI Z/Irak/P 432, AD; La Sablière, *Dans les coulisses du monde*, 217; and personal interviews. See also above, chap. 4, 156. On the sequel of this episode, see Epilogue, 307 and note 38.

10. TD DFRA Vienne 107, March 4, 2003; TD DFRA New York 720, March 5, 2003, and 735, March 7, 2003; and TD Washington 820–21, March 7, 2003, NUOI, Z/Irak/P 434, AD; Woodward, *Plan of Attack*, 329–34; and Le Maire, *Le Ministre*, 234–35.

11. Dominique de Villepin's remarks at the UN Security Council, New York, March 7, 2003, available through the French Ministry of Foreign and European Affairs Documentary Database, http://basedoc.diplomatie.gouv.fr/exl-doc/e011648.pdf; see also TD DFRA 688–89 and 737–38, March 4 and 7, 2003, and TD Diplomatie 17522, March 8, 2003, NUOI, Z/Irak/P 434, AD.

12. TD DFRA New York 739–40, March 7, 2003; see also TD DFRA New York 702, March 4, 2003, 736, 737–38, March 7, 2003, and 752, March 8, 2008, NUOI, Z/Irak/P 434, AD.

13. TD Diplomatie 17530 and 17531, March 9, 2003, and TD Santiago 149, March 10, 2003, NUOI, Z/Irak/P 434, AD.

14. TD Yaoundé 133, February 25, 2003; TD DFRA New York 645, February 27, 2003; and TD Londres 395, March 6, 2003, NUOI, Z/Irak/P 434, AD. See also Vernet and Cantaloube, *Chirac contre Bush*, 237 *ff.*; and personal interviews.

15. MAE, Direction Afrique et Océan indien, note pour le cabinet du ministre, a/s Comment rallier l'Angola à notre position sur l'Irak?, and note a/s Cameroun-position sur l'Irak, February 25, 2003; and TD Diplomatie 16589, March 6, 2003, NUOI, Z/Irak/P 434, AD; Vernet and Cantaloube, *Chirac contre Bush*; and personal interviews.

16. TD Luanda 194, March 12, 2003; TD Yaoundé 180–81, March 11, 2003; and TD Conakry 193, March 13, 2003, NUOI, Z/Irak/P 434, AD; and Vernet and Cantaloube, *Chirac contre Bush*.

17. Jacques Chirac, interview with TF1 and France 2 television channels, Paris March 10, 2003, available through the French Ministry of Foreign and European Affairs Documentary Database, http://basedoc.diplomatie.gouv.fr/exl-doc/e011640.pdf.

18. Blair, *Journey*, 426–27.

19. Woodward, *Plan of Attack*, 337–38 and 340–41; Blair, *Journey*, 430; and TD Londres 417 and 440, March 10 and 12, 2003, NUOI, Z/Irak/P 434, AD.

20. TD DFRA New York, 764, 790–91, 800, and 801–2, March 10 and 12, 2003, and TD Diplomatie 18587, March 12, 2003, NUOI, Z/Irak/P 434, AD; Woodward, *Plan of Attack*, 344–45; and personal interviews.

21. TD DFRA New York 823–24 and 825 and TD Bagdad 366, March 13, 2003, NUOI, Z/Irak/P 434, AD.

22. TD Londres 422, March 11, 2003, NUOI, Z/Irak/P 434, AD.

23. TD Londres 429, 432, and 439, March 11 and 12, 2003, NUOI, Z/Irak/P 434, AD. See also the declassified documents from the Chilcot Inquiry: "12 March 2003 Rycroft to Powell, Manning, Campbell, Pruce and Wall e-mail – 'French veto – Urgent,'" March 12, 2003; "13 March 2003 FCO telno 53 'Iraq – Foreign Secretary's conversation with French Foreign Minister,'" March 13, 2003; "13 March 2003 Paris telno 127 'France – Iraq,'" March 13, 2003; and "13 March 2003 Ricketts to Holmes letter 'France and Iraq,'" March 13, 2003, all at http://www.iraqinquiry.org.uk/transcripts/declassified-documents.aspx.

24. "13 March 2003 FCO telno 53 'Iraq – Foreign Secretary's conversation with French Foreign Minister,'" March 13, 2003.

25. Sir Stephen Wall, oral evidence to the Chilcot Inquiry, January 19, 2011, 68–70, http://www.iraqinquiry.org.uk/media/51760/20110119-wall-final.pdf; see also TD Londres 464, March 14, 2003; and TD Diplomatie 19565, March 15, 2003, NUOI, Z/Irak/P 434, AD.

26. Woodward, *Plan of Attack*, 346–47 and 357–60; Jacques Chirac, interview with US television channels CBS and CNN, March 16, 2003, available through the French Ministry of Foreign and European Affairs Documentary Database, http://basedoc.diplomatie.gouv.fr/exl-doc/e011596.pdf; and TD Washington 930, March 16, 2003, NUOI, Z/Irak/P 434, AD.

27. Woodward, *Plan of Attack*, 364–65; and TD DFRA New York 845–86, March 17, 2003, NUOI, Z/Irak/P 434, AD.

28. TD Washington 964, March 18, 2003, NUOI, Z/Irak/P 434, AD; and "President Says Saddam Hussein Must Leave Iraq Within 48 Hours," George W. Bush White House, March 17, 2003, http://georgewbush-whitehouse.archives.gov/news/releases/2003/03/20030317-7.html.

29. TD London 484, 485, and 486, March 18, 2003; TD Diplomatie 20213, March 19, 2003; and Blair, *Journey*, 433–37. British attorney general Lord Goldsmith had suddenly changed his position during the lead-up to the war, recognizing the legality of the war even without a second resolution. Previously, he had defended the opposite thesis. Goldsmith's change of opinion would long remain at the center of the Iraq war controversy in the United Kingdom.

30. Woodward, *Plan of Attack*, 312 and 314; MAE, ANMO, note de Bernard Emié, a/s Irak et Proche-Orient, January 15, 2003; and note a/s Perspectives de la situation en Irak, February 13, 2003, ANMO, Irak III C3 01-02/2003, AD.

31. Personal interviews; TD Diplomatie 13319, February 24, 2003; TD Moscou, 355 and 651, March 11 and 13, 2003; TD Le Caire 300, March 13, 2003; TD Bagdad 386, March 18, 2003, NUOI, Z/Irak/P 434, AD; and Woodward, *Plan of Attack*, 369.

32. Woodward, *Plan of Attack*, 376–99; and "President Bush Addresses the Nation," George W. Bush White House, March 19, 2003, http://georgewbush-whitehouse.archives.gov/news/releases/2003/03/20030319-17.html.

33. Woodward, *Plan of Attack*, 401–3; and Ricks, *Fiasco*, 116–17.

34. Woodward, *Plan of Attack*, 402–3; Ricks, *Fiasco*, 117–18; TD Diplomatie 25177, April 7, 2003, NUOI, Z/Irak/P 435, AD; and ANMO, note a/s Guerre en Irak – Premières analyses, March 25, 2003, NUOI, Z/Irak/P 428, AD.

35. MAE, Note du directeur politique pour le directeur de cabinet, A/S Irak–CS-Position allemande, March 17, 2003; TD Diplomatie 19854, March 17, 2003, NUOI, Z/Irak/P 434, AD; MAE, ANMO, and NUOI, note pour le ministre, a/s Irak – Consultations à trois, March 28, 2003, NUOI, Z/Irak/P 435, AD; and MAE, Direction des affaires juridiques, note pour le directeur de cabinet, a/s Irak – Situation juridique créée par l'intervention militaire, April 11, 2003, NUOI, Z/Irak/P 428, AD.

36. MAE, ASD, note a/s Demandes des États-Unis et d'autres alliés concernant les opérations en Irak, March 19, 2003, NUOI, Z/Irak/P 428, AD.

37. Jacques Chirac, Declaration on Iraq, Paris, March 18, 2003, available through the French Ministry of Foreign and European Affairs Documentary Database, http://basedoc .diplomatie.gouv.fr/exl-doc/e011582.pdf; Jacques Chirac, Declaration on Iraq, Paris, March 20, 2003, ibid., http://basedoc.diplomatie.gouv.fr/exl-doc/e011566.pdf; and TD Diplomatie 23360, March 29, 2003, NUOI, Z/Irak/P 435, AD.

38. Woodward, *Plan of Attack*, 405–6; Ricks, *Fiasco*, 118–25; and TD Washington 1100, March 27, 2003, NUOI, Z/Irak/P 428, AD.

39. TD Diplomatie 22205, 23358, and 23687, March 25 and 29 and April 1, 2003, NUOI, Z/Irak/P 435, AD.

40. TD Diplomatie 23360, 25978–79, and 25099, March 29 and April 4 and 5, 2003, NUOI, Z/Irak/P 435, AD.

41. Woodward, *Plan of Attack*, 407–8; Ricks, *Fiasco*, 125–27 and 133–35; and TD Washington 1242, April 4, 2003, NUOI, Z/Irak/P 435, AD.

42. TD Diplomatie 26798, April 11, 2003, NUOI, Z/Irak/P 435, AD.

43. TD Washington 1333–34, April 11, 2003, NUOI, Z/Irak/P 428, AD; and TD Diplomatie 27318 and 30460, April 14 and 25, 2003, NUOI, Z/Irak/P 435, AD.

44. Woodward, *Plan of Attack*, 409–10; and Ricks, *Fiasco*, 138–44.

45. Ricks, *Fiasco*, 145; and "President Bush Announces Major Combat Operations in Iraq Have Ended." George W. Bush White House, May 1, 2003, http://georgewbush -whitehouse.archives.gov/news/releases/2003/05/20030501-15.html.

46. TD Washington 1254, April 6, 2003, NUOI, Z/Irak/P 435, AD.

47. MAE, ANMO and NUOI, note pour le Ministre, a/s Irak – Déclaration conjointe de MM. Bush et Blair à Belfast: synthèse et commentaires, April 9, 2003, NUOI, Z/Irak/P 435, AD; TD Washington 1035, March 24, 2003, and TD RPAN Bruxelles 398, March 31, 2003; and MAE, ASD, Réunion de Bruxelles-Force de stabilisation en Irak-Rôle de l'OTAN, April 24, 2003, NUOI, Z/Irak/P 428, AD.

48. Woodward, *Plan of Attack*, 346.

49. TD Diplomatie 23360, March 29, 2003; see also Vernet and Cantaloube, *Chirac contre Bush*, 225 *ff.* and 269 *ff.*; and Woodward, *Plan of Attack*, 346.

50. See Justin Vaïsse, "Anonymous Sources: The Media Campaign Against France," Brookings Institution, July 1, 2003, http://www.brookings.edu/research/articles/2003/07 /france-vaisse.

51. Jean-David Levitte, "La crise franco-américaine sur l'Irak: leçons apprises pour le fonctionnement de l'ambassade à Washington," n.d., AFEW; see also Vernet and

Cantaloube, *Chirac contre Bush*, 272–78.

52. TD Washington 1372, April 14, 2003, NUOI, Z/Irak/P 435, AD.

53. TD Londres 651–52 and 723, April 8 and 17, 2003, NUOI, Z/Irak/P 435, AD.

54. Jacques Chirac, *Mémoires 2*, 437–38; Note, Entretien du président de la République avec le président Bush, April 15, 2003, 5AG5 AP/6, AN; and Rice, *No Higher Honor*, 212–13.

55. Bush-Chirac telephone conversation, April 15, 2003, 5AG5 AP/6, AN; and Chirac, *Mémoires 2*, 438–41.

56. TD Diplomatie 29931, April 24, 2003, NUOI, Z/Irak/P 435, AD; and Brian Knowlton, "U.S. Officials Consider Ways to Punish France," *New York Times*, April 23, 2003.

57. MAE, NUOI, note pour le directeur de cabinet, a/s Irak – Liens entre enjeux humanitaires, questions de désarmement et sanctions, April 18, 2003.

58. Personal interview; see also Chirac, *Mémoires 2*, 442; TD Washington 1772 and 1836, May 13 and 19, 2003; TD Diplomatie 33128, 32408, 33796, 35243, 36462, and 36825, May 9, 15, 20, and 21, 2003; and TD DFRA 1335, 1392-4, 1548, May 5, 8, and 22, 2003, NUOI, Z/Irak/P 435, AD.

59. TD Washington 1960, May 26, 2003, AD, ED. See also Vernet and Cantaloube, *Chirac contre Bush*, 287–89; Chirac, *Mémoires 2*, 442–49; and personal interview.

60. TD Diplomatie 40050, June 4, 2003, private papers; and personal interviews.

61. On all this, see Ricks, *Fiasco*, 149–88. `

62. TD Washington 2498-9, 2631, July 4 and 17, 2003, NUOI, Z/Irak/P 435, AD.

63. Dominique de Villepin interview in *Le Figaro*, July 10, 2003; TD Diplomatie 47308 and 47671, July 4 and 11, 2003; and TD Washington 2631, July 17, 2003, NUOI, Z/Irak/P 435, AD.

64. TD Washington 2507–8, 2648, and 2678–79, July 5, 18, and 21, 2003, NUOI, Z/Irak/P 435, AD.

65. MAE, NUOI, note, Irak-Post-conflit: quelles conditions pour une participation de la France à une force de stabilisation?, July 2, 2003, and ANMO, note a/s Force de stabilisation ou de gendarmerie en Irak: Hypothèse d'une participation française, July 7, 2003, NUOI, Z/Irak/P 428, AD; and TD Diplomatie 47308 and 47671, July 4 and 11, 2003, NUOI, Z/Irak/P 435, AD.

66. TD Washington 2507–8, 2631, 2648, and 2678–79, July 5, 17, 18, and 21, 2003, NUOI, Z/Irak/P 435, AD.

67. TD Diplomatie 53801 and 54572, August 5 and 11, 2003; TD DFRA New York 2277, 2308, and 2342, August 8, 14, and 20, 2003; and TD Washington 2986, August 22, 2003, NUOI, Z/Irak/P 435, AD.

68. Ricks, *Fiasco*, 176 and 215–16.

69. TD Diplomatie 58711, September 5, 2003, NUOI, Z/Irak/P 436, AD.

70. TD Diplomatie 58948, September 8, 2003; and TD DFRA New York, 2646 and 2697–98, September 18 and 23, 2003, NUOI, Z/Irak/P 436, AD.

71. TD DFRA New York 2713–14, September 23. 2003, ED, AD.

Epilogue

1. On this period, see Bob Woodward, *State of Denial* (New York: Simon & Schuster, 2006).
2. Quoted by Ricks, *Fiasco*, 362.
3. Ibid., 290.
4. *9/11 Commission Report*, 66.
5. On the March 2004 Madrid train bombing and its connections with al-Qaeda, see Fernando Reinares, *Al-Qaeda's Revenge: The 2004 Madrid Train Bombings* (Washington, DC: Woodrow Wilson Center Press; New York: Columbia University Press, 2016).
6. Ricks, *Fiasco*, 321 *ff.* and 380.
7. Paul Starobin, "The French Were Right," *National Journal*, November 7, 2003.
8. Note de Pierre Lellouche, Compte-rendu d'entretiens avec MM. Robert Blackwill et Paul Wolfowitz, November 3, 2003; and note a/s Entretien avec Mme Condoleezza Rice (Londres, 21/11/03), 5AG5 AP/6, AN; TD Diplomatie 67308 and DFRA New York 3217, October 16, 2003, NUOI, Z/Irak/P 435, AD.
9. Gourdault-Montagne–Rice meeting, November 21, 2003; Chirac-Biden meeting, December 2, 2003, 5AG5 AP/6, AN.
10. Chirac-Bush telephone conversation, December 10, 2003; TD Washington 4436, December 15, 2003; and note a/s Conversation avec James Baker, December 16, 2003, 5AG5 AP6, AN; Vernet and Cantaloube, *Chirac contre Bush*, 311. On all this, see also Nouzille, *Dans le secret des présidents*, 427 *ff.*
11. Gourdault-Montagne–Rice meeting, January 31, 2004, 5AG5 AP6, AN.
12. Chirac-Brahimi meeting, April 24, 2004, TD Diplomatie 26309, April 27, 2004, 5AG5 AP/15, AN; Note, entretien avec le président Bush (25 mai, 13h45), May 23, 2004, 5AG5 AP/6, AN; see also Nouzille, *Dans le secret des présidents*, 446.
13. Note, Chirac-Bush meeting, June 5, 2004, 5AG5 AP/6, AN; and Chirac-Bush meeting, Sea Island, June 10, 2004, private papers.
14. Letter from Laura Bush to Chirac, October 12, 2003; and letter from George H. W. Bush to Chirac, June 15, 2004, 5AG5 AP/6, AN.
15. Jean-David Levitte, "La crise franco-américaine sur l'Irak: leçons apprises pour le fonctionnement de l'ambassade à Washington," n.d., ANMO 5 Irak, AFEW; and Vernet and Cantaloube, *Chirac contre Bush*, 291 *ff.*
16. André Parant, Note a/s Visite en France du représentant Houghton, January 12, 2004; TD Washington 596–97, February 11, 2004; and TD Diplomatie 10641, February 17, 2004, 5AG5 AP/6, AN.
17. Gourdault-Montagne–Rice meeting, January 30, 2004; and TD Washington 413, January 30, 2004, 5AG5 AP/6, AN.
18. In 2002, France and the United States, as well as four other Western countries, had established a close antiterrorist cooperation in the form of an intelligence exchange structure called "Alliance Base," which was established in Paris. Not only did the Iraqi conflict not interrupt this cooperation, but it was intensified afterward, leading notably to the arrest in July 2003 of Christian Ganczarski, a German who had converted to Islam and was involved in the attack on the synagogue of Djerba in April 2002: Dana Priest,

"Help From France Key in Covert Operations; Paris's 'Alliance Base' Targets Terrorists," *Washington Post*, July 3, 2005; and personal interview.

19. Note a/s Entretien avec une délégation du "Caucus" sur la France au Congrès des États-Unis, February 16, 2004; see also Note, Entretien et dîner de travail entre le président de la République et M. George W. Bush, June 5, 2004; and TD Washington 2217–20, May 27, 2004, 5AG5 AP/6, AN.

20. Chirac-Biden meeting, December 2, 2003, 5AG5 AP/6, AN; TD Washington 596–97, February 11, 2004; and TD Diplomatie 10641, February 17, 2004.

21. Gourdault-Montagne–Rice meeting, November 21, 2003, and January 30, 2004; Chirac-Bush meeting, June 5, 2004; and personal interviews.

22. Gourdault-Montagne–Rice meeting, January 30, 2004; Note a/s Entretien avec les sénateurs Stevens, Warner et Hollings, March 19, 2004; and Chirac-Bush telephone conversation, TD Diplomatie 18779, March 19, 2004, 5AG5 AP/6, AN.

23. Chirac-Bush meeting, June 5, 2004, private papers; and personal interview.

24. Woodward, *State of Denial*, 378.

25. See Justin Vaïsse, "États-Unis: l'hiver du néo-conservatisme" [United States: The winter of neoconservatism], *Politique internationale* 110 (February 2006), http://www.politiqueinternationale.com/revue/article.php?id_revue=25&id=285.

26. Chirac-Bush telephone conversation, November 9, 2004, 5AG5 AP/6, AN.

27. Chirac-Rice meeting, February 8, 2005, 5AG5 DB/5, AN.

28. TD Washington 618–19, February 17, 2005, 5AG5 DB/5, AN.

29. Chirac-Bush telephone conversation, March 16, 2005, 5AG5 DB/5, AN; see also Nouzille, *Dans le secret*, 433–36.

30. Chirac-Bush meeting, February 21, 2005; see also the preparatory notes for the trip by Maurice Gourdault-Montagne to Washington, June 1, 2005, 5AG5 DB/5, AN. See also Aeschimann and Boltanski, *Chirac d'Arabie*.

31. Note a/s Conversation avec M. George W. Bush, lundi 21 février à Bruxelles, February 21, 2005; and note a/s Conversation téléphone avec M. George W. Bush, March 30, 2006, 5AG5 DB/5, AN.

32. Letter from Rice to Chirac, November 7, 2005, 5AG5 DB/5, AN.

33. Woodward, *State of Denial*, 422 and 472–73; and Ricks, *Fiasco*, 412–29.

34. Chirac-Bush meeting, February 21, 2005; notes préparatoires au déplacement de Maurice Gourdault-Montagne à Washington, June 1, 2005; note a/s Conversation avec Mme Condoleezza Rice, October 14, 2005; and Chirac-Rice meeting, October 14, 2005, 5AG5 DB/5, AN.

35. Chirac-Rice meeting, February 8, 2005; note, sommet de l'Alliance, February 23, 2005, 5AG5 DB5, AN.

36. TD Washington 4104, November 9, 2005, ANMO 5 Irak, AFEW.

37. See CIA, *Comprehensive Report of the Special Advisor to the DCI on Iraq's WMD* (Washington, DC: US Government Printing Office, September 2004), 40–41; Independent Inquiry Committee into the United Nations Oil-for-Food Programme, *Manipulation of the Oil-for-Food Programme for the Iraqi Regime* (October 2005), chap. 2, 47–78; TD Washington 1407, 1826, 1833, 1854, 1856, and 1891, April 14, May 11–13 and 17, 2005, and TD Diplomatie 29520 and 29841, May 10 and 13, 2005, ANMO 5 Irak, AFEW; and personal interviews. The trial of the French branch of the

"Oil-for-Food" scandal opened on January 21, 2013, at the Paris Criminal Court. The defendants included, among other individuals, former Interior Minister Charles Pasqua and former ambassadors Jean-Bernard Mérimée and Serge Boidevaix, as well as Christophe de Margerie, the chief executive officer of the Total oil company, who had been head of Total's Middle East division at the time of the Oil-for-Food program. In July 2013, the trial led to a surprise first-instance acquittal of these individuals, but the public prosecutor appealed the court's decision, except for de Margerie and Pasqua. See *Le Monde*, January 22 and July 18, 2013. (De Margerie died in 2014; Pasqua died in 2015.) In February 2016, however, the court in the second instance fined Total, Boidevaix, and Mérimée €750,000, €75,000 and €50,000, respectively; see "'Pétrole contre nourriture': Total condamné en appel à 750.000 euros d'amende" ["Oil for food": Total sentenced on appeal to 750,000-euro fine], *Le Figaro*, February 26, 2016, http://www.lefigaro.fr/actualite-france/2016/02/26/01016-20160226ARTFIG00108-petrole-contre-nourriture-total-condamne-en-appel-a-750000-euros-d-amende.php

38. TD Washington 4194, November 17, 2005, and TD Diplomatie 70228, December 2, 2005, ANMO 5 Irak, AFEW. The Americans observed in particular that the French—at least the Quai d'Orsay—had not formally denied the existence of a contract between Iraq and Niger concerning the supply of uranium, even if they thought it had not been executed. See US Senate, Select Committee on Intelligence, *Report on the U.S. Intelligence Community's Prewar Intelligence Assessments on Iraq* (108th Congress, 2nd sess., July 2004), 59, http://www.intelligence.senate.gov/108301.pdf; see also note 9 in chapter 7 of this volume. The Niger affair would give rise a little later to a rather comic Franco-Italian episode when SISMI, against all the evidence, accused the French of having been the source of false documents, which they supposedly had transmitted to the Americans to induce them into error, in order then to be able to denounce the war. See Faligot, Guisnel, and Kauffer, *Histoire politique des services secrets français*, 546–47; and "Nigergate: lo 007 francese che smonta la tesi del SISMI" [Nigergate: The French 007 that debunks the SISMI theory], *La Repubblica*, December 1, 2005.

39. David Ignatius, "Bush's New Ally: France?," *Washington Post*, February 1, 2006.

40. Chirac-Bush telephone conversations, February 22 and November 27, 2006; note a/s Conversation avec le président Bush, July 16, 2006, 5AG5 DB/5, AN; and Sylvie Kauffmann and Natalie Nougayrède, "France – États-Unis: histoire d'un retournement" [France–United States: History of a turnaround], *Le Monde*, April 5, 2006, http://www.lemonde.fr/a-la-une/article/2006/04/05/france-etats-unis-histoire-d-un-retournement_758328_3208.html.

41. Frédéric Bozo and Guillaume Parmentier, "France and the United States: Waiting for Regime Change," *Survival* 49, no. 1 (2007): 181–98; and Woodward, *State of Denial*, 456.

42. TD Washington 3526, October 20, 2006, ANMO 5 Irak, AFEW; and Woodward, *State of Denial*, 453 and 472.

43. *The Iraq Study Group Report: The Way Forward – A New Approach* (New York: Vintage Books, December 2006); and TD Washington 4115 and 4205, December 6 and 13, 2006, ANMO 5 Irak, AFEW.

44. TD Washington 950 and 2393, March 20 and July 13, 2007, ANMO 5 Iraq, AFEW.

Afterword

1. For an up-to-date account of recent French foreign policy, see Frédéric Bozo, *French Foreign Policy since 1945: An Introduction,* trans. Jonathan Hensher (Oxford: Berghahn Books, forthcoming, September 2016).

Sources and Bibliography

Archives

French National Archives (Paris)

Archives of the Presidency of the Republic, Presidency of François Mitterrand (5AG4), box CDM33/1.
Archives of the Presidency of the Republic, Presidency of Jacques Chirac (5AG5), boxes AP/6, AP/7, AP/15, AP/19, BE/11, BE/66, BE/73, DB/5, JFG/11, JFG/32, and JFG/34.

French Diplomatic Archives (French Ministry of Foreign Affairs, Paris and La Courneuve)

Série ANMO, Irak, boxes C3 A/B+III A1 2002, C3 IIIA1 01-02/2003, C3 IIIA1 03/2003, C3 A1 1999-2002, III B Political issues, political relations with France 1999/2002.
Série NUOI, Z/Irak/P, boxes 428, 430, 431, 432, 433, 434, 435, and 436.

Archives of the Embassy of France in the United States (Washington, D.C.)

Série ANMO 5 Irak.

Private Archives

Documents given to the author by former French officials.

Government Reports and Inquiries

United Nations Special Commission (UNSCOM) English-language website. 1999. https://www.un.org/Depts/unscom/.

United Nations Special Commission (UNSCOM) French-language website. [1999]. https://www.un.org/french/Depts/unscom/.

United Nations Monitoring, Verification, and Inspection Commission (UNMOVIC) English-language website. 2003. http://www.un.org/Depts/unmovic/.

The 9/11 Commission Report: Final Report of the National Commission on Terrorist Attacks Upon the United States. New York: W. W. Norton, July 2004. http://govinfo.library.unt.edu/911/report/index.htm.

Review of Intelligence on Weapons of Mass Destruction [Butler Review]. London: The Stationery Office, July 2004.

U.S. Senate. Select Committee on Intelligence. *Report on the U.S. Intelligence Community's Prewar Intelligence Assessments on Iraq.* 108th Congress, 2nd sess., July 2004. http://www.intelligence.senate.gov/108301.pdf.

Central Intelligence Agency (CIA). *Comprehensive Report of the Special Advisor to the DCI on Iraq's WMD* [Duelfer Report]. Washington, DC: US Government Printing Office, September 30, 2004. http://www.gpo.gov/fdsys/pkg/GPO-DUELFERREPORT/content-detail.html.

Independent Inquiry Committee into the United Nations Oil-for-Food Programme. *Manipulation of the Oil-for-Food Programme by the Iraqi Regime* [Volcker Report]. October 2005, http://www.iraqwatch.org/un/IIC/un_iic_final_report_27Oct2005.pdf.

U.S. Senate. Select Committee on Intelligence. *Report of the Select Committee on Intelligence on Postwar Findings about Iraq's WMD Programs and Links to Terrorism and How They Compare With Prewar Assessments.* 109th Congress, 2nd sess., September 8, 2006. https://www.gpo.gov/fdsys/pkg/CRPT-109srpt331/pdf/CRPT-109srpt331.pdf.

The Iraq Study Group Report: The Way Forward – A New Approach [Baker-Hamilton Report]. New York: Vintage Books, December 2006. http://media.usip.org/reports/iraq_study_group_report.pdf.

United Nations Monitoring, Verification, and Inspection Commission (UNMOVIC) French-language website. 2008. http://www.un.org/french/Depts/unmovic/.

The UK Iraq Inquiry [Chilcot Inquiry, 2009]. http://www.iraqinquiry.org.uk.

Documents Published by the National Security Archive, Washington, D.C.

Battle, Joyce, ed. *The Iraq War, Part I: The U.S. Prepares for Conflict, 2001.* National Security Archive Electronic Briefing Book No. 326. Washington, DC: National Security Archive, September 22, 2010. http://nsarchive.gwu.edu/NSAEBB/NSAEBB326/index.htm.

———, ed. *Saddam Hussein Talks to the FBI: Twenty Interviews and Five Conversations with "High Value Detainee #1" in 2004.* National Security Archive Electronic Briefing Book

No. 279. Washington, DC: National Security Archive, July 1, 2009. http://nsarchive
.gwu.edu/NSAEBB/NSAEBB279/index.htm.

Central Intelligence Agency. "Iraq's Continuing Program for Weapons of Mass Destruction."
National Intelligence Estimate (NIE) 2002-16HC, October 2002. http://nsarchive
.gwu.edu/NSAEBB/NSAEBB129/nie.pdf.

Prados, John, and Christopher Ames, ed. *The Iraq War, Part II: Was There Even a Decision?*
National Security Archive Electronic Briefing Book No. 328. Washington, DC:
National Security Archive, October 1, 2010. http://nsarchive.gwu.edu/NSAEBB
/NSAEBB328/index.htm.

——, ed. *The Iraq War, Part III: Shaping the Debate*. National Security Archive Electronic
Briefing Book No. 330. Washington, DC: National Security Archive, October 4, 2010.
http://nsarchive.gwu.edu/NSAEBB/NSAEBB330/index.htm.

Personal Interviews with Author

Benoît d'Aboville, Paris, February 11, 2010.
Kathleen Allegrone, Paris, February 2, 2011.
Michèle Alliot-Marie, Paris, July 19, 2010.
Gilles Andréani, Paris, October 29, 2008.
Gérard Araud, Paris, October 31, 2007, and March 6, 2009.
Richard Armitage, Washington, D.C., February 16, 2011.
Denis Bauchard, Paris, October 27, 2009.
Antonin Baudry, New York, December 2, 2010.
Jacques Baute, Vienna, August 22, 2011.
Henri Bentégeat, Paris, January 19, 2010.
Laurent Bili, Paris, April 23, 2010.
Pierre Brochand, Paris, March 14, 2012.
François Bujon de l'Estang, Paris, October 1, 2009.
Alain Chouet (by telephone), June 10, 2011.
Catherine Colonna, Paris, June 18, 2010.
Jean-Claude Cousseran, Paris, December 16, 2009, and May 18, 2011.
Alain Dejammet, Paris, December 4, 2009.
François Delattre, Washington, D.C., July 22, 2011.
Thérèse Delpech, Paris, November 6, 2009, and September 22, 2011.
Tyler Drumheller, Washington, D.C., July 6, 2011.
Charles Duelfer, Washington, D.C. March 1, 2011.
Michael M. Dunn, Washington, D.C., January 6, 2011.
Eric Edelman, Washington, D.C., July 13, 2011.
Gérard Errera, Paris, January 20, 2010.
Philippe Errera, Paris, October 26, 2007.
Douglas Feith, Washington, D.C., May 11, 2011.
Jean Félix-Paganon, Paris, March 22, 2010.
Carl Ford (by video-conference), May 17, 2011.

Daniel Fried, Washington, D.C., March 10, 2011.
Jean-Patrick Gaviard, Paris, February 12, 2010.
Jean-Louis Georgelin, Paris, November 12, 2009 and July 13, 2010.
Jean-François Girault, Paris, January 14, 2010.
Maurice Gourdault-Montagne, London, January 22, 2010.
Camille Grand, Paris, February 16, 2010.
Jeremy Greenstock, Ditchley, United Kingdom, October 23, 2008.
Mark Grossman, Washington, D.C., January 11, 2011.
Bruno Gruselle, Paris, April 12, 2012.
André Janier, Nice, August 8, 2012.
A. Elizabeth Jones, Washington, D.C., December 17, 2010.
Craig Kelly, Washington, D.C., February 8, 2011.
Ann Korky, Washington, D.C., March 29, 2011.
Yves Aubin de La Messuzière, Paris, February 3, 2010.
Jean-Marc de La Sablière, Rome, October 6, 2009.
Stanislas de Laboulaye, Rome, December 10, 2009.
Jean-Pierre Lacroix, Paris, April 1, 2010.
Manuel Lafont Rapnouil, Washington, D.C., November 18, 2008.
Bruno Le Maire, Paris, August 24, 2010.
Pierre Lellouche, Paris, November 3, 2009, and March 30, 2010.
Jean-David Levitte, Paris, March 3, 2010.
Don Loren, Washington, D.C., May 9, 2011.
Jean-Claude Mallet, Paris, March 25, 2010.
Robert Malley, Washington, D.C., April 11, 2011.
John McLaughlin, Washington, D.C., April 11, 2011.
Franklin C. Miller, Washington, D.C., January 24, 2011.
Jérôme Monod, Paris, April 12, 2010.
John D. Negroponte, Washington, D.C., January 12, 2011.
André Parant, Paris, April 23, 2010.
Robert Pelletreau, New York, January 20, 2011.
Thomas Pickering, Washington, D.C., March 24, 2011.
Kenneth Pollack, Washington, D.C., April 26, 2011.
François Richier, Paris, September 29, 2011.
Bruce Riedel, Washington, D.C., March 8, 2011.
Kori Schake, Washington, D.C., November 19, 2008.
Edouard Scott de Martinville, Paris, January 12, 2012.
Hubert Védrine, Paris, February 22, 2010.
Dominique de Villepin, Paris, July 26, 2012.
Kurt Volker, Washington, D.C., January 13, 2011, and July 20, 2011.
David Welch (by telephone), May 16, 2011.
Wayne White (by telephone), February 7, 2011.
Lawrence Wilkerson, Washington, D.C., January 26, 2011.
N.N., Paris, January 27, 2012.
N.N., Paris, October 5, 2012.

Memoirs, Testimonies, and Diaries

Albright, Madeleine, with Bill Woodward. *Madam Secretary: A Memoir*. New York: Miramax Books, 2003.

Annan, Kofi, with Nader Mousavizadeh. *Interventions: A Life in War and Peace*. New York: Penguin Books, 2012.

Balladur, Edouard. *Le Pouvoir ne se partage pas. Conversations avec François Mitterrand* [Power cannot be shared: Conversations with François Mitterrand]. Paris: Fayard, 2009.

Blair, Tony. *A Journey: My Political Life*. New York: Alfred A. Knopf, 2010.

Blix, Hans. *Disarming Iraq: The Search for Weapons of Mass Destruction*. London: Bloomsbury, 2004.

Bush, George H. W., and Brent Scowcroft, *A World Transformed*. New York: Alfred A. Knopf, 1998.

Bush, George W. *Decision Points*, New York: Crown Publishers, 2010.

Cheney, Dick, with Liz Cheney. *In My Time: A Personal and Political Memoir*. New York: Threshold Editions, 2011.

Chirac, Jacques. *Chaque pas doit* être *un but. Mémoires 1* [Each step should be a goal: Memoirs, vol. 1]. Paris: NiL, 2009.

———. *Le temps présidentiel. Mémoires 2* [The presidential years: Memoirs, vol. 2]. Paris: NiL, 2011.

Chouet, Alain, with Jean Guisnel. *Au cœur des services spéciaux: La menace islamiste, fausses pistes et vrais dangers* [At the heart of the special services: The Islamist threat, false leads, and real dangers]. Paris: La Découverte, 2011.

Clarke, Richard A. *Against All Enemies: Inside America's War on Terror*. New York: The Free Press, 2004.

Drumheller, Tyler. *On the Brink: An Insider's Account of How the White House Compromised American Intelligence*. New York: Carroll & Graf Publishers, 2007.

Duelfer, Charles. *Hide and Seek: The Search for Truth in Iraq*. New York: Public Affairs, 2009.

ElBaradei, Mohamed. *The Age of Deception: Nuclear Diplomacy in Treacherous Times*. New York: Metropolitan Books, 2011.

Feith, Douglas J. *War and Decision: Inside the Pentagon at the Dawn of the War on Terrorism*. New York; Harper-Collins, 2008.

Fischer, Joschka. *"I am not convinced". Der Irak-Krieg und die rot-grünen Jahre* ["I am not convinced": The Iraq war and the red-green years]. Cologne: Kiepenheuer & Witsch, 2011.

Haass, Richard N. *War of Necessity, War of Choice: A Memoir of Two Iraq Wars*. New York: Simon & Schuster, 2009.

Indyk, Martin. *Innocent Abroad: An Intimate Account of American Peace Diplomacy in the Middle East*. New York: Simon & Schuster, 2009.

La Sablière, Jean-Marc de. *Dans les coulisses du monde: Du Rwanda à la guerre d'Irak, un grand négociateur révèle le dessous des cartes* [In the world's backstage: From Rwanda to the Iraq war, a great negotiator reveals the untold stories of international politics]. Paris: Robert Laffont, 2013.

Le Maire, Bruno. *Le Ministre. Récit* [The minister: A tale]. Paris: Grasset, 2004.

McClellan, Scott. *What Happened: Inside the Bush White House and Washington's Culture of Deception.* New York: Public Affairs, 2008.

Obeidi, Mahdi, and Kurt Pitzer. *The Bomb in My Garden: The Secrets of Saddam's Nuclear Mastermind.* Hoboken, NJ: John Wiley & Sons, 2004.

Pitt, William Rivers, with Scott Ritter. *War on Iraq: What Team Bush Doesn't Want You to Know.* New York: Context Books, 2002.

Rice, Condoleezza. *No Higher Honor: A Memoir of My Years in Washington.* New York: Simon & Schuster, 2011.

Rodman, Peter W. *Presidential Command: Power, Leadership, and the Making of Foreign Policy from Richard Nixon to George W. Bush.* New York: Alfred A. Knopf, 2009.

Rove, Karl. *Courage and Consequence: My Life as a Conservative in the Fight.* New York: Threshold Editions, 2010.

Rumsfeld, Donald. *Known and Unknown: A Memoir.* New York: Sentinel, 2011.

Schröder, Gerhard. *Entscheidungen. Mein Leben in der Politik* [Decisions: My life in politics]. Hamburg: Hoffmann und Campe, 2006.

Tenet, George, with Bill Harlow. *At the Center of the Storm: My Years at the CIA.* London: HarperCollins, 2007.

Villepin, Dominique de. *Le Requin et la mouette* [The shark and the seagull]. Paris: Plon/Albin Michel, 2004.

Selected Bibliography

Aeschimann, Eric, and Christophe Boltanski. *Chirac d'Arabie. Les mirages d'une politique française* [Chirac of Arabia: Mirages of French policy]. Paris, Grasset, 2006.

Alfonsi, Christian. *Circle in the Sand: The Bush Dynasty in Iraq.* New York: Vintage Books, 2007.

Bacevich, Andrew. *The New American Militarism: How Americans Are Seduced by War.* Oxford: Oxford University Press, 2005.

Balis, Christina V., and Simon Serfaty, eds. *Visions of America and Europe: September 11, Iraq, and Transatlantic Relations.* Washington, DC: Center for Strategic and International Studies, 2004.

Bozo, Frédéric. *French Foreign Policy since 1945: An Introduction.* New York: Berghahn Books, forthcoming September 2016.

Brands, Hal. *From Berlin to Baghdad: America's Search for Purpose in the Post-Cold War World.* Lexington: University Press of Kentucky, 2008.

Brenner, Michael, and Guillaume Parmentier. *Reconcilable Differences: U.S.-France Relations in the New Era.* Washington, DC: Brookings Institution Press, 2002.

Chollet, Derek, and James Goldgeier. *America Between the Wars: From 11/9 to 9/11.* New York: Public Affairs, 2008.

Cockburn, Andrew, and Patrick Cockburn. *Saddam Hussein: An American Obsession.* London: Verso, 2002.

Cogan, Charles. *French Negotiating Behavior: Dealing with la Grande Nation.* Washington, DC: United States Institute of Peace Press, 2003.

———. *La République de Dieu* [The republic of God]. Paris: Jacob-Duvernet, 2008.

Collins, Joseph J. *Choosing War: The Decision to Invade Iraq and Its Aftermath*. Washington, DC: Institute for National Strategic Studies/National Defense University, 2008.

Coudurier, Hubert. *Le Monde selon Chirac* [The world according to Chirac]. Paris, Calmann-Levy, 1998.

Daalder, Ivo H., and James M. Lindsay. *America Unbound: The Bush Revolution in Foreign Policy*. Washington, DC: Brookings Institution Press, 2003.

Davidson, Jason W. *America's Allies and War: Kosovo, Afghanistan, and Iraq*. New York: Palgrave Macmillan, 2011.

Delafon, Gilles, and Thomas Sancton. *Dear Jacques, Cher Bill. Au cœur de l'Elysée et de la Maison Blanche 1995–1999* [Dear Jacques, Dear Bill: Inside the Elysée and the White House, 1995–1999]. Paris, Plon, 1999.

Dettke, Dieter. *Germany Says No: The Iraq War and the Future of German Foreign and Security Policy*. Washington, DC: Woodrow Wilson Center Press; Baltimore: Johns Hopkins University Press, 2009.

DeYoung, Karen. *Soldier: The Life of Colin Powell*. New York: Alfred A. Knopf, 2006.

Eisner, Peter, and Knut Royce. *The Italian Letter: How the Bush Administration Used a Fake Letter to Build the Case for War in Iraq*. New York: Rodale, 2007.

Faligot, Roger, Jean Guisnel, and Rémi Kauffer. *Histoire politique des services secrets français* [Political history of the French secret services]. Paris: La Découverte, 2012.

Favier, Pierre, and Michel Martin-Roland. *La Décennie Mitterrand* [The Mitterrand decade] 4 vol. Paris: Le Seuil, 1990–1999.

Gelman, Barton. *Angler: The Cheney Vice Presidency*. New York: Penguin, 2008.

George, Roger Z., and Harvey Rishikof, eds. *The National Security Enterprise: Navigating the Labyrinth*. Washington, DC: Georgetown University Press, 2011.

Gordon, Michael R., and Bernard E. Trainor. *Cobra II: The Inside Story of the Invasion and Occupation of Iraq*. New York: Vintage Books, 2006.

Gordon, Philip H., and Jeremy Shapiro. *Allies at War: America, Europe, and the Crisis over Iraq*. Washington, DC: Brookings Institution Press, 2004.

Guedj, Mikaël, and Yoanna Sultan-R'bibo. *11 Septembre. Paris, 14h46* [September 11: Paris, 2:46 pm]. Paris: Stock, 2011.

Hoffmann, Stanley, and Frédéric Bozo. *L'Amérique vraiment impériale? Entretiens sur le vif* [Is America really imperial? Conversations on the spot]. Paris: L. Audibert, 2003. Translated as *Gulliver Unbound: America's Imperial Temptation and the War in Iraq* (Lanham, MD: Rowman & Littlefield, 2004).

Howorth, Jolyon. *Security and Defence Policy in the European Union*. London: Palgrave, 2007.

Jentleson, Bruce. *With Friends Like These: Reagan, Bush, and Saddam, 1982–1990*. New York: W. W. Norton & Company, 1994.

Jervis, Robert. *Why Intelligence Fails: Lessons from the Iranian Revolution and the Iraq War*. Ithaca, NY: Cornell University Press, 2010.

Kampfner, John. *Blair's Wars*. London: Free Press, 2003.

Krasno, Jean E., and James S. Sutterlin. *The United Nations and Iraq: Defanging the Viper*. Westport, CT: Praeger, 2003.

Kuisel, Richard. *The French Way: How France Embraced and Rejected American Values and Power*. Princeton, NJ: Princeton University Press, 2011.

Labévière, Richard. *Le grand retournement. Bagdad-Beyrouth* [The great turnaround: Baghdad-Beirut]. Paris: Seuil, 2006.

Lang, W. Patrick. "Drinking the Kool-Aid." *Middle-East Policy* 11, no. 2 (2004): 39–60.

Leffler, Melvyn P. "The Foreign Policies of the George W. Bush Administration: Memoirs, History, Legacy." *Diplomatic History* 37, no. 2 (2013): 190–216.

Lequesne, Christian, and Maurice Vaïsse, eds. *La politique étrangère de Jacques Chirac* [The foreign policy of Jacques Chirac]. Paris: Riveneuve, 2013.

Litwak, Robert S. *Regime Change: U.S. Strategy through the Prism of 9/11*. Washington, DC: Woodrow Wilson Center Press; Baltimore: Johns Hopkins University Press, 2007.

Lundestad, Geir, ed. *Just Another Major Crisis? The United States and Europe since 2000*. Oxford: Oxford University Press, 2008.

Malone, David M. *The International Struggle over Iraq: Politics in the U.N. Security Council 1990–2005*. Oxford: Oxford University Press, 2006.

———, ed. *The U.N. Security Council: From the Cold War to the 21st Century*. Boulder, CO: Lynne Rienner, 2004.

Mann, James. *Rise of the Vulcans: The History of Bush's War Cabinet*. London: Penguin Books, 2005.

Marr, Phebe. *The Modern History of Iraq*, 3rd ed. Boulder, CO: Westview Press, 2012.

Melandri, Pierre. "'The French Were Right': la guerre d'Irak et la brouille franco-américaine," ["The French were right": The Iraq war and the Franco-American spat], in Lequesne and Vaïsse, *La politique étrangère de Jacques Chirac*, 131–58.

Melandri, Pierre, and Justin Vaïsse. *L'Empire du milieu. Les États-Unis et le monde depuis la fin de la guerre froide* [The Middle Kingdom: The United States and the world since the end of the Cold War]. Paris: Odile Jacob, 2001.

Nouzille, Vincent. *Dans le secret des présidents. CIA, Maison-Blanche, Élysée: les dossiers confidentiels, 1981–1990* [Presidential secrecy: Confidential files of the CIA, the White House, and the Elysée, 1981–1990]. Paris: Fayard, 2010.

Péan, Pierre. *L'Inconnu de l'Élysée* [The unknown at the Elysée]. Paris: Fayard, 2006.

Pearson, Graham S. *The Search for Iraq's Weapons of Mass Destruction*. New York: Palgrave, 2005.

Pisar, Leah. *Orage sur l'Atlantique. La France et les États-Unis face à l'Irak* [Storm over the Atlantic: France and the United States faced with Iraq]. Paris: Fayard, 2010.

Pollack, Kenneth M. *The Threatening Storm: The Case for Invading Iraq*. New York: Random House, 2002.

Pond, Elizabeth. *Friendly Fire: The Near-Death of the Atlantic Alliance*. Washington, DC: Brookings Institution Press, 2004.

Prados, Alfred B. *Iraq: Post War Challenges and U.S. Responses, 1991–1998*. Report for Congress 98-386 F. Washington, DC: Congressional Research Service, 1999.

Prados, John. *Hoodwinked: The Documents That Reveal How Bush Sold Us a War*. New York: The New Press, 2004.

Ricks, Thomas E. *Fiasco: The American Military Adventure in Iraq*. New York: Penguin Books, 2006.

Risen, James. *State of War: The Secret History of the CIA and the Bush Administration*. New York: Free Press, 2006.

Sassoon, Joseph. *Saddam Hussein's Ba'th Party: Inside an Authoritarian Regime*. Cambridge, UK: Cambridge University Press, 2011.

Shawcross, William. *Allies: The United States, Britain, Europe and the War in Iraq*. London: Atlantic Books, 2003.

Styan, David. *France and Iraq: Oil, Arms and French Policy in the Middle East*. London: I. B. Tauris, 2006.

———. "Jacques Chirac's '*non*': France, Iraq and the United Nations, 1991–2003." *Modern & Contemporary France* 12, no. 3 (2004): 371–85.

Sur, Serge. *Le Conseil de sécurité dans l'après-11 Septembre* [The Security Council after September 11]. Paris: LGDJ, 2004.

Suskind, Ron. *The One Percent Doctrine: Deep Inside America's Pursuit of Its Enemies Since 9/11*. New York: Simon & Schuster, 2006.

Szabo, Stephen F. *Parting Ways: The Crisis in German-American Relations*. Washington, DC: Brookings Institution Press, 2004.

Timmerman, Kenneth R. *The Death Lobby: How the West Armed Iraq*, 2nd ed. London: Bantam Books, 1992.

———. *The French Betrayal of America*. New York: Three Rivers Press, 2004.

Tripp, Charles. *A History of Iraq*. Cambridge, UK: Cambridge University Press, 2007.

Vaïsse, Justin. *Histoire du néoconservatisme aux États-Unis* [History of neoconservatism in the United States]. Paris: Odile Jacob, 2008.

Vaïsse, Maurice. *La Puissance ou l'influence? La France dans le monde depuis 1958* [Power or influence? France in the world since 1958]. Paris: Fayard, 2008.

Vernet, Henri, and Thomas Cantaloube. *Chirac contre Bush. L'autre guerre* [Chirac versus Bush: The other war]. Paris: JC Lattès, 2004.

Woodward, Bob. *Bush at War*. New York: Simon & Schuster, 2002.

———. *Plan of Attack*. New York: Simon & Schuster, 2004.

———. *State of Denial*. New York: Simon & Schuster, 2006.

Index

Baath Party, 20; "de-Baathification," 281
Baathism, 21
Baghdad Fair, 58
Bahrain, 104
Baker, James A., 26, 122, 293; Baker-
  Hamilton Report, 309
Balkenende, Jan Peter, 225
Balladur, Édouard, 239
Bandar bin Sultan, 186
Barak, Ehud, 111
Barnier, Michel, 297
Barroso, José Manuel, 262
Baute, Jacques, 116, 253
Beghal, Djamel, 88
Belgium, 227–28, 273
Bentégeat, Henri, 126, 160–62, 170–71,
  268, 280
Berlusconi, Silvio, 75, 207, 222, 244, 301
Biden, Joe, 293
bin Laden, Osama, 52, 73, 79, 323n17;
  post-9/11 US attacks against, 76, 83,
  86–87, 90
biological weapons. *See* weapons of mass
  destruction (WMDs)
Biya, Paul, 216, 256
Blackwill, Robert, 292
Blair, Tony, 50, 263–64; Azores meeting
  and, 262; British public opinion and,
  163, 207, 263–64; British-French
  relations and, 221–22, 257–58, 275;
  Chirac and, 128, 139, 258; European
  Union and, 225; following US invasion
  of Iraq, 269; reelection of, 301;
  relationship with Bush, 91, 130–31;
  September 11 attacks and, 75; UN
  and, 248, 258; US invasion of Iraq
  and, 105–6, 114, 119, 130–31, 181,
  207, 222, 260–61, 301, 320n17
Blix, Hans, 57, 115–16, 137, 173,
  180–81, 183, 191, 200–204, 217–19,
  251–52, 262–63; French support
  of, 192–94; Resolution 1284 and,
  192; Resolution 1441 and, 162–63,
  165–66; US invasion of Iraq and,
  203–4, 254–55

Boidevaix, Serge, 328n106, 353n37
Bosnia, 7
Boutros-Ghali, Boutros, 36
Boyce, Sir Michael, 119
Brahimi, Lakhdar, 294
Brazil, 216–17
Bremer, Paul, 281, 290
Britain. *See* Great Britain
Brzezinski, Zbigniew, 236
Bujon de l'Estang, François, 7, 67, 78, 91,
  107–8, 113–14, 124, 138
Bulgaria, 214, 223, 250, 292
Bundesnachrichtendienst (BND), 147
Burns, Nicholas, 228
Bush, George H. W., 1, 24; attempted
  assassination of, 4, 35–36, 93; Chirac
  and, 67–68, 70, 77–81, 84–86,
  110–12, 128, 138, 159, 208, 234–35,
  273, 276–77, 279–80, 285–87, 294,
  296, 299, 302–3; decision to invade
  Iraq and, 170; electoral defeat of, 35;
  Franco-American relations and, 15–17,
  35; Gulf War (1991) and, 25, 27–28,
  140; September 11 attacks and, 81;
  United Nations and, 25–26
Bush, George W., 17, 65–66; 2000 election
  and, 65–66; 2002 visit to Paris, 110–12;
  2003 State of the Union address, 204–5,
  207–8, 211; 2004 election and, 289,
  293, 299–300; anti-French backlash
  and, 273–74; "axis of evil" speech
  and, 101–2, 109, 112; Azores meeting
  of, 262; Blair and, 91, 104, 130–31,
  258–60, 262; cabinet of, 68; "coercive
  diplomacy" of, 95, 97, 125, 169, 173;
  decision to invade Iraq and, 4, 9–10, 90,
  95, 116, 119, 139, 168–70, 184–87,
  204–5, 207, 215, 234, 244, 253,
  260, 262; declaration of victory by, 1,
  247–48, 271–72, 312; Iraqi WMD and,
  151–52; meeting with Powell, 119–21;
  NATO and, 228; "new Europe" and,
  222; normalization of Franco-American
  relations and, 299; Powell's UN speech
  and, 212; regime change and, 244–45;

detect, 2–3, 145, 271, 282, 291; use of in Iran-Iraq war, 23–24; used against Iraqi Kurds, 23; VX nerve agent, 38, 51–52, 60, 202, 204–6, 217, 248, 252, 263. *See also* United Nations Special Commission (UNSCOM)
Weiner, Sharon, 240
Wilkerson, Lawrence, 210
Wilson, Joseph, 146
Wolfensohn, James, 302
Wolfowitz, Paul, 40, 45, 89, 325n47, 331n71; decision to invade Iraq and, 90, 93, 106, 190–91, 204; Franco-American relations and, 190–91, 275, 302; Iraqi WMD and, 151; NATO and, 82, 226; UNMOVIC and, 115; US invasion of Iraq and, 271; US-Iraq relations and, 71–73
Woodward, Bob, 169

yellowcake. *See* uranium enrichment
Yemen, 77, 104
Yugoslavia, 7

Zapatero, José Luis, 292
Zarqawi, Abu Musab al-, 205, 211, 213, 237
Zinni, Anthony, 123, 147–48, 290